A Compendious History of the Reformation in France

by Stephen Abel Laval

A Compendious

HISTORY

OF THE

REFORMATION in *France,*

AND OF THE

Reformed Churches in that Kingdom.

FROM

The Firſt Beginnings of the REFORMATION,

TO THE

Repealing of the Edict of *NANTZ.*

WITH

An ACCOUNT of the late Perſecution of the *French* Proteſtants under *Lewis* XIV. Extracted out of the beſt Authorities.

A WORK never before publiſhed.

Wherein the many Falſifications of the Jeſuit *Daniel,* Author of the Hiſtory of France, in Matters relating to Religion, are ſet forth in their full Light, and proved by his own Quotations.

By the Reverend

STEPHEN ABEL LAVAL,

One of the Miniſters of the United Chapels of *Caſtle-ſtreet* and *Berwick-ſtreet.*

VOL. III. The Firſt Part.

LONDON:

Printed by H. WOODFALL, for the AUTHOR.
MDCCXXXIX.

110. j. 82.

THE
PREFACE.

THIS First Part of the Third Volume of our History of the Reformation in France, and of the Reformed Churches in that Kingdom, contains the most considerable Events from the Peace of *Amboise* to Charles the Ninth's Death in 1574. It will seem surprising that in a Book that promises the History of the Reformation one is continually to meet with Events having little or no Relation to Religion, most part of them being of a political Nature, such as Manifestos, warlike Preparations, Sieges, Battles, Negociations of War and Peace, &c. But that flows of course from the State and Circumstances the Reformed were in, in France.

Reformation had been settled in that Kingdom as much out of a political View, as out of any other Motive. CATHERINE of MEDICIS aimed at being absolute Mistress of the

A 2   Government,

Government; and whereas she could not cope alone with the Guises' powerful Faction, which was supported even by the first Prince of the Blood, she endeavoured to strengthen herself by bringing over to her own Interest the Reformed Party, which had till then grown and been kept up amidst Fires and Flames, and yet was in a Condition of withstanding the other; she draws them, *one may say*, out of the Ashes, she undertook sincerely or feignedly their Protection, and to make them fully assured of her Sincerity, she gave her Consent to an Edict which the General Estates had required in their Behalf, whereby, not only Liberty of Conscience, but the publick Exercise of their Religion were granted them in the Suburbs of those Cities they lived in; and as for the Temporal, they were to have the same Privileges the other Subjects did enjoy.

Nothing could be more Authentick than this Edict. It was granted to the Sollicitations of the General Estates, wherein, as it is well known, resided the Sovereign Authority, and whose supreme Power Kings themselves were obliged to submit to, and who had more than once taken Cognizance of Religious Matters, and of what belonged to the Liberties of the Gallican Church, as in the Dispute between Philip the Fair, and Pope Bonifacius VIII, in 1300 or 1301,

Nothing could be more proper to foment and maintain Peace, Union and Concord amongst the Subjects, to make the Kingdom flourish flourifh anew, to reftore the Church to thê Purity of the firft Ages, and the State to its ancient Splendour, than fuch an Edict, which, leaving to Confcience its Rights, or-dained Punifhments, only againft thofe petu-lant Spirits, who defirous of gratifying their Paffions at any rate, or following the furi-ous Inftigations of a blind-fold Zeal, would have attempted to difturb the Peace of the Society whereof they were Members. But it was not the Fate of *France* to be happy under the Government of Henry II's Pofte-rity. The Nation's enormous Sins called aloud for Punifhment, and the Sons and Grandfons of Claudius of Guife, who had retired amongft them in Francis I's Time, were for many Years the Rods of the Lord's Anger, and the Staff of his Indignation againft that un-righteous and perverfe Generation.

The unbridled Ambition of Francis Duke of Guife, fupported and incited by the vio-lent Counfels, Cabals and Intrigues of Charles Cardinal of Lorrain his Brother, found no-thing too high for his afpiring Thoughts ; no-thing fo Sacred, but what he would violate, to bring his Defigns about. Whereas the great-eft Oppofition, the unjuft Projects of his Am-bition met with, was the Peace and Tran-quility the State enjoy'd, the Union and Con-cord that was brought infenfibly amongft the Subjects of both Religions ; he fet all his Engines at work to difturb the one and to deftroy the other, and to plunge the King-dom in a Confufion and Diforder, the Ad-

vantages

vantages whereof his Family alone was to reap, to the perpetual Prejudice of the Royal House, and of the Prince's Authority that posseſſed the Throne.

The Pretence he covered his Deſigns with, could not be more plauſible, nor more proper to dazle the People's Eyes, to produce in them his deſired Effects, to gain the Clergy's Affection, and to make it intirely devoted to him, viz. RELIGION. Factious People have in all Times, generally ſpeaking, compaſſed their Ends by ſuch Means. *You ſee*, ſays Demetrius to his Journeymen, *that not alone at Epheſus, but almoſt throughout all Aſia, this* PAUL *hath perſuaded and turned away much People, ſaying, that they be no Gods which are made with Hands : So that, not only this our Craft is in danger to be ſet at nought, but alſo that the Temple of the great Goddeſs* DIANA *ſhould be deſpiſed, and her Magnificence ſhould be deſtroyed, whom all Aſia and the World worſhippeth.* Acts xix. 26, 27. THE CHURCH IS IN DANGER, has always been the Topick which Ringleaders have uſed to trouble the State and ſubvert it, if poſſible. That Pretence our Duke made uſe of to ſet all his Wheels in motion, to make the People rebel, and trample the ſacred Authority of Laws under-foot. Whereby he aimed at two different Effects, the one to deprive the Queen Regent of her Power, by repreſenting her as favouring and protecting Hereſy, the other of riſing himſelf upon her Downfall, by ſetting up himſelf for Protector of the Church

and

and a Defender of the Faith. VASSY was the firſt Stage whereon he opened the tragical Scene; the Groans of the Miſerable, that periſhed in it, was the Alarm-Bell that was heard all over the Kingdom, and the Drops of Blood ſpilt there, became as many Rivers that overflow'd it for ſo many Years.

We have ſeen in our ſecond Volume the Iſſue of that audacious Attempt, fatal to the Author of it, and to his chief Adherents. His Sons treading in his Steps, followed the ſame ambitious Projects, nay, carrying them, may be, farther than their Father had done, left in their tragical End a dreadful Example of God's juſt Judgment againſt Uſurpers, that uſe the ſacred Veil of Religion to cover the moſt deteſtable Deſigns, it is what we ſhall be informed of by Hiſtory.

To return to the Effects of the firſt Civil War : On one hand, Catherine, being delivered from thoſe ſhe the moſt feared, did not think herſelf obliged to all thoſe regards ſhe had had for the Reformed, as long as ſhe thought herſelf to be in need of their Aſſiſtance ; ſhe gave herſelf up intirely to her true Inclinations, and having then, properly ſpeaking, no Religion at all, ſhe adhered outwardly to that that ſuited beſt with her immoderate Paſſions, and procured her, as ſhe thought, the greateſt Worldly Advantages, and ſacrificed to it the Intereſts and Concerns of the other, as contrary to her political Views, and whoſe Maxims were no leſs contrary to thoſe ſhe followed, either in the Admini-

ſtration

ſtration of the Government, or in her private Deportment, than Light is to Darkneſs. On the other hand, the two Parties having once tried their ſtrength, grew the bolder by it, the one in attacking, and the other in defending itſelf; the latter having found by Experience, that if they were not in a condition to ſubdue the other Party, they were at leaſt to withſtand it; if they could not increaſe their Privileges, they could however preſerve thoſe that had been ſolemnly granted to them; they did not think themſelves obliged to give way to the other's Violence as often as thoſe their Enemies had a mind to deſtroy them, and trample them under their Feet, but drove to it by neceſſity, they took up Arms for their juſt Defence, as often as was neceſſary.

But it will be ſaid, Is it ever lawful for Subjects to reſiſt their Sovereign's Will, to take up Arms againſt him for the Defence of their Religion, and to oppoſe Force to Force? It would be more eaſy to anſwer that Objection, had the Reformed Religion and Church been the National Religion and Church in *France*. But whereas the Reformed have been always the ſmaller Number in the Kingdom, whatever can be ſaid in behalf of the whole Body of a Nation that riſes in Arms againſt its Sovereign for oppoſing his tyrannical Government, would be of none or very little Service to the preſent CAUSE. For ſuppoſing that we ſhould be able to prove, that it is lawful, in certain Caſes, for the whole
Body

Body of a Nation to refift their Sovereign, when he perverts Royalty into an open Tyranny, whatever is lawful in certain Cafes for the whole Body, cannot be fo for the lefſer part of it, unlefs it fhould be authorized by the whole, much lefs when the Caufe of that fmall part is quite of another Nature than the whole.

It is true, the Reformed had fome Grievances to redrefs which were common to them with the whole Nation ; and as to thefe, if it was lawful for the other part of the Nation, to have them redreffed by force of Arms, when all other means proved ineffectual, to be fure it was no lefs lawful for the Reformed to join themfelves with their Countrymen for obtaining the fame end by the fame means ; in fuch a cafe they acted not as Reformed, but as Members of the French Nation.

But the Reformed had alfo private Grievances of their own, occafioned by their Religion, their very Name, wherein the greatest part of the Nation was not ingaged ; could they with a fafe Confcience endeavour to have thefe redreffed with open force, feeing that by fuch means they involved the whole Nation into the utmoft Miferies ? Would it not have been better, and more Chriftian-like, either to fubmit themfelves patiently to the fierceft Perfecutions, or to flee into another Country ? The Objection is in its full force.

But

The PREFACE.

But without blaming thofe who think themfelves obliged to take either of thefe Courfes,
I fay that there is fome Circumftances which
might render lawful the Refiftance even of
the fmall part of a Nation; an Edict folemnly and freely granted by the advice of the
Reprefentatives of the whole Nation lawfully
affembled, by the King's Proclamation, or a
Capitulation made with the faid part, how
inconfiderable foever, in order to quiet them,
and engage them to defift from profecuting
their Rights: When thefe things, which
have been always deemed moft facred a-
mongft Men, are made ufe of only for de-
ceiving a Party, and betraying it with more
eafe to Deftruction and Ruin, I fay that in
fuch Cafes, the abufed Party has a Right of
refifting and oppofing force to force.

Now the Edict of January 1561 had been
granted to the Reformed by the Advice, and
at the Inftances of the States General. They
confidering wifely, that though fires had been
kindled in the Kingdom for almoft forty
Years together, yet far from having been able
to deftroy the Profeffors of the Reformed Doctrine, they had only ferved to increafe their
Number to fuch a degree, that it exceeded
Two Millions of People of every Rank and
Condition in France. They thought it was
high time to put a ftop to thefe violent methods ufed againft them, and no lefs contrary to Humanity than to Chriftianity, left
they fhould be provoked to fome defperate
Attempt. That Edict included nothing con-
trary

trary to the fundamental Laws of the Kingdom, or to the Liberties and Privileges of
the Gallican Church; the King had as much
Right to grant it, at leaft as the Pope has
to grant the Jews the free Profeffion of their
Religion in his own Territories. That Edict
was very beneficial to the Catholicks themfelves, it afforded them a fair opportunity of
delivering themfelves, if they had a mind, from
that fhameful Bondage whereunder they are
detained to this day, and of attaining the
true Knowledge of God and of the Chriftian
Religion: In a word, that Edict was noxious only to thofe obdurate and bafe Demetrius's and their Journeymen, who for lucre
fake don't ftick at any thing. Now that E-
dict having been granted and fworn to in fo
folemn a manner, I fay that it could not be
repealed but by the fame Authority whereby
it had been enacted, I mean the King advifed, not by his Privy Council or any of
his Courts of Parliament, but by the States
General freely called and affembled.

Neverthelefs a private Man, and a Foreigner
too, undertakes to break it in its moft tender Points, and far from obtaining any Satisfaction, the Deputies of the Reformed received only hard Words and unkind Ufage
at Court. But for all that, I queftion much
whether the Reformed would have ftirred,
had it not been for the preffing Inftances and
repeated Orders of the Queen-Mother, Regent of the Kingdom. But it is certain, that
as foon as they thought to have obtained fome
Security

Security for Liberty of Confcience and free
Exercife of their Religion, they accepted readily the offers of it when tendered unto them,
without minding any further Intereft.

Such was the Edict of Amboife publifh'd
in 1563, much lefs favourable than that of
1561. This Amboifian Treaty would have
been as advantageous as the firft, had they
tarried fome time longer, or at leaft had their
principal Chief fhown a greater Refolution.
It was obtained Sword in hand, it is true,
but befides the Queen-Regent's preffing and
pofitive Orders, had they not the right on
their fide? Were they not obliged in good
Policy to fhow publickly that they were in
a condition of preferving what Privileges had
been freely granted unto them in the moft
folemn manner, in fpite of thofe who were
no lefs the King's and the State's Enemies than
theirs? However, as that confideration came
into their heads feveral Months only after
the breaking out of the firft Civil War, and
that at firft they acted only out of a principle of Duty to their King, his Mother and
the Royal Family, detained, as fhe faid herfelf, in Captivity, it would not be reafonable
to charge them with a view of revenging the
publick Injury they had received by the Vaf-
fiacan Maffacre.

Whatever Abftractions, Reftrictions and
Modifications were made to the faid Edict
by the fecond, the Reformed, generally fpeaking, were fatisfied with it, but their Enemies were not. On one hand the Bullies

lies of the Court, on the other, the Spanish and Romish Emissaries, instilled these two abominable Principles into the young King's mind: The first gave him continually to understand, that Princes were not obliged to keep their Treaties contracted with their own Subjects, and that even it is honourable for them to revenge themselves of a Treaty which they have been constrained to, by breaking it at the first favourable Opportunity. The others whispered every day in his Ears, that a Catholick is not obliged to keep Faith with Hereticks. True it is, that these pernicious Counsels made very little impression upon the King's mind as long as Chancellor de L'Hospital had any Credit at Court, and that his Majesty listen'd to his prudent Advices, always full of Moderation; but when that great Man had once lost his ground at Court, and was left in a kind of Exile at his Country Seat, then it was that the Disturbers of the publick Peace, sailing before the Wind, bore down whatever Oppositions they could meet, and ensnared the young King so well, that hence-forward he had so little regard for his Treaties, that he made but a jest to break, without the least Provocation, those he had the most solemnly sworn to.

But how detested those Maxims were by every sober Man, appears by the Judgment which Agricola (Le Laboureur) Prior of *Juvigné* makes of them in the first Chapter of the VIIth Book of his Additions to the Memoirs of Castelnau, and which I have

transcribed

tranfcribed in this Book, page 248, 249, 50,
to which I refer the Reader, whereby every
one will be fatisfied of the falfhood of that
Hypothefis, that it is difhonourable for a King
to capitulate with his Subjects, or to keep faithfully the Capitulation Articles, when he has
been obliged to grant any.   But methinks
fuch a Judgment is fufficient for clearing the
Reformed's Innocence,   when they were obliged to oppofe force to force.

Had they attempted to fettle their Religion by force of Arms, that would be odious before God and Men, but that is not the
Cafe, they fuffered patiently the moft exqui-
fite Torture, and the bittereft Pains, without murmuring againft God, or reviling their
Perfecutors, or offering any Refiftance, but
they only endeavoured to preferve what Settlement had been granted unto them ; nay,
they did not take any Steps towards that
Prefervation, unlefs at the laft extremity, and
when they faw that there was no other means
or way left for keeping themfelves, their Wives
and Children alive.   Had they been the firft
Aggreffors, they would be guilty; but let it
be proved, and then we fhall believe it.   Had
they rifen in Arms for Trifles, or at the
firft Provocation, we would forfake their Caufe;
but nothing lefs than the Honour and Lives
of their Wives, Children, and their own,
lay at ftake, and feveral of their Neighbours Houfes had been burnt down to Afhes
before they thought of preferving their own.

True

True it is, that when they began the second Civil War, the Court did not expect it, the Ministry was fully persuaded that they should surprize the Reformed unawares, so it seems that they were the first Aggressors; but the only reading of History will clear them of that Imputation; besides the Modifications, Restrictions, &c. put upon the Amboisian Edict by way of Explanations, as they stiled them, whereby they made it void and of no force: Besides the many Murders and Massacres committed in several Places, and for which no Satisfaction could be obtained, They saw the vast Preparations made against them, six thousand Switzers in the very heart of the Kingdom, all ready to put the Plot laid at *Bayonne* in Execution, and they had so many repeated Warnings from the best hands, of what was hatching in the Queen's Secret Council against them, that really they could do no less, without being too far wanting to themselves, than to put themselves in a posture of Defence, lest they should be prevented by their Enemies. As to the attempt they made to seize upon the King's Person, I have freely delivered my Opinion upon that Subject, in its proper place, and blamed what appears unto me blameworthy.

Now who can be properly called the Aggressor; he who plots secretly the ruin and destruction of the other, or he, who being warned of it, endeavours to avert the threatning Danger? I leave the Decision of that Query, even to a Jesuit. Had the Reformed been

been the firſt that had riſen in Arms for
the defence of their Rights and Privileges,
their Proceeding would appear very ſtrange,
and may be criminal ; but how many times
did not the French before and after the Reformation riſe in Arms againſt their Sovereign, even upon leſs Provocation, under the
Reign of Charles VI. VII. Lewis XI. Lewis
XIII. and XIV ? And thoſe who pretend
to render the Reformed odious that way,
what can they ſay for proving the lawful-
neſs of their unnatural Rebellion againſt their
lawful Sovereigns Henry III. and IV. which
laſted for eight Years and better, and of their
barbarous Parricide committed on the Perſons of theſe two Princes ? What then, will
they be like that impudent Fellow in Syl-
la's Proſcription, and arraign the Reformed
becauſe they did not ſtretch their Necks of
their own accord to have their Throats cut
with more eaſe, becauſe they did not expoſe
their own Wives and Daughters ſtark naked
to ſatiate their Enemies brutiſhneſs ? How
then, ſhall nine or ten Highwaymen and Murderers indite two or three harmleſs Travellers
for the Wounds which five or ſix of them
have received in the fray ? How impudent,
unjuſt and wicked ſuch an Inditement would
be, is obvious to every thinking Man : Therefore the Reformed cannot, with any ſhadow
of Reaſon and Juſtice, be charged with the
Miſeries and Calamities, the Kingdom groaned
under for above 36 Years, ſince they were not
the Aggreſſors, and ſince they were forced to

fight

fight for the defence of what is deareft a-
mongft Men.

And it is needlefs to oppofe the Patience
of the Chriftians during the three firft Centuries, their Circumftances were not the fame.
Tho' fome of the Emperors, as Trajan, An-
toninus Pius, Alexander Severus, and a few o-
thers, have not been fo rigorous againft the
Chriftians, as many of their Predeceffors and
Succeffors, yet they never granted them the
free publick Exercife of their Religion, which
was always ftrictly forbidden by the Laws of
the Empire, till the time of Conftantine the
Great; therefore as there was no ftanding
Laws in their behalf, as they could not meet
together for Divine Worfhip without viola-
ting the ftanding Laws, they would have been
extremely blamable, had they attempted to
oppofe force to force : But that was not the
Cafe of the Reformed in France after the
firft Edict in their behalf : That Edict was
a ftanding Law, whereby they were authorized to meet publickly together, and to perform all other parts of their Religious Worfhip, and whereby it was forbidden to any
Perfon of what Rank and Quality foever to
difturb or moleft them on account of their
Religion, as long as they kept themfelves in
the bounds prefcribed by that Law. Confequently the Reformed being affaulted againft
their Privileges, and without any Provocation
on their Part, had a Right of refifting their
King, and oppofing force to force.

VOL. III. a The

The Nature of a Preface doth not allow me to enlarge myfelf any further upon that Subject, it would be an eafy matter to prove that thefe our Enemies Charges proceed rather from their hatred againft us, than from any fettled principle of Duty and Allegiance to Kings and Magiftrates, or from any Conviction of their Confcience; but that would be needlefs, THEY SHOW THEIR FAITH BY THEIR WORKS.

Now to come to this part of our Hiftory: I have been obliged to divide this Volume into two Parts. This firft hath been fwelled up with fome Relations which may appear, at the firft fight, to be fomething foreign to our main defign. The fhort Account I give of the Council of *Trent*; of the Rife, Progrefs and Settlement of the Jefuits in *France*; of the Reformation in the *Low Countries*, and the cruel Government of the Duke of Alva, could have been omitted, it is true, but not eafily, without leaving the Reader at a lofs, when he will fee in this Hiftory, that how favourable foever to the Popes the Kings of France have been, the Parliaments, efpecially that of Paris, could never be prevailed upon to receive the Council of *Trent*, and to publifh it in the Kingdom; That the Jefuits, whereof no mention is made before this time, have done fuch and fuch things; That the Reformed of *France* and thofe of the *Low Countries*, did mutually affift one another in feveral Occafions. Therefore I hope he will excufe thefe necefſary Digreſſions, intended
only

only for saving him the trouble of perusing other Books, for getting an Information of these things.

If I have been some thing out of humour in speaking of the Duke of Alva's cruel Government, and in relating the Massacre of Bartholomew's-Day, and other Particulars bearing some Resemblance with these ; I hope again, that the Reader will excuse me, considering that such Villanies as these cannot be thought of without Horrour, and that it is next to impossible for a feeling Man to relate them without the utmost Detestation : *What the Heart feels, the Mouth speaks, and the Hand writes.*

An Author must not be deemed Partial, unless when he magnifies the Objects on each side, when he conceals the right and good Actions of the contrary Party, and good Qualities and Virtues of an Enemy; and the Wrongs and Injustices of his own, the Vices, bad Qualities and Faults of Friends, and it is what I have not done, as far as I remember; and if I am guilty in that respect, and shewn of my Faults, I am ready to submit. But for venting one's Indignation by some scornful or odious Epithet, that I don't take to be Partiality, provided it should be deservedly bestowed upon the Actor.

And now it remains only to warn the Reader, that the next Contents are the most correct, exactly the same Articles as contained in the Margents of the Book.

HISTORY

HISTORY
OF THE
REFORMATION,
AND OF THE
Reformed Churches in *France*.

VOL. III.
The First Part.

BOOK V.

Containing the History of eleven Years, two Months, and eleven days, from the 19th of March 1563 to the Death of Charles IX. on the 30th of May 1574.

CONTENTS.

INTRODUCTION. *Means made use of by the Queen-Mother to extricate herself out of her fears. She sent Deputies into the several Provinces of the Kingdom. The Parliament of Thoulouse refractory. Edict for raising a vast Sum upon the Clergy. The Queen endeavours to corrupt the Prince. War proclaimed against England. Havre de Grace taken from the English. The English Embassadors arrested. Peace made between the two Crowns. Charles IX. declared of Age at Rouën. The Parliament of Paris opposes in vain. The Dowager of Guise*

Vol,   B.   *petitions*

The CONTENTS.

The CONTENTS.

her

The CONTENTS.

The CONTENTS.

The

The CONTENTS.

#6

The CONTENTS.

HISTORY
OF THE
REFORMATION,
AND OF THE
Reformed Churches in *France*.

VOL. III.

Containing the History of 47 Years, one Month, and
twenty-five days, from the Edict given at Amboise on the 19th of March 1563, to the Death
of Henry IV. on the 14th of May 1610.

BOOK V.

Containing the History of 11 Years, two Months,
and eleven days, from the 19th of March 1563
to the Death of Charles IX. on the 30th of May
1574.

CONTENTS.

B

The CONTENTS.

Execu-

The CONTENTS.

The CONTENTS.

The CONTENTS.

B 3   and

6   *Hiftory of the Reformation, and of the* VOL.III,
   and executed.   CIII. Charles IX's *Death.*
   Character of that Prince.

Charles
IX.
1563.
Pope Pius
IV.
⁓⁓⁓
Introduc-
tion.

THE Peace concluded at Amboife was
no lefs neceffary to the Catholicks than
to the Reformed ; this we muft infer
from the pathetick Defcription of the fad Condition the Kingdom was in, given by the Lord
Caftelnau de Mauviffiere in his Memoirs written
for the ufe of his own Son (*a*).

The Queen Regent was not ignorant of it, but
what induced her chiefly, to be in fuch a hurry
for concluding the Treaty, was, her Greedinefs
after Power and Authority ; fhe thought that
fhe could never enjoy foon enough the Sweetnefs
of Governing without any Controul ; for the
Heads or Support of the Triumvirate being dead,
there remained only the Conftable, whofe old
Age fecured her from all Apprehenfions of his
undertaking any thing againft her own Authority.

As to the Prince of Condé, fhe was in great
hopes of winning him to her Intereft one way or
another, fuch being the fituation of her Mind,
fhe dreaded nothing more than to fee the Treaty
thwarted before concluded ; or unperformed after its Conclufion, whereby the Reformed would
have been obliged to ftand in Arms, or to take
them up again, and renew a War, which then
would have put the greateft Obftacles to the execution of her Defigns.

She declared her fears upon that account to
Mr. de Gonnor, Super-Intendant of her Exchequer, (known afterwards by the Name and
Title of Marfhal de Coffé) dated the 27th of A-
pril, 1563 (*b*).

There-

(*a*) Memoires de Caftelnau, Liv. V. ch. 1.
(*b*) Le Laboureur Additions aux Mem. de Caftelnau,
Vol. II. liv. IV. ch. 12. pag. 246.

Therefore in order to avoid the firſt Inconvenience, the Prince had no ſooner concluded the Treaty with her, but ſhe ſent ſome of her moſt truſty Confidents to Paris for engaging the Parliament in a Compliance with her Deſires, and to ratify the Edict of Pacification ; wherein, after ſome ſtruggles, ſhe ſucceeded better than ſhe expected, and the Peace having been publiſhed in the Camp and at Orleans, the King made his publick Entry into that City on the 29th of April.

Then for avoiding the ſecond Inconvenience, ſhe ſent ſome Deputies into ſeveral Provinces, eſpecially into Guienne, Languedoc, Provence, and Dauphiné, with Orders to ſettle every thing according to the Edict, and to cauſe it to be obſerved by every one. Beſides that, Orders were ſent on the 18th of June to the ſaid Deputies enjoining them to recal without delay, the Reformed that had been exiled for their Religion ſake, or on account of the late Troubles, to return to them the price of thoſe of their Goods that had been ſold by Auction ; not to delay upon any account ſoever the Reſtitution of thoſe of their Moveables that had not been ſold ; the ſame thing was ordered as to their Immoveables ; which however was to be underſtood only of thoſe Goods, Moveables or Immoveables, which had not been plundered by the Soldiery at the taking of the Cities, &c. Furthermore, it was ordered, That all the Captives for Religion ſake ſhould be immediately ſet at liberty. Laſtly, they were ordered to inquire into the Conduct of thoſe Judges or other Magiſtrates who ſhould ſhow themſelves remiſs, or partial and unjuſt in the diſcharge of their Office as to the execution of the Edict, and to puniſh them according to Law (c).

Charles IX. 1563. Pope Pius IV.

I.
Means made uſe of by the Queen Mother to extricate herſelf out of her fears.

II.
She ſent Deputies into the ſeveral Provinces, &c.

B 4　　　　　　　　The

(c) Thuani Hiſt. lib. XXXV. p. 241, 242.

Charles
IX.
1563.
Pope Pius
IV.

III.
The Parli-
ament of
Thoulouse
refractory.

The Parliament of Thoulouse was one of the most refractory, and when they had published the Edict, they expelled from their House the Counsellors Arnold Cavagne and Gabriel Du Bourg, whose Religion was suspected ; but upon proper Application of the Plaintiffs to the King's Council, they were after several Jussions restored to their Dignities ; and a few days after the Decrees of the same Parliament against *Lanta, Pastorel,* and several others of their Body who had been deprived the Year before, and against *Mandinelli* who had been beheaded, were reversed by the King's Council, and likewise whatever the said Parliament had done against them, or their Families, and they were all restored to their good Name and Fame, Honours and Estates.

While those things were a doing at Thoulouse, *Damville,* Son to the Constable of Montmorancy having obtained the Reversion of the Government of Languedoc, which his Father enjoyed, went into that Province, and behaved himself towards the Reformed with a great deal of Injustice and Severity, nay with the greatest Cruelty ; and indeed he deprived them of several things that had been expresly granted by the Edict, and explained the remaining part in a way quite contrary to the obvious meaning of the Words ; the worst of all was, that his Conduct was approved of by the Court, and no Redress of their Grievances could be obtained by the Reformed. But more of this afterwards, when we shall relate on a thread the many just Subjects of Complaints the Reformed had (*d*).

IV.
Edict for
raising a
vast Sum
upon the
Clergy.

On the seventh of *May* an Edict was published, whereby one hundred thousand Crowns of
                                                        yearly

(*d*) Thuan. ubi supra.

yearly Rent (*) over the Church's Lands and other immoveable Goods belonging to it, were mortgaged to the beft Bidder for the difcharge of the publick Debts, which was executed with great Rigour : If the Clergy were incenfed already againft the Court for having granted Liberty of Confcience to the Reformed, they were put almoft out of all patience at this Step.

But a little time after they were much appeafed by Chancellor de l'Hofpital granting them the Faculty of redeeming the fame, and caufing another Edict to be publifhed whereby the Reformed were obliged to pay them the Tythes (*e*).

Two things remained ftill which made the Queen Regent uneafy ; the Conduct of the Prince, and the Havre de Grace which was in the poffeffion of the Englifh.

How artfully foever the Queen-Mother behaved herfelf, it was not in her power to part the Prince from the Admiral, nor to dazzle him with an idle Fancy of a Kingdom of Sardinia, as his Brother the King of Navarr had been : But fhe endeavoured to win him to her own Intereft by the Allurements of Senfuality, and the fair LIMEUIL one of her Maids of Honour was the unfortunate Victim fhe offered up to her own Ambition. And indeed fhe fucceeded fo well by thefe means, that for a time the Prince feemed to have quite forgotten the care of his own Reputation and Honour ; the Princefs his Confort not able to recal him from this evil Courfe,

V.
*The Queen
endeavours
to corrupt
the Prince.*

died

<hr>

(*) Mr. Jurieu fays, that there was for two Millions five hundred thoufand Livres of Church Lands, &c. fold at a very low rate, and that the temporal Jurifdiction over the City of Lyons, enjoyed till then by its Archbifhop, was bought for the King for thirty Thoufand Livres. Abregé de l'Hift. du Concile de Trente, Tom. II. lib. viii. p. 395.

(*e*) Idem ibid. pag. 245, and 250.

died with Grief. Then it was that the Queen conceived greater hopes than ever of succeeding in her Designs, doubting not but that she would prevail with the Prince to marry one that was in her Interest. She pitched upon MARGARET DE LUSTRAC, Widow of the Marshal of St. Andrew; as she was the richest Party in the Kingdom, it was very likely that the Prince, whose Income was not sufficient for maintaining him according to his Rank and Dignity, would be glad of an opportunity which should enable him to discharge his Debts, and to live after a Way suitable to his Condition, as well as to his Humour: Therefore, as the Lady was very ambitious, it was not a difficult Task to engage her to do all in her power for inspiring the Prince with Love for her. But it succeeded quite contrary to her Expectation; for instead of inspiring the Prince with Love for her, she fell herself into such a violent Passion for him, that she bought the Gratification of her unlawful Desires at the price of her own Estate of St. Valery, one of the finest in the Kingdom, and of many thousand Livres of yearly Rent (f).

The Admiral being very sensible of the great Mischiefs which might ensue from such a disorderly Life of the Chief of the Party, prevailed at last by his Intreaties with him, and engaged him to forsake it, and to marry Frances of Orleans, Sister to the Duke of Longueville; notwithstanding the Endeavours of the House of Guise, who, in order to win him to their Interest, flattered him with the hopes of marrying MARY their Niece, Queen of Scotland. I have a little anticipated the times, for the Prince was married only the next Year (g).

Now

(f) Idem Ibid. pag. 243, 244.
(g) Id. Ibid. Mezeray, 3d Part, Tom. V. p. 77, 78.

Now every thing was ready for the Siege of Havre de Grace. A Trumpet had been sent to the Earl of Warwick, Governor of that Place, summoning him in the King's Name to surrender it ; to which having answered, that if *Calais* was restored to England, he would readily surrender the *Place* ; but if not, he would keep it and be upon the Defensive ; a War against Queen Elizabeth was proclaimed on the 5th of July, the King being at *Gaillon*. On the 20th the Constable came to the Camp, with the Marshal of Montmorancy his Son, and the Marshal of Bourdillon, and other Lords, and the Chiefs of the Nobility. The Prince of Condé and the Duke of Montpensier arrived likewise, and it was observed, that, of the whole Army, none shewed so great a Zeal, nor fought with so much Chearfulness and Ardour, as the Reformed did, whereof great Notice was taken at Court ; whereupon I shall relate here the Reply made by MONEINS an Officer of the Reformed Religion to Sir———LEIGHTON ; Leighton perceiving Moneins in a Parley, told him, *That he was surprized to see him, and so many others, amongst their Enemies, since they had fought together at Rouën against the same Enemies.* To which Moneins replied, *As you do now stand in Arms for the Defence of your Queen, so we do for that of our King ; it is no more a question of our Religion, for which the King has made sufficient Provisions by his late Edict, but it is a question of the Limits of the Kingdom ; therefore do not be surprized, if the Reason of our Union being ceased, we are suddenly turned Enemies, ready to destroy one another, except you would give a speedy Satisfaction to his Majesty for the controverted Place now in your possession.*

However it cannot be denied that the Prince of Condé had been very ungrateful to the Queen

of

Charles
IX.
1563.
Pope Pius
IV.

of England his good Friend, and at the same time he shewed himself a very bad Politician ; for not only he concluded his Treaty with the King, without taking any care to have that Princess included in it, nay, without giving her any previous Notice of it, as he was obliged to do by the Articles of the Treaty of London, to which he had subscribed ; but he displayed all his Might to have her driven out of a Place which he himself had put into her hands. Very likely for these Reasons it was, that the Admiral and D'Andelot his Brother did not think proper to assist in the King's Army.

VII.
Havre de Grace taken from the English.

The Earl of Warwick defended the Place some time with great Bravery and Intrepidity, but the Plague which raged in the Town, daily swept away many of his Men, and besides that a Letter of SMITH, Embassador of England, directed to the Earl, (whereby he gave him Notice of the sudden arrival of the Succours sent from Queen Elizabeth) having been intercepted, and another sent in its stead, whereby the said Earl was made to believe that he ought not to expect any Succour from England ; these two Considerations reduced him to the Necessity of a Capitulation, whereby the Town was to be restored to the King ; the Prisoners on both sides to be set at liberty ; the Earl, with the Garison, and all the People with him in the Town, and all the Ammunitions and other Effects belonging to the English, to retire with all Safety to England, &c. These are the chief Articles of the Capitulation, which were to be fully executed in six days (*b*).

The very next day arrived in the Road a Succour of 1800 Men coming from England, which were followed two days after by a Fleet of 60 Sail

(*b*) Mem. de Castelnau, liv. V. ch. 2, 3. Thuan. lib. 35. p. 246, &c.

Sail commanded by Admiral CLINTON. But understanding that the Capitulation was signed, they did not attempt to make a Descent, and waited only for the remaining part of the Garison, which to the Number of above 3000 came on board on the 30th of July, and put to sea immediately.

At the beginning of the Siege the Garison was six thousand strong, besides a body of French Reformed Soldiers, who detesting the Ungratefulness of their Chief, offered their Services to the Earl of Warwick, and were admitted in the Town, six Hundred whereof perished during the Siege either by the Plague or by the Sword, and the rest came over to England with the Earl, and were kindly received by Queen Elizabeth. The next day SARLABOS was made Governor of the Place for the King (*i*).

The English Forces which had served in France bringing the Plague with them into England, it made a terrible havock especially in London, where above twenty Thousand died of it in a little time.

Havre de Grace being taken, the French and English were for some Months rather in a State of Inaction than of Peace. Queen Elizabeth had sent Orders to her Embassadors THROCKMORTON and SMITH to make all haste they could to meet the King in Normandy. But his Majesty, or rather the Queen Regent, unwilling to receive them, had sent CASTELNAU DE MAUVISSIERE with Orders to arrest them, because they were come over without a Pass, the War being declared against England ; but it was done especially by Reprisal, because DE FOIX, the French Embassador had been arrested at London, and the King was advised to do the same with Smith ;

VIII. *The English Embassadors arrested.*

(*i*) E.J. Ib id. D'Aubigné Hist. Univ. liv. III. di. 2.

Smith ; and not to receive Throckmorton upon any account foever, but rather to send him Prisoner into some strong Hold, as a Disturber of the publick Peace. Castelnau executed his Commission ; Throckmorton was sent to the Castle of St. Germain en Laye under a strong Guard ; and Smith to the Castle of Melun.

IX.
*Peace made
between
the two
Crowns.*

This last shewed a great deal more of Moderation under this Misfortune than the first, and it was he who made the first Overture of a Peace, which came at last to a happy Conclusion the next Year 1564, and was proclaimed at Troyes in Champaign on the 13th of April (k).

By this Treaty the King of France and the Queen of England preserved entire all their Pretensions, without mentioning any in particular, not even the Restitution of Calais : (for tho' by the Treaty of Chateau-Cambresis in 1559, Henry II. had agreed to restore that Place to the Crown of England, or to pay down 500,000 Crowns in eight Years, during which time neither of the Parties ought to attempt any thing against the other, nevertheless the French Council pretended, that Queen Elizabeth had forfeited her Right to that Place, because she had relieved the Reformed with her Forces and Money :) There were only some separate Articles which were left unsigned till the next day, concerning the Hostages delivered to Queen Elizabeth, after the Treaty of Chateau ; she restored them to their Liberty for the Sum of one hundred and twenty thousand Crowns.

X.
*Charles
IX. declared of Age
at Rouën.*

During the Siege, King Charles came to the 14th Year of his Age, and being arrived at Rouën, the Queen Regent in order to put the Prince of Condé and the Constable out of all hopes of having any Share in the publick Administration

(k) Mem. de Castelnau, liv. V. ch. 4. & 7.

miniftration of the Government, and to engrofs it Charles
IX.
1563.
Pope Pius
IV.
all to herfelf, under the King's Name, refolved,
by the Chancellor's Advice, to have the King
declared of Age, and for that end to renew the
Conftitution of Charles V. King of France, whereby, after the Example of *Joas, Jofias, Solomon,*
&c. the Kings, having attained the 14th Year
of their Age, are declared capable of the Admif-
ftration of their Kingdom ; which Conftitution
bears date the 20th of May, 1374 (*l*).

This Conftitution very likely has never been
well underftood, for it is not faid exprefly, whether the King muft have fourteen Years compleat,
or whether he fhall be of Age at the beginning of
the fourteenth Year. By the Common Law the
fourteen Years compleat are requifite to be declared of Age ; but the Chancellor willing to pleafe
the Queen, perfuaded her not to ftay for the
fulnefs of the fourteen Years, and faid, that in
fuch Cafes favourable, when the Year is begun,
it is to be reckoned as compleat ; and whether
he was afraid left the Parliament of Paris would
oppofe that Opinion, becaufe it was doubtful
whether it was advantageous for the Good and
the Welfare of the Kingdom, or not ; he advifed her Majefty to bring the King to the Parliament of Rouën for performing that Ceremony.

Accordingly the King came to the Parliament
on the 17th of Auguft, with the Queen his
Mother, the Duke of Orleans, the Princes of
the Blood, and all the Lords then at Court ; and
after a feafonable Speech on the prefent juncture,
which had been compofed by the Chancellor, he
was proclaimed of Age ; then he publifhed an
Edict, which was afterwards regiftered in all the
Parliaments of the Kingdom, whereby he declared that the Edict which he had granted before
for

(*l*) Thuan. lib. XXXV. pag. 248.

for the Liberty of Conscience ought to be obſerved, till the Points controverted ſhould be decided by the Council, or till he himſelf ſhould order otherwiſe ; that whoſoever ſhould break it would be treated as a Rebel ; that every one in the Kingdom ſhould diſarm, and renounce all manner of League or Aſſociation with Foreigners ; that he would ſpare no body, not even his own Brethren, if they acted contrary to this.

XI.
The Parliament of Paris oppoſes in vain.

The Edict of the King's Age was not regiſtered by the Parliament of Paris without much ado: The firſt Preſident De Thou and two others were deputed to make their Remonſtrances to the King upon that account. But the King, having received his Leſſon of his Mother, bid them with a very ſevere Countenance to obey, and not meddle with the publick Adminiſtration of the Kingdom ; and to renounce that old Error, That they were the King's Tutors, the Defenders of the Kingdom, and the Guardians of the City of Paris. His Majeſty would not come to Paris till the Parliament had obeyed, which it did at laſt after the ſecond Command, on the 28th of September (*m*). La Hode places this Event on the 28th of October (*).

XII.
The Dowager of Guiſe petitions for Juſtice.

The King arrived in his Capital about the latter end of October, and the Mother of the late Duke of Guiſe, his Widow, his Children, ſeveral of his Relations attended by a vaſt number of his Adherents, walking two by two along the Streets, all in deep Mourning, came to Court in December next, to require Juſtice againſt the late Duke's Murderers. That doleful Sight

(*m*) Id. Ibid. Mezeray, 3d Par. Tom. V. p. 80.
(*) There is no Law in the Kingdom for preferring one Parliament to another for the Performance of that Ceremony. De La Hode. Faſtes des Roix de France, p. 148.

Sight was prepared purposely to move the Affections of the People towards that illustrious Family, yet more Ambitious than Noble, and they succeeded to their Wishes, for the Mob ran after them, and followed the Procession to the Palace : Being admitted to the King's Presence, they all fell upon their Knees; the King was much moved at that Sight, however he received them very kindly, and having raised up again the Duchess Mother and the Widow, he hearkened to their Complaints with a great deal of Compassion, either real or affected, and promised to do them Justice in a proper time. The young Dowager, in her Speech, had directly pointed at the Admiral, tho' she had not named him; and the Prince of Condé had already declared in the King's Council, by a publick Instrument, on the 15th of May, that considering that the said Admiral was his good Friend, Uncle to the Princess his Consort, and great Uncle to his Children, who, besides that, had deserved very well of the King and the Kingdom by his glorious and generous Feats; he took him so far under his Protection, that whosoever should attack him otherwise than as Law directed, he would deem him his own Enemy. The Marshal of Montmorancy had spoken to the same effect at the same time, and in the Name of his Father, and of his whole Family.

The Queen-Mother was not a little puzzled at this Affair; she knew very well that she could not gratify the Plaintiffs in their Requests without kindling anew the civil War; on the other hand, she knew that the Admiral, who refused not to stand his Tryal, had challenged all the Parliaments in the Kingdom for their notorious Partiality against him; therefore she advised the King, to bring that Case before him, and to have it tried in his great Council. But the Guises, much diffatisfied, complained loudly that they were wronged in that refpect, inafmuch that the Cafes of the Peers could not be tried but by the Parliament of Paris, which was the fupream Court of the Kingdom: The King tired with their Importunity brought back again the Cafe to himfelf, and put off the Decifion of it for three Years longer; when being at Moulins, where he had fummoned a general Affembly of the Nobility and the Deputies of all the Parliaments to meet there in January 1566, and there being no Evidence againft the Admiral, who cleared himfelf by a folemn Oath, he interpofed his own Authority, and bid both Parties to be Friends again, whereupon they embraced one another in token of a Reconciliation, and promifed to forget whatever was paft. Thefe things were tranfacted between the Widow and the Duke of Guife, the Cardinal of Lorrain his Brother, and the Admiral; Henry Duke of Guife Son to the deceafed was prefent, being lately arrived from Hungary, but he was filent, and fhewed by his Countenance that he waited only for a more proper time to vent out his Refentment, which opportunity he met with at laft, fix or feven Years after, on Bartholomew's day (*n*).

The fourth National Synod of the Reformed Churches was held this year at Lyons: The firft Seffion whereof begun on the 10th of Auguft, Peter Viret then Minifter of Lyons being Moderator. Wherein nothing very material was tranfacted befides what concerned the Difcipline. Cenfures were decreed againft Minifters contracting unfitting Marriages (either as to the Age, or as to the Condition, or the Morals of the Bride) it was ordered that Marriages fhould

---

(*n*) Thuan. lib. XXXV. p. 245, and lib. XXXIX. p. 391.

should be celebrated in the Church ; and in case
one of the Parties should be disabled, either by
Sickness or otherwise, to walk to the Church, it
was said, that he or she should be carried thither.

Several Regulations were made, several Cases
of Conscience decided, and several Queries a-
bout that Matter answered ; and whether they
were not too severe, or whether they stretched
not their Authority too far, that I do not take
upon me to determine, neither is it of my Province, in the capacity of an Historian, to determine. For example, a Man who forsakes his
Wife afflicted with the Leprosy, and marries another, this second Marriage is declared void, and
the Man is excommunicated till he comes again
with his first Wife, and has done publick Penance. All Promises of Marriage made between
Parties of a competent Age, and with the Consent of their Parents, are declared indissoluble,
tho' the Marriage has not been solemnized, nor
even the Banns published : Nay, tho' both Parties should unanimously consent to their Separation.

The Ministers of Geneva consulted upon that
Point, are of Opinion, That the Promise is sacred and irrevocable, even tho' the Parents should
oppose, the Parties concerned are in Conscience,
and by the Laws of God, obliged to go on notwithstanding these Oppositions, &c.

As to Baptism, it was ordered that it should
be celebrated publickly in the Church. The
Church of Geneva having been consulted about
the Validity of Lay-baptism, their Answer was
to the following purpose :

,, We Ministers and Divines of the Church
,, of Geneva, with those of our Brethren coming
C 2   ,, from

„ from the Synod of Lyons, being met together
„ in the Name of the Lord, after having exa-
„ mined that Cafe of Confcience, viz. *Whether*
„ *the Baptiſm adminiſtred by a Lay-Man is to be*
„ *reïterated or no?* we do declare, that we
„ believe unanimouſly that ſuch a Baptiſm agree-
„ ing not with the Inſtitution of our Lord Jeſus
„ Chriſt, is confequently invalid and of none ef-
„ fect, and that the Child muſt be brought to
„ the Church of God, there to be baptized ;
„ forafmuch that to feparate the Adminiſtration
„ of the Sacraments from the Paſtor's Office,
„ it is the fame as to take off a Seal from an
„ Inſtrument, in order to make uſe of it with-
„ out the Commiſſion of the Letters Patent, and
„ to this Cafe we may apply what Jeſus Chriſt has
„ ſaid upon another Occcafion, *Let no Man put*
„ *afunder what God hath joined together.* This
„ for and in the Name of all the Aſſembly.

John Calvin.

Befides that the fame Aſſembly fully anſwered
a Letter directed to the faid Synod in defence of
Lay-Baptiſm, fetting forth the weakneſs of the
Arguments made uſe of by the Author thereof,
for the fupport of his Hypothefis, and ſhewing
evidently that the bringing of the Child that had
been baptized after that manner to the Church,
could not be termed a *Rebaptization,* fince he
had not been baptized before ; that Ceremony
performed by a Lay-Man, being no more than
a Mockery, the requifite Qualification for anſwer-
ing the Inſtitution of Jeſus Chriſt, being wanting, viz. the Character of the Perſon that ad-
miniſters that Sacrament, &c.

It was enacted likewife in the Synod, That
the feveral Churches of the Kingdom fhould be
warned to make a faithful Collection of whatever

ever had happened in their Diſtricts, worthy of Obſervation, and ſend the relations thereof to their Reverend Brethren of Geneva with all poſſible diligence.

Furthermore it was enacted, That Mr. De Beze ſhould be deſired to ſet in writing in Latin and French the Cauſes and Proteſts of Nullity, againſt the Council of Trent, and to ſend them to the Miniſters at Court, that they might tender them to his Majeſty.

Four or five Books were cenſured and condemned by this Synod as full of Blaſphemies, Hereſies, &c. Their Titles were, *The Declaration of the Myſtery of God demonſtrated by two Figures.* Item, *The Mirrour of the Antichriſt.* Item, *Counſel to poor France.* Item, *The Queſtions propoſed by the Miniſters of Geneva to thoſe who deſire to be admitted to the Lord's Supper* (o).

Then a Liſt of twenty-four Miniſters, Vagrants or Depoſed, was publiſhed in the Synod's Name.

On the 4th of December ended the Seſſions of the Council of Trent. The Cardinal of Lorrain put an end to it, in a way much unbecoming his high Station and Character ; for he not only compoſed the Acclamations and Anthems, but he tuned them in the Cathedral, which Office belonged properly to the Deacons ; wherein he ſhewed very little regard even for the honour of his King, inaſmuch that, I don't know for what, he made a particular mention of the Emperor only, and put together all the Catholick Kings of Europe, without ſo much as ſpecifying the King of France his Maſter. But it was not the only thing whereby he became obnoxious to the Cenſures of the King's Council, and of the Par-

C 3　　　　　　liament

(o) Quick Synodicon, Vol. I. Aymon Synodes Nationaux, Tom. I.

Charles IX. 1563. Pope Pius IV.

liament of Paris. For that Prelate, [who, at his setting out for Trent, had made the Pope upon his Throne, and the whole Confistory at Rome to tremble, left he should perform what he bragged he would, as to the Reformation of the Church, in its Head, and in its Members] did no sooner hear of the Duke his Brother's death, but all his Zeal cooled apace, and to ingratiate himself with the Court of Rome, he suffered many things to be done in the Council, contrary to the Prerogatives of the Court of France, and the Rights of the Gallican Church; and we shall prove, in its proper place, by undeniable Authorities, that the Embryo of that dreadful Monster which appeared under Henry III. and put the Kingdom on the very brink of its utter Destruction, (I mean the League) was formed at Trent, by the Intrigues of this brave Cardinal (*p*).

XV. *A short Account of that Council.*

The History of that Council written by that great Man Fra. Paolo, having been translated into English, I shall not enlarge myself too much upon that Subject. I shall only give a sketch of it, and of the most remarkable Transactions in it, referring my Reader to the Book itself.

The means whereby Pope Leo intended to stop the Progress of the Reformation in Germany proving ineffectual, and Charles V. having been obliged to grant them Liberty of Conscience, till the Determination of a free general Council; Clement VII. consented at last in 1531, to convene one, but upon such unreasonable Terms that he knew very well the Protestants would never agree to; for he intended to appoint it in some City of the Ecclesiastical State then in his power, as *Bolonia*, *Parma*, or *Placentia*. 2dly. That none but the Bishops, Abbots, and those who

(*p*) Mezeray, 3d. Par. Tom. V. pag. 83. Fra. Paolo, liv. VIII. p. 670.

who were privileged by Popes, fhould vote deliberately in that Affembly ; and as to the Proteftants that fhould defire to be heard, they fhould be obliged to ftand by the Decifions of others, and fubmit themfelves to them.

All the Remonftrances which the Emperor made to the Pope upon that Subject, either by his Embaffadors, or in the Conference he had with him at Bolonia in 1532, and at another in June 1534 were fruitlefs ; Clement would not fwerve a jot from his Opinion. So the Proteftants refufing to fubmit themfelves to thefe hard Terms, there was no more Talk about the Council, till Paul III. Clement's Succeffor, being promoted to the Papal Chair on the 13th of October 1534, he feigned, at firft, to be much defirous of holding a Council, and readily confenting to the Emperor's Requeft, on the 12th of June 1536 he appointed one at *Mantua.* But the Duke refufing upon feveral Pretences to lend his chief City for that ufe, the Council was put off till November, when the Pope appointed it at Vicenza, for the 1ft of May 1538 ; but Henry VIII. having protefted againft the Bull of Convocation, and the Emperor, together with the King of France, having refufed to fend their Prelates thither, the Pope was obliged to recall his Legates from that Place where they were alone, and by his Bull of the 28th of July he put off the Council again to the Eafter Holidays of the next Year ; but that Convocation was without effect, therefore by his Bull of the 13th of June 1539, the Pope prorogued it at his own and the Holy See's pleafure.

In the Year 541, the Emperor and the Pope agreed together to convene it at the fame laft place, and to appoint it for the beginning of the Year 1542. But the Venetians having fome

reafons

reafons for not allowing that the Council fhould meet at *Vicenza*, which belonged to them, the Pope appointed it at *Trent* for the Month of November. But the Proteftants of Germany were much offended at the Pope taking upon him to publifh a Council in his own Name, and would not confent to it. On the other hand, the Emperor took amifs that the Pope had directed his Bull to the King of France as well as to himfelf, forafmuch as the faid King had declared War againft him, whereby he put an infuperable Obftacle to the celebration of the Council.

But the Pope little regarding thefe Complaints, fent his Legates to Trent on the 26th of Auguft, viz. the Cardinals PETER PAUL PARIS, JOHN MORON, and REGINALD POLUS, with pofitive Orders to make all the hafte they could, that they might arrive in time at *Trent*, there to receive and entertain the Prelates and the Embaffadors that fhould come; however without making any publick Act, till they fhould have received their Inftructions, which fhould be fent unto them in proper time.

Notwithftanding the great buftle the Emperor had made, he was not forry in his Heart that the Pope would not recede from his Refolution; he was in hopes that this Step would ferve him as a pretence for eluding the Inftances which he forefaw the Proteftants would make at the Diet of *Nuremberg*, for redreffing their religious Grievances, referring them to the Decifions of the Council; therefore he fent his Embaffadors to *Trent*, and fome Bifhops of his Kingdom of *Naples*. Befides the Legates, the Pope fent likewife fome Italian Bifhops on whom he might entirely depend, but with Orders to proceed only by little Journeys.

Never-

Nevertheless the Italians, as well as the Imperialists were arrived at Trent at the appointed time, viz. the 1st of November. The Emperor's Embassadors delivered their Credentials to the Legates, and insisted much to have the Council opened without any further delay : But the Legates excused themselves, saying that it was not fit to begin a Council with such a small number of Prelates, but the true reason was, that they waited for the Success of the Diet of Nuremberg, which having been fruitless, the Emperor's Embassadors withdrew themselves from *Trent*, the *Neapolitan* Prelates followed them, the *Italians* went away on several Pretences, and the Legates themselves were obliged at last to set out for Rome (*q*).

So the Council was put off again to another time. The War being kindled between the Emperor and the King of France, there was no talk of it, till the Treaty of *Crespy*, September 24th 1544, whereby the two Crowns engaged themselves to require the Pope to summon a Council without any delay, for to cure the Church's Diseases. The Pope having got Intelligence of this Article, was not surprised at it, knowing how the two Princes stood affected towards him ; but left he should be looked upon as having been forced to such a thing, without waiting for the two Princes Request, he appointed again the Council at *Trent* for the 15th of March 1545. He knew very well that the time was too short for giving notice of it to all the Princes and States of Europe, and much more for the Prelates to dispose themselves for that Journey, and to arrive at Trent by that time ; but he knew likewise very well, that it was vastly for his Advantage to have the Council opened with

a

(*q*) Fra. Paolo Hist. du Concile de Trente, liv. I.

a small Number of Prelates, and they even *Italians* and of his own Dependants, for they could settle the Form and Manner of proceeding in the Council to his own liking, whereto those who should come afterwards would be obliged to submit themselves.

Accordingly he dispatched in all haste his Legates JOHN MARY DEL MONTE Cardinal Bishop, MARCEL CERVIN Cardinal Priest, and REGINALD POLUS Cardinal Deacon; they received their Brief of Legation, but not their Instructions, the Pope reserving to himself to send them as the Cases should require. Their Powers were large enough, as well as the Faculties given to the Council, since they were authorized to constrain even the Pope himself: But to avoid the Inconveniences which could arise from such an Authority, the Pope, after the Example of MARTIN V. gave to his Legates a secret Brief whereby they were empowered to prorogue, dissolve, or transfer the Council to another Place, whenever the Fathers should undertake any thing against the *Holy See*, and by that means all the good Intentions of the Council were frustrated, if they were contrary to the Designs of the Court of Rome; and the Legates failed not to make use of that Power for transferring the Council from *Trent* to *Bolonia*, as we shall say in its proper place.

They arrived at *Trent* on the 13th of March 1545, and made their publick Entry, being received by MADRUCE Cardinal of Trent: They granted three Years, and as many Quarantains of free Pardon or Indulgences, to all those that were present at that Ceremony: No Prelate was arrived as yet, nevertheless they caused their Legantine Bull to be regiftered.

Dom Diego de Mendoza the Emperor's Embaffador, arrived at *Trent* on the 23d of the fame Month, and was received by the Legates, by the Cardinal Bifhop of *Trent*, and three other Bifhops, for there was no more arrived as yet in that City. On the 27th the Embaffador delivered his Credentials, and opened his Commiffion, whereto the Legates anfwered.

After that, they were very bufy to find out means for difpenfing themfelves with the imparting to others the Difpatches which they received from Rome, and they could find no better than to advife the Pope, that for the future he would be pleafed to write apart, whatever he thought proper, to be kept fecret from others.

On the 8th of April arrived the Embaffadors of Ferdinand, King of the Romans. That Prince had much infifted with the Proteftants at the Diet of *Worms*, held on the 24th of March, to put off the Refolutions upon the points controverted, till they had feen what Turn the Affairs would take at *Trent*, and in the mean while to grant the neceffary Subfidies for the War againft the Turks; but they could not be prevailed on, becaufe they were afraid, left after having exhaufted their Purfe, the Emperor would fall upon them unawares. The Pope being much diffatiffied with that, endeavoured to engage the Emperor in a religious War.

In the mean while the Legates, who had received Orders of the Pope for opening the Council without waiting for a greater number of Prelates, if they underftood that any point of Religion was debated in the Diet, feeing by what was tranfacted in the faid Diet that there was no great Occafion for opening the Council, and on the other hand, that the fmall number of Prelates, then at *Trent*, (they were but four) afforded
them

them a fair Opportunity of doing Service to the Pope, they sent a Messenger to him to know his pleasure, and how they ought to behave themselves in this Occurrence.

The Pope having maturely examined all the reasons for and against the opening of the Council, resolved at last for the affirmative, and accordingly sent his Orders to his Legates ; which Orders however were countermanded, and the Council was opened only seven Months or thereabout after, viz. on the 13th of December 1545. The Legates with 25 Prelates in their *Pontificalibus*, attended by several Divines, the Clergy and the People, either Foreigners or Inhabitants, went in Procession from Trinity Church to the Cathedral ; there the first Legate Cardinal DEL MONTE sung the Mass of the Holy Ghost, the Bishop of *Bitonte* preached a Sermon ; then followed a long Exhortation upon the present Occasion ; after that the Pope's Bulls and Briefs were read ; Prayers were said ; and at last the first Decree declaring the opening of the Council was read by the first Legate, and the second Session appointed for the 7th of January 1546, all which was registered by the Notaries of the Council, then the *Te Deum* was sung, and so ended the first Session.

This Council lasted under five Popes, viz. Paul III. Julius III. Marcel II. Paul IV. and Pius IV. eighteen Years and a few days from this first Session to the 25th, which was the last, held on the 4th of December 1563. It was transferred twice, and interrupted once. The first Translation was on the 11th of March 1547, when the Bishops in the Pope's Interest followed the Legates from Trent to Bolonia, while the Imperialists and their Adherents remained at Trent. The second Translation from Bolonia to Trent

Trent again on the firſt of May 1551. It was
interrupted the next Year by the War of Mau-
rice Electour of Saxony againſt the Emperor : At
laſt the 15th Seſſion was held at the ſame place,
on the 18th of January 1562, after an Interrup-
tion of about ten Years.

Now whoſoever will be at the trouble of reading the Hiſtory of that Council, written by
Fra. Paolo, nay, by Pallavicini himſelf,
will readily ſubſcribe to the Title given to it
by Visconti, a ſecret Miniſter to Pius IV. in
the Council, who ſays in one of his Letters to
Cardinal Borromeo the Pope's Nephew, *that
he could find nothing of an Œcumenical Council,
in that* Croud *of Trent ; that Matters were debated and determined in a tumultuous manner, and
that, even ſeveral of the Fathers did not underſtand the Matters in debate.*

In order to have a right Notion of that Council, and of its Deciſions, one needs only to conſider, 1ſt, The great Reluctancy of the Popes
againſt the convening any, wherein the Points
controverted ſhould be freely propounded, impartially conſidered, debated, and decided ; the
remembrance of the Councils of Conſtance and
Baſil, eſpecially of this laſt, wherein their uſur-
ped Authority was ſo much depreſſed, was too
freſh in their Mind, they dreaded leſt any thing
like it ſhould be attempted againſt them, which
would have proved of a worſe Conſequence for
them, than any thing done at Baſil ; becauſe the
times were much changed. 2dly, The fraudu-
lent and ſcandalous Means whereof they made
uſe, for rendering ineffectual that Remedy, when
they were forced to apply it to the Diſeaſes of
the Church : They ſpared nothing in order to
have the majority of Votes, either by Threats
or Promiſes, they bribed as many Foreigners as
they

they could ; and they fent fuch a number of
Italian Prelates, intirely at their Devotion, that
no wonder if they carried their Point, feeing
that inftead of voting by Nations, they reckoned
the Votes by Heads, whereof the Italian and
other Penfioner Bifhops made the greateft Number. 3dly, Their way of proceeding ; nothing
was propounded in the Council but by the Legates ; no freedom in the Examination of Matters ; no freedom in delivering their Opinion ;
and when they had refolved the Matters in fome
private Congregations, their Refolutions and De-
terminations were fent to Rome in order to be
approved, altered or rejected by the Pope, and
then fent back to Trent, to be there publifhed
as Articles of Faith.

We have the following Letter of Monf. De
Lanssac, French Embaffador to the Council,
directed to Monf. De l'Isle, French Embaffador at Rome, dated from Trent the 19th of
May, wherein he complains bitterly of the illegal
proceedings of the faid Council.

,, S I R,

,, I Muft tell you one thing, viz. that if by
,,   your means we cannot obtain the two next
,, Points, I am afraid left we fhould not get
,, much by this Council. The firft is that the
,, Pope would order his Legates not to be in fuch
,, a hurry ; but to wait patiently till the Pre-
,, lates, and namely ours, fhould be arrived——
,, they will not ftay, I am fure, any longer than
,, two or three Months at the furtheft ; for I
,, hope that before that time they will find pro-
,, per means for pacifying the Kingdom. The
,, fecond is, that according to our Holy Father's
,, reiterated Promifes, he would be pleafed to
,, grant the Prelates the freedom of propound-
,,   ing,

,, ing, voting and deliberating, without prescri-
,, bing to them any Restriction or Limitation,
,, or SENDING THE HOLY GHOST IN THE
,, MAIL OF ROME : And that whatever shall
,, be proposed or determined in this Council,
,, should not be blamed, calumniated, or adul-
,, rated at Rome, &c (r).

To this I shall subjoin another Letter of Dr.
DE XAINTES to Dr. D'ESPENCE, dated from
Trent the 15th of June 1563.

,, SIR,

,, NEVER was you better inspired than
,, when you resolved not to come hither.
,, For I believe that you would have been dead
,, by this time, had you seen all the ENOR-
,, MITIES AND BASENESS made use of for ob-
,, structing a Reformation. The French carry
,, themselves in this Affair with a greater Sin-
,, cerity and Vigour than the others, who very
,, often laugh at them when they see them in
,, such Perplexities. When we came here at
,, first, the Point under debate was about the *Sa-*
,, *crament of Orders.* The Spaniards insisted
,, much to have it decided so, that THE BISHOPS
,, ARE INSTITUTED BY CHRIST, AND ARE
,, SUPERIOR TO THE PRIESTS BY DIVINE
,, RIGHT. The French joined in the same Opi-
,, nion with them : But for avoiding the Con-
,, sequence of such a Declaration, the Italians
,, mixed together in that Canon ten or twelve
,, Titles for the Pope, whereby they declared
,, him to be the only one Bishop instituted im-
,, mediately by Christ, and that all others had

,, no

(r) Instructions & Missives des Roix tres Chretiens & de
leurs Ambassadeurs & autres pieces concernant le Concile de
Trent, pris sur les originaux, pag 100.

„ no Power but what derived from his own, and
„ from himself.   There is none of us that chufes
„ not to be in the Sorbonne, even in danger of
„ death, rather than to be here : It is impoffible
„ for me to give you an Account of whatever
„ I have feen and heard in this Council (*s*).

I fhall not infift upon the Inftructions given
to the French Embaffadors ; they had received
Orders to require that the whole Communion
fhould be reftored to the Lay-Men ; that the
Adminiftration of the Sacraments fhould be performed in the French tongue ; that the ufe of
Homilies (*Prône*) fhould be reftored in all Paro-
chial Churches, for the Inftruction of the People, with the reading and explaining the Holy
Scripture, and the Catechifm for the young ones ;
that the ufe of Pfalms and other fpiritual Songs
in the French tongue, revifed and approved by
the Bifhops, fhould be allowed in the Church :
finally, that the Priefts fhould be allowed to
marry.   Neither of thefe Points were granted ;
nay, tho' the Emperor and the Duke of Bavaria's
Embaffadors joined with the French in the fame
Petition for reftoring the whole Communion to
the Lay-Men, the Council was fo unjuft as to
pronounce a Curfe againft all thofe who fhould
fay, that by the Commandment of God, or in
order to be faved, every Chriftian, of what Order or Quality foever, ought to receive the Wine
as well as the Bread in the Sacrament of our
Lord's Supper.
They followed the fame Method as to the
other Points controverted between the Proteftants, the Reformed, and the Catholicks, as
Tranfubftantiation, Image-Worfhip, &c. and ana-
thematized

(*s*) Idem pag. 294. Both thefe Letters are to be found in
D'Aubigné Hift. Univ. liv. III. ch. xxi.

thematized all thofe who differed from them :
Being however very cautious, not to offend the
Scholafticks.   Let us hear Palavicini himfelf, in
his Preface to the Hiftory of the Council of
Trent.

„ The Method of the Council has been to re-
„ gulate its Decifions in fuch a manner, and to
„ word them with fo great a choice of nice Ex-
„ preffions, that they could not prejudice the
„ various Opinions of the School, whereupon
„ the Chatholick Doctors were divided ; and
„ indeed the Wifdom of the Council required
„ that they fhould not expofe the Church to any
„ new Troubles, by the Heats that would have
„ been raifed amongft the Divines, had the
„ Council undertook to examine and cenfure
„ their Tenets.

He fays further, *That it was one of the Articles
whereupon the Pope had particularly infifted, having fhown that he had nothing more at heart than
to manage the Matters in difpute amongft the Scholafticks, in fuch a manner that neither of them
fhould take offence, in order thereby to reunite all
the Catholick Forces againft the Sectaries.*

That Confeffion of Cardinal Palavicini is a
Weapon which he had very unwifely provided
us with againft that Council.   And indeed what
other Inference can be drawn from what he fays,
befides this, viz. that the faid Council, infpired
by the Pope, had no thoughts at all to enter fincerely into the Examination of the Points controverted, which ought to have been the chief
fubject of their Convocation.   To be fure they
were come to Trent fully refolved to condemn,
to anathematize whatever fhould not agree with
them ; but on the other hand, to keep fair with
the Scholafticks, left they fhould increafe the

number of their Adversaries, if they did molest them.

Is it not plain, that the main scope of that Council was not to unfold the TRUTH, but to hinder the discovery of it, at any rate ; not to reform the ERRORS and ABUSES, but to authorize them as much as they could ; not to pacify the TROUBLES, but to crush those that were unjustly stiled Innovators, and Disturbers of the publick Peace ? Let every one judge now, whether there is any ground for believing, that the Holy Ghost, that Spirit of Truth, of Holiness, Union and Concord, has presided in that Assembly ?

Amongst other things six Points were debated in the Council, which put the Court of Rome in a terrible fright, lest the Pope should lose his ground.

I. The Clause PROPONENTIBUS LEGATIS, (the Legates proposing) was contradicted as long as the Council lasted ; and indeed it was a foul Encroachment on the Rights and Freedom of the Fathers present in the Council, that none but the Legates should be at liberty to propose what they pleased.

II. Whether the Residence of the Bishops is a divine Institution ? the question would have been carried in the Affirmative, had not the bribed Votes prevailed.

III. Whether EPISCOPACY proceeds directly from Jesus Christ ? It seems that all the Bishops should have voted for the Affirmative, seeing that the very Soul and Substance of their Dignity was called in question, by such an Alternative ; and indeed all the learned Prelates agreed together in the Affirmative ; but the Pope's crafty Devices succeeded so well, that by virtue of a

captious

captious Decree, the Bishops were much amazed, to find themselves under the Dependance of the Pope, who by that Decree usurped the power of the Sovereigns, and for ever has deprived the private Churches of their natural Right of E-lection.

IV. How far the Pope's Authority goes ? That was the Rock dreaded by the Court of Rome ; nevertheless she avoided it by the means of Equivocation, and with the ambiguous Expressions of the Decision : the Popes pretend that the Councils hold of them all their Authority ; that to them it belongs to explain arbitrarily their Decrees ; and to speak the thing as it is, the Church of Rome has no other Foundation but the Pope's Will.

V. The general Reformation of the Head as well as of the Members. The Court of Rome having so many mighty Reasons to oppose that Scheme, and being in danger of losing so much, had it succeeded, had the pleasure to see it miscarry.

VI. As to the Indulgencies, the Abuses whereof had occasioned the Reformation of Luther, nothing was decided upon that point.

Never a more ridiculous Play had been seen in the World, than that which the Pope and his Adherents represented upon the Stage of Trent ; and one who undertakes the Defence of it, is much like to the Spectator of a Farce, who would believe that the Actors are such as they seem to be upon the Stage.

That the Canons of that Council have been drawn with all the Artifice and Subtilty agreeable to the Prudence *of the Children of this World* ; that they knew how to manage slily the contradictory Opinions of the School between the Divines ; so much we will own and acknowledge. But to assert that such Decrees grounded only

upon

upon Politicks, have been equally inspired *for interpreting*, as the Holy Scripture *for settling*; such an Assertion, I say, includes in itself a manifest Outrage to the Glory of Almighty God; it is such an absurd Pretension, that every Man of any Capacity, who has read the History of that Council, is obliged in Honour and Conscience to place it amongst the greatest Extravagancies, if his faculty of Reasoning is not strangely byassed and prepossessed with the Opinion of the Infallibility either of the Councils, or of the Popes.

Great Disputes arose in that Council between the French and the Spanish Ambassadors, about the Precedency, wherein Pius IV. shewed so great Partiality for Spain, that France was upon the point of following the Example of England under King Henry VIII. and Du Ferrier and Pibrac, French Embassadors to the Council, after a very eloqent Speech, wherein they vehemently inveighed against the Pope, and disclosed the manifold Iniquities committed in the Transactions of that Assembly, in the King's Name, protested against it, and whatever should be done in it, and withdrew themselves to *Venice*; and whereas that Protest is very remarkable for its Singularity, as it gives us a just Notion of the true Character of that Council, I shall insert it in the next Note (*t*).

That

(*t*) After having recited the many Wrongs and Injustices done by Pius IV, he goes on so. *Num hæc sunt Petri, Lini, Damasi, Gregorii, aliorumq; summorum Pontificum facta & gesta? Num Pium IV pro summo Pontifice & Petri successore habere debeat Gallia? qui ut antiquam dignitatem & majestatem Pupilli regis minueret, omnia divina & humana jura pervertit? Num nobis, etsi ingratissimo animo, justâ tamen & necessariâ causâ, hinc discedendum sit, ubi nullum legibus locum, nullum antiquorum Conciliorum libertatis vestigium Pius IV. reliquit? Quid enim vobis judicandum proponitur, aut a vobis judicatum publicatur quod non prius Romam missum, & Pio IV. placuerit? Quam*

That Difpute was not decided till about an hundred Years after ; and that Decifion was oc-cafioned by the Affront which the Baron of Batte-ville, the Spanifh Embaffador to the Court of England, put upon the Count d'Eftrades, French Embaffador to the fame Court, at the publick Entry of the Swedifh Embaffador into London, in the Year 1661. Amongft other Articles of Satisfaction, Lewis XIV. obliged the King of Spain to acknowledge in the moft authentick manner, his Right of Precedency, which was accordingly done the next Year with all the fo-lemnity poffible.

D 3   That

Quam putabis aliam effe caufam toties dilati & procraftinati judicii petitionum noftrarum, quam quod ille ex Epiftolâ Adri-ani VI. Pontif. Max. *optime noverat ;* CURATIS QUAN-TUMVIS MEMBRIS, CORPUS SANUM ESSE NON POTEST, NISI ETIAM CAPUT CURETUR ? *Huic autem capiti quæ quantaq; immineant, in aliud tempus dicendum refervamus. Hic eft igitur Pius* IV *ad quem folum hominum præfens hæc noftra denunciatio & proteftatio pertinet. Sedem Apoftolicam, fummum Pontificem, fanctam Rom. Ecclefiam, pro cujus digni-tate augenda Majores noftri fanguinem fuderunt, & adhuc hodiè in Gallia acriter pugnatur, veneramur, reveremur, fufpicimus & maximis ad Cælum laudibus efferimus : Pii autem* IV. *Im-perium detractamus, quæcumq; fint, ejus judicia & fententias rejicimus, refpuimus, & contemnimus. Illum pro vicario Chrifti, pro capite, pro Petri legitimo fucceffore afpernamur & rejicimus. Et quanquam,* PATRES SANCTISSIMI, *veftra omnis religio, vita, eruditio magnæ femper fuit & erit apud nos autoritatis,* CUM TAMEN NIHIL A VOBIS, SED OMNIA MAGIS, ROMÆ QUAM TRIDENTI AGANTUR, *& hæc quæ publi-cantur magis* PII IV. PLACITA QUAM CONCILII TRI-DENTINI DECRETA *jure exiftimantur, denunciamus & tefta-mur, quæcumq; in hoc conventu, hoc eft Pii* IV. *motu decreta funt & publicata, decernentur & publicabuntur, ea neq; regem Chriftianiffimum probaturum, neq; ecclefiam Gallicanam pro decretis Oecumenicæ Synodi habituram. Interea quotquot eftis Galliæ Archiepifcopi, Epifcopi, Abbates, Oratores, Theologi, Vos omnes hinc abire rex Chriftianiffimus jubet : redituros ut primùm Deus Opt. Max. Ecclefiæ Catholicæ Generalibus Con-ciliis antiquam formam & libertatem reftituerit, rex autem Chriftianiffimus debitum dignitati & majeftati fuæ locum re-ceperit.* Thuan. Hift. lib. XXXV. pag. 267.

That freedom of the French Embassadors ex-asperated the Pope, and being sollicited by the Court of Spain (*u*), he resolved to revenge himself; for that end he attempted anew to encroach upon the King's Rights, and the Liberties and Privileges of the Gallican Church, summoning the Queen of Navarr, the Cardinal of CHATILLON, JOHN OF ST. CHAMOND Archbishop of Aix, *John of St. Gelais* Bishop of Usez, *John De Montluc* Bishop of Valence, *Claudius Régin* Bishop of Oleron, *Lewis of Albret* Bishop of Lescar, *Charles Gaillard* Bishop of Chartres, *Anthony Caracciol* Bishop of Troy, *Francis of Noailles* † Bishop of Daqs; to appear before him, and give account of their Faith and Behaviour.

Those Prelates had been already summoned at Rome in the Month of April, and on the 20th of October the Pope pronounced Sentence of Deposition against some of them, and of Suspension against the others.

As to the Queen of Navarr, the Instrument whereby she was summoned to appear at Rome in six Months time, for to give an Account of her Religion, and answer to the Crimes laid to her Charge, was published in the latter end of September, and affixed to the Gates of St. Peter's Church, and of the Holy Office of Inquisition. The Pope desired that Sentence should be passed against her in the Council; but the Legates's Remonstrances caused him to alter his Mind. In the Summons the Pope declared, that if she refused to obey, she would forfeit all her Dominions and Estates, and be obnoxious to all other Penalties decreed against the Hereticks.

The Court of France heard no sooner of this, by Cardinal DE LA BOURDAISIERE, Embassador

at

(*u*) Addit. aux Mem. de Casteln. liv. III. ch. ix. p. 777. to 810.

at Rome, but she sent orders to D'Oysel to let the Pope know, that he acted directly against the Honour of the Crown of France, and the Liberties and Privileges of the Gallican Church, in virtue whereof no Archbishop or Bishop can be tried for any Crime soever, without the Limits of the Kingdom ; and as to the Queen of Navarr, he was ordered to tell him, that he had no Authority or Jurisdiction over Kings and Queens, and that it did not belong to him to deprive them of their Kingdoms and Dominions, nor to deliver them to be a Prey to the first Conqueror, &c (w).

Now Castelnau says, that the Pope was not at all moved by these Remonstrances, and refused obstinately to revoke the Sentence (x). But Fra. Paolo says positively, that he complied (y). Nay, according to Thuanus, D'Oysel's Remonstrances were so efficacious with the Pope, that the Proceedings against the Bishops, and the Sentence against the Queen of Navarr, were so entirely abolished, that nothing of that Affair could be found amongst the Constitutions of Pope Pius IV. in his own time, (that is, about 30 or 40 Years after) (z). D'Avila says likewise, that the Pope's Prosecutions were abated by the King's Opposition (a). And indeed the Pope would have acted very imprudently had he insisted any more upon an Affair of that Consequence wherein all the Princes (the King of Spain excepted) were concerned, and who very likely would not have suffered such Indignities to be put upon their Character.

D 4　　　　　　　　　　　　At

(w) Addit. aux Mem. de Castelnau, liv. III. ch. ix. pag. 783. Thuan. lib. XXXV. p. 260, &c.
(x) Liv. V. ch. ix.
(y) Liv. VIII. pag. 635. de Diodati.
(z) Liv. XXXV. p. 263.
(a) Liv. III. p. 143.

Charles
IX.
1563.
Pope Pius
IV.

XVII.
*A general
Interview
of the Ca-
tholick
Powers
propoſed.*

At the ſame time a Rumour was induſtriouſly and maliciouſly ſpread by the Pope's Nuncio, and the Embaſſadors Granvelle and Chantonay, that the Queen-Regent was premeditating a League with the Emperor, the King of Spain, the Pope and other Catholick Princes, for the extirpation of the Proteſtant and Reformed Religion ; that piece of Forgery was invented on purpoſe to kindle anew the Fire of the civil Diviſions in the Kingdom, which was not as yet quite extinguiſhed. The Queen reſented it highly, as it appears by her Letter to the Biſhop of *Rennes*, then Embaſſador of France to the Court of Vienna, dated at Paris the 23d of December 1563, whereby ſhe owns, that ſhe had ſollicited the Pope for a Conference with the Catholick Princes, not for making a League to work the Deſtruction of the Proteſtants ; which Deſign could but render her odious to all the Potentates of Europe, nay, intolerable even to her own ſelf : but to find out ſome mild ways for reconciling the Diſputes about Religion, ſeeing that no ſuch thing could be expected from the Council, wherein the Pope's Party was always the uppermoſt, being ſuperior in number to all the reſt, ſhe ordered Monſ. of *Rennes* to do his beſt endeavours for perſuading the Emperor and the King of the Romans his Son, that ſhe had no other Intention in the propoſed Interview but of procuring, by all fair means, Peace, Union and Concord amongſt the Chriſtians (b).

In order to clear this Point, one muſt know that the Cardinal of Lorrain's Zeal being cooled, either by the Duke of Guiſe's Death, or becauſe he was but fickle in his Reſolutions, or becauſe his Ambition found better its Account in ſerving the

(b) That Letter is to be found in the Additions to Caſtelnau's Mem. Vol. II. Book V. ch. ix. pag. 328, 329.

Book V. *Reformed Churches in* France. 41

Charles
IX.
1563.
Pope Pius
IV.

the Pope than his King, or for these three Reasons together, it is certain, that the Council, instead of working out the Reformation of the Ecclesiastical body, undertook to reform the Princes, whereby the Kings of France would have been the greatest Sufferers, because of the many great Privileges they do enjoy over the Gallican Church. That was attempted on purpose to oblige the Princes, and especially the French King, not to insist any longer upon the Reformation of the Ecclesiastical body, seeing that it would be to their own detriment, and to bring them to consent to, nay, to desire the breaking up of the Council ; and whether that Devise had been contrived by the Cardinal of Lorrain, and by him communicated to the Court of Rome, in order to ease the Pope of the great Anxieties he was in, on the Council's account, left he should not succeed according to his Wishes, that I cannot say with a thorough certainty ; tho' the Affirmative seems to me very probable, because he was then and afterwards much caressed by the Pope, who had promised him the Legateship of France, with as great a power as he could desire, as he owns himself, in one of his Letters to the Emperor ; and because likewise he was so remiss in the Affairs relating to the Crown of France, that it seemed rather to approve than to disapprove the Attempts made by the Pope, and by his Council. However, having agreed with the Pope upon an Interview between the Catholick Princes and his Holiness, wherein he thought to find his own Account for the Gratification of his own Revenge against the Reformed of France, he took the Opportunity of these Attempts of the Council against the Princes, to dispose the Queen-Mother, by his Letter, to the breaking up of the said Council, giving her to
under-

underſtand, that the King and other Princes would diſpatch more Buſineſs, and obtain more Redreſs in a ſingle Conference with the Pope than in many Seſſions of the Council ; but he was very cautious to hide the true Motives which induced him to take that Step, viz. to form a League between all the Catholick Princes againſt the Proteſtant, and to work the Deſtruction of the Reformed of France, whom he looked upon as the greateſt Oppoſers of the ambitious Views of his Houſe. He did conceal likewiſe from the Queen, that according to his Agreement with the Pope, that Interview was to be preceded by a ſolemn Embaſſy from the Pope, and the moſt conſiderable amongſt the Catholick Powers, to intreat the King to receive and publiſh the Council of Trent in France ; that was to be the beginning of the Tragedy which the Cardinal intended to act for revenging his Brother's death : for he doubted not but that he would be able by his own Credit to compaſs his Ends, and to oblige the Parliaments of the Kingdom to publiſh the ſaid Council ; but he found himſelf much miſtaken in that.

The Queen taking for granted, that ſuch a Conference with the Catholick Princes could be but very uſeful for compounding the Differences about Religion, and diving not into the Cardinal's ſecret Intentions, accepted of it, and ſpoke of it to Cardinal *St. Croix*, the Pope's Nuncio, and teſtified to him her Inclination of ſeeing the Council's end. The Nuncio, who had Orders from Rome to diſturb, as much as he could, the Peace made with the Reformed, took the Queen at her Word, thinking that it would be a means very proper for forming a League againſt them, and at random he gave out his own Conjectures in order to raiſe Jealouſies amongſt the King's

Sub-

Subjects, and to plunge again the Kingdom in a Civil War. That Affair made such a Noise in Germany, as well as in France, that the King was obliged to write to Monf. of *Rennes*, his Embaffador at Vienna, for contradicting what was induftriously and malicioufly reported ; and the fame Rumour occafioned the Queen's Letter above-mentioned to the fame Embaffador : and feeing fo many infuperable Obftacles to a general Conference with the Princes, fhe defired earneftly a private one with the King of the Romans for the fame end ; that Prince (Maximilian by Name) fhewing a great defire to give fome Satisfaction to his Proteftant Subjects of *Bohemia* and *Hungary*, and having much infifted, by his Embaffadors to the Council, to have the Communion *fub utraq*; and the Marriage of the Priefts allowed to them, liftened very readily to the Queen's Propofition, and promifed to improve the firft Opportunity that would offer itfelf for that Conference. [*And indeed it appears by that Princefs's Letters, that fhe was in earneft at that time, for finding out fome means of reconciling the Differences, or, at leaft, of giving fome Satisfaction to the Reformed of France, by granting them fome of the moft effential Points controverted between them and the Catholicks.*] But feveral things obftructed her good Intentions, and the Emperor Ferdinand, his Father, being dead, that intended Conference was put off ; and then, either becaufe the new Emperor had obtained his Ends, or becaufe he miftrufted the Queen (*for indeed fhe was quite altered three or four Months after*) it was no more talk'd of (c).

At

(c) See the Letters of the King and the Queen-Regent, and thofe of Monfieur de Rennes, as well as Agricola's Reflections, in his Additions to the Mem. of Caftelnau, Vol. II. Book V. ch. ix. from pag. 319, to 339.

Charles
IX.
1564.
Pope Pius
IV.

XVIII.
*The King is
intreated
by several
Powers to
receive the
Council of
Trent.*

At the beginning of February, the Court being at Fontainebleau for the Winter Season, arrived the abovesaid Embassy from the Pope, the King of Spain, and the Duke of Savoy ; they had Orders from their Principals to intreat the King to receive the Decrees of the Council of Trent, and to cause them to be received and observed throughout the Kingdom ; they were put off to the Assembly of the Catholick Princes, which were to meet together at Nancy on the 25th of March, (as the Queen thought) in order to look for some Remedy for healing the present Diseases of the Church. They required further, that the King should forbid the Alienation of the Church's Lands and Estates ; and in order to take off the pretence of discharging the National Debts, the King of Spain and the Duke of Savoy declared themselves ready to remit their Rights, as much as they could, in behalf of the Church ; that the King was to be satisfied with a free Gift from the Clergy ; that he ought to punish with Banishment or some other Penalty all Seditious and Schismaticks, and to punish severely all those who had destroyed the Churches, plundered the Priests Goods, and introduced in the Kingdom the Enemies of the State ; that he ought to repeal the Act of Grace granted to them by the Edict of Peace, and especially those who should be found guilty of High Treason against God ; because such Crimes being committed not against Princes, but against God, to God only it belongs to forgive them ; that he would do justice impartially to all his Subjects, and punish severely and without delay the Authors and Abettors of the most execrable murder of the late Duke of Guise. The Embassadors promised to the King, in the Name of their

Prin-

Principals, all manner of Aid and Affiftance for compaffing thefe Ends.

To this the King, inftructed by his Mother, and by the Chancellor, anfwered, That he was much obliged to their Mafters for the wholefome Advices they imparted to him, and efpecially to them (*the Embaffadors*) who had vouchfafed to come to him for that purpofe ; that he affured them, that he was firmly refolved to live according to the ancient Conftitution of the Roman Church, and to oblige his Subjects to follow his Example ; that he had made Peace with them for that very purpofe, and to expel the Enemies out of his Dominions ; that for the prefent he had nothing more at heart, than to do juftice impartially to all his Subjects ; as for the reft he defired to be excufed, for the Reafons which he would fet in writing, that they might be imparted to them ; thefe things were tranfacted on the 12th of February (*d*).

But whereas they infifted upon a pofitive Anfwer, the King, on the 27th of March, let them know, that he wanted to advife with the Princes and the chief Men of his Council, before he could anfwer peremptorily.

The Queen-Mother had been at firft much puzzled at this ; fhe fufpected that fome Bufybodys had affectedly managed that Embaffy, in order to make themfelves neceffary, and to get Reputation abroad, and a great Power at home ; therefore fhe endeavoured to render their Attempt vain and fruitlefs, and after feveral delays fhe difmiffed the Embaffadors with ambiguous Words.

The Prefidents of the Parliament and the *Why he did* King's Council, having been fummoned for exa-*not comply.* mining the Decrees of the Council of Trent, their

Opinion

(*d*) Thuan. lib. XXXVI. pag. 292.

Opinion ~~was~~ that it could not be received as to the Difcipline, inafmuch that feveral Decrees of it were derogating to the Privileges of the Crown, and the Liberties of the Gallican Church; and for thefe very fame reafons, the faid Council has never been received in France (*e*).

And whereas the Pope's Creatures infifted at that time, that it fhould be received, CHARLES DU MOULIN, a Man extraordinarily well learned in the Law, and a great Stickler for the ancient Liberty, publifhed a Confultation upon that Subject, whereby he fhewed forth, that for many Reafons the Council of Trent was to be deemed null, as having been affembled, held, and concluded, in a way contrary to the Decrees of the ancient Fathers, and to the Dignity and Liberty of the Kingdom of France. The Pope's Champions were much offended at this Author's boldnefs, and prevailed fo far in the Parliament of Paris, that Du Moulin was ignominioufly fent to Goal, as an Heretick, and an Abettor of Sedition: But few Months after he was releafed, by the King's Orders, while he was at Lyons; however, upon thefe terms, that for the future he fhould publifh nothing without the King's Licence; and the Parliament was forbidden to take any further Cognizance of that Affair. That Gentleman was fallen under the Parliament's Disfavour, becaufe, being an Upright Man, he had afferted of late the Rights of the Nobility and Commoners of confenting to the Election of a Bifhop, againft ANTHONY DE CREQUI Bifhop of *Nantz,* a great Enemy to the Reformed, who had been tranflated to the See of *Amiens* without fuch a previous Confent; tho' Du Moulin's

(*e*) The King of Portugal, and the Republick of Venice, were the firft that received the Council, and after them the King of Spain.

lin's Opinion was grounded upon the Decrees of the ancient Fathers, and of the Councils, upon the Conſtitutions of CLOTARIUS, CHARLEMAIGN and LEWIS the Good, and upon the Regulations lately made in the Aſſembly of the States-General held at *Orleans* (*f*).

Charles
IX.
1564.
Pope Pius
IV.

The King publiſhed an 'Edict in February, whereby he ordered to begin the Year by the firſt of January, whereas he begun before by Eaſter-day ; and tho' that Edict was not regiſtred by the Parliament, nevertheleſs it was obſerved.

XIX.
The King's
Edict for
beginning
the Year by
the firſt of
January.

On the 31ſt of March, his Majeſty being attended by the Queen-Mother, began to viſit his Kingdom. Amongſt the Reaſons which obliged Queen Catharine to undertake that Journey, the frequent Complaints the Reformed made of the Violation of the Edict, eſpecially in the Southern Provinces, was one of the chiefeſt ; ſhe was afraid leſt their Patience being tired, they would riſe again in Arms ; beſides that ſhe knew very well, that they begun to miſtruſt her, they ſuſpected that ſhe had a mind to break the Edict ; and their Suſpicion was not, at this preſent time, without Foundation, notwithſtanding all her Demonſtrations to the contrary.

XX.
He begins
the Viſit of
his King-
dom.

And indeed the Behaviour of the Duke of Damville, Governor of Languedoc, being approved by the Court, could but afford them a juſt Subject of Jealouſies.

XXI.
Injuſtices
of Dam-
ville in
Languedoc.

That Lord, (in order to blot out the Impreſſions which his own, and his Father, and Brother's proceeding in behalf of the Admiral had made upon the Minds of the Catholicks, as if they countenanced the Reformed Party ;) behaved himſelf in his Government not only with great Injuſtice, but even with the greateſt Barbarity,

(*f*) Thuan. lib. XXXVI. pag. 293.

rity, without any regard to the Edict lately made. For, with the Conſent and Approbation of the Parliament of *Thoulouſe*, he entered in an hoſtile manner into the Cities that had formerly been poſſeſſed by the Reformed, putting Gariſons at the Gates, and fixing the flying Colours and Standards upon the Walls, as if they had been taken by Storm; then he commanded the Inhabitants to bring all their Arms to the Town-houſes, their Swords not excepted; and left any Arms ſhould be left, he ſent ſome of his Men to ſearch the Reformed Houſes. At *Nimes* a Gentleman having delayed a little to bring his Sword, was publickly and ſeverely whipt through the Streets by his Orders. It was a Cuſtom amongſt the Reformed, while they were Maſters of that City, that the Magiſtrates before they undertook any thing in the Town-houſe, put up their Prayers to God for imploring his Aſſiſtance; Damville ordered that this Cuſtom ſhould be aboliſhed, and when CALVER, the firſt Conſul of the City, oppoſed ſuch Order, ſaying, *Who then ſhall teach us juſtice, or under whoſe Auſpice ſhall we render it, if not in the Name of God?* he anſwered only, That if they and their Followers were ſo ſollicitous about that Uſe of praying to God, the King was unwilling to impoſe ſuch a burden upon thoſe who cared not for it. Tho' he, with his Attendants, lived with an intolerable Licentiouſneſs in the City, his Guards, compoſed of Troops from *Albania* and *Sclavonia*, went continually a plundering the Country, juſt as they would have done during the War. Mean while he interpreted the Edict according to his fancy. Tho' liberty had been granted to the Reformed to meet together for Religious Worſhip, in all the Cities and Places where they were uſed to reſort, before the 7th of March 1563, Damville reſtrained that
liberty

liberty to thofe Places, the Lords whereof would grant fuch a Licence. Whereas by the fame Edict, every one was to enjoy a full Liberty of Confcience every where, he weakened fo much that Conceffion, that he obliged all the Priefts, and religious Perfons, who had renounced their Priefthood, or their Fraternity, and confequently the Roman Religion, to forfake their Wives or Husbands if they had any, and to return to their refpective Monafteries; and if they difobeyed, they were banifhed out of the Kingdom : and that Order was given not only for thofe who had renounced the Roman Religion during the late Troubles, but even for thofe, who, from the beginning of the Reformation, had turned Proteftants ; he condemned one Mouton, Minifter of Ufez, to be hanged; for having fpoke too freely in his Sermons. For which Caufe Mr. De Clauson, a Counfellor of Nimes, was deputed to Court to complain of thefe Violences, but by the Conftable's Credit he was fent to Jail.

The City of *Pamiers* in the County of *Foix* was one of the moft feverely handled by Damville. The Inhabitants whereof dreading the Licentioufnefs and Cruelties of that Governor's Troops, had writ to him, fhewing forth that they had no need of a Garifon ; that they were ready to obey all other Orders he would give them, and to obferve ftrictly the Edict. But Damville infifted that he fhould be admitted into the City without any Condition foever ; and faid, that thofe were not as pacifick as they pretended to be, who undertook to impofe Conditions on a Governour fent to them by their King ; and he notified to the Confuls, that unlefs they would obey without delay, and admit him into the City, they fhould anfwer for their Fellow-Citizens Obftinacy. The Confuls, frightned at thefe Threatnings, were willing to admitthat Governour; but the Citizens oppofed, dreading the Confequences of admitting a proud and cruel Governour, irritated by their Refiftance, and attended by a band of Soldiers, plunged in all manner of Diffolutenefs: the Debate between the Confuls and the Inhabitants came to fuch a degree of Heat and Paffion, that thefe laft expelled their Magiftrate out of the City; abfolutely denied admittance to Damville, and put themfelves, the beft as they could, in a pofture of Defence. Damville fent to Court to complain of this Ufage, and the Queen dreading the Confequences of fuch an Example, difpatched Rambouillet to Pamiers, for bringing the Inhabitants to a Compliance with their Governour. He prevailed with them, upon promife that he would obtain their free Pardon from the King; and perfuaded them to receive Damville in the City, without any Condition. But they paid very dear for their Refiftance, and for their Compliance too; they were gone too far, and had complied too foon: Damville was no fooner entered into the City, but he made them fenfible what fort of Man he was; tho' he was received with the utmoft Refpect, he treated them as the fierceft Enemy would have done; he deprived them of their Privileges; pulled down their Walls; inflicted feveral Penalties upon the moft fubftantial Citizens; caufed fome of them to be put to death, and their Minifter Taschard to be hang'd; gave the City to be plundered by the Soldiers; forced the Women and Virgins; and having expelled eight hundred of the Inhabitants out of the City, and put a Garifon into it, he went to Thouloufe, there to receive the Congratulations of a bloody Parliament on fuch a Feat, fo much to their liking.

liking (g). No wonder then if the Reformed were full of Fears and Jealoufies; if they doubted of the Queen's Sincerity, feeing that far from obtaining any redrefs of their Grievances, their Deputies were clapt in Jail, or filenced by fuch like Methods.

The King went thro' Champaign into Lorrain, outwardly under pretence of ftanding God-father to the new-born Son of the Duke of Lorrain, but really to treat with the German Princes, fome of whom became Penfioners of France, and obliged themfelves to find a certain number of Troops in cafe of need ; but others refufed generoufly, among whom were the Duke of WIRTEMBERG, the ELECTOR PALATINE, and the Duke of DEUX-PONTS. From Lorrain the King proceeded to Burgundy, where the States of the Province affembled at Dijon, infifted much to his Majefty, that the laft Edict in behalf of the Reformed fhould not take place in Burgundy ; but they were refufed. And now the Queen was much ftaggering at the Inftances of the Houfes of Lorrain and Guife, and of feveral others, who endeavoured to engage her to repeal that Edict, and to enter into a League with the Catholick Princes for the utter Extirpation of the Hereticks. But if fhe durft not as yet to act in an open Defiance to the King's Royal Word and Promifes, we fhall fee prefently what a terrible Breach fhe made on the Edict, and how at laft fhe entered the next Year into that fo much defired League with the King of Spain.

The King proceeding in his Journey arrived at Lyons about the 15th of June, and made great Alterations in that City, wherein the Reformed were the ftrongeft, in order to fecure it

E 2   to

(g) Thuan. lib. XXXV. p. 242, 244.

to his own Intereſt, he took the Government of it from the hands of the Count of SAULT, who was a very meek Man, and who countenanced the Reformed, and gave it to DE LOSSES, Captain of his Guards, only for a time ; for it was deſtined for the Duke of NEMOURS. Then he cauſed two Citadels to be built in it ; and tho' the Plague raged in the City, the King departed not from it till the Works were in a great forwardneſs.

The Queen could not diſſemble ſo well, but the Reformed dived into her moſt ſecret Thoughts, as it appears by theſe Lines in proſaick Rhimes directed under the Name of John Philoglutius, Doctor of Sorbonne, to Mr. Pandolphus Verunculius, Batchelor, dated the 9th of July 1564 ; and whereof, for humour's ſake, I ſhall inſert here the following Abſtract.

I.

In noſtra urbe Regina
Se oſtendit multùm bona,
Et videtur ad placitum
Velle mutare Edictum :
Sed Rex ſemper dicit altè,
Quod vult conſervare ſtrictè,
Et promittit non fracturum,
Puto quòd non erit verum.

2.

Nam ego multa video
Quæ vix dicere audeo,
Sed præſtat ea tacere,
Et parumper exſpectare
Reginæ novum decretum
Adverſus Regis Edictum.
Hoc nobis eſt pollicita
Credo quod faciet ita :

Hoc

Hoc nobis ſatis eſt notum
Per recens ſuum adventum.

3.

Huguenoti Lugdunenſes
Non ampliùs portant Enſes,
Neque ivere per viam
Regi futuri obviam :
Sed . . . . . . Genuenſes,
Florentini & Lucenſes,
Antè eum exiverunt
Et eum comitaverunt.
Hoc benè fecit prudenter
Catherina Regis Mater,
Nam in quibus fiduciam
Poneret quàm in Patriam.

4.

Indè pro conſuetudine,
Tuba eſt clamatum manè,
Ut Huguenoti ceſſarent
Nec ampliùs predicarent ;
Unde ſunt valdè territi.
Nam putabant Huguenoti
Quod Rex eos non turbaret,
Sed Contrarium apparet,
Et non ſunt ubi putabant
Neque de hoc diffidebant.

5.

Verum ipſi nihil audent,
Et Papiſtæ eos rident :
Quoniam Regina Mater
Ita gubernat potenter :
Quod benè eis indicat
Nam in urbe ædificat,

E 3

Duas

Duas bonas Turres fortes
Ad † retrahendum milites,
Quos ad urbis præsidium
Fecit venire Lugdunum.
Sed benè fecit ampliùs,
Quod est illis molestiùs,
Quia vult Nemorum Ducem
Urbis habere Regimen.

6.

Præterea hic dicitur
Quod plurimi exspectantur,
Alphonsus Dux Ferrariæ
Et Cosmus Dux Florentiæ,
Cum Principe Philiberto.
Ipsi huc venient citò,
Et tunc Regina mutabit
Edictum & non timebit,
Illud frangere apertè ;
Nam habet de sua parte
Omnes Reges Catholicos
Adversus istos iniquos.

7.

Per Deum si hoc Edictum
Non est celeriter fractum,
Sed servetur in Gallia,
Actum est de Ecclesia,
Et oportet quod Facultas
Rescribat litteras multas
Ad Papam, & hunc moneat
Sedulò manum teneat,
Ut Regina hoc Edictum,
Omninò reddat irritum :
Nam si diù habet cursum,
* Marmita cadet deorsum.

8. Aliud

---

† For receiving Soldiers.　　　* Seething-pot.

8.

Aliud eft quod timemus
In hac urbe multùm trifte,
Nam hic moriuntur pefte.
Regina eam non timet
Quia Peftis eft ipfamet,
Neque hinc eft abitura,
Quin omnia reliétura
Sit, ficut ipfa decrevit.
Dudum totus Clerus novit
Quantùm ipfa vult curare
Ecclefiam fuftinere :
Jam jam nobis eft cognitum
Et Huguenotis moleftum, &c.

During the ftay of the Court at *Lyons*, Mifs
LIMEUIL, the Prince's Miftrefs, above mentioned, was delivered of a Son. The Queen had not
been forry to fee that young Lady, of the beft
Nobility of the Kingdom, fuffering the Prince's
Addreffes ; it may be, that fhe did not think that
that Inclination would go any further than Court-
fhip : but whether the Lady could not refift the
Prince's Quality, or for the Value fhe had for
him, or that fhe expected to marry him after
Princefs Eleonor's death, as it is faid fhe had been
promifed by the Prince ; howbeit, being overcome by Ambition and Love, fhe furrendered
herfelf to his Royal Highnefs. The Queen
was fo much the more offended at that Scandal,
that it happened fo publickly, that it was impoffible to conceal it ; fhe was fhut up in a Nunnery
by the Queen's Orders, but releafed, and married advantageoufly fome Years after. The following Lines were made by the fame Author as
the laft, and fent in the fame News.

Puella

1.

Puella illa Nobilis
Quæ erat tàm amabilis,
Commifit adulterium,
Et nuper fecit filium.
Sed dicunt Matrem Reginam
Illi fuiffe Lenam,
Et quod hoc patiebatur
Ut Principem lucraretur.
At multi dicunt quod Pater
Non eft Princeps, fed eft altor,
Qui Regi eft a fecretis,
Omnibus eft notus fatis.

2.

Contra hanc tamen Regina
Se oftendit tantum plena
† Cholerâ, ac fi nefciffet
Hoc quod Puella feciffet,
Et dedit illi cuftodes
Superbos nimis & rudes,
Mittens in Monafterium
Quærere refrigerium.
Sed certè pro tàm levi re,
Sic non deberet tractare,
At excufare modicum,
Tempus, Perfonam & Locum,
Aliis non fit taliter
Quæ faciunt fimiliter.

3.

Pridiè venit Nuncium
Puellum effe mortuum,

Et

† Anger.

Et fuit magna jactura
De tàm pulchrâ Creaturâ
Quæ nunc eft cum Cœlitibus
Rogans Deum pro Patribus
Et ut Patri fit meliùs (b)

From *Lyons* the Court came, in the Month of July, to *Rouffillon*, a place in *Dauphiné*, belonging to the Counts of Tournon, where the King ftayed for fome time. There he received many great Complaints from the Reformed about the general infraction of the late Edict almoft in every Province, and about the ill ufage they received from the Governours: and indeed they had great reafon to complain ; we have already feen how the Parliament and the States of *Burgundy* ftood affected towards them. Furthermore, the Fraternity of the Holy Ghoft fettled in that Province, obliged thofe who were admitted into it, to promife with a folemn Oath, not to ceafe till they had intirely deftroyed the *Hereticks*. Nothing was to be heard in the Pulpits but the praifes of King Philip, and confequently of the Spaniards, whofe Piety was extolled to the skies ; every where, and in every thing Philip's Name was intermixed, to the great difhonour of the King of France, and of the French Nation ; as if the King of Spain had been the fole Arbitrator of Religion, and as if to him it had belonged, to interpret the King's Edicts. At *Crevant* in the *Autunefe*, the Reformed were affaulted as they went to Church, and if it had not been for fome Gentlemen of the Country that came to their affiftance, they would have been very feverely handled ; the Queen, by her Letters to D'Andelot dated from *Lyons*, had made fome Excufe

XXII.
The King comes to Rouffillon.

(b) Addit, aux Mem. de Caftel. Tom. II. lib. V. ch. x. p. 240, 241, 242.

Excuse for the Fact. Besides that, heavy Complaints were sent to Court on the 8th of August, against Claude D'Angennes, Bishop of Mans, who having usurped the Government of that Province, made use of it, to oppress in a thousand ways more odious one than the other, not only those who professed openly the Reformed Religion, but likewise those whom he suspected to countenance them. The Marshal of Vielle-ville having been commissioned by the King to take cognizance of these Matters, he received a Petition tendered to him in the Name of the whole Province, wherein the many Villainies of that Bishop and his Followers, were set in their full Light. At *Tours* the Reformed were likewise assaulted as they were assembled in the place appointed for them by the Edict, for their Religious Meeting, some of whom were killed, and their Minister murdered in the Pulpit. The Parliament of Paris deputed several Members of its body to inquire into the Fact; but very little justice could be obtained. About the same time happened the Murder of Gilbert De la Cure'e, a Gentleman no less conspicuous by his Virtue than by his Nobility; he was Lieutenant of the Duchy of Vendosme for the Queen of Navarr; may be, he was too partial to the Reformed, and too severe against the Catholicks: however, he was murdered in treason at a hunting-match, with the Knowledge of the Bishop of Mans; some say, with his Consent. The Widow petitioned the Court for Justice; but after many delays, many injustices and hardships undergone by her Friends, she was forced to desist. By these repeated breaches of the Edict, and the denials of Justice, the Queen fomented the Discontents of the Reformed, and afforded them a just pretence of rising up in Arms; but this was but the beginning

ning of their Miseries, and we shall see present-ly a great deal more; whereby their Patience was at last tired (*i*).

In order to weaken more and more the Reformed Party, the King published an Edict, whereby it was ordered to demolish the Citadels and Fortifications, raised in the Cities on account of the last War; to the end that every one might live peaceably according to his Profession, without fear, and without any other safe-guard but that of the Laws. Accordingly Cipierre was sent to *Orleans* to see that the Fortresses of that City should be demolished, but some Engineers went at the same time along with him, by the Court's Order, for taking a View of the Place, and for taking the squaring of a Fortress which they intended to build at the Gate that leads to Paris. Furthermore, the Court considering of what great Importance that City was, and for other private Considerations, which had no place under the following Reigns, gave the Duchy of *Anjou* instead of that of Orleans, for an Apanage to the King's eldest Brother.

The new Fortifications of *Montauban, Valence* and *Cisteron*, were likewise demolished. The Reformed were also forbidden to keep School; and their Ministers were obliged to take Lodgings near their Churches (*k*); they were not allowed to assemble for divine Worship, nearer than ten Leagues from the place where the Court made any stay; the Noblemen and Gentlemen of the Reformed Religion, who had right to have

(*i*) Thuan. lib. XXXVI. pag. 294.
(*k*) These Articles were very hard, and done on purpose to hinder the Pastors to visit their Flock, to instruct and comfort them in their Sickness; and so the Nerves of the Doctrine and Discipline being cut asunder, as the Emperor Julian had done in the former times, nothing could be expected but to see all sense of Religion extinguished amongst the Christians.

have a Chapel in their Caſtle, were forbidden to admit any into it but their own Families and Vaſſals or Tenants, under the penalty of forfeiting their Right : No Synod could be held without calling ſome of the King's Officers to be preſent at their Conſultations and Deliberations ; no Money to be raiſed amongſt themſelves upon any account ſoever, without the King's ſpecial Licence ; all Marriages contracted by or between Perſons in Holy Orders, or engaged in monaſtical Life, not only during or ſince the late Troubles, but even long before, were made void ; and ſuch Perſons, Men or Women, obliged to go back into their Cloyſters in two Months time, or to depart the Kingdom ; and in caſe of Diſobedience, Men were condemned to the Galleys, and Women to a perpetual Confinement.

It is clear that this Edict, under pretence of interpreting the former of *Amboiſe*, was a downright violation of it, as any one might be convinced, if he does but compare them together. And indeed the Article which forbad the Reformed to aſſemble for divine Service, nearer than ten Leagues from the Court, was very troubleſome to them, and expoſed them to very great Inconveniences, and to many Dangers. Thoſe againſt their Synods, and aſſeſſing themſelves for the Maintenance of the Miniſtry, deprived them of the moſt proper means of repreſſing the Diſſoluteneſs of Manners, and of providing for their own Security. What a Tyranny was it, to oblige married People to part from their Wives, or from their Husbands, and to take again upon them a Yoke which they had found intolerable by their own Experience, and which they could not bear any longer without wounding their Conſcience ?

The

The Prince of Condé having got notice of this, while he was at his Caſtle of St. Valery, wrote to the Queen, complaining of the manifold Infractions of the Edict, cauſed either by Interpretations contrary to the obvious Senſe of the Words, or by other Edicts quite oppoſed to that, and by the Decrees of the Courts of Juſtice ; he complained likewiſe of the wilful Murders which were paſs'd by unpuniſhed ; and ſhewed forth, that ſince the Peace no leſs than 132 Innocents had been put to death by the Malice and Hatred of their Enemies : to this he added the many Injuſtices and Vexations of the Governours againſt the Reformed.

The King anſwered to this Letter, and aſſured him that he had nothing more at heart than to do Juſtice to every one impartially ; and as to the Interpretations of the Edict, he ſays, that it had been done for ſo good Reaſons, that he himſelf would approve of them, was he acquainted with them : beſides that, he could not believe that the Prince ſhould preſume that his own Will ought to be a Rule for his ; but if the Governours or others of his Officers had offended againſt the Edict, he would bring them to Juſtice, that they might receive a condign Puniſhment, &c.

From Rouſſillon the Court went to *Valence*, then to *Montelimar*, where the King was received with great Pomp and Solemnity ; from thence he entered into Provence, and going through *Orange* he came to *Avignon*, where he was received with great Magnificence by Cardinal D'ARMAGNAC, Governour of that City for the Pope.

Henry, Prince of Navarr, was then at Court, where the Queen his Mother had ſent him for his Safety, after ſhe had been providentially delivered from the threatning Danger ſhe had been in by the Treachery of her own Catholick Subjects,

Charles
IX.
1564.
Pope Pius
IV.

XXIV.
*Plot a-
gainst the
Queen of
Navarr
discovered.*

jects, and whereof I shall give here a short Account, tho' the Plot was discovered some Months before.

No bolder Attempt had ever been seen in the Kingdom before this, nor more happily prevented. The King of Navarr being dead, the Enemies of his House, who imagined no other ways of settling and strengthening the ancient Religion, but what were conducive to their own private Interest, and thought that there was no better than to destroy, under that specious pretence of Religion, the Heads of the Kingdom that supported the Reformed Religion, or to reduce them under the power of some Catholick Prince ; and by the same means thinking to ingratiate themselves with the King of Spain (with whom they kept a strict Correspondence) by some signal Service, plotted to seize the Queen of Navarr (she resided then at *Pau* in Bearn) with Prince Henry her Son, and Princess Catherina her Daughter, and to carry them to the Prisons of the Inquisition in *Spain :* they thought that they had a fair Opportunity for executing their Plot, because the King of Spain was then assembling his Troops at *Barcelona* for the War of *Africa.* They made no doubt, but that Philip would the more readily listen to their Scheme, that by that means, not only the Interest of the Religion, whereof he boasted to be a zealous Defender, would be secured ; but he would likewise secure to himself the Possession of the Kingdom of Navarr, which he so unjustly detained : for the lawful Heirs being once taken out of the way, there would be no more Dispute about it for the future. They settled the order of execution in such a manner that the Success seemed to them infallible ; for they intended to send part of the Troops that were at *Barcelona* to *Tarascon,*
and

and from thence, by the narrow Paſſages of the
Mountains, to *Pau*; and indeed by that means
they could have introduced the Troops into
Bearn without the leaſt Suſpicion, and have ſurpriſed the Mother and the Children unawares.

They imparted their Scheme to the King of
Spain, and the Duke of Alva, by a certain Captain, Dominic by Name, a Bearneſe, a Man
who had been let into the Secret, and was very
well acquainted with the People, and the Roads
and By-ways of the Country. The Murder of
the Duke of Guise, which was perpetrated about
this time, relented not their Hatred againſt the
Queen of Navarr, only it obliged them to delay the Execution of their Plot: Dominic ſtayed
in Guienn till further Orders; which having received, he went directly to the Duke of Alva,
who, with the King's Licence, was retired at
that time to *Alva*; he had frequent Conferences
with him about that Affair, and after having
weighed the importance of it, he diſpatched him
to Philip, being attended by Francis de Alava. Philip was then at *Monçon*, where he
waited for the general States of *Catalonia*, *Arragon* and *Valencia*, that were to be held in that
place.

But as Dominic was upon his Journey, he fell
dangerouſly ſick at *Madrid*, and was obliged to
ſtay there, ſending, however, Alava before him,
in order to prepare every thing with Philip. During his Sickneſs, Annas Vespiers, (a Gentleman born at *Nerac*, and belonging to Elizabeth Queen of Spain) was introduced by his
Landlord to him. and by his continual Attendance, and good Offices, he got into his moſt
inward Familiarity, ſo far that Dominic diſco-
vered to him the Plot, and the Names of the
Accomplices. Veſpiers, ſtruck with horror, conſidered

sidered in himself how he could prevent that fatal Blow; he thought proper to impart that Affair to St. Esteve, great Almoner to Queen Elizabeth, that he might give notice of it to her Majesty. The Queen when she heard of this, struck with the atrocity of the Crime, could not forbear Tears; being united with Queen Joanna, not only by the Ties of Blood, but also by those of a sincere Love: and thinking that the Honour and Welfare of the Kingdom of France was concerned in the Danger that Princess was in, she wrote without any delay to St. Sulpice, the French Embassador, who was then at *Monçon* with the King her Husband. Her Letter was in Cypher, and St. Esteve, by the Queen's Command, wrote likewise to him to the same purpose, and let him know the House where Dominic was to lodge at Monçon, described his Face, his Mien, and Clothes, as he had been told by Vespier. The Express that was sent with those Letters, made such great diligence, that he arrived at Monçon before Dominic. Saint Sulpice having received his Letters, sent some trusty Friends to the Inn, and being certain by the Description given of him, that he was arrived, he took care to get Intelligence of his doings by proper Persons which he had set in his way, and found that in one Night only after Midnight, he had been introduced three times by Alava to Philip; whereby he judged that there was no time to be lost for preventing Dominic. Therefore he dispatched Rouleau his Secretary to the Court of France, to acquaint the King and the Queen of what was hatching at the Court of Spain against the Queen of Navarr; he charged him likewise to warn this last as he went through Guienn, to provide for her own and her Children's Security. Which he

enter

carefully executed; for when he arrived at *Bayonne*, he sent a trusty Man to the Queen of Navarr with Letters, whereby she was informed of whatever was plotting against her.

Rouleau being arrived at Court, and the Queen understanding the subject of his Message, she would scarce believe him; so sturdy that Attempt appeared to her: however being plainly certified of the Truth of it, she gave proper Orders to stop Dominic as he came from Spain, that she might hear from himself the whole Plot, and take the proper measures in such cases. But Dominic having got Intelligence of these Resolutions, by some of Philip's Pensioners, at the Court of France, took another Road than that whereby it was thought that he should pass, and so escaped the just Reward due to his execrable Treason. It was rumoured that Montluc the Marshal, and the Viscount of Ortez were in the Plot; Montluc denied that he had any hand in it, but not that he was acquainted with it; and whereas the Evidences are not clear enough against him, we must wait till the Doom-day, when God Almighty shall reveal the secret of every Man's heart. As to the Queen-Mother, it was said, that she was very glad of the Discovery of that Plot, but that she would have been sorry, had Dominic been taken, lest the Credit and Authority of the Authors and Abettors of that Plot, whereof she intended to make use, should have been sunk too low. This Discovery was made while the Court was still at Fontainbleau: The Queen of Navarr, as we have said, sent the Prince of Navarr her Son to Court, for the greater Safety; she had gave him Governours and Tutors to watch over him, and not suffer him to be ensnared by the Allurements of the Court (*l*).

Vol. III.   F   From

(*l*) Thuan. XXXVI. pag. 290. and p. 296.

From *Avignon* the Court came to *Marſeilles*, where the many Complaints of the Reformed obliged the King, for preventing ſome Inſurrection, to publiſh an Edict to inforce the ſtrict Obſervation of the Articles of *Rouſſillon*. From *Marſeilles* the King came back to *Avignon*, which place was very delightful to him, and having forded the Rhône he entered Languedoc, and came to *Nimes*. There was a great Concourſe of Reformed in that City, who, for the moſt part came from Provence, where they had ſo many Wrongs and Hardſhips to undergo. The Reformed renewed here their Complaints, eſpecially againſt the Marſhal DAMVILLE, which, however, were ſmothered by the Conſtable's Intereſt. The Court came to *Beziers* by the latter end of this Year, and the King's reception put the Inhabitants to a vaſt Expence, which was very prejudicial to them.

While the Court ſojourned at *Avignon*, the Affairs of *Guienne* were in a very bad Condition, and very near to break out in a civil Commotion ; for FREDERICK DE FOIX, Count of CANDALE, liſtening to the violent Counſels of GASTON de FOIX, Marquis of TRANE, a turbulent Man, which having imparted to CHRISTOPHORUS, Biſhop of *Aire*, MONTLUC, DE CAUMONT, DE LAUSUN, DESCARS and MERVILLE, they had made a League amongſt themſelves at *Cardillac*, in the laſt Month of Auguſt, againſt the Reformed, under a falſe pretence that they exceeded the Liberty granted to them by the Edict of Amboiſe, and that they had committed ſome Murders. But the Court having got notice of that League, by JAMES LARGEBASTON, firſt Preſident of the Parliament of *Bourdeaux*, ſent into Guienne Marſhal de BOURDILLON, for ſuppreſſing theſe Commotions ; but ſhowing himſelf

self too partial in behalf of the Catholicks, the Reformed complained of him to the King no less than of the Count of Candale. However, having repressed by his Presence the Efforts of the Confederates, the State of that Province was more quiet for a time.

At the beginning of the Year 1565, the Court came from *Beziers* to *Narbonne*, and from thence to *Carcassonne*, which is divided into two parts by the River *Aude*, the upper Town and the lower; the first was under the Jurisdiction of the Bishop, and the second under the Kings: That Year the Winter was very severe, and the King being arrived in the upper Town, waited there till the Preparations for his publick Entry into the lower Town should be ready; but the Night preceding the Day appointed for that Ceremony, which was the 13th of January, there fell such a vast quantity of Snow, and the Wind blew so hard, that all the Preparations were either carried away, or otherwise spoiled, so that the King was obliged to stay ten Days longer in the upper Town, being besieged, as it were, with the Snow, and could not make his publick Entry till St. Vincent's Day. Old People in that City say, that they had been told by their Grand-fathers, that something like it had happened about 123 Years before this, and that Mary of Anjou, Consort to Charles VII. had been forced to stay for three Months in their City, because of the Snow that fell that Winter six feet high: Strange thing indeed! Carcassonne lying in the 42d Degree of Latitude.

While the Court was at Carcassonne, came the News of a Tumult happened at Paris, on Cardinal of Lorrain's account. That Prelate coming from *Rome* after the Council of Trent, and before he went to see his Mother at *Joinville*, had written to the Queen-Mother, setting forth the

the

the danger he was in from the great Number of his Enemies, who might play him a foul Trick, and deſiring that the King would grant him the Licence of being attended with a Troop of Guards at his own Charge; which Licence had been granted to him, ſigned by one of the Secretaries of State. (That Step of the Cardinal was then neceſſary, and ſuch a Licence requiſite, becauſe of the King's Edict in 1563, whereby it was forbidden under ſevere Penalties to go with Arms along the Streets, the Nobility and others to whom it ſhould belong being allowed to bear a Sword only, and the Governours of the Provinces or of the Cities were ſtrictly charged to watch narrowly upon the due Obſervation of that Edict.) Now the Cardinal being arrived at

Why?

Joinville, had a mind to ſee his Friends at *Paris*, but out of an unſeaſonable Wantonneſs, he was willing to make a ſhow of his power; for that end he ſent to the Duke of AUMALE his Brother, then at *Anet*, deſiring him to meet him at *Nanteuil*, where he was coming, with as many armed Men as he could, which was complied to; and the Cardinal, being ſo well attended, came to *St. Denis* with Henry Duke of Guiſe his Nephew. But the Marſhal of Montmorency, Governour of *Paris* and of the *Iſle of France*, having notice of the Cardinal's deſign, ſent him word not to proceed any further with ſuch Attendance, and not to inſiſt upon his entering the City with armed Men contrary to the King's Edict, during his Majeſty's abſence, and at a time when there was a diſpoſition in the People's mind towards an Inſurrection; this the Marſhal did with the Advice and Conſent of the Parliament of Paris.

But the proud Cardinal, little acquainted with any Compliance to the Laws, was affronted at
this

this Meſſage, and deſiſted not from his Attempt, not vouchſafing ſo much as to give notice to the Marſhal of the Licence the King had granted him. The Marſhal underſtanding this, thought that it was his Duty to hinder him by force from coming into the City ; but he was prevented by the Cardinal, who having rejected with Scorn all the prudent Advices given to him, was entered by the Gate of St. Denis ; and was met in the Street by the Marſhal, and the Prince of Porcian attended with a great number of Nobility on Horſe-back. They ſtopt the Van of the Cardinal, and obliged them to ſurrender their Arms, one of them refuſing to obey was killed upon the ſpot, whereat the Cardinal, a downright Coward, thinking that they ſought his own Life, alighted quickly with his Nephew, and ran for ſafety into a Mercer's Shop hard by ; his Men fled as faſt as they could, ſome to one place, and ſome to another, and the Marſhal forbad to purſue them, being very well ſatisfied with having chaſtiſed the Haughtineſs of the Cardinal with the terrible fright he was in. He had been in great hopes that the Mob would have riſen for him, but he had the mortification of ſeeing no body ſtirring to his Aſſiſtance. The Marſhal, and he, ſent to Court ; the firſt for juſtifying what he had done, the other for making his Complaints ; but by the Conſtable's Intereſt, the King condemned not the Marſhal, and ſaid only, that he would examine the Matter, and whereas he underſtood that both Parties were aſſembling their Friends and Adherents, he ſent them Orders to diſarm, to diſmiſs their Friends, and not to bear Arms in Paris ; he was obeyed. The Prince of Condé's Opinion was, that the Marſhal had gone too far if he had a mind only to frighten

the

the Cardinal; but that he had not done enough, if he was in earneft.

From *Carcaffonne* the Court came to *Thouloufe*, whither the King had appointed the States of that Province, and the Deputies of the neighbouring. Many Complaints were brought thither from the Reformed againft MONTLUC; but that Gentleman being come to Court in order to clear himfelf, no body durft appear againft him. It was at Thouloufe that, by the Queen's Orders, the Names of the King's Brothers were changed; he who had been called ALEXANDER took the Name of HENRY, and the youngeft, who was named HERCULES, received the Name of FRANCIS.

From *Thouloufe* the Court came to *Bourdeaux*, where the King was received with a greater Pomp and Magnificence than any where elfe, on the 9th of April. Three hundred Men at Arms went to meet him out of the City, with Troops of Men reprefenting feveral foreign Nations, as Grecians, Turks, Arabians, Egyptians, Sumatrafians, Indians, Canarians, Moors, Ethiopians, Cannibalians, Americans and Brafilians, that were led like Captives. The Chief of each Troop made a Compliment to the King in the Language of the Nation which the faid Troop reprefented, which was turned into French by an Interpreter.

The Reformed Inhabitants of the City, had obtained fince the laft Year, while the King was at Valence, fome Articles of their Demands, but the Parliament had refufed to regifter and publifh the Letters-Patent which the King had granted to them upon that fubject, notwithftanding all the Inftances of the King's Attorney, and of the Mayor, and the Sheriffs. Now the King being in the City, the Parliament, willing to fhow their Obfequioufnefs to his Majefty, took a middle

middle way, and caused these Letters-Patent to
be published by the Governour of *Guienne*. These
Concessions were to the following purport : That
the Reformed should be at liberty to sing Psalms,
even out of their Churches, without being molested for that Cause, either by the Governours
of Provinces, or by the Mayors and Sheriffs of
the Cities ; that they should not be constrained
to pay any thing towards the making of what
they called the *Holy Bread* ; nor to set Hangings
before their Houses or Windows on Corpus
Christi Day ; and that in those places where
the Reformed should refuse to put such Hangings, the Captains or other Officers of the Ward
should do it at their own Charge ; that the Reformed should not be compelled to pay any thing
to the Parish towards the Relief of the Catholick
Beggars and Poor ; nor for the Maintenance of
the Fraternities ; that being summoned in Judgment, they should not be obliged to swear upon
St. Anthony's Arm ; (a Relique much reverenced
at Bourdeaux) that the Reformed should be admitted to the publick Offices, as well as the Catholicks ; and few other Articles of less moment
than these. Castelnau differs a little from Thuanus in these Articles ; he don't speak of St. Anthony's Arm, nor of the Admittance of the Reformed to publick Offices. 2dly, He don't say
that these Articles were granted at the Instances
of the Reformed of Bourdeaux ; but that the
Queen-Mother, seeing that the heats of the two
Parties (which he ascribes in a banter to the scorch-
ing heat of the last Summer) increased every day,
she sent orders to the Governours of Provinces,
&c. about the Articles above-mentioned. But
one must consider that Castelnau writes only some
Memoirs wherein he insists only upon the most
material Events, whereas Thuanus writes a com-

F 4 pleat

pleat History of his own times, wherein he omits nothing worthy to be mentioned, when he has been acquainted with the Matter, so both might be very well reconciled ; those Articles above-mentioned were granted to the Reformed in general, as Castelnau says, but at the Instances of the Bourdelese, as Thuanus says, and as to the number of the Articles, as those in Castelnau are agreeable to those in Thuanus, no matter, me-thinks, if there is two or three more in this last than in the former (*m*).

The Complaints against the Count of *Candale* and his Adherents were renewed at Bourdeaux ; but whereas the King saw that too many Lords and Great Men of the Kingdom were Accom-plices with him, he thought proper to forget every thing, and to forbid all sovereign Courts to take any further notice of it.

Then the King set out from *Bourdeaux* in or-der to go to *Bayonne*, there to meet his Sister Elizabeth Queen of Spain, sent thither attended with the Duke of Alva, for conferring with the Queen-Mother about the means of compassing the Destruction of the Reformed in France and in the Low Countries, As the King was at *Mont de Marsan* he received Advice of a League between some of the greatest Men in the Kingdom against THE COLIGNIES and MONTMORENCIES, which was confirmed by some intercepted Letters, from the Duke of AUMALE to his Brother the Marquis of ELBEUF, written on the 24th of Fe-bruary, wherein mention was made of the Duke of MONTPENSIER, the Viscount of MARTIGUES, the Duke of ESTAMPES, CHAVIGNY, and the Bishop of MANS, as being concerned in the Con-federation. The Queen dreading the Conse-quences

(*m*) Casteln. liv. V. ch. x. Thuan. lib. XXXVII. p. 320.

quences of it, left the King's Name and Authority fhould be fubverted by fuch Factions, advifed the King in his Council on the 18th of May,
to draw a form of Oath, whereby every one fhould
folemnly promife to reveal whatever he knew or
fhall know of any fecret Confederacy, raifing of
Money, Treaties with foreign Princes, and warlike Preparations ; that being required of it by
the King, they fhould obey with all Humility,
befeeching his Majefty not to believe them guilty
of any fuch thing, which they look'd upon with
the utmoft Abhorrence, and wherein they never
had any hand, being ready to fpend their Goods
and fhed their Blood for maintaining the Royal
Authority, and the Obfervation of his Edicts
and Commands. Befides that, that they engage
themfelves never to rife in Arms but at the King's
Command. Such an Inftrument having been
drawn, the Lords then prefent at Court fubfcribed
to it, amongft whom there was fome named in
AUMALE's Letters, who were come to Court of
late : It was added further, that the King willed
and commanded that the faid Inftrument fhould
be tranfmitted to thofe Princes and great Lords
of the Kingdom, then abfent from Court, to be
fubfcribed by them ; and that thofe who fhall
refufe to fubfcribe fhall be deemed Accomplices
of the Factions, Scorners of his own Authority,
Difturbers of the publick Peace, and Traitors to
their King ; ordering that whoever fhall know
any thing of the Premifes fhall repair immediately
to him in order to reveal it, promifing to receive
. and keep them under his Royal Protection.

MONTLUC fays in his Commentaries, that the
Queen having bid him to fpeak his own Opinion
upon that Affair, he faid, that the King ought
to reject and condemn that Affociation, and to
form a new one, whereof he fhould be the Chief,

and

and that he fhould oblige all the Princes, Lords, and Great Men of the Kingdom, to enter into it, and to tie themfelves with a folemn Oath. Since Montluc fays himfelf, that this was his own Opinion, we muft believe him. But that the King, *as he faid*, followed it as the beft and the moft wholefome, that is not true, at leaft there is no Sign of it left in the Records of thofe days; and fuch a Step would have been directly contrary to thofe Acts mentioned above, and related in the Journal of the King's Council, whereby all fuch fecret Confederacy of the Subjects amongft themfelves were condemned and forbidden, as pernicious to the King, and contrary to the publick Tranquility. As to what Montluc fays, that the King caufed an Inftrument of that Affociation to be drawn, which was put in his Trunks, and that he believed it was not loft : That Evidence is very weak in order to prove a Fact fo extraordinary, and of fo great a Confequence, and being done fo publickly, it ought to have been recorded in the Council's Regifters, where being not to be found, we muft infer, that if Montluc or any other ever made fuch a ftrange Propofition in the King's Council, it was rejected (*n*).

The Court having received notice that the Queen of Spain was coming, the King fet out for *Bayonne*, from whence he fent his Brother Henry to meet their Sifter on the borders of *Bifcay*. On the 9th of June the Queen arrived at *St. Sebaftian* ; where Ferdinand Alvarez de Toledo, Duke of Alva, repaired immediately after, with a great Attendance, carrying the Collar of the Golden Fleece to the King in the Name of the King of Spain his Mafter ; hiding under that

(*n*) Thuan. lib. XXXVII. p. 320, 321. Comment. de Montluc, liv. VI. fol. 431, 432.

that specious pretence the true motive of his Embassy, which was to engage the King of France and the Queen his Mother in a League against the Reformed.

At this time the Queen shewed a greater Inclination for it than she had done before ; and was very glad to know what Philip intended to do with the Reformed of the *Low Countries*, who began then to form a great Party there.

Before that time the said King had seen with pleasure the civil Commotions in France, which he had endeavoured to foment as much as he could. But now that he saw himself exposed almost to the same Diseases, he altered something his Behaviour, lest theReformed of France being in peace at home, should keep Correspondence with those of the Low Countries, called by the nick-name of Beggars. Nay, lest in order to keep peace at home, the Reformed should be allowed to relieve their Brethren of the Low Countries. That was the true Reason which induced the King of Spain to consent to that Interview between the Queen his Consort, and the Queen his Mother-in-Law, which he had cunningly delayed till this time, in order to increase the Jealousies amongst the Reformed of France, and to countenance the Suspicions they were in, of a League between the two Crowns formed against them, whereby they would be obliged to think of their own Safety, and be deterred from granting any Relief to others. The Queen-Mother would have been very glad, had the King of Spain come himself, as for a long time he had given her hopes, only to amuse her, and to engage her upon that account to be severe with the Reformed ; and if it had not been for that, he would not even have consented to the Journey of the Queen his Consort, which he granted

granted only as a favour to the Importunities of St. Sulpice, the French Embassador at his Court, according to what the said Gentleman wrote to the Bishop of *Rennes.*

So all that great bustle about that intended Interview of all the Catholick Princes came to this only between the two Crowns of France and Spain, which even cost very dear to the first, not only by the extravagant Expences made on that account, but more by the Troubles and Miseries which were the Consequences of it (*o*).

The Queen-Mother had taken her Lodgings in the Bishop's Palace, adjoining to which she had caused a House of Bricks to be built in haste, adorned with the finest Hangings, for the Queen her Daughter's reception; she came in frequently in the Night by a Back-Door known only by those which were in the Secret, and there she conferred with the Duke of Alva, who was intrusted with his Master's Intentions. There the League between the two Crowns was made, for the Restoration of the old Religion, and the Destruction of the Reformed; and they promised their mutual Assistance one to the other for the execution of that Design. Thuanus, in the relation of this, could have spared to the Reformed the Title he gives them, calling them *a kind of mistrustful People,* and speaking of them as if they had been the Authors of the Rumours spread abroad about the said League, seeing that he himself, four or five Lines afterwards, acknowledges, that the Event shewed that they were in the right : but the Protestant Historians are not the only ones that have said the same (*p*). Thuanus himself quotes John Bapt. Hadrianus, as an Historian of great Fidelity and Capacity, according to
Guic-

(*o*) Addit. aux Mem. de Casteln. liv. VI. ch. 1.
(*p*) *Genus hominum Suspicax*, lib. XXXVII. p. 322.

GUICCIARDINE, and to whom very likely Cosmo, Duke of *Tuscany*, had imparted his Memoirs. But that Historian says, that it had been proposed in that Conference (held at the Pope's Instances, who earnestly desired that the King of Spain should be present at it :) to deliver the Kingdom of France from that plague of the Reformed, and that at last, Alva's Opinion had been agreed to, viz. to strike down the Heads of the Chiefs, and to put to the Sword all the Reformed, without exception, after the way of the SICILIAN VESPERS ; and whereas they began to talk at Court of an Assembly to be held at Moulins, it was thought that no better opportunity could be found for executing that barbarous Plot, than that, when the greatest Princes and Lords of the Kingdom would be assembled at that Place to have them murdered all at once ; and that Signal once given, to have the rest murdered likewise throughout the Kingdom.

But, either because all the Nobles which had been pitched upon to be the Victim of that Fury, did not come to *Moulins*, or for some other reason, that Execution was put off to another time ; and was effected seven Years after at Paris, just as it was now projected at *Bayonne (q)*.

La Noüe says, that he had been told by the Duke of Alva himself, *that it was needless to be so busy in catching the little Frogs, but that they ought to endeavour to catch the great Salmons and such other large Fishes.* The Duke required further, in Philip's Name, that the King should repeal the free Exercise of their Religion, granted by his Edict to the Reformed inhabiting in the frontier Towns, left that *Plague* should spread and communicate itself to the Subjects of the King of Spain ; but whereas the Court of France thought

(q) Thuan. Hist. lib. XXXVII. p. 322.

thought not proper at this time to gratify Philip in that respect, the Court of Spain took that pretence afterwards for obliging the Pope to take away from the Diocese of *Bayonne* the Provinces of *Guipuscoa* and *Biscay*; the same thing had been done not long before, as to the Bishopricks of *Cambray* and *Tournay*, which were formerly of the Diocese of *Rheims*.

Such were the Transactions of that famous Conference at *Bayonne*, which might be looked upon as the Original of all the Calamities that befel the Kingdom under this and the following Reign. For the Queen henceforward had very little or no regard at all for the Reformed Party, she did stick at nothing for compassing her Ends, as we shall see; and on the other hand, the Prince of Condé and Admiral de Coligny, having got Intelligence from their Friends at Court of whatever was transacted in that Conference, consulted together with their Friends about the means of averting the threatning Danger, and of providing for their own Security, so the King of Spain obtained his Ends, viz. to keep the Kingdom of France in a perpetual Division amongst the Subjects.

Then the King proceeding in his Journey arrived at *Nerac*, where he restored the Catholick Religion, the exercise whereof had been forbidden by the Queen of *Navarr*; from thence, going through the *Agenese*, *Perigord*, Angoumois, *Poitou*, *Anjou*, he took his Winter Quarters at *Blois*; and appointed an Assembly of the Notables at *Moulins* for the beginning of the next Year.

XXVII.
*A Law-Suit
between
the Univer-
sity of Paris
and the Je-
suits.*

This Year there was a great Law-Suit tried before the Parliament of *Paris*, between the University of that City, and the Jesuits. They had tendered a Petition to that Court for obtaining the Licence of instructing the Youth, being

being opposed in that by the Rector of the said
University. But before I proceed, I think proper to give a short and impartial Account of the
Origin, Institutes, Progress and Settlement of
that famous Society in France, abstracted not
only out of Paquier (Lettres, & Recherches
de la France) but likewise out of Thuanus,
which last seems to me more impartial.

PETER ANTHONY CARAFFA, who was afterwards Cardinal, then Pope under the Name of
PAUL IV. had instituted a Fraternity of Priests,
who, renouncing the Society of Men, lived in
a perpetual Contemplation, and were named
THEATINES, from the place where they inhabited in *Apulia*. IGNATIUS LOYOLA, a Biscay-
an, tired with the military Life, whereby he
had got nothing else but a sore Leg, gave up himself to a kind of Life more retired (*r*) ; after
having travelled in *Italy*, and in the *Holy Land*,
he came back into his own Country in the Year
1524, and being thirty-three Years of Age, he
began to learn the Latin Grammar at *Barcelona*;
there he had for Companions in his way of living, one CALLISTUS, who had been along with
him at *Jerusalem*, ARTIAGUES and CAZERE,
both Spaniards, and a young Frenchman named
JOHN. Being sensible of the little Improvement
he had made in his Studies at *Barcelona*, Alcala,
and *Salamanca*, (tho' he had earnestly desired
his Regent at Barcelona, to whip him soundly,
as any other School-boy, if he did not learn his
Task) he came to Paris four Years after, and resolved

Charles
IX.
1565.
Pope Pius
IV.

XXVIII.
*A short Ac-
count of the
Rise, Pro-
gress and
Settlement
of the Je-
suits in
France.*

(*r*) He consecrated himself to the blessed Virgin's Service,
and followed in that Ceremony, all the Rules and Prescrip-
tions of the antient Knight Errantry. Whosoever has a
mind to know what he did on that Occasion might read it
in Stillingfleet's Fanaticism of the Roman Church; and
Jurieu, Apol. pour la Reform. 1st part, ch. i. he copies after
Stillingfleet.

solved to begin again with the Grammar; then he learned Philosophy under JOHN PENA, one of the greatest Mathematicians and Philosophers of his Age, then he learned Divinity in the Dominicans College; he got by this time some new Companions, viz. PETER FAVRE, a *Savoyard*, JAMES LAINEZ, born at *Siguenca* in *Spain*, ALFONSUS SALMERO of *Toledo*, NICHOLAS BOBADILLA of *Palentia*, SIMON RODRIGUEZ, a *Portugueze*, CLAUDIUS LE JAY and JOHN CODUR of the Diocese of *Geneva*, PASQUIER BROET of *Ambrun* (*s*), and FRANCIS XAVIER, one of his own Countrymen (*t*). They obliged themselves by a solemn Vow, after having received the Sacrament, that when they should have finished their Studies in Divinity, they would entirely renounce the World, and serve in a perpetual Poverty to the Glory of God, and the Salvation of Men's Souls; and especially that they would go to Jerusalem at a certain time, there to convert the Infidels, and to endeavour by all means to get the Crown of Martyrdom; that if it was impossible for them to put this their Design in execution, then a Year after they would go to *Rome*, and offer their Services to the Pope, without any Condition, or restriction of times and places. This was transacted in the Church of *Montmartre*, a Suburb of Paris, on the 16th of August 1534 (*u*).

The

(*s*) Pasquier says, that he was born at *Dreux*; but I follow Thuan. See Pasquier Recherches de la France, liv. III. ch. 43. p. 319.

(*t*) This Man, at the request of John King of Portugal, was sent by the Pope into the East for converting the Infidels: he travelled through the maritime Countries of India, went into Japon, and having undergone many Dangers, he died in China, as he was entering that Country in the Year 1556.

(*u*) Bayle puts this on the 15th of August. See Art. Loola.

The next Year Loyola went into Spain, then he came by Sea to *Genoa*, and from thence he arrived at Venice, where he was met by his Af- sociates on the 8th of January 1537, in order to fulfil their Vow. While Loyola waited for them at *Venice*, he became acquainted with Peter Anthony Caraffa, afterwards Pope Paul IV. who was very serviceable to him and his Society. Now before they embarked for their intended Voyage to the Holy Land, they went to Rome to ask the Pope's blessing, and his Licence, which having obtained they came back to *Venice* ; but finding no Opportunity for embarking, and the War being kindled with the Turks, they desisted from that Pilgrimage. Whereupon they dispersed themselves into the Territories of the Venetians. As to Loyola, he went back to Rome with Favre and Lainez. His Biographers relate, that being enter'd a Church hard by that City, to make his Prayers, he fell into a rapture, and saw God the Father recommending to Jesus his Son, (who carried a Cross and suffered the bitterest Pains) the said Loyola and his Companions, and that he doubted not but he would be favourable to them at Rome : From that Vision it is, that he gave to his Society the Name of Jesus.

They were received by Quirino Garzoni, a Citizen of Rome, in his Country-house. Here it was that Loyola drew the Scheme of a new Society ; which was approved of, with some Limitations, by Paul III. on the 3d of November 1540, and without any Limitation by another Bull published in 1543 ; at first their number was fixed at 60, but by this last Bull their number was not fixed. Loyola was created General of the Society in the Year 1541. He stayed at Rome while his Companions went up and down almoſt throughout the World ; he was taken up with ſeveral kinds of Buſineſs, either for the Converſion of the Jews, or that of the lewd Women, or for the Orphans.

ISABELLA ROSELLA, a Gentlewoman who had taken much care of him while he was in the College at *Barcelona*, was ſo fond of him, that ſhe came from Spain to Rome with ſome other Women, to pay him a Viſit, and to form a Society after the model of his own, and under the ſame Rules and Preſcriptions. But Loyola refuſed to take care of Women, and obtained at laſt of the Pope, that his Society ſhould be for ever exempted from that trouble. He obtained ſome other Privileges from Pope PAUL III. which were confirmed by JULIUS III. Then Paul IV. having been raiſed to the Papacy, increaſed much the Society ; and it was under his Pontificate that Loyola died on the laſt day of July 1556, aged about 65 Years, being born in 1491. Three-ſmall Stones were found in the Vein of his Liver. Such was the Life and Death of Ignatius de Loyola, the Founder of a Society, which afterwards increaſed to that degree, that it began ſoon to be dreadful to the Kings themſelves.

Near about the ſame time WILLIAM DU PRAT, Biſhop of *Clermont* in *Auvergne*, and Son to the Chancellor of that Name, being exceſſively fond of that Society, allowed them the College of Clermont at Paris ; and by his laſt Will, bequeathed to them 36000 Crowns, on condition that a School being erected at *Billon*, and *Mauriac* in *Auvergne*, they ſhould inſtruct the Youths. Therefore Paſquier BROET above-named had obtained of King Henry, at the recommendation of the Cardinal of Lorrain, and ſix Years before Loyola's death, that the Society ſhould be received
in

in the Kingdom, according to the Pope's Bull, and that the Fellows might build a House, and have a College at Paris, and not in any other Towns, out of the Alms which they fhould receive. Which Letters-Patent of the King being read in the Parliament four Years afterwards on the 3d of Auguft, it was refolved to fend the faid Letters-Patent, together with the Pope's Bull, to the Bifhop of Paris, and to the Faculty of Divinity, in order to be read and examined by them, and to have their Opinion upon the whole Matter.

Accordingly the Sorbonne delivered her Opinion in writing on the firft of December in the fame Year 1554, whereby fhe declared, that that new Society which went by the Name of the Society of Jefus, unheard of before, feemed to be a very dangerous one in regard to Religion, as difturbing the Peace of the Church, fubverting the Monaftical Difcipline, and tending more to Deftruction than to Edification : for they admitted without any diftinction into their Body all forts of Perfons how infamous, villainous and wicked foever ; befides that, they had been endowed by the Popes with fo many Privileges, Liberties and Immunities, efpecially as to the Adminiftration of the Sacraments, and to the prejudice of the Rights of the Bifhops and Clergy ; nay, to the detriment of Princes themfelves, and to the great grievance of the People, &c. Therefore they concluded that they could not, nor they ought not to be admitted.

The Jefuits, being ftunned at this Decree, thought proper to comply with the times, in hopes that the Hatred conceived againft their Society might relent with length of time, and they ftirred not till Francis IId's acceffion to the Throne ; then it was that the Guifes being all-potent,

potent, and countenancing that Society to their utmost, undertook the defence of their Cause; and first of all they asked the Opinion of the Bishop of Paris, who delivered it in writing, which was to the very same purport as that of the Sorbonne, only he insisted a little more upon the Title of SOCIETY OF JESUS, whereby they ascribed to themselves only, what does belong to the whole Christian Church; and in so doing it seemed that they declared that they only composed the Church: from the Premises he inferred, that whereas they had been bound by the Pope for instructing Mahometans and other Infidels, and preaching the Gospel amongst them, some places of Abode ought to be appointed for them in the Frontiers of those Countries, as formerly the Knights of Rhodes had been settled upon the Borders of Christendom, for watching over the Motions of the Infidels.

These Opinions having been read and examined in the King's Council, at the Cardinal of Lorrain's Instance, a Decree was sent to the Parliament, on the 25th of April 1560, whereby they were enjoined, that, without any regard to the Opinion of the University or the Bishop of Paris, they should publish the Pope's Bull, and the King's Letters-Patent granted in the Jesuits behalf.

But tho' the Society offered, by their Petition to the Parliament, to submit themselves to the Common Law, and to renounce all Immunities and Privileges to them granted by the Popes, that were contrary to the Rights and Privileges of the Bishops, Priests, Colleges, University, and of the Gallican Church, and to the Covenants made between the Kings and the Popes: Nevertheless the Parliament, on the 22d of February 1561, referred the whole Matter to the Decision cifion of a General Council, or to the Affembly of the Gallican Church.

At laft the Bifhops being affembled at Poiffy, by the King's Command, as we have faid in our firft Volume, the Cardinal of Tournon, Arch-bifhop of Lyons, being Prefident, and that Affembly being impowered by the Parliament for deciding finally the Queftion, the new Society was admitted and approved of under the Name both of Society and College, upon condition that they fhall take another Name than that of *Society of Jefus*, or Jefuits ; and that they fhall be fubject as well as other Priefts to the Jurifdiction of the Bifhop of the Diocefe wherein they fhall live ; that they fhall do nothing to the prejudice of the Bifhops, Priefts, Colleges and Univerfities ; that they fhall govern themfelves according to the Common Law, and renounce all Privileges to the contrary. Adding, that if they do not obey, or if for the future they did obtain new Privileges, they fhall lofe *ipfo facto* the Benefit of this Decree as if it had never been granted.

Accordingly the Society opened their College of Clermont at Paris. But whereas the Univerfity of Paris entered an Action againft that Liberty, the Affair was brought again before the Parliament, and the Society tendered a Petition to that Court, to the end that it fhould interpofe its Authority, that for the future they fhould be no more difturbed in their Calling. Before that Caufe was debated in the Parliament, CHARLES DU MOULIN had been confulted by the Univerfity, and had anfwered, that their Caufe was very juft, which he evinced by many ftrong and unqueftionable Arguments.

The Caufe was learnedly argued in full Parliament, PETER VERSORIS was Advocate for the

Jefuits,

Jeſuits, and STEPHEN PASQUIER for the Uni-
verſity. This laſt ſhewed forth, that that ambitious SECT, full of Hypocriſy, was born in
Spain, grown at Paris, raiſed at Venice, received
at Rome, and had been endowed with great Privileges contrary to the Common Law; then
condemned by the Sentence of the Sorbonne,
and rejected by the Biſhop of Paris; that now
under the ſpecious pretence of teaching the
Youths for nothing, it ſpreadeth itſelf like a
Peſt, and then by their Flatteries winning the
Affections of People, they engaged them to make
a laſt Will in their behalf, and ruined the Families by that means; then they corrupted the
Youths under pretence of Religion, and having
bewitched the minds of Children by their Super-
ſtitions, they diſpoſed them to Seditions, which
would break out in time to the Deſtruction of
the Kingdom. Then, in ſpeaking of their Vows,
he took notice of that whereby they do promiſe
a blind Obedience in every thing to their General, always choſen by the King of Spain, and
whom they worſhip as a God upon Earth: then
he compared Loyola with Luther, and ſaid, that
both conſpired to attain the ſame end, tho' by
different ways, viz. to undermine the lawful Authority of the Magiſtrates, to weaken the Church's
Diſcipline, and to confound all human and divine Rights (*v*). Then he inveighed againſt the
proud Name they took to themſelves; which
having been taken by ſome other Hereticks about
200 Years before, they had been expelled out
of the Church, and been deſtroyed by the juſt
Judgment of God; that they very likely intended to cauſe a Schiſm between thoſe who profeſſed

(*v*) That is very true as to the Jeſuits, but is utterly falſe
as to the Lutherans; and very likely Paſquier had never read
the Books of Luther, and ſpoke at random of his Opinions.

feffed the fame Religion, that fome of them would be Jefuits, while others would be Chriftians; that rendering themfelves fo far obfequious to the Popes, they ought to be the more fufpicious to the French Nation, which indeed confidered the Pope as Head and Prince of the Church, but in the mean while as inferior to the Councils, and therefore as bound to obey their Decrees; having no Power nor Authority of pronouncing any thing againft Kings or Kingdoms, or the Decrees of the Parliament; nor of decreeing any thing to the prejudice of the Bifhops in their Diocefe; then he fubjoined, that if thefe new Sectaries were once admitted, it would be felt by experience that they had fed fo many Enemies in the very bowels of the Kingdom, who would take up Arms againft the King and his Subjects, whenever a paffionate and hot-headed Pope fhall declare War againft both. Then directing his Speech to the Prefidents and Counfellors of the Parliament, You, fays he, who do now tolerate the Jefuits, the time will come when you will repent, but too late, of your Credulity; when you will fee that by your Connivance the publick Tranquility, not only of this Kingdom, but of all Chriftendom, will be endangered by the Frauds, Craft, Superftition, Hypocrify, Delufions, and wicked Tricks of thefe Men.

When Pafquier had done, Versoris replied, and then Baptist du Mesnil, the King's Attorney, a Man of great Sagacity and Probity, having at firft blamed the too great Bitternefs of the two Advocates; after having fet forth the Danger there was in admitting new Societies, not only as to Religion, but even as to the civil Government, he fpoke againft the Jefuits, who being obliged by a Vow, could not be admitted into the Body of the Univerfity, for teaching the

Youths,

Youths, and defired the Parliament to fee to what ufe the Legacy of the Bifhop of Clermont could be converted, which might anfwer his Intention and Meaning.

That Caufe was argued for two days together, and the Parliament, either becaufe they were not fenfible of the Confequences, or rather out of Hatred againft the Reformed, and becaufe they took the Jefuits to be the fitteft Men for fubduing them, decreed to take more time for confidering the Matter, and in the mean while granted to them the Liberty of opening their College to teach publickly the Youths : This was done on the 5th of April 1565 (*w*).

Seven Years afterwards Pope Gregory XIII. granted them another Bull, whereby they were allowed to chufe for themfelves fome JUDGES CONSERVATORS, as they call them, for all fort of Caufes either Civil, or Criminal, or Mixt, even for thofe wherein they fhall be Plaintiffs ; forbidding to all other Judges, even to the Cardinals themfelves, to take any cognizance of them. Which Bull derogated from the general Councils and apoftolical Conftitutions, and from the Ufes and Indults granted to the Kings and other Princes. In the Year 1578 on the 24th of March the Society having petitioned to be admitted into the Univerfity, the Rector and fome other Members being commiffioned to examine the Matter, declared, that the Jefuits Conftitutions and Rules, could not be tolerated without fubverting the ancient Difcipline, and abrogating the Statutes of the Univerfity ; therefore they were caft off (*x*).

The

(*w*) I have tranfcribed almoft all that I have faid till now upon this Subject out of Thuan. lib. XXXVII. p. 315 ——320.

(*x*) Le Mercure Jefuite, pag. 310.

The same Year on the 7th of May they obtained another Bull from the Pope, granting them the faculty of conferring Degrees, and of reading publickly in concurrence with the Fellows of the University, and NOTWITHSTANDING all Decrees, Laws, and Constitutions to the contrary.

In the Year 1594, Henry IV. having been acknowledged by the City of Paris, the University pursued again their Cause against the Jesuits, which had lain dormant for almost 30 Years: ANTHONY ARNAUD was their Advocate, who discharged his Duty as well as could be expected from a Man of his Parts. The Society, if we may give credit to Pasquier, had been the first Firebrands of that cruel League which had put the Kingdom to the very brink of its utter ruin. They had suborned one BARRIERE to murder King Henry IV. when they saw that, having embraced the Roman Religion, he had removed the greatest Obstacles to the peaceable Possession of the Throne of his Ancestors. They had confessed the said Barriere in their College, and administred unto him the Sacrament of the Lord's Supper; and having promised unto him the Crown of Glory, if it happened that he should die in the Attempt, they sent him to execute that bloody and detestable Murder; three times he had been like to execute his Design, and had been providentially hindered, and at last he was taken at the Gate of Melun on the 27th of August 1593, and the last day of the same Month, being convicted, he was brought to condign Punishment (y). He had charged, amongst many others,

(y) He was executed in the great Market-place of Melun, he had his Hand burnt to Ashes, holding in it the Knife found upon him when taken; then he was pinched with red-hot Pinchers along the Streets, in all the musculous parts of his Body, and then broken alive upon the Wheel.

others, the Curate of St. Andrew at Paris, his Vicar, but above all the Jesuit VARADE. All these new Productions of Jesuitism, occasioned the Pursuits of the University. And as the Parliament were about to judge the Cause, there happened a new Attempt against the King's sacred Person, which forwarded the final Decision of it. John Chastel, a Youth of 19 Years old, born at Paris, and brought up by the Jesuits, attempted to murder the King in his Palace of Louvre, and amidst his Nobility, but missed his end, and wounded him only in the Lip; he was taken, and brought almost to the like Punishment as Barriere But the Parliament decreed and inhibited to all Persons, of what Quality and Condition soever, upon pain of High Treason, to say or utter the following Propositions; That it is lawful to murder Kings; that Henry IV. then reigning, was not a Member of the Church till he should be approved by the Pope, *(which Propositions had been asserted by Chastel in his Trial, and owned to have been taught to him by the Jesuits;)* which Propositions the Court declared to be scandalous, seditious, contrary to the Word of God, and condemned as Heretical by the Holy Decrees. Commanded all Priests and Scholars of the College of Clermont, and all others of the same Society, as Corrupters of the Youth, Disturbers of the publick Peace, Enemies to the King and the State, to depart the City of Paris, and all other Cities, or places wherein they had Colleges, three days after the Intimation of the Sentence, and to depart the Kingdom a fortnight after; which time being expired, they were to be punished as guilty of High Treason, wherever they should be found in the Kingdom.

Their Goods, Moveable or Immoveable, were to be laid out in charitable Uses, and distributed as the Court fhould think proper. Furthermore, all the King's Subjects were forbidden to fend any Scholar to the Colleges of the faid Society without the Kingdom, upon the faid Pain of High Treafon. Done on the 29th of December 1594.

During the Trial the Court fent fome Lords to fearch the College of Clermont, and having feized upon feveral Papers, they found amongft them fome Books whereof Father John Guig-nard was Author, containing feveral Arguments whereby he endeavoured to prove, that it had been lawful to murder the late King Henry III. and feveral Inductions for committing the like horrid Crime upon his Succeffor Henry IV. (z).

But that Sentence was reverfed fome time after, and they came again into the Kingdom more powerful and dreadful than before, as we fhall fee hereafter ; and Henry IV. paid very dear for his Compliance.

After their fecond Admittance into the King-dom, it is not to be conceived what Incroach-ments they made every where upon the Univer-fities, and upon the Clergy ; and what is the more furprizing is, that the Succefs attended al-ways their Attempt according to their Wifhes, and they bore down all Oppofitions before them, as it is to be feen in the Book quoted in the Note *x*, which is nothing elfe but a Collection of many authentick Deeds and Inftruments for and againft them.

Such were the Origin, Beginnings, Progrefs and Settlement of that famous Society, which being intirely devoted to the Popes, muft be of courfe the more dreadful to the Kingdoms and States, which by the Conftitutions of their Go-vernment, or by Principle of Religion, don't acknow-

(z) Pafquier Rech. de la France, liv. III. ch. xlii.

acknowledge them as the supreme Lords of the Church, as having an arbitrary Power over it.

I do really believe that many things have been charged upon the Jesuits, whereof they are not guilty, and very often the Actions of a private Member are ascribed to the whole Body, which is very wrong. There are just subjects of Complaint against them, more than enough for passing Sentence upon them ; their Ambition, their greediness after Power and Authority, their manifold Attempts at several times, and in several places, to gratify that predominant Passion, render them justly obnoxious to the Abhorrence of any sober and truly virtuous Man.

And indeed such a great Power as theirs cannot be acquired in so short a time, and preserved so long, without the help of the most refined Politicks. And is not that Society the Encyclopædia of the bad Morality as to spiritual Sins ? Besides that, they are those who stretched so far, and with the greatest Ardour, the Consequences of several Doctrines taught before their time, and which do expose the Sovereign to continual Revolutions, the Protestants and Reformed to the Slaughter, and Christian Piety to the most deplorable Decay. But it is time to come to the main Subject of this History.

XXIX.
The Cardi-
nal's War.

While the Court was still at the *Mount of Marsan* in Guienne, the Queen received the News of an Attempt made by the Cardinal of Lorrain, which was an evident Testimony of his Affection to the King and the Kingdom. The Cardinal had some time before let the Emperor know, that as Bishop of *Metz* he was his Vassal, and Prince of the Holy Empire ; and therefore he put the Jurisdiction and Territory of Metz under his Imperial Protection, desiring to be defended against the Violences, Incursions and Vexations

tions of his Enemies. Whereupon the Emperor had granted to him his Letters of Patronage, dated on the 5th of May of this Year; which Letters he attempted out of feafon to have publifhed in the *Meffine Country*. But Salcede, Bailif of *Vic*, and Governour of *Marfal*, tho' one of the Cardinal's Creatures, oppofed him with all his Might, until he had received Orders from the King for fuch a Publication ; and feized upon fome places belonging to the Cardinal, faying that he had reafon fo to do, fince the faid Cardinal had put himfelf under the Protection of the Emperor, without any regard to the King his Sovereign ; neverthelefs, Salcede being too weak to cope with the Cardinal, who had raifed a fmall Army for executing his Defign, was at laft obliged to furrender *Vic* and Marfal (*a*).

On the 13th of December died Pope Pius IV. after a Reign of five Years 11 Months and 13 Days, having been elected on the 26th of December 1559. He was fucceeded by Michael Gisleri, known by the Name of Cardinal Alexandrine, who was elected on the feventh of January following, and took the Name of Pius V.

On the 25th of December this Year was held at *Paris* the fifth National Synod of the Reformed Churches of France ; Nicholas de Galars, Minifter of the Church of *Orleans*, was chofen Moderator ; and Lewis Capel, Minifter of *Meaux*, with Lewis le Clerc, Elder of the Church of *Paris*, Secretaries.

XXX. *The fifth National Synod of the Reformed Churches.*

A Book and other Writings of one J. Morelly concerning the Polity and Difcipline of the Church was cenfured and condemned, as containing evil and dangerous Opinions, fubverting that Difcipline which is agreeable to the Word of God, and at that day received in the Reformed

(*a*) Thuan. Hift. lib. XXXVII. pag. 323.

formed Churches of the Kingdom ; and indeed delivering up the Government of the Church unto the People, he would bring in a new tumultuary Government, full of Confusion, upon it, from whence would follow many great and dangerous Inconveniences, which were demonstrated unto him ; and he was further admonished to renounce such Opinions, which he refused to do, but persisted in his Assertions, saying, that he was persuaded, that those his Opinions were grounded upon God's Holy Word. Nevertheless, whereas, upon all other Points, his Opinions were agreeable to the Doctrine received by the Churches ; he was tolerated, promising to live peaceably for the future, and not to publish any thing against the Discipline received and followed by the Churches, &c.

Then they declared the manner of proceeding in Ecclesiastical Censures, which were to be accommodated to the Nature of the Offences ; some are publick, others private and secret : As to the publick, some are more enormous and crying than others, therefore a great deal of Discretion .is requisite in the Censures and Reprehensions, and it was ordered to proceed always with Meekness and a Christian Charity. As for Excommunication, no private Man, either Minister or Elder, was allowed to make use of it out of his own Authority, but by the Advice and Consent of the Consistory, to whom it belongs to judge of these Matters, and whether the Sinner had been first admonished in a suitable manner, whether the Offence is publick ; in a word, whether the Sinner deserves such a Punishment.

Those who were excommunicated, were deprived of all Communion with the Church, and of all its Privileges, and the Members of it were to be admonished neither to converse familiarly
with

with them, nor to frequent their Company, that so they might be ashamed, humbled, and brought to Repentance; the Truth whereof ought to be demonstrated not only by Words, but by Works too, and unexceptionable Evidences, known unto the Consistory, who was to judge whether they ought to be admitted again into the Church; and having summoned, seen, and heard them, and found them truly penitent, the Minister was to declare it unto the whole Congregation, that so they might be stirred up to praise God, for having recovered them unto Repentance. Then those Penitents were to come before the whole Congregation, to give Satisfaction for their past Scandal, confessing and detesting their former Sins and Rebellions, humbly begging pardon of God and of the Church; and thus they were received into the Church's Peace and Fellowship with Joy and publick Thanksgiving. N. B. That none but obdurate Sinners, that could not be brought to a Sense of their Duty by any other means, were excommunicated. 2dly, That that dreadful Act was always publickly done; but as to the Suspension from the Sacrament, sometimes it was published from the Pulpit, sometimes only in the Consistory, according to the Merit of the Cause and the Offender's Dispositions.

Then the Synod proceeded to the examination of several Cases of Conscience; for instance, whether a beneficed Person, who had embraced the Reformed Religion, could be admitted to the Lord's Supper as long as he held the *Benefice?* Answer. Such as hold Benefices under a feigned Name, cannot be admitted to the Lord's Supper. But if they hold it in their own Name, they may be admitted, provided they employ the third part of their Income to holy and pious Uses. All secret Promises of Marriage were declared null.

null. The Churches guilty of a notorious Ingratitude towards their Ministers were to be deprived of their Ministry. Children under twelve Years of Age could not be admitted to the Lord's Supper ; but above that Age, the Minister was to judge of their fitness for it. A Man might marry the Sister of his deceased Spouse with whom he was only betrothed. The Accounts for the Church's Money ought to be always settled before the Ministers of the Church, and even, if possible, before all the People. The Consistories were not allowed to intermeddle themselves with the Execution of Dissolution of Marriage, because it belongs of right to the Civil Magistrate. Care was ordered to be taken that Vagrants, by feigned Certificates, might not rob the Church's Charity. Such as would not submit themselves to the Church's Discipline, were not to be reckoned for Members of that Church. Such as would be received into a Church were obliged first to acquaint the Elder of their Ward with it. No other Council besides the Consistory could be established in the Church. Imposition of Hands at the Confirmation of the Ministers was recommended to be observed in those places where it was not formerly observed. It was left to the prudence of the Consistories to admit the Students in Divinity to hear the Debates in their Assemblies.

Parents were to be exhorted to bring other Sureties besides themselves, for their Children, at their Christning.

Judges, Notaries, Scriveners, and others, who by the Duty of their Callings are bound to judge, sign and seal all Matters brought to them, were not to be censured for having given Judgment, or received a last Will, or passed a Contract, or dispatched Writings about Idolatrous Concerns.

I

But

But Advocates, Arbitrators, and all others, who were free to undertake a Bufinefs or not, were to be admonifhed, wholly to forbear pleading for, or any other ways to treat of Beneficiary Caufes, or fuch like Matters.

All the Churches in the Kingdom were ordered to be conformable in point of Common publick Prayers. No Perfon could be married without a fufficient Certificate ; and the Banns were to be publifhed in the very places where both the Parties had their Refidence. Provincial Synods, and Colloquies were to be eftablifhed according to the extent of the Government in the State ; and if the Government was of too large an extent, and the number of the Minifters too great in it, then they might divide themfelves into two Provinces, and as many Synods.

One John Du Bard, alias Du Gar, alias Du Gast, a Socinian Minifter, who had vented and defended his Tenets at Poitiers, made a Retraction and an Abjuration of his Errors in full Synod.

It was enacted that the following Order fhould be obferved for the future in the Convocation of the National Synods.

1. As it was ufual, there fhall be one certain Church appointed, which fhall have the power of fignifying unto the Provinces the day and place of meeting. 2. Whatever Matters are to be debated in a National Synod, fhall be fent up by the feveral Provinces unto that appointed Church. 3. The faid Church fhall call the National Synod within a Year, in a convenient time and place, and give notice thereof three Months before to all the Provinces ; and fhall fend a Duplicate of difficult Matters which are to be propounded and debated, unto the faid Provinces, to be confidered by them. 4. Such as are charg-

ed with the Power of calling the said Assembly
must know, that it is fitting that one particular
Church be nominated in every Province, to
which they might direct their Letters; which
Church having received them, shall assemble the
Provincial Synod within three Months, where
the transmitted Difficulties shall be maturely examined, and the Arguments on both sides urged, being fair and carefully written down, shall
be sent unto the National Synod. 5. And forasmuch as our present Circumstances will not admit any great number of Ministers and Elders in
the National Synod, we are of Opinion, That
for this time only, and during these Difficulties,
the Brethren assembled in each Provincial Synod
should choose from among themselves one or two
Ministers, and as many Elders, of the ablest and
most expert in Church-Affairs, to be sent in the
Name of the whole Province, who shall come
furnished with the Powers, Memorials, and with
all the Instructions requisite for determining those
Difficulties which had been imparted unto them.
6. The Provinces shall not prescribe any set time
or term unto these their Deputies for returning,
but shall let them tarry in the said Synod as long
as there may be need of them, and the Charges
of the said Deputies shall be defrayed by their
respective Provinces. 7. And that the National
Synod may be no more imployed in Matters already decided by former Synods, the Provinces
shall be exhorted to read over carefully the Acts
of the past Synods, before they prepare their Memorials, and to send nothing but what is of a
general and common Concern to all the Churches,
or what deserves the Attention and Resolution
of a National Synod. And the Church of Poic-
tiers which is charged by this present Synod with
the calling of the next, shall be informed of all
this,

this, that she might conform herself to these Orders and Regulations.

Then followed some general Advertisements unto the Church, as not to discharge their Elders, but for great Causes, whereof the Consistories were to take cognizance.

No Book in defence of the Truth of our Religion was to be written, in a ridiculous or scurrilous manner, but with Modesty. The Churches were to be admonished to maintain some hopeful Scholars at the Universities, who being educated in the Arts and Sciences, may be fitted for and employed in the sacred Ministry. The Noblemen were to be exhorted not to carry along with them the Chaplain of their Houses, when the Places and Churches of the ordinary Residence of these Lords would be thereby left unprovided. They whose Brethren and Sisters have quitted the Monasteries to serve God with Liberty of Conscience, shall be exhorted to admit them into a part of their Estate, at least they shall be compelled by all Censures to afford them Maintenance, and a competent Pension according to their Ability: For they would otherwise shew themselves void of Natural Affection.

This is the short Account of the Transactions and Regulations of the first general Synod, which was the second held at Paris, and which may be found at large in Quick's Synodicon in *Gallia Reformata*, Vol. I. And Aymon Synodes Nationaux de France, Vol. I.

Now we must come to Blois, where we have left the Court. The King came to Moulins in the Month of January, where he had appointed the Nobles and Peers of the Kingdom, to procure a Reconciliation, first between the Houses of Guise and Chatillon, and then between the Houses of Montmorency and the Cardinal of

H 2   Lor-

Lorrain; but left such an Assembly should be looked on as convened for some private Designs rather than for procuring the publick Good, the Presidents of all the Parliaments of the Kingdom had been likewise summoned, that by their Advice some Remedy might be found for healing the great Diseases of the Kingdom, and for redressing the Grievances of the People; whereof the King had taken notice during his Circuit.

The Summons were directed to Christophorus De Thou, first President of Paris, Peter Seguier, President, and John Dasi of Thoulouse, James Benedict Largebaston of Bourdeaux, John Truchon of Grenoble, L. Favre of Dijon, and H. Fornari of Aix in Provence. Being called in the Hall to the King, present the Queen-Mother, the Duke of Anjou, the Cardinal of Bourbon, the Prince of Condé, the Duke of Montpensier, the Dauphine of Auvergne his Son, the Cardinals of Lorrain and Guise, the Dukes of Nemours, Longueville and Nevers, the Constable of Montmorency, Odet, Cardinal of Chatillon, the Admiral, and D'Andelot, the Marshals of Damville, Bourdillon, Vielleville, St. Gelais Lansac, the Counts of Chaulnes, Crussol and Villars, Des Gordes, the Bishops of Orleans, Valence and Limoges.

The King told them, that he had visited his whole Dominions, in order to hear the Complaints of his Subjects distressed by so many Evils, and to redress their Grievances the best way he could; that for that end he had convened them into that place, to hear their Advice, desiring and commanding them, to apply themselves earnestly and vigorously, and as much as he expected from their wonted Zeal and Fidelity to his Service, to find out some proper means, whereby the Will of God should be obeyed, his

Con-

Conscience unburthened, his People relieved, and Justice restored to its former Splendor and Purity.

Then Chancellor de L'Hospital, in a set Speech, shewed forth the great and manifold Disorders that were crept into the Kingdom, which he ascribed especially to the bad Administration of Justice, whereto it was absolutely necessary to apply proper Remedies ; that the King had been made sensible of it during the two Years past in his Travels, that he had seen nothing in the Provinces but Concussions and Robberies, committed even by those who are called to administer Justice ; and that he could not without Sin dissemble any longer such Crimes, which were fomented and entertained by Impunity and too great a Licence.

After many other Considerations concerning the Origin, Authority and Appointment of the several Courts of Justice in the Kingdom, he examined whether it would not be very proper to decrease the superfluous number of the Chambers, and to reduce them to their primitive Institution ; and whether it was more proper that the Parliaments were stable as they were, than Ambulatories, as they had been formerly ; and that the Members of it should receive greater Salaries from the Exchequer, if it was possible, than to receive Fees, as it was usual. Whether it was not fit that the Judges should submit themselves to the Censure, and every one of them be obliged to give Account of his Conduct in the discharge of his Office. From whence he inferred, that it would be better if the Judges were only named for two or three Years, than to be for their Life. Many things he said further concerning the Reformation of the Judges, and the Administration of Justice ; whereupon, after several

veral

veral Debates, each Member of that Assembly having delivered his Vote, the famous Edict, which from the *Place* was called the Edict of *Moulins*, was drawn in eighty-six Articles, most of which concern the Administration of Justice, the cutting off the tediousness and length of the Process, and such other useful Regulations tending to the Welfare of the Subjects: Amongst these Articles I shall pick out these two only ; by one of them the Money or other things lost by Minors at any hazardous Play was to be recovered by their Tutors, Curators, or their Parents, and the Winner was obliged to restore it to a Farthing. By the other, all Fraternitys instituted amongst the People on any religious pretence, riotous Banquetting and Revelling, breaking of Glasses, were entirely forbidden, as occasioning Superstition, Troubles, Quarrels, Lascivity and Monopolies. That Edict was registered and published by the Parliament of Paris on the 23d of December the same Year.

Then was made the feigned Reconciliation between the Houses of Guise and Chatillon abovementioned, pag. 18, and that of the House of Montmorency with the Cardinal of Lorrain : The Cardinal was obliged to declare that it was not out of Contempt of the Governour's Authority that he had delayed to show him the Letters-Patent he had obtained from the Queen. And the Marshal of Montmorency answered, that in what he had done he had no mind to offend or affront the Cardinal, but only to maintain the King's Authority, as he was obliged by the duty of his Charge. But how far that Reconciliation was sincere, especially on the Cardinal's side, we shall see when we come to speak of the supposed Conspiracy of LA MOLE and Coconnas (*b*).

Another

(b) Thuan. Hist. lib. XXXIX. p. 389, 390, 391.

Another Quarrel of no lefs moment than the former was decided at Moulins. About fix Years before, the Duke of NEMOURS, upon a promife of Marriage, had received the laft favours of the Lady of ROHAN, furnamed at Court Mademoifelle DE LA GARNACHE, firft Coufin to the Queen of Navarr; he begot a Son of her, who bore the Title of Prince of GENEVOIS. The Duke of Nemours kept no Account of his Promifes which he refufed to perform, notwithftanding all that the King of Navarr could do to compel him. Now the Queen of Navarr having accompanied the King to Moulins, renewed the purfuits of that Affair; but the Intereft of Nemours being then united with that of the Guifes, prevailed fo far, and the Hatred againft the Reformed, whofe Religion the Lady of Rohan profeffed, was fuch, that the faid Lady was caft off, and by the Pope's Licence the Promifes were declared void and null, and the Duke at liberty to marry another if he pleafed.

Therefore the faid Duke married the late Duke of Guife's Dowager, and the Ceremony was performed at *St. Maur des Foffez*, near Paris, where the King and the Queen-Mother affifted in Perfon: A little after were celebrated the Nuptials of the Duke of Montpenfier with Renée of Anjou, Heirefs to Nicholas of Anjou, Marquis of Mezieres, to whom the King and Queen-Mother did the fame Honour as to the Duke of Nemours.

Now, whereas the Duke of Montpenfier could not endure to fee Frances of Bourbon his Daughter, and Confort to the Duke of Bouillon, following the Reformed Religion, to which he was fo averfe; in order to reclaim her, he caufed a Conference to be held between SIMON VIGOR, afterwards Archbifhop of Narbonne, CLAUDIUS

H 4   DE

DE SAINCTS, afterwards Bifhop of Evreux, and JOHN DE L'ESPINE, CHARLES BARBASTE of *Bearn*, both Minifters ; and whereas this laft could not be prefent, HUGUES SUREAU, furnamed du Rozier, took his place ; the Conference was held at Paris, in Nevers's Houfe, prefent two Publick Notaries, and the Acts of that Conference were afterwards publifhed at Paris : All the benefit received from that long and tedious Conference was the Confirmation of the Duchefs of Bouillon in the Reformed Religion.

XXXII.
*Execution
of Simon
May at
Paris.*

An Incident happened this Year which was like to have broken the Reconciliation made at Moulins between the Noblemen, and which caufed great Troubles at Court. One Simon May, a Rake and an Inn-keeper, that lived not far from *Chatillon* upon *Loin*, (where the Admiral refided) in a place out of the Way, and very proper to commit Robberies and Murders, was arrefted under Sufpicion, that, being fuborned by the Admiral's Enemies, he had fome ill Defign againft him ; but being in hopes to conceal his real Crimes under the appearances of a fictitious one, and fave his Life by that means, he charged the Admiral with an Attempt to bribe him, in order to murder the Queen Mother, for which, he faid, he had offered to him a large Sum of Money, which having refufed to do, he had drawn upon himfelf the Admiral's Hatred, who profecuted him for Crimes whereof he had never been guilty. But the Judges having thoroughly examined the Evidences, and taking for granted that a greater regard ought to be had to the Actions and the whole Tenor of the Life, than to the Words of a Man, which he fpeaks in order to fave or prolong his Life ; and befides that, having not the leaft proof againft the Admiral, condemned the Calumniator to be broken

upon

upon the Wheel; he acknowledged his Crime before his Death, and confessed that what he had said against the Admiral was intirely false, and spoken on purpose to save his own Life, thinking that it was the only way remaining.

This very same Year began the Troubles of the Low Countries, which ended at last by the loss of the seven United Provinces. In order to have a true Notion of this admirable Change we must go a little higher.

The Report of the League between the Kings of France and Spain, for the extirpation of the Protestants and the Reformed, concluded at *Bayonne*, being spread abroad, those of the Low Countries thought proper to make one amongst themselves for the preservation of their civil and religious Rights, invaded by the tyrannical Government of Philip. That League had had its first Beginning at *Bruxelles* in *Kulembourg's House* on the 3d of November 1565, between about twenty Nobles only, which Number increased so fast, that on the third of April following they were above five hundred Lords or Gentlemen that came to *Bruxelles*, in order to tender a Petition to the Governess. But before I proceed any further, I think proper to give a short Account of the Beginnings and Progress of the Reformation in those Provinces.

The Disputes of Luther in Germany were attended with the same Success in the Low Countries as in France; many who wanted only an opportunity, improved this for declaring themselves, and forsaking the Roman Communion, followed the Doctrine of Luther; that went so far, and this Progress was so quick, that Charles the Vth published a Placaert dated from *Worms* on the 8th of May 1521, to put a stop to this Progress, (Margaret of Austria being then Governess

XXXIII. A short Account of the Reformation in the LowCountries.

verness of these Provinces) whereby it was forbidden to publish any Book, wherein mention was made of the Holy Scripture, or which contained the Explanation of some Passages, without being licensed by the Ordinary of the place or others commissioned by him, with the Consent and Approbation of the Faculty of Divinity in the nearest University.

The next Year he commissioned FRANCIS VAN DER HULST, his Counsellor in *Brabant*, for examining exactly the Opinions and Faith of the People in all the *Low Countries*, and he associated himself with one NICHOLAS VAN EGMONT ; the first was a great Enemy to all manner of Learning, and the last a Mad-man trusted with a Sword in his Hands. These two Inquisitors sent People to Jail under the least suspicion of Heresy, and then they thought of the Charges they should lay upon them. CORNELIUS GRAPHEUS, Secretary of the City of *Antwerp*, was one of the first Victims of their Fury. In 1523, the Austin-Fryars of Antwerp were violently persecuted. They had read and approved the Books of Luther. Several of these Monks were sent to Prison. The Prior, named HENRY of ZUTPHEN, made his escape out of the Jail. Some of them recanted ; but three persisted in their Opinions. They were degraded, and declared Hereticks upon a Scaffold at BRUSSELS, on the first of July 1523, and the same day two of them expired in the midst of the Flames with an undaunted Courage. As they were led to the Execution-place, they said loudly, *That they suffered for the Christian Religion sake.* Being tied to the Post, and the Fire being kindled, they said the *Apostles Creed*, and sung the *Te Deum*, till the Flames had deprived them of the use of their Tongues. The third Augustine was brought back to Prison, and

I

executed

executed in private. This was the first Blood that was shed in the *Low Countries* for Religion sake since Luther's attempts for reforming the Church. As to HENRY of ZUTPHEN, he was massacred the next Year by the Peasants in the Country of *Holstein*, at the instigation of the Clergy.

At the same time several Persons forsook their Monasteries. Most part of the Inhabitants of *Holland*, *Zeeland*, and *Flanders*, adhered to the Lutheran Doctrine; whereat the Monks were extremely incensed. The Lutherans continued their Assemblies without the City of Antwerp, notwithstanding the *Placaerts* of the Emperor. MARTIN DORPIUS, a learned Dutchman, Professor in Divinity at *Louvain*, suspected of countenancing Lutheranism, and ERASMUS, were both in great danger of their Lives. PHILIP DE LENS, Secretary to the Emperor in the Court of *Brabant*, was thought likewise to countenance the Reformation. WALTER DELEEN, a learned Man, afterwards Professor of Greek at *Embden*, declared himself for the same Opinions in Brabant. ANTHONY FREDERICKS embraced the same Doctrine at *Naerden*, and was followed by many of the chief Inhabitants. JOHN or HENRY RHODIUS, Principal of the College of St. Jerome, at *Utrecht*, CORNELIUS HONIUS, a learned Civilian, and Counsellor in the Courts of *Holland*, renounced the Roman Religion, and followed the Lutheranism. The said Honius, with a Monk named BERNARD, GERARD WORMER, WILLIAM of UTRECHT, JOHN DE BACKER of *Woerden*, who was entered into Holy Orders to please his Father, and WILLIAM GNAPHEUS, Rector of the College of the *Hague*, were imprisoned in this last Town with JOHN SARTORIUS of *Amsterdam*. John de Backer, not yet twenty-seven Years of Age, was tied to a Post, strangled,

gled, and his Corpse burnt to Ashes in September 1565, for having preached, notwithstanding the Prohibitions, and because he was married; he was first degraded upon a Scaffold, then they put on him a yellow Cassock, and yellow Hat; and so he was led to the place of Execution. As he passed by the Prison, where many Persons were shut up for the Faith, he said loudly unto them, *See, my dear Brethren, I am ready to suffer Martyrdom; chear up, as faithful Soldiers of Jesus Christ; and being incited by my Example, maintain and defend the Truth of the Gospel against all Unrighteousness.* When the Prisoners had heard these words, they clapt their Hands, uttered joyful Acclamations; and to honour their Friend's Martyrdom, they sung the *Te Deum*, the *Certamen Magnum*, and the Hymn, *O beati Martyrum Solemnia*; and they ceased not till the Martyr had expired. When he was tied to the Post, he said, *O Death, where is thy Sting? O Grave, where is thy Victory? Death is swallowed up by the Victory of Christ.* At last the Martyr expired, after having uttered these words: *Lord Jesus! forgive them, for they don't know what they do. O Son of God remember me; have Mercy upon me.*

The Monk Bernard, Gerard Wormer, William of Utretcht, and may be Gnapheus too, would have been condemned to death, had it not been for the Constancy and Stedfastness of the young de Backer, whereby the Judges themselves had been extremely moved. Gnapheus and Honius had been imprisoned without any Examination. They were set at liberty three Months after, upon Securities not to go out of the Hague for two Years together. Honius died during that time; and when the two Years were expired, Gnapheus was set at full liberty, having promised that he would appear whenever he should

be

be required.   But a little after, he was arrested a
second time, on account of a certain Book by him
composed for the comfort of a Widow, wherein
they pretended that he ridiculed the monastical
Life ; after a long Examination, he was condemned to do Penance in a Monastery for three
Months, living upon Bread and Small Beer
only.

Some time after Gnapheus, considering the
Persecution which raged in the *Low Countries*,
and the War of the Peasants in *Germany*, composed a small Book, the Matter whereof he had
extracted out of the Bible, and intitled it, *Mirrour for comforting the Sick* ; *or, a Dialogue between Theophilus, Tobias, and Lazarus*.   That
Book was published without his Knowledge, and
was a great prejudice to the Church of Rome.
There were several Editions of it printed in a little time ; and one of the Printers was condemned to death for it.   At last Gnapheus was obliged to leave his own Country.   After he was
gone from the *Hague*, his Family was exposed to
a new Persecution ; for a Sausage was found at
his House boiling in a Pot with Pease, and it was
Lent : it had been put in by a Woman with
child, who longed for it.   The Judges were
very busy about that Affair for two days together ; the Physicians were called for, and asked,
*Whether it was possible for a Woman with child to
long for Flesh in Lent ?*   After having maturely
debated the Question, the Judges pronounced
the Sentence, whereby Gnapheus was to be seized dead or alive, wherever he could be found ;
but very luckily for him he was then very far off
from the *Hague*.

The Emperor published another Placaert a-
gainst the Lutherans in July 1526.

In

In 1527 a Widow of *Monickendam* in North-Holland was strangled, and burnt to Ashes at the *Hague* for her Religion.

It was about this time that the Anabaptists began to spread their Tenets in the Low Countries; and caused so great Troubles and shedding of Blood for several Years, as I have hinted before in the first Vol.

But we must not confound those Anabaptists with these of our days, who are a peaceable People, faithful Subjects, Lovers of Virtue, and Enemies of Enthusiasm.

The Reformed too, must not be charged with the Extravagancies of the Anabaptists and other Sectaries of those times, for they have been always condemned with the utmost Abhorrence by them.

John Waden and two other Persons were the first Martyrs of the Anabaptism condemned by the Roman Catholicks in Holland, and burnt little by little at the Hague in the Year 1527.

The Dean of *Louvain*, Inquisitor of *Brabant*, Holland, and the adjacent Countries, condemned about sixty Persons to death, or to do Penance, this Year.

On the 28th of January 1528, a new Placaert was published against the Lutheran Books, and against the Monks, who had deserted from their Convents.

HENRY, an Austin-Fryar, was burnt alive at *Tournay*, for having deserted his Order, and having married a Wife, and preached against the Church of Rome. His pardon was offered unto him, if he was willing to declare that his Wife was only his Concubine; which refusing to do, he was executed.

On the 14th of October 1529, a new Edict was published against the Lutherans, whereby those who
who

who had relapfed were condemned to be burnt.
As to the others, Men were condemned to die
by the Sword, and Women to be buried alive.
Life was offered to all thofe who fhould forfake
the Reformation, if they had not relapfed, or were
not actually Prifoners. It was forbidden by that
Edict to receive or entertain any Heretick, upon
pain of Death and forfeiture of Goods. All
Perfons fufpected of Herefy were excluded from
all Honourable Employments ; and for the better difcovery of Hereticks, half of their Goods
forfeited was promifed to the Informer, if they
did not exceed a hundred Florins of Flanders.

The 30th of the fame Month, Willi am of
Zwol was burnt at Mechlin for Religion fake.

In the Year 1530, a young Man of Naërden,
twenty-four Years old, was burnt at the *Hague*.
He had made his Study at *Louvain*, and had been
very profligate. When he was come back to his
own Home, he fell down fuddenly one day as he
was walking, juft as if he had been ftruck with a
Thunder-bolt ; he was carried to his own Houfe,
thinking he was dead ; but he recovered, and
from that time he forfook his diforderly Life and
the Roman Religion. He went from one place
to another, preaching the Reformation ; and being fummoned to appear at the Hague, he came
there of his own accord. The firft time he got
off entirely fafe ; the fecond he was chided only
for his Obftinacy ; at laft he was clapt in Prifon,
and would not improve the opportunities of mak
ing his efcape offered unto him. When he was
led to the place of Execution, he fung a Canticle
to the Glory of God ; then he pulled off his
Shoes and Stockings, which he gave to fome
Beggars.

Margaret of Austria, Daughter to the
Emperor Maximilian I. died in the Month of
Decem-

December 1530; she had governed the Low Countries with great dexterity for about eighteen Years. MARY, Sister to Charles V. succeeded her in October 1531. She was Widow of LEWIS King of Hungary. That Princess loved Learning, and especially the Latin Tongue.

The Clergy of the Low Countries were very little acquainted with the Bible. The Lutherans translated into Flemish the New Testament of Luther, and then his whole Bible ; but it was published some Years afterwards : and it has been observed that that important Work is defective in several places. A Printer was beheaded for having had a Hand in the printing of that Bible. An anonymous Author published a Collection of Passages from the Scripture, which he intitled, *The Well of Life.* That Book extremely displeased the Church of Rome's Adherents : it was printed at Amsterdam. A *Jacobine* of *Brabant* went to that City, and bought a certain quantity of Copies, and burnt them ; but it was reprinted again in several places. Nothing could be more prejudicial to the Church of Rome than the prohibiting to the People the reading of the Holy Scripture. Seeing that Holy Book is the Original of the Christian Religion, why doth she forbid to the Christians the reading of it ? Is it not because many of her Tenets are not to be found in it ? since the Clergy are so cautious to conceal it from the People.

A new Edict against the Lutherans was published at this time, confirming that of the 14th of October 1529, with this further Clause : ,, That for the future no body should attempt to ,, write or print, or cause to write or print, any ,, new Book upon what subject soever, without ,, having obtained Letters of Licence, upon pain ,, of being pillory'd ; and besides that, of being
　　　　　　　　　　　　　　　　,, branded

„ branded in the Forehead with a hot Iron, or
„ of having one of his Eyes plucked out, or one
„ of his Hands cut off, at the difcretion of the
„ Judge, who ought to execute that Sentence
„ without any delay, and without any mercy."

About the fame time nine Men were taken out of their Beds at Amfterdam, and brought to the Hague, where they were beheaded by the Emperor's Command, being fufpected of Anabaptifm.

The Magiftrates of *Limbourg* had fhown themfelves very moderate towards the Lutherans ; but in the Year 1532, at the Inftances of the Emperor's Commiffaries, fix Perfons of one and the fame Family, the Father, Mother, two Daughters and their Husbands were burnt alive. They fung Pfalms as they went to the Place of Execution, and called upon Chrift to their laft Breath.

In the Year 1533 three Men were burnt at *Arras* for having refufed to worfhip the *Holy Candle* of that City, and for having fpoken againft thofe and fuch like Superftitions. Four Men were likewife executed at *Bois-le-Duc* for Lutheranifm.

The Courts of Juftice of *Holland* having reprefented to the Governefs of the *Low Countries*, that fometimes it would be very proper and neceffary to execute in private the Hereticks that were obftinate, for avoiding the Impreffion which their Conftancy made upon the People's minds, that Princefs left it to their Prudence, to do as they fhould think proper.

In the Year 1534 a Potter of *Bois-le-Duc* was beheaded for Lutheranifm, and many other Perfons were condemned to undergo feveral Penances in the fame City. WILLIAM WIGGERTSON was beheaded privately in the *Fort of Schagen*.

ISBRAND SCHOL, a Priest of Amsterdam, conspicuous for his Eloquence and Integrity, was burnt at *Bruſſels.*

The Church of Rome became every day more and more odious for her Cruelties : nothing was to be seen for many Years in the Low Countries but barbarous Executions of the Lutherans, and others. Charles V. being come into theſe Provinces in the Year 1540, for ſuppreſſing the Sedition of Ghent, publiſhed a very ſevere Edict againſt the Lutherans and the Anabaptiſts at the Inſtances of the Monks and the Clergy ; which Edict occaſioned a very cruel Perſecution. In the Year 1542 ſeveral Women with child were executed in Holland for the pretended Crime of Hereſy, and were delivered in the midſt of the Flames, For the better diſcovering of thoſe who preached againſt the Roman Church, their Pictures were poſted at the City-Gates, and in other publick places. In the Year 1547 a new Placaert was publiſhed in the Emperor's Name, forbidding all Heretical Books, among which were ſeveral Latin, Dutch and French Bibles, printed in France, Switzerland and the Low Countries.

In the Year 1549 the Emperor ſent for his Son PHILIP from *Spain,* into the *Low Countries,* and cauſed the States of thoſe Provinces to pay Homage unto him. While that Prince was at *Rotterdam* with the Governeſs of the Low-Countries, he had the Curioſity to ſee the Houſe and the Chamber wherein ERASMUS was born.

An Attempt was made for introducing the Spaniſh *Inquiſition* in the Low Countries. The City of *Antwerp,* and ſome others of *Brabant* oppoſed it. There was already an Inquiſition in the *Low Countries,* but it was far different from that of Spain. In the Year 1555 Charles V. reſigned the Crown of Spain and the Low Countries
tries

tries to his Son Philip. This laft Prince publifhed a Placaert, whereby he ratified all thofe publifhed by his Father againft the Hereticks. He
endeavoured by this Edict cunningly to introduce
the Spanifh Inquifition, inferting, (without the
Knowledge of the Council of the Low Countries)
a Claufe in the Letters-Patent granted to the
Magiftrates for taking poffeffion of their Office;
but the City of *Antwerp*, and the other great
Cities of *Brabant* would not fuffer the publifhing
of it.

It would be endlefs to give an Account of all
the Martyrs that fuffered at this time and the
following Years, amongft whom was the moft
celebrated ANGE MERULA, who fuffered in the
Year 1557, being 75 Years old; but it is obfervable, that when he came to the place of Execution, having obtained the liberty of making his
prayers, he did it with fuch a great Zeal and Fer-
vour that he fell down dead: His Corpfe was
burnt to Afhes.

The bafe, cruel and crying Injuftices put in
ufe againft this learned Man, one of the beft of
his Age, and his Meeknefs, his Submiffion and
Refignation to the Will of Almighty God, were
fuch, that certainly they deferve a place in this
Hiftory.

,, ANGE MERULA was born at the *Brille*, in
,, the Year 1482. He entered into Holy Orders
,, at *Utrecht*; being a Man of great Learning and
,, of an exemplary Life, a Lord of the Province
,, of *Utrecht* gave him the Living of *Henfteet*.
,, He applied himfelf to the Study of the Bible,
,, and very foon difcovered the Errors of the
,, Roman Church. In the Year 1552 he made
,, fome Alterations in that part of the Office
,, wherein mention is made of the Merits, and of
,, the Interceffion of Saints. Nay, he was bold

I 2 ,, enough

,, enough to fay in his Sermons, and in his
,, private Difcourfes, that the Church wanted to
,, be reformed. The next Year, his Books and
,, Manufcripts were feized, and he himfelf was
,, put into Prifon. He was charged with having
,, faid, *That it was better to neglect ten Maffes*
,, *than a fingle Sermon ; that every thing neceffary*
,, *to Salvation is to be found in the Scripture ;*
,, *that Faith without Charity is not a true Faith ;*
,, *that one muft live according to the Gofpel-rules,*
,, *without following any other Rule ; that thofe*
,, *who forfook their Goods wilfully, to go a beg-*
,, *ging of others, were not truly poor ; that the*
,, Salve Regina *was a Canticle blafphematory*
,, *againft God and Jefus Chrift, feeing that things*
,, *which belong only to God and his Son, are afcri-*
,, *bed to a Creature ; that in Italy the Immorta-*
,, *lity of the Soul and the Refurrection of the Body*
,, *were not believed ; that the Commandments of*
,, *God are far above all the Synods and Councils,*
,, *how numerous foever they be,* &c.

,, Merula anfwered to all thefe Charges with
,, a great deal of Wifdom. He was transferred
,, to the *Hague :* and was obliged to anfwer to
,, 108 Articles exhibited againft him. In vain
,, was he intreated to abjure his Opinions ; he
,, was ftedfaft. The States of *Holland* bewailed
,, the fate of that good old Man ; they admired
,, his Learning, his Eloquence, his Probity and
,, his Charity towards the Poor ; thefe laft la-
,, mented publickly, *We are deprived of our Fa-*
,, *ther, of our Patron, our Defender, and our*
,, *Comforter in our needs,* did they fay. Amongft
,, other his Charities he had erected an Hofpital for
,, the Poor at the Brille. Every one complain-
,, ed of the Inquifitors Injuftice, and faid loudly,
,, that they violated the Rights of the Courts of
,, Juftice in Holland.

,, The

,, The Inquifitors defired earneftly to burn
,, that poor Man, but they were afraid of the
,, People. To avoid the danger, and rid them-
,, felves of that Affair, they devifed a Trick as
,, fingular in itfelf as it was bafe and wicked.
,, A titular Bifhop of *Hebron* came and fell upon
,, his Knees before the Prifoner, his Head unco-
,, vered, his Arms croffed, and, with Tears in
,, his Eyes, he made a very moving Speech un-
,, to him, *You are,* fays he, *a hundred times more*
,, *learned than we are all ; we are perfuaded that*
,, *you mean well, and we agree with you as to the*
,, *principal Articles. We differ only about fome*
,, *Ufes and Ceremonies of the Church, which are*
,, *indifferent things, depending only upon the Con-*
,, *ductors of the Church. Submit then yourfelf, to*
,, *the Church and its Decifions, I do befeech you.*
,, *You fee that the People are much exafperated a-*
,, *gainft us : Will you expofe us to the Violence*
,, *and Fury of the Mob ? Preferve your Life for*
,, *the Poor's fake, who defire your Prefervation*
,, *with fuch abundance of Tears. Preferve our*
,, *Lives that depend on you. The only thing that*
,, *we do require of you, is, that you would own,*
,, *that you have imprudently undertaken to abolifh*
,, *fome Ufes and Ceremonies, which, in their na-*
,, *ture, are indifferent, and that you are forry for*
,, *it : If that Confeffion offends your own Confci-*
,, *ence, we do take all the blame upon us.* Utter-
,, ing thefe laft words, the Bifhop gave one of
,, his Hands to the Prifoner, and put the other
,, upon his Breaft.

,, Merula was fo much moved by that Speech,
,, that he promifed to do what he was required.
,, A little after he was brought upon a Scaffold,
,, but inftead of reading before him the Articles
,, agreed with the Bifhop of Hebron, they read
,, the chief Articles of his own Opinion, and that

I 3　　　　　　　　　　　　　,, with

,, with such a low Voice, and so fast, that the
,, poor old Man, who was deaf, could hear no-
,, thing of what they said. To which they add-
,, ed without any stop, and in the same man-
,, ner, that he abjured the Errors of Luther ;
,, that he believed sincerely whatever was taught
,, in the Church of Rome, and promised upon
,, his Oath to live and die in its Communion ;
,, declaring that whoever should do the contrary,
,, would be damned eternally ; and if he had for
,, the future any other Opinion he submitted him-
,, self to the utmost rigour of the Ecclesiastical
,, Laws ; that he besought the Assistants to pray
,, God that he would forgive his former Here-
,, sies, which he heartily abjured now ; and beg-
,, ged pardon of all those whom he had de-
,, ceived.

,, Then he was asked loudly, Whether he did
,, not consent to whatever had been read to him ?
,, he, mistrusting of nothing, and thinking that
,, nothing had been read but what had been
,, agreed between him and the Bishop of He-
,, bron, answered affirmatively. He desired to
,, read the Paper before he should sign it ; but
,, the Inquisitors told him that they were in haste,
,, because the People made a great noise. It is
,, remarkable, that a great Alteration was obser-
,, ved in the People. Love and Compassion
,, were changed into Hatred and Wrath against
,, Merula, because they thought that he had ab-
,, jured really. That Abjuration was followed
,, by a Sentence whereby Merula's Manuscripts
,, were condemned to be burnt ; himself to be
,, deprived of his Living, declared uncapable of
,, performing any of the Ecclesiastical Functions ;
,, that he should read his Abjuration from the
,, Pulpit in his Church on a Sunday, or some
,, other Holy-day ; that he was condemned to

,, a

,, a perpetual Imprisonment, and to do Penance all
,, the days of his Life ; and should pay all the
,, Charges of his Trial.

,, When that unfortunate Man understood that
,, he had been so basely imposed on by the In-
,, quisitors, he was so grieved for it, that he fell
,, sick, and was transferred from the Prisons of
,, the Hague to a Convent at *Delft*, where he
,, composed a Refutation of the Sentence pro-
,, nounced against him.

,, In the Year 1555 he was brought from
,, *Holland* to Louvain, and obliged to feed upon
,, Bread and Water only, every Monday, Wed-
,, nesday and Friday. He declared openly there,
,, that he believed whatever he had preached, or
,, written, and that he was resolved to defend
,, it to the last.

,, The next Year they endeavoured in vain, by
,, some Conferences and Threatnings, to bring
,, him to a Recantation of his Opinions. Every
,, one admired his Constancy, and even several
,, Members of the University said publickly, that
,, that old Man was treated with great Injustice
,, and Cruelty. The Inquisitor TAPPER caused
,, him to be transferred from Louvain into an
,, Abby of *Hainaut*, where he stayed for about
,, a Year. The King being made to believe
,, that Merula had relapsed, ordered that he should
,, be brought from that Abby to the Prisons of
,, *Mons*, and to make an end of that Trial.
,, The Inquisitors desired no better. That Or-
,, der was executed on the 4th of June 1557,
,, and Merula was shut up in a hideous Dun-
,, geon. At last TAPPER had him declared a
,, *Heretick Relapse*, and as such condemned to be
,, burnt.

,, Merula was transferred to *Mons* very secret-
,, ly, that they might put him to death, before

I 4   ,, his

,, his Friends in *Holland* could be in a condition
,, of oppoſing the Deſigns of the Inquiſition ;
,, for TAPPER and his AGENTS were afraid leſt
,, the States of Holland would revindicate their
,, Rights which had been violated in Merula's
,, Trial.   His Nephew knew not that he had
,, been put in Priſon at *Mons :* he arrived in that
,, City on the 27th of July at ten o'clock in the
,, Morning, juſt at the time when Merula was
,, led to the place of Execution.   That good
,, Man was leaning upon his Stick, but was ſo
,, waſted by the long and cruel Sufferings he
,, had been expoſed to in the Priſons for about
,, five Years, that his Nephew did not know
,, him at firſt.   As ſoon as his Uncle ſaw him,
,, what Joy did he not feel ? for he loved him
,, intirely.   He ſpoke to him to the following
,, purport :
,, *My Son,* ſays he, *here is the time that God*
,, *calls me to ſeal up with my blood the Truth*
,, *which I have drawn out of his Holy Word. I have*
,, *been carried out of my Country, and after hav-*
,, *ing been transferred from one place to another,*
,, *at laſt I have been brought here : I am prepared*
,, *to be offered up as a pure Victim to Jeſus Chriſt.*
,, *My Soul longs to be with my God.   The High-*
,, *waymen and Murderers are treated with more*
,, *Lenity than I am.   Give notice to our Relati-*
,, *ons and Friends in our dear Country of what you*
,, *have ſeen. You have been always faithful unto me.*
,, *You would have been my Heir ; I beſeech you to*
,, *bear with Patience, the loſs of that Inheritance,*
,, *and with the ſame Conſtancy that I bear the*
,, *loſs of my Life. You do not want either good*
,, *Senſe or Learning, and you know that I took*
,, *care to cultivate both theſe Qualities in you.*
,, *You are of Age ; marry that Woman whom I did*
,, *deſtine for you.   Truſt in God ; take care of the*
                                        ,, *Hoſpital*

,, *Hospital founded by me for the Poor at the*
,, *Brille. I hope they will let the Poor enjoy peace-*
,, *ably what I have given unto them ; and that*
,, *the Procurator-Fiscal of the States will be more*
,, *merciful than the Inquisitors.* Could greater
Temper, Calmness, and good Sense, be found in
any other Martyr in such Circumstances?

,, When Merula had done speaking, it is
,, impossible to express what Tenderness, what
,, Love and Compassion both the Uncle and the
,, Nephew felt when they parted one from an-
,, other. That Holy Martyr continued his
,, March, walking between a Monk and the
,, Executioner, exhorting the People, as he went,
,, to fear God, and to love the Truth. Being
,, arrived at the Wood Pile, he asked leave for
,, putting up his Prayers to God ; which being
,, granted, he did it with such a Fervency, that
,, he fell down dead as abovesaid (c).

The Sufferings and Constancy of the Martyrs
moved the People to so great pity for them,
that many comforted them as they went to be
executed, and sung Psalms with them. Nay, in
several Places whole Communities of Protestants
undertook to rescue the Confessors, as they were
ready to be put to death.

XXXV.
Continua-
tion of the
State of
Religion in
the Low
Countries.

In the Year 1559 died suddenly the cruel
Tapper at *Brussels* ; he was about 71 Years of
Age ; born at *Enchuysen*, Dean of *Louvain*, and
Great Inquisitor of the *Low Countries*. It is pretended that that detestable Monster said : *It is*
no matter whether those who die for Religion sake,
are guilty or not, provided that we could frighten
the People with such Examples ; and we cannot
fail

(c) Merula, is *Merle* in French : He was great Uncle to
Paul Merula, once Professor of History at Leyden, and
known by several Works. Hist. Abregée de la Ref. des
Pays-bas, trad. du Holl. de Gerard Brandt, liv. IV.

fail to succeed, *when Persons conspicuous for their Learning, or Riches, or Nobility, or their great Employments, are sacrificed in that manner.* To which he added, *that such Executions were necessary, especially at Amsterdam.*

One of the secret Articles of the Treaty concluded this Year at *Chateau-Cambresis,* between the two Crowns of France and Spain, was, (*as we have said in our first Vol.*) That the said Princes should use unanimously all their endeavours to extirpate Heresy out of Christendom. Henry II. King of France, told it to the Prince of Orange ; which Indiscretion, very likely, was the occasion of the following Troubles and Revolutions.

This same Year King Philip resolved to go to Spain, inasmuch that the Reformation began to be introduced in that Kingdom. He trusted the Government of the *Low Countries* to MARGARET, Duchess of *Parma,* his Natural Sister ; and he commanded that Princess and the Privy Council to put in execution all the Edicts published by his Father and himself against the Hereticks : he gave the same orders to the Governours of each Province. He made some Regulations in the University of *Louvain,* for stopping the Progress of the new Opinions. And it was with the same view that he founded an University at *Douay,* the Inhabitants whereof spoke French ; that his Subjects should not be obliged to send their Children into foreign Countries, to learn that Language. And whereas he knew that the Dissoluteness of the Clergy was in great part the Cause of that Abhorrence, which had been conceived against the Church of Rome ; he endeavoured with all his Might to have the Council assembled again at *Trent,* in hopes that they would find some proper Remedies for that
Dis-

Difeafe. He framed the Defign of erecting fome new Bifhopricks in the *Low Countries* ; and it is faid that there was in that Scheme fome great Myftery of State hidden under the fpecious pretence of Religion. The States of the Low Countries were affembled at *Ghent*, in the Month of Auguft. The Lords required the King to withdraw the foreign Troops out of the Provinces ; to give the Government of the ftrong Cities and Caftles to none but Natives ; and that no Foreigner fhould be admitted to the Government of the *Low Countries*. The King was much furprized and angry at thefe Demands ; he doubted not but that the Prince of *Orange* was the chief Inftigator thereof : However, diffembling his Refentment, he fed them with fair words. The Bifhop of *Arras* infifted much upon the receiving of the Spanifh *Inquifition*. Several Members of that Affembly fhewed their Reluctancy againft it ; fome of them declared openly, *that the Low Countries were not ufed to bear fuch a Yoke ; that the very Name of* Inquisition *was dreadful to them ; that Herefy was a Difeafe that might be cured by fome Remedies more lenitive than Sword and Fire, &c.* One of Philip's Minifters told him, that he ran the hazard, by his Severity, to lofe the *Low Countries*, at leaft part of thefe Provinces ; he anfwered, *that he chofe to fee himfelf deprived of all his Dominions, rather than to poffefs them imbibed with Herefy.* He embarked at *Flufhing*, and having efcaped a great Storm upon the Coaft of *Bifcay*, wherein moft part of his Fleet perifhed, he faid, that *Providence had preferved him, that he might forward the Glory of God by the Deftruction of Herefy.* He was prefent at fome Auto's da Fe at *Seville* and *Valladolid* ; wherein feveral Perfons of great Diftinction were made Victims to the Fury of

I   the

the Inquisitors, and Hardheartedness of their King.

About this same time Paul IV. erected, by his Bull, three new Archbishopricks, viz. *Mechlin, Cambray* and *Utrecht.* By the same Bull the Bishops with their Chapters were to perform the Office of *Inquisitors* in their respective Dioceses. Every one was frightened at this News; but the worst of all was, that Anthony Perrenot of *Granvelle*, Bishop of *Arras*, named to the Archbishoprick of *Mechlin*, had been promoted to the Cardinalship. A *Burgundian* by Birth, intirely sold to the Court of *Rome!* every thing was to be feared for the liberty of the Provinces, over which it was foreseen, that he would rule after the *Italian* and *Spanish* Method. And since that Man, by his Pride, and his cruel Counsels and Deportments, gave birth to the Liberty of the *United Provinces*, it will not be improper to insert here his Character, such as I found it in Agricola's Additions to the Memoirs of Castelnau, Book VI. ch. i.

XXXVI.
Of the Cardinal of Granvelle.

„ Those who judge of Ministers of State, „ says he, by their Actions, or great Undertak- „ ings, and praise all their bad Qualities, provi- „ ded that they keep their Ground, and main- „ tain themselves in their Credit to the last, „ will, to be sure, allow the first place to An- „ thony Perrenot, Son to Nicholas Per- „ renot, *Sieur* of *Granvelle*, born at *Nozeroy*, „ from whence he removed to *Besançon*; a „ Man of low Extraction, but who, for his great „ Capacity and Experience, was raised by „ Charles V. to be his Secretary of State, „ and was made by him Count of the Holy „ Empire, with the Faculty of coining Money „ of Gold and Silver. He took great care to „ train up his Children that they might succeed „ him

,, him in the Miniſtry, with the ſame Reputa-
,, tion, and his Labour was not in vain ; for
,, Anthony Perrenot and Thomas Perrenot, Sieur
,, of *Chantonay*, his Brother, anſwered ſo well
,, their Father's Expectations, that Spain could
,, boaſt that ſhe never had before greater Poli-
,, ticians, nor more faithful Partizans. I ſhall
,, add, that ſhe never had before a more learned
,, Man, nor more able Speaker than the Cardi-
,, nal was ; but far from aſcribing to him the
,, Title of *Defender of the Faith, and Protector*
,, *of Religion* ; whereof he made uſe, as a pre-
,, tence to juſtify his own Conduct in the Go-
,, vernment of the *Low Countries* : contrariwiſe,
,, I think myſelf obliged to ſpeak here of him
,, as of the firſt Author of the Progreſs of He-
,, reſy (*he means the Reformation*) by the Seve-
,, rity of his Adminiſtration, and by his Haugh-
,, tineſs, whereby he drew upon himſelf the Ha-
,, tred of the People, and of all the Great Men
,, in Flanders ; which obliged the King of Spain
,, to recal him. We have already ſeen that he
,, and his Brother de Chantonay ſtirred up the
,, Fire, during our religious Wars, inſtead of en-
,, deavouring to put it out, as they were in duty
,, bound, had they been ſo good Catholicks, as
,, they boaſted ; and that they deſired to ſee us
,, deſtroying one another, for attempting after-
,, wards upon this Crown with more eaſe. Now
,, can we not ſay with a great deal of reaſon, that
" the Concerns of the Faith which he took upon
,, him to defend with ſo much Violence, was but a
,, pretence for oppreſſing the remains of the great
,, Lords in the Low Countries who oppoſed
,, their long Services, and their Qualities to the
,, Attempts of that *New-Comer*. And indeed
,, the Chancellor of *Burgundy* was much in the
,, right, more wiſe than the *Flemiſh* that made
,, Bon-

„ Bonfires for the accession of their Prince to
„ the Crown of *Spain* ; he told them, *that these*
„ *Bonfires could not be named otherwise than the*
„ *first Flames of the future Combustions of their*
„ *Country, under the Tyranny of the Governours,*
„ *and even of a foreign Government.* This they
„ experienced, especially under the Cardinal of
„ Granvelle and the Duke of Alva, this last be-
„ ing only the Avenger of the Quarrels of the
„ first, and the Executor of his Designs and
„ Maxims. The Inquisition, whereof he intend-
„ ed to make use, was rather to serve for the
„ Crimes of State than for that of Heresy ; and
„ it was on purpose to render it more general,
„ that he undertook to alter, nay, to trouble
„ the Ecclesiastical State by the Erection of these
„ new Bishopricks, that they might be as many
„ Sees of Inquisition, whereof he was the Chief
„ as Archbishop of *Mechlin.* And whereas what
„ he did in that respect was against the People's
„ Privileges and Liberties, he stirred them up,
„ and in that violence of Passion, he occasioned
„ the Change of Religion in several who embraced
„ the new Opinions almost out of spite. To this
„ the Discontents of the great Lords was much
„ conducive ; they had warmly opposed his De-
„ signs, but in vain, and saw themselves expo-
„ sed, as well as the Commoners, to the said Ef-
„ fects of that Authority which he exercised in
„ the Country, and of that dreadful Influence
„ which he had in the King's Council : There-
„ fore they thought that it was their best way to
„ support that Party (*the Protestant*) for their
„ own Security, rather than out of any Principle
„ of Conscience (*d*). For every one knows that
„ „ the

(*d*) That is not true as to the Prince of Orange, who had
been brought up in the Protestant Religion, till Charles V.
took

,, the Religion of the Great Men lies commonly
,, on their own Interest. To that Disorder the
,, Republick of Holland is beholden for its
,, Birth ; and it owes to that Cardinal a Statue
,, amongst those that have set it at liberty. All
,, that can be said in that Man's behalf, is, that,
,, may be, he would have compassed his ends,
,, had he not been recalled, and put the Noble
,, to a *non-plus*. But, tho' even that is dubious,
,, can any body deny that he was much in the
,, wrong to bring Matters to such an extremity,
,, as to occasion a civil War, and to venture the
,, State and Religion upon a private Quarrel ?
,, and can it be found that it is lawful for a prime
,, Minister to embroil the Affairs to such a de-
,, gree, that he should be the only Man able to
,, disintangle them, without being justly suspect-
,, ed of attempting against his Master, and with-
,, out being justly charged with an Ambition per-
,, nicious to his State, whereby he intends to
,, make himself more necessary than the King
,, himself. Therefore I shall oppose to the praise
,, of his *Stedfastness*, the blame of his wicked and
,, untoward Obstinacy ; I shall ascribe to his
,. Pride and Haughtiness, the ill usage the Peo-
,, ple received at his Hands, and the Quarrels he
,, had with the Nobility, rather than to his Af-
,, fection for the Service of his Prince ; I shall
,, affirm, that he had less Religion than Policy in
,, his Attempt for settling the Spanish Inquisi-
,, tion ; which he did rather for encreasing the
,, number of Hereticks than for destroying them ;
,, to the end that he might have a pretence for
,, keeping up *Tribunals* and *Prisons* out of the
,, ordinary forms and uses of Justice, from
,, whence

took him into his Court ; nor of the Lord de Brederode,
and some others, who adhered to the Protestant Religion
out of Principle.

„ whence they could not claim the Laws and Privi-
„ leges of their Country, nor their natural Judges,
„ and where the misfortune of being suspected
„ for too great a Merit and good Qualifications,
„ and may be for too great a Love for his Coun-
„ try, would be more cruelly punished than the
„ blackest Crimes of all, by the foreign Gover-
„ nour who attempted to oppress the said Li-
„ berty. (*He proceeds to prove that the Cardi-*
nal acted not out of Principle of Religion, because
he kept secret Correspondence with the Reformed of
France, and endeavoured to set them and the Ca-
tholicks together by the Ears.) „ But for all
„ that he has been the most praised Man of his
„ time, and that too by the ablest Writers. And,
„ may be, shall he be so too in the future, be-
„ cause of the habit of suffering every thing in
„ Persons of a publick Character, even to that
„ degree as to submit Religion to their Interest.
„ I shall observe further a thing very remarkable,
„ viz. that he gave up himself intirely to world-
„ ly Affairs, and secular Employments, and scarce
„ has he been seen twice performing any of the
„ Functions of so many Ecclesiastical Dignities,
„ which served only to afford him Titles that he
„ might appear greater to the World. He was
„ Canon and Archdeacon of *Besançon* without
„ residing, and Bishop of *Arras*, at the Empe-
„ ror's Court, which he followed constantly :
„ He assisted at the Council of *Trent*, as Em-
„ bassador, was Archbishop of *Mechlin*, per-
„ forming the Functions of a Minister of State in
„ the *Low Countries* ; from whence being recal-
„ led a little after, he kept his Dignity for about
„ two Years ; then he was made a Cardinal (*e*),
                               „ Viceroy

(*e*) There must be some Mistake either in Agricola, or
in Brandt's Abbreviator, as to the time when Granvelle was
made a Cardinal ; for this last places it twenty Years before,
which is more likely.

" Viceroy of *Naples*, Prefident of the Council Charles
" of Italy for the Catholick King, wherein he IX.
" fignalized his Zeal by a Perfecution againft the 1566.
" Archbifhop of *Naples*. At laft he was made Pope Pius
" Archbifhop of *Befançon*, where he never refi- V.
" ded but after his death, which happened at
" *Madrid* on the 21ft of September 1586, being
" 70 Years old. And even he ordered by his
" Will that he fhould be buried hard by his
" Father, in the Carmelites Church, rather than
" hard by his Predeceffors in his Cathedral. And
" in his Life-time he chofe the Name of Cardi-
" nal of *Granvelle*, (his Father's Name) before
" that of *Mechlin*, or of *St. Sabine*, or of *Befan-*
" *çon*, as having had always a greater regard for
" temporal Titles. He ended his days in the
" midft of the Court, and of the management
" of publick Affairs, as he had lived, and with
" fuch a Succefs which would make me to con-
" clude, that he has been the happieft Man of his
" Age, was it not that Moral Philofophy for-
" bidding us to pronounce a Man happy before
" his death, the Chriftian Religion raifes very
" juft doubts in our Minds as to the ftate of a
" Man, who is to anfwer for the performance of
" the Duties incumbent with fo many different
" Charges and Offices, and who is to juftify fo
" many Maxims before a God who requires that
" Kings fhould reign by him, and who does not
" fuffer with Impunity that Policy fhould attempt
" upon Providence, whereby he difpofes of the
" Government of the States."
Such is the Character which Agricola gives
us of the Cardinal of Granvelle; if it is not tranflated word for word, I may fay that I have rendered it faithfully as to the true meaning of the
words.

Charles
IX.
1566.
Pope Pius
V.

XXXVII.
Continua-
tion of the
Affairs of
the Low
Countries.

The King of Spain had given him for Counsel unto the Duchess of Parma, Governess of the Low Countries, with positive Orders to take and follow his Advices in every thing. This was the Man who begun the Work whereof the DUKE OF ALVA made an end some Years afterwards.

The Erection of the nine new Bishopricks had much irritated the Monks, because they had been obliged to part with some of their Lands and other Revenues for the Maintenance of these new Sees. The Magistrates of *Antwerp, Louvain, Ruremonde, Deventer, Groningue* and *Lewar-den,* being sensible of the weakening of their Authority, by that of the Bishops, opposed them with such a Resolution that they did not enter into their Cities, or they were expelled out of them. These Oppositions of the Catholicks gave Courage to the new Sects; they increased considerably. The Persecution was renewed against the Protestants in the Year 1559, and a vast number of them suffered Martyrdom. Amongst whom was one JOHN HEERWIN. He had been formerly very profligate, but had amended his Life since he had frequented the Protestant Meetings at London. His change was fatal to him, as to this present Life. Being come back into Flanders his native Country, in the Year 1560, he was arrested, and condemned to death for his Religion. The Reflection which he made upon his Condemnation deserves to be taken notice of in this place. *There is,* says he, GENTLEMEN, *the Recompense which this wretched World gives to the Servants of Christ. While I gave up myself to Drunkenness, while I did pass Days and Nights at play, and lived in the most shameful Dissolutions; then I ran no hazard of being loaded with these Fetters, I was welcomed every where, and every one was glad of my Company.*
But

But I no sooner began to lead a more sober Life, than the World hath declared itself against me. So the best sort of Men were condemned to death, while the Profligate did find Mercy and Favour. No wonder if on certain Occasions the People rose up against the Executors of such Injustices, as it happened at *Valenciennes* in 1561.

The first Confession of Faith of the Protestants of the Low Countries was published that Year, it had been drawn up by GUI DE BRES, with the help of Adrian Savaria, and three or four other Ministers. It contained thirty-seven Articles, much like to that of *Geneva*. For which reason the Churches that received it took thenceforward the Title of Reformed Churches, as those of France.

So many things concurred then to the general Discontent of the Provinces, that a general Assembly of the States was earnestly desired; in hopes that it would restore Order and Tranquillity. But Philip had expressly forbidden the Governess to convene any during his Absence; and all that she could do for remedying the inward Diseases, and for obviating the outward, wherewith the Country was threatened, was to assemble in the Year 1562, the Knights of the *Golden Fleece*, and the Stadtholders or Governours of the Provinces. These Lords took secret measures between themselves for frustrating the Designs of Granvelle; and they deputed publickly the Lord Montigni to the King for informing his Catholick Majesty of the State of Affairs. He represented *that all the Evil came from the Erection of the new Bishopricks without the Consent of the States; from the dread of a Spanish Inquisition, and from the general Hatred conceived against the Cardinal's Administration.* To all this the Spanish Ministry answered in general; excusing the

K 2   Car-

Cardinal ; ſaying that the People did not take right the King's meaning in the Erection of the Biſhopricks ; that they had no mind to ſettle the Spaniſh Inquiſition in the *Low Countries* ; and as to the reſt, that the King was reſolved to go very ſoon into thoſe Provinces, that he himſelf might take away all occaſion of Complaints from his beloved Subjects.

But while they talk'd at that rate at Madrid, Orders were ſecretly diſpatched from the Court to the Governeſs for increaſing the Perſecutions ; and Granvelle carried his Pride and Cruelty ſo far, that the greateſt Lords declared themſelves openly againſt him. The PRINCE OF ORANGE, and the COUNTS OF EGMONT and HORN, abſented from the Council ; they wrote to the King againſt the Cardinal, and then they made an Aſſociation between them and the principal Nobility. Philip was obliged to recal his Miniſter in 1564, but to avoid ſome part of the Shame, he went out of *Bruxelles* on pretence of going into *Burgundy* to pay a viſit to his Mother.

The confederated Nobility were mightily pleaſed with theſe Advantages they had obtained over the Favourite. The Lords that had abſented themſelves from the Council, took again their places in it, and the Prince of Orange was willing to manifeſt unto all the World the defects of the laſt Miniſtry. For that end, he made uſe of one FRANCIS BAUDOUIN, a learned Civilian, who, in a Diſcourſe written on purpoſe upon the Matter, aſſerted that *Religion could not, nor ought not to be maintained by Violence ; and that the Proteſtants got more ground every day by the Perſecution than by a Toleration.* That Gentleman was one of the two, whom the Lords aſſociated, who were reſolved to conſult about Religious Matters.

Matters. The other was Cassander, who had been recommended by the Count of Horn.

We muſt not imagine that theſe Lords had at this time forſaken the Roman Religion ; ſome of them forſook it but few Years after, and ſome others never ; the Prince of Orange had been brought up in the Proteſtant Religion in his Childhood, but Charles V. as aboveſaid, having taken him to his Court, cauſed him to be educated in the Roman Religion, which he profeſſed ſtill at this time. But they thought that the beſt way for ſtopping the progreſs of the Reformation, was to reform the Clergy, to inſtruct the People, and to aboliſh the penal Laws. Nay, they went further, for they propoſed to allow to every one Liberty of Conſcience, and to grant the Communion *ſub utráque.* The Prince of Orange explained himſelf very plainly, and with a great deal of Vivacity, in an Aſſembly called by the Governeſs about the latter end of 1564. There he declared, ,, That the Severity of the
,, Government, the Inquiſition, and the Biſhop-
,, ricks newly erected, could be but of very bad
,, Conſequence ; that the Corruption of the Cler-
,, gy was very ſcandalous, and that it was time
,, to put a ſtop to it ; that the Royal Authority
,, would prove inſufficient for introducing the
,, Council of Trent, in a Country ſo near *Ger-*
,, *many* ; and that tho' he had himſelf a great
,, Zeal for the Catholick Religion, nevertheleſs
,, he could not be of Opinion, that the Sove-
,, reigns had any Juriſdiction over the Conſci-
,, ence of their Subjects."

It was reſolved in that Aſſembly to ſend the Count of Egmont into Spain, and he ſet out out at the beginning of the Year 1565. He was very graciouſly received at the Court of *Madrid,* in a view of taking him off from the Aſſociation.

Nothing

Nothing was neglected for that end. He had several Audiences of the King, who feigned to refer much to his Counsels, tho' he never went so far as to abate a single Tittle of the Articles concerning Religion. And to show him that it was not out of Infatuation, he called an Assembly of some of his Divines, and consulted them about the Liberty of Conscience, which some Cities of the *Low Countries* desired. Most part of the Divines having answered, *that considering the Circumstances of the times, the King could grant it without sinning against God* ; the King told them, *that his Query was not whether he could do it, but whether he was obliged to do it in Conscience ?* Then the Divines answered plainly, *that they did not think that any indispensable Duty obliged him so to do it.* The King strengthened by that Decision, so much agreeable to his own Inclination, kneeled down before a Crucifix, and spoke to it to this purport ; *I beseech you, O God and Lord of all things, that I might persevere all the days of my Life in the same Mind as I am now, never to be a King by Name, or by Fact of any Country, where you shall not be acknowledged for Lord.*

The Count of Egmont received an Answer in writing, the purport whereof was ; *That the King would never suffer to make any Alteration in Religion, that however he gave leave to the Council of the Low Countries for calling three or four Bishops, some Divines and some Civilians, for advising together about the means of instructing the People, as well by the exposition of Truth, as by the Reformation of Schools ; that he commanded to work without delay the extirpation of Heresy ; that however if it was found that the penal Laws did not answer the end they had been made for, he would not oppose the Substitution of some others more efficacious.*

Ac-

Accordingly the Divines and the Civilians of the Low Countries were consulted ; the first having prevailed in the Resolutions taken, they declared themselves for Persecution against Hereticks, and added that the Council of Trent had done whatever could be done towards the Reformation so much desired : it remained only to put its Canons in execution, for keeping the Clergy in the bounds of their Duties, and that nothing could be done better for the Reformation of the Schools than what had been prescribed by the Council.

Nothing could be better pleasing to the King than such a Decision. He intended really to introduce the Council of Trent in the *Low Countries* ; and the positive Orders for executing that Design arrived at *Bruffels* very little after the Count of Egmont's. The Governess having received them, advised with the Bishops, the Stadtholders, the Civilians, and the Universities. All of them voted for the Reception of the Council ; save only in what concerned the Rights and Privileges of the King and of his Subjects either Ecclesiastical or Lay-men. That Reftriction was very necessary to bridle the Licence of the Inquisitors. For by the Decision of the Council of Trent it was enacted, that no civil Authority had power either of suspending or annulling Excommunications pronounced by spiritual Judges, to whom only the cognizance thereof do belong. Such a Decision was no wise agreeable to a People who had ever enjoyed the Privilege of appealing to the secular Magistrate from the Sentence of their Bishops, when they thought that they were wronged by them. Therefore the Court of Holland insisting upon the Concordate, opposed warmly that Article.

K 4   The

The Governefs fent notice of that Oppofition to the King her Brother, and told him by the fame Meffenger that the Count of EGMONT was one of thofe who complained the more, that he feemed to have expected fome Mitigation in the Affairs concerning Religion ; and that he faid, that the King had promifed fuch a thing unto him. But Philip did not alter his Courfe for all that, he reiterated the moft fevere Edicts he had publifhed. The Governefs fent to the Bifhops and the Stadtholders of the Provinces, and to all the Magiftrates of the Cities, the Placaerts whereby the Eftablifhment of the Inquifition, and the Publication of the Council of Trent were confirmed.

Some of thofe who received thefe things, dreading the confequences thereof, wrote to the Governefs. The Prince of Orange was one of them ; his Letter is dated from *Breda* the 24th of January 1566. *Louvain, Bruffels, Antwerp,* and *Bois-le-Duc* made their Remonftrance to the fovereign Council of *Brabant.* Which being confulted by the Governefs upon that Affair, anfwered freely, *that the Province was not obliged to fubmit itfelf to the Inquifitors Authority.* The Council of State anfwered to the fame purpofe, and in general every one was fo fenfible of the Injuftice of the laft Orders fent from Spain, that the Magiftrate durft not publifh them at Bois-le-Duc, and that in feveral other places it was with much ado that they prevented an Infurrection. And even in fome places the Executions of the Inquifition were done in fecret, and in a way far different from that which had been obferved before ; for inftead of burning or hanging, they drowned ; and for that purpofe they kept in the Prifons fome large Tubs full of Water, wherein they

they threw the wretched Heretick, Hands and Feet tied, till he was entirely fuffocated. It is faid, that that moft Christian Invention owed its Original to the Catholick Brains of the glorious King Philip.

Great Oppofitions were made to the Eftablifhment of the Inquifition: And the Pride, Haughtinefs and exceeding Cruelties of the Inquifitors, brought Matters to almoft a general Confufion; the Cities of *Flanders* infifted two or three times with the Governefs, and fhewed forth, that what was required of them was quite contrary to their Privileges and Liberties; that Inquisition had never been admitted either by the General States, or by the four Members; and that they defired that it fhould be abolifhed, at leaft, as to the Authority which it had ufurped over the Lay-men. Their Remonftrances having not the defired Effect, they prefented another Petition, but no greater regard was paid to it, only Orders were fent to the Inquifitor at Bruges not to proceed in his Purfuits againft the Reformed in that City till new Orders from the King.

This Year 1566 the Reformed of the Low Countries printed again their Confeffion of Faith, which they dedicated to the King, and made their Apology as to the Crimes laid to their charge.

The dread of the Inquifition had fo much feized upon every one, that the chief Nobility made a League between themfelves for hindering its Eftablifhment. The more zealous Catholicks were admitted into it as well as others. That could not be done fo fecretly, but the Governefs had fome hint of it; and whereas Fame magnifies ordinarily the Objects, that Princefs was told that the League was already more than fifteen thoufand Men ftrong, who were all ready

to

to revenge themselves upon the Provinces; if Liberty of Conscience was not allowed. At this News the Governess being frightened, she summon'd the Knights of the Golden Fleece, and the Stadtholders of the Provinces : And above all, she invited in a very obliging manner the Prince of Orange and Count of Horn, who had absented from Court, to be present at that Assembly. Every Member voted for MILDNESS, and for LIBERTY. The Governess, who was better acquainted than any body else with her Brother Philip's Intentions, knew very well that the only way to please him, was to make use of the most violent methods. But what could she do? She was obliged by her Circumstances either to yield, or to take up Arms; but in the last case, to whom could she give the Command of the Army? She mistrusted the Prince of Orange; and the Count of Egmont being sollicited to take that Charge upon him, answered, *that he would never fight for the penal Laws and the Inquisition.*

It was while that Assembly was upon deliberating what to do, that the Confederates arrived in Numbers at Brussels, as abovesaid, and presented their Petition to the Governess, whereby they required chiefly the Inquisition's proceedings should be superseded till the King had answered their Petition.

At first the Governess answered in a way too general, wherewith they were not at all satisfied; and at last she was obliged to promise that the Inquisitors would proceed for the future with all possible lenity in religious Affairs, the Cases of Tumult and Sedition being excepted, and that even in such Cases nothing should be done without the Court's Advice. She promised further to send their Petition to the King, back'd with proper Representations from her upon the matter.

Where-

Whereupon the Nobility were more eafy, and refolved to feparate themfelves. But they took proper meafures for fecuring to themfelves the Advantages they had procured. They named for that purpofe four Perfons of their Body, to whom they trufted the general Direction of their Affairs. They named three or four others more in each Province, who were to give notice of every thing to the Directors-General, and to execute the Orders they fhould receive from them. And they charged them all with the care of preventing all popular Infurrections, and of preffing the Performance of what had been promifed unto them. Laftly, they engaged themfelves to alter nothing in the Government civil or ecclefiaftical, till the King had ordered it in the Affembly of the States.

Tho' many of the firft Nobility were in the Confederates Company when they prefented the faid Petition to the Governefs, that hindered not the Count of BARLEMONT to call them *B E G-G A R S*, when willing to remove the Fears which the Governefs had of them, he told her, *What do you fear,* MADAM, *from thefe Beggars?* The confederated Nobility gloried in that Title, it ferved as a Mark of Diftinction for animating the Party by the Refentment of the Injury. They caufed feveral Medals to be ftampt, which they hung on their Neck, on one fide whereof the King's Effigy was to be feen ; and on the reverfe was a Bag with this Motto, FAITHFUL TO THE KING, EVEN TO BEGGARY : It is faid likewife that while they were at *Bruffels*, the Lord BREDERODE gave them an Entertainment, where Health to the Beggars was drunk feveral times in a wooden Cup, and that at every time they repeated thefe two Verfes,

,, Parce

,, Par ce Pain, par ce Sel, & par cette Besace,
  By this Bread, by this Salt, and by this Bag,
,, Les Gueux ne changeront, pour chose que
  l'on fasse.
  The Beggars shall not change for any thing.

The Marquis of BERGUE and the Baron of MONTIGNY were sent into *Spain,* for presenting to the King the said Petition, and a Scheme that had been drawn for answering the Expectation of the People. But the Reformed acquainted with the pernicious Designs of the Court, and seeing themselves threatened with an utter Destruction, if they did not make a Show of their Number, began on a sudden to meet together in publick; in some places they appeared to the number of seven thousand, in some others to that of fifteen thousand. The Governess thinking to repress them by some Act of Severity, increased their Number. The Insurrection of *Antwerp* would have proved of worse consequence than it did at this time, had it not been for the Prince of Orange, Governour of that City, who was sent thither by the Duchess of Parma for quelling the Sedition.

About the middle of July the Nobility met together at *St. Tron,* in the Diocese of *Liege,* according to their own Appointment; being assembled to the number of about two thousand, they considered what they were to do, in case they were declared Rebels by the King, and what new measures they ought to take for the Affairs of Religion. The Governess deputed unto them the Prince of Orange and the Count of Egmont, in order to bring them to a Conference, whereto the Confederates having consented, nothing material was done, only the Princess promised unto them that their Remonstrances should be examined

in

in an Assembly of the Knights of the Golden Fleece, which would be held at *Brussels* on the 29th of August next.

King Philip's Answer to the Petition of last April was not at all conformable to what had been expected, and under some appearances of Mildness, his resolutions were as much severe as any of the former.

On the 14th of August began a Sedition in the District of *St. Omer*, where a Mob being got together, out of a false Zeal, or out of Hatred against the Roman Clergy and the Monks, fell to plundering the Convent of the Nuns of *Wolvergben*; they broke the Images to pieces, and took away whatever served to superstitious Use, or could gratify their Greediness. Their Success raised up their Courage, and of those like them, almost in an instant the *Iconcclostical* Spirit spread itself throughout most part of the Provinces, and in three days time plundered above four hundred Churches. That Fury was blamed and condemned by every sober Man, as quite contrary to the spirit of the Gospel. Some were of opinion that these Tumults had been excited under-hand by the Nobility, in order to oblige the Governess to grant them better Terms: if that is true, they succeeded to their Wishes. For in the Assembly of the 24th of August held at Brussels, she promised to abolish the Inquisition; to settle the Affairs of Religion to the Satisfaction of every one; to assemble without delay the General States, or at least to sollicit the King for the Convocation of that Assembly; to molest no body for whatever had been done in consequence of the Union of the Nobles. Such were the Articles promised on the Governess's side. The Nobility promised on their own, to return to their Allegiance; to do their utmost to engage others to do the same; to

put

put a ſtop to the Abuſes done to the Clergy ; to hinder the plundering and prophanation of the Churches ; not to ſuffer the Reformed to ſeize upon any more Churches ; and to do what they could that their Aſſemblies ſhould not be tumultuary : Laſtly, on both ſides they engaged reciprocally to lay down their Arms.

That Treaty was not kept on either ſide ; the Nobles excuſed themſelves oftentimes on account of the breach of the Articles, and they were in the right ; when they parted, they had expreſsly ſtipulated amongſt themſelves, that their Union ought to be deemed as ſubſiſting yet, if any breach was made to the aboveſaid Treaty.

Very likely they ſuſpected that it would not be long before their Enemies would break their word ; and that Suſpicion proved to be well grounded, being confirmed by a Letter intercepted, which was brought to the Prince of Orange. It was written by FRANCIS ALAVA, Miniſter of Spain at the Court of France, and directed to the Governeſs. It was ſaid in it, that
,, the junctures of times were the moſt favour-
,, able for executing the Deſign of ſettling an
,, arbitrary Government in the Low Countries.
,, Which Deſign the preſent King and his Pre-
,, deceſſors had had always in view ; that for ſuc-
,, ceeding in it, nothing more was requiſite than
,, to know how to flatter, and to threaten *à pro-*
,, *pos*; that they ought to copy after the Example
,, of the Prince of Orange, the Counts of Egmont
,, and Horn, to diſſemble as they did, to flat-
,, ter them ; but that the King would treat them
,, very ſoon as they deſerved ; that he had not
,, forgotten that they were the three Chiefs of the
,, Sedition ; and that he had made an Oath to re-
,, venge upon them the Affronts he had received
,, in the Low Countries, and to revenge himſelf
,, in

,, in such a manner that all Europe would be
,, frightened at it."

The Prince of Orange did not fail to impart
that Letter to his Friends; being assembled at
Dendermonde at his own Appointment, they conferred together about it, and considered likewise
the Advices which they had received from Spain.
They weighed the Matter for six Hours together, but could not come to any tolerable Conclusion, only they resolved to behave themselves
in such a manner that their Enemies could have
no just Occasion of doing any harm unto them,
and so they parted.

The Governess having gathered some Troops
sent them to *Valenciennes*, under the Command
of the Lord St. Aldegonde, Baron of *Nor-
kermes*, with Orders to the Inhabitants to receive a
Garrison into their City; whereto having refused to
submit, it was besieged, and obliged at last to
surrender at discretion, upon a promise however,
that they should be treated with lenity; that lenity was such as could be expected from a Catholick Prince, a Bigot, and a Man irritated; the
Cruelties put in use against the Inhabitants of
what condition soever, cannot be represented;
the Governor of the City and his Children perished in it, the Elders and Deacons of the
Church, and some of the chief Members thereof
were put to death, the Assemblies were inter-
dicted, and the two Ministers condemned to be
hanged, and executed. It was said then, *that the
Duchess of Parma had found at Valenciennes the
Keys of all the other Cities*; and it was true, for
Cambray, Hassels, Maseik, and *Maestrich* surrendered themselves, as well as *Bois-le-Duc.* The
surrender of *Valenciennes* happened on the latter
end of December 1566.

In

In Spain the Council was divided between two Opinions; and Philip followed that of the Duke of Alva, as the most agreeable to his unmerciful and proud Temper, viz. to make use of the utmost Severity for repressing these Tumults, and not to receive the Inhabitants of these Provinces to any Mercy, till they had submitted all their Privileges, Goods, and Life, to the King's Discretion. Accordingly having feigned for three Months as if he had a mind to go himself into the Low Countries, he sent thither the Duke of Alva with Orders to execute the bloody Resolution whereof he was the Author.

He went thro' *Savoy, Bressia,* the County of *Burgundy* and *Lorrain,* with the Troops of the *Milanese,* and of the Kingdom of *Naples.* Being still in Italy, he sent word to the Queen-Mother to arm on her side for exterminating the Hugonots, while he would do the same with the Beggars in the Low Countries.

Before he set out from Spain the Marquis of Bergue and the Baron of Montigny, the two Deputies of the Low Countries, had been arrested; the first died in Prison with Grief, or with Poison; the second was beheaded; nevertheless both were Catholicks. Which shewed forth that the Council of Spain was as much, if not more, intent to deprive these Countries of their Privileges and Liberties, as to the Extirpation of Heresy (f).

XXXVIII.
The Queen-Mother makes great Preparations for oppressing the Reformed.

However, it is certain, that the Duke of Alva's Army occasioned the breaking out of the second Civil War, for the Queen-Mother on pre-

(f) What I have said in this long but necessary Digression concerning the Reformation of the Low Countries, is abstracted out of the Abridgement of Brandt's History, but compared with Thuani Hist. lib. XL, XLI. Meteren Hist. Belgica, lib. I. II, III. Petit Chron. Anc. & Mod. de Hollande, Zelande, &c. Tom. II. Lib. ix.

pretence of putting the Frontiers of the Kingdom in a ſtate of Defence, in caſe the Duke of Alva ſhould attempt any thing in his way, ſent Orders to the Governours of the Provinces to aſſemble the Companies of Ordnance, and to raiſe ſome new ones; beſides that, ſhe ſent for ſix thouſand Men out of Switzerland.

I don't know from whence *Caſtelnau* had learned that all theſe Levies were made by the Advice and Counſel of the Prince of Condé, and of the Admiral; Thuanus, D'Aubigné, D'Avila, nor La Noüe ſay not a word of ſuch Advice; contrarywiſe they ſay, that theſe Levies gave them great Suſpicions that ſome ill Deſign was hatching at Court againſt them, and the noble Hiſtorian above-mentioned acknowledges ſo much himſelf three or four Lines after; *Notwithſtanding that,* ſays he, *they took great Jealouſies and Miſtruſts leſt that Army of the Duke of Alva ſhould come into the Low Countries, and the ſix thouſand Switzers, levied by the King's Command, ſhould fall upon their Backs.* If the Prince and the Admiral had adviſed theſe Levies, how could they be frighten'd at them, ſince the King would have done nothing in that regard but by their Counſel (g)?

D'Avila tells us, that the Queen took the opportunity of Alva's paſſage thro' the Frontiers for raiſing the Troops above-mentioned, to execute the Scheme agreed on between the two Crowns of France and Spain, (*for the Extirpation of the Reformed of France and the Low Countries, of which Scheme ſhe ſaid Alva was the Author.*) He ſays further, that the King of France diſſembled as much as poſſible his real Sentiments, and his Deſigns, waiting for the arrival of the Switzers; that the Queen-Mother likewiſe endeavoured

(g) Memoirs de Caſtelnau, liv. VI. ch. ii.

deavoured to conceal from the Reformed what she intended to do, and the Plot laid against them ; that for that end she made use of the publick Fame that King Philip was coming into the Low Countries ; she added much of her own to that Tale, as if she had been very sorry for it, and as if she thought that such a Journey was intended for some greater Design ; and so she persuaded the most part, that all these Preparations of War which she made, were only upon that account.

And in order to render the thing more likely, she summoned to Court several Lords, and she held an Assembly, whereto she had invited several Lords of the Reformed Religion. There it was proposed not only to be upon the Defensive, but to act Offensively against the Spaniards, in case their King should come into the Low Countries with some ill Design. Nay, it was unanimously resolved to send the young L'Aubespine Express to *Madrid*, either to dissuade the King of Spain from his intended Journey into the Low Countries, or to dive into the Design of it ; but all this was a Sham. The Queen went further, for left Philip, for want of being thoroughly informed of every thing, should disclose the Mystery one way or another, she sent Post to him Father Hugues, a Franciscan Fryar, who having imparted to the King the Resolutions of the Court of France, they agreed together that in order to impose the more easily upon the Reformed of France, he would receive very indifferently L'Aubespine. That was done, and Philip refused Audience for some Weeks to the said Embassador, and when he was admitted, he received him with an apparent Coolness, as if he made no account of his Master : In all other occurrences he told the Envoy that he mistrusted the King and the Queen.

In

In France the Court made outwardly great Complaints against the King of Spain, and took great care to have it published every where, that they would very soon declare War against Spain. In short, that Dissembling went so far, that the Pope was deceived by it, and thinking that they were in earnest, he sent a Nuncio to the Queen-Mother, with Orders to remonstrate to his Majesty, that the King of Spain had attempted nothing against her Son ; and therefore that there was no occasion of raising so many Troops, and making so many Preparations of War. The Queen answered with such ambiguous words, that it was impossible to dive into her true Design. However she told the Nuncio, that she did not trust much to the King of Spain, having so many reasons of Complaint against him, since he had not answered to her sincere Affection, and to the care she had taken to hinder her Son's Subjects from assisting the Rebels of the Low Countries ; that nevertheless she declared that the King her Son would not resolve upon a War, unless he should be provoked to it. But for all that she could say, the Pope was not satisfied at all, and he was not alone deceived by these outward Demonstrations ; for the Prince of Condé thinking that it was in earnest, desired the King to improve this opportunity for declaring War against Spain, offering for that purpose a great number of French Reformed ; which Offer much displeased the King, who could not bear that any other should have more Credit and Authority amongst and over his own Subjects, than himself. Therefore tho' the Queen intreated him always to dissemble, and that the Catholick Lords at Court did the same, nevertheless he could not forbear shewing his Resentment to the Prince

L 2   in

in the private Diſcourſes they had together (*b*). This is the full Account of that Intrigue given by D'Avila, whereby it is evident, 1. That a Treaty was really concluded between France and Spain for deſtroying the Reformed ; at leaſt, the Chiefs of them, and then oblige the reſt to conform themſelves to the Will of their King. 2. That in order to execute that Plot, the Queen, making uſe of a Diſſimulation of the deepeſt dye, careſſed the Reformed, feigned to them that ſhe was much afraid of the King of Spain's Deſigns ; and all that for having a fair pretence for raiſing Troops within and without the Kingdom, and be in a condition of ſurpriſing the Reformed unawares. 3. That the Prince had no hand at all in the raiſing of the 6000 Switzers, ſeeing the Orders had been given for it by the Queen-Mother, before ſhe aſſembled the Lords to conſult them upon that imaginary Emergency.

XXXIX.
*Several
Occurrences of this
Year.*

The Duke of Alva's March through Savoy obliged the City of Geneva to put themſelves in a poſture of Defence. Emanuel Philibert, Duke of Savoy, willing to improve that opportunity of making himſelf Maſter of that City, levied a great Number of Soldiers, which being known in France, the Prince of Condé ſent ſome Officers and Troops to relieve that place. But Alva, acquainted with the condition it was in, and that he could not ſurpriſe it, refuſed to attack it, and continued his March (*j*).

About this time the Proteſtant Princes of *Germany* ſent a ſolemn Embaſſy to King Charles, requiring that he would deal with more Equity and Juſtice with his Reformed Subjects, and not

to

(*b*) D'Avila Hiſt. des Guerres Civiles, liv. IV. p. 164—167.
(*j*) Sponde Hiſt. de Geneve, liv. III. p. 46, 47.

to perfecute them, and to allow a Church and fome Minifters to thofe of *Paris*. But the King underftanding that they had had fome private Conferences with the Prince of Condé and the Admiral, even before they had prefented their Credentials, received them very coldly, and anfwered, that he would be always ready to cultivate a Friendfhip with the Princes their Mafters, if they would ceafe to interfere with the Affairs of his Kingdom ; and that he would grant their Demands, if at the fame time they would allow to the Catholicks the free Exercife of their Religion in their own Dominions, and let the Priefts fay Mafs therein.

It is faid, that about this time the Conftable of Montmorency defiring to refign his Office in behalf of his Son the Marfhal Duke of Montmorency, and having been refufed, the Prince of Condé asked that place for himfelf, with the confent of the Conftable, and that the King and the Queen his Mother being puzzled at this, in order to be rid of the Prince's Importunities, bid the Duke of Anjou to ask the Lieutenancy-General of the Kingdom for himfelf, if the Conftable's old Age obliged him to leave the Court.

That young Prince not yet fixteen Years old, being prefent when the Prince of Condé renewed his Petition, waited not till the King had anfwered, but replied in a Paffion, (as he had been taught before by the Queen his Mother) that his Majefty having promifed to make him his Lieutenant-General, he ought not to fuffer that another fhould prefume to ask the Command of his Armies (*i*).

But Brantome relates this paffage otherwife, which is not at all likely ; he fays, that the Queen being at Supper at *St. Germain des Prez*,

L 3   the

(*i*) D'Avila, liv. IV. p. 167.

the Prince of Condé was there ; that the Duke of Anjou took him aside, and left him uncovered, and spoke to him with great Heat and Passion, concerning the boldness he had to aspire to a Dignity which belong'd to himself, and which no body could presume to dispute with him ; and that at last he threatened him, that if ever he had any thought about it, he would make him repent of it, *and make him as little and low a Companion as he would feign to appear great.* Though Brantome says, that he was present in the same Room, when the words were spoken, I must beg his pardon for my not believing him ; it is not at all likely that a Youth like the Duke of Anjou, who was a Subject as well as the Prince, should have offered such abusive Language to a Prince of the Blood, of the Age, Capacity and Credit, as the Prince of Condé was ; as much a Darling as he was of the Queen his Mother, she would never have suffered such an Affront to be put upon the Prince, whom she had Interest to manage still, because the Pear was not full ripe as yet.   D'Avila's Account is much more likely. A little after the Prince left the Court, the Admiral and D'Andelot his Brother did the same.

About the beginning of June the Reformed attempted to seize upon *Metz*, Montbrun was Chief of that Enterprize : he had counterfeited an Order from the King, to the Governour of that place, for sending away the Troops that were in Garrison in it, and to receive some which were supposed to come from *Piedmont*. But the Marshal of Vieilleville was so strict in the Questions he asked, to the Officers of these Troops, that the Cheat being discovered, they miscarried in their Attempt.

The sixth National Synod of the Reformed Churches was held at *Vertueil* in *Angoumois*, and be-

began its Seffions on the firft of September, Mr. De Leftre being Moderator.

Amongft the feveral Regulations made in this Synod the following are to be noted. Excommunicated Perfons and Infidels were not permitted to marry without a previous Penance done in publick. Nothing befides the Holy Scripture fhould be read in the Church. The Bread was not to be given in the Lord's Supper to them who refufed to receive the Cup. A Minifter charged with having left his Church, fhall be obliged to appear before the Synod of his Province at the firft Summons, there to give an Account of his Conduct; and if he is not guilty, the Charges of his Journey fhall be borne by the Church who had accufed him. A Woman could not be compelled to cohabit with her Husband attacked with Leprofy. The Church, or the Province wherein that Church lies, was obliged to provide for the Maintenance of the Minifter's Widow and Children.

Several Orders and Decrees concerning Marriages were received by this Synod, which had been drawn up before by John Calvin (*k*).

The firft Query moved about it, was, Who are thofe that cannot marry without firft having asked and obtained leave of their Parents or Guardians ?

Anfwer. All thofe of both Sexes who have never been married before, and have not as yet attained the Age prefcribed by Law ; twenty Years for young Men, and eighteen for Girls in France : and though they are come to that Age, then they are in duty bound to ask leave, either by

L 4 them-

(*k*) Quick and Aymon miftook grofsly, when they faid that the following Decrees had been drawn by Calvin *at the requeft of the Fathers of the Synod of Vertueil*, for Calvin was dead fince the 27th of May 1564. Therefore he could not write in September 1567.

Charles
IX.
1567.
Pope Pius
V.

themſelves, or by ſome other ; and if their Parents ſhould make no aecount of their Requeſt,
then they may proceed, and marry without their
Conſent.   The ſame Rule ſhall be obſerved as to
the Pupils and Orphans, who are under the Authority of their Truſtees and Guardians.   Mo-
thers nor Guardians ſhall not diſpoſe at their own
Will and Pleaſure, of their Children or Pupils,
for marrying them, without the Advice of their
Relations or Kindred, if they have any.

In caſe two young Perſons under Age ſhould
raſhly contract Marriage together, without the
conſent of their Parents or Guardians, they ſhall
be puniſhed for it, and the ſaid Contract ſhall be
reſcinded, and the Marriage declared void, at the
requeſt of the ſaid Parents or Guardians.   And if
they have been inticed to it by ſome Man or Woman, the Inticer, Man or Woman, ſhall be proſecuted by the Parents or Guardians, and obliged
to acknowledge their Crime before the Magiſtrate, and to beg pardon, and be puniſhed with
faſting for three days together, feeding only upon
a ſmall quantity of Bread and Water.   The Witneſſes who have conſented to ſuch Marriages ſhall
be likewiſe puniſhed with faſting a whole day,
upon a ſmall quantity of Bread and Water.

Let the Promiſes made between two young
Perſons who are not of Age, be always condi-
tional, and before two Witneſſes, or elſe they
ſhall be deemed void and null.

When young Perſons come to the Age required by the Law ſhall marry without the conſent of their Parents or Guardians ; let the Magiſtrate take cognizance of the Matter : and if
the Parents have refuſed to interfere with it, or
if they have been too ſevere towards them, and
ſo have obliged their Children to act as the Law
directs, then and in ſuch Caſe let the Parents be
com-

compelled to give them a Portion, or to settle them in such a way and condition, that they might live in the World as if they had given their consent unto the Marriage of their Children.

Parents shall not constrain their Children to marry against their Will : And in case a Son or a Daughter should refuse the Party offered them by their Father, let that refusal be expressed with all Modesty and filial Reverence ; and let them not be punished for this their refusal. The same thing shall be observed as to those who are under Guardians.

Parents or Guardians shall not be allowed to engage their Children or Pupils for Marriage, till such time as they are come to Age capable of ratifying the said Engagement. However, if a Child who is not of Age, having refused to marry a Person of his Father's choice, should a little while after marry another, who is less advantageous, the Father shall not be obliged to give any thing, during his Life, unto that disobedient Child.

The second Query. Who are the Persons that may marry without leave ?

Answer. Such as having been once married, be they Men or Women, tho' their Parents be living, provided they be of Age ; as it has been declared in the first Article, twenty Years for a Widower, and eighteen for a Widow : provided likewise that they have been emancipated, and that they kept House by themselves apart. Yet it would be always more decent for Children to do nothing in that respect without the Advice of their Parents.

Let all Promises of Marriage be made decently, and in the fear of God, not in Dissolution, nor lightly over a Bottle of Wine, but with all possible
ble

ble Serioufnefs, after they have well confidered of it, and are perfectly refolved about it; and in cafe any one fhould do otherwife, let them be corrected. And in cafe the Minifter declares that he has been furprifed, let the Marriage be diffolved.

If a Man fhould fue a Woman at Law, alledging, that fhe has promifed to marry him, unlefs there be two Witneffes, Perfons of Credit and Probity to atteft it, the Defendrefs fhall be put upon her Oath, and if fhe denies the faid Promife, fhe fhall be abfolved.

The third Query. For what Caufes a Marriage-promife may and ought to be refcinded?

Anfwer. There are two Cafes wherein fuch Promifes may be refcinded, when made betwixt Perfons capable of them.   1. When upon good Evidence it fhall appear that the Girl is not a Virgin, and that before the Marriage fhe was taken to be a Virgin, and fhe declared herfelf to be fuch.   2. When one of the Parties is utterly unfit for Generation. But the non-payment of a Dowry or Portion, or Wedding-Clothes, cannot be a reafon for hindering the performance of Marriage-promifes, becaufe fuch things are not of the Effence, but Accidents, and Acceffories unto Marriage.

The fourth Query. What diftance of time is there to be obferved between the promife of Marriage and its performance?

Anfwer. Not above fix Weeks after the promife is made. And in cafe the Parties fhould delay beyond that time, they fhall be fummoned before the Confiftory, and be admonifhed to fulfil the Marriage; and if they prove difobedient, they fhall be deliver'd over to the Magiftrate, who may compel them to the performance.

In cafe the Marriage fhould be oppofed, the Minifter fhall refer the oppofing Party to the
Con-

Confiſtory.   Nevertheleſs no oppoſition ſhall be admitted, unleſs the Opponent ſhould live in the ſame place, or be a Perſon well known, or that he brings with him ſome Perſon well known to teſtify to his Character, left an honeſt Maid ſhould ſuffer in her Reputation.

If the Opponent do not appear at the appointed day, the Banns ſhall be publiſhed without any further delay, as if there had been no oppoſition ; for preventing and avoiding thereby all manner of Frauds, which might be committed in this Matter.

Let no Foreigner coming from a far diſtant Country be admitted unto Marriage, unleſs he brings with him good Certificates, or undoubted Letters of Credence, or that he have a Teſtimony from Perſons of an undoubted Character, who certify that he is not married elſewhere.

The fifth Query. What is to be done before the Celebration of Marriage?

Anſwer. Let the Banns be publiſhed on three ſeveral Sundays in the Church before the Marriage be ſolemnized ; and let the firſt Magiſtrate give it under his hand, that he knows both the Parties, ſo that immediately after the third Publication, the Marriage may be then celebrated. If one of the Parties belongs to another Pariſh, let him bring a Certificate from that Pariſh he belongs to.

Let not the Betrothed cohabit together as Man and Wife till ſuch time as they ſhall be ſolemnly married in the Church. If they do otherwiſe, let them be impriſoned for three days, and feed upon Bread and Water only ; then they ſhall appear before the Conſiſtory, where they ſhall be convicted of their Sin, that they may be aſhamed of it, and humble before God.

The

The sixth Query. How is the Marriage to be celebrated ?

Answer. Let the Persons to be married come
modestly to the Church, without Drums or Min-
strels, demeaning themselves orderly and gravely
as becometh Christians, and let them come before
the Bell hath done tolling, that so the Marriage
may be solemnly blessed before the Sermon ;
but if they are negligent, and come too late, they
shall be sent back unmarried.

It shall be lawful to celebrate Marriages on any
day of the Week, provided there be a Sermon,
or upon the Lord's day by Nine in the Morning ; the days when the Lord's Supper shall be
administred only excepted, that so there may be
no distraction, and that every one may the
better prepare himself for receiving.

The seventh Query. About the Man's dwelling
with his Wife.

Answer. Let the Man and his Wife cohabit
together in one and the same House, having all
things in common between them.   And if either
of them separate from the other to live apart, let
the Party that separates himself be summoned to
appear before the Consistory, that he or she may
be convicted of their Sin ; and in case of Quarrels
or Differences betwixt them, let them be made
up, and sent home reconciled one with the other.

The eighth Query. What are the Degrees of
Consanguinity forbidden in Marriage ?

Answer. No Marriage can be contracted in direct line between a Father and his Daughter, or
the Mother and her Son, nor any other of their
Descendants ; because that is destructive of natural Modesty and Piety, and is expresly forbidden by the Laws of God, and the civil Laws.

In like manner an Uncle cannot marry his
Niece or Grand-Niece, nor the Aunt her Nephew

phew or Grand-Nephew ; *becaufe an Uncle repre-
fents the Father, and an Aunt the Mother.*

Nor can a Brother marry his Sifter, or even
Half-Sifter. As for thofe other degrees, tho'
they are not forbidden neither by the Law of
God, nor by the civil Law of the *Romans* ; yet
becaufe fuch Marriages have not for many Years
been in ufe, (*at Geneva he means*) and for fhun-
ning the Scandal which ignorant Perfons might
take at it, let not *firft Coufins* contract Marriage
together, till fuch a time that a better opinion
concerning thefe Marriages fhall prevail amongft
us. As for Intermarriages in other degrees, let
them not be hindered.

The ninth Query. What are thofe degrees of
Affinity forbidden in Marriage ?

Anfwer. A Father fhall not marry his own Son's
Widow, nor a Mother her own Daughter's Widower, and fo in the degrees defcending in a direct Line.

A Man fhall not marry his Wife's Daughter,
nor a Woman her Husband's Son, and fo in the
degrees defcending in a direct Line.

A Man fhall not marry his own Nephew's Widow, or the Widow of his Grand-Nephew.

A Man fhall not marry his Brother's Widow,
nor a Woman her Sifter's Widower.

A Man having committed Adultery with his
Neighbour's Wife, if it be afterwards difcovered,
he fhall not marry the Adulterefs, in cafe fhe
became a Widow, becaufe of the Scandals and
Dangers that will enfue upon fuch a Marriage.

The tenth Query. What is to be done in cafe of
Difcords, Variance and Contentions between married Perfons ?

Anfwer. In cafe a Man doth not live peaceably
with his Wife, but that there be Strifes, Jealoufies
and Quarrels betwixt them, they fhall be fummoned
before the Confiftory, and be admonifhed to live in

a

a godly Concord, Union, and Love together; and each of them shall be reproved for their Faults, as the Case shall require.

If a Man uses his Wife ill, beating and tormenting her, if he threatens her with some great Mischief, and that it should be known that he is a disorderly Fellow, he shall be turned over to the Magistrate, who will be most humbly intreated to interpose his Authority, and to forbid him most expresly, upon some penalty, to abuse his Wife any more.

The eleventh Query. For what Causes may a Marriage be declared null?

Answer. In case a Woman should complain that her Husband is *bewitch'd*, (NOTA BENE) or naturally Impotent, and that by his own Confession, or upon his being searched, it should be found true, the Marriage shall be declared void, and the Woman shall be separated from her Husband, and he strictly forbidden not to deceive any other Woman for the future.

If a Man should make the same Complaint of his Wife, that she hath some bodily Defect which hinders the Cohabitation, and that she refuses to be cured; the Matter of the Complaint being proved true, the Marriage shall be declared null.

The twelfth Query. For what Causes a Marriage can be dissolved?

If a Man charges his Wife with Adultery, and proves it by irrefragable Evidences, and requires to be separated from her, he shall be divorced, and be at liberty to marry with whom he best pleaseth. However, he may be exhorted to forgive his said Wife; but not urged to it with too great Importunity; much less shall he be compelled in any wise to keep her.

Tho' in ancient times the Privilege of a Wife was not equal to that of her Husband, in case

of

of Divorce ; yet forasmuch as the Apostle says (*l*), that the Obligation is mutual and reciprocal as to Bed and Board, and that in neither of these the Wife is more subject to her Husband, than he is to her ; therefore, if a Man is convicted of Adultery, and his Wife demands to be separated from him, she shall be divorced, unless she can be prevailed on by godly Advices to be reconciled to him. Nevertheless, in case the Wife should be found to have committed Adultery through a meer suspicion of her Husband being in the fault, or the Husband of his Wife, so as both should be guilty ; or in case it should appear, by their dealings, that they have a mind to be separated, they shall not be hearkened to in either of these cases. (IF ANY ONE REFUSES TO GIVE HIS ASSENT TO THIS DECISION, AND DEEM IT NOT ONLY ABSURD, BUT EVEN CONTRARY TO DIVINE AND HUMAN LAWS, I WILL NOT GAINSAY, NOR UNDERTAKE THE DEFENCE OF IT).

If a Man undertakes a long Journey either upon his Trade or Traffick, or any other business, and that he is not a Debauchée, nor alienated in his Affections from his Wife, and that he be absent for a very long time, without being known what is become of him, only there are some probable Conjectures that he is dead ; for all that his Wife shall not be allowed to marry again till the term of ten Years be expired, reckoning from the day of his setting out, unless there should be certain Evidences of his death. And yet notwithstanding this Licence should be granted her at the end of ten Years, if there is any Suspicion, or News, or other Indicaitons, that this Man has been detained Prisoner, or that he has been hindered

dered

(*l*) (*It is but an inference, which is not sufficient for building a Law so contrary to the Uses of all the World at all times*).

dered by some other means from returning home, the said Woman shall live as a Widow, till a greater light can be had in that Affair.

If a Man through Debauchery, or some other evil Affection should forsake the place of his Abode, his Wife shall inquire diligently after him, and where he is to be found ; and then she shall ask a Warrant from the Magistrate to recal him, or to constrain him to return, or at least to give him Notice, that unless he would return home unto his Family, he will be proceeded against in his Absence. And this being done, tho' there be no possible means to compel him to return, nevertheless, he shall be prosecuted, and a Proclamation shall be read on three Sundays, (a Fortnight intervening betwixt each Proclamation) the same Proclamation shall be read likewise in the Lieutenant's Court, and it shall be notified unto two or three of his nearest Friends and Relations, (if he hath any) that in case he do not appear, his Wife shall be at liberty to make her Address unto the Consistory, and sue for a Separation, which shall be granted her ; and for that end she shall be directed to the Magistrate, and that Person who shall have rebelled in this manner, shall be banished for ever out of the City and its Territories. But if he doth return within the prescribed time, all Endeavours shall be used to reconcile him to his Wife.

A Man of a roving Temper that uses to forsake his Wife, and to wander up and down the Country, shall be imprisoned for the second Offence of this kind, and fed upon Bread and Water only ; upon the third Offence he shall be punished with the utmost rigour, and if he does not amend, his Wife shall be divorced from him.

A

A Debauchée, who, without any Provocation, forsakes his Wife, the said Wife, upon a full Evidence of the Truth of her Complaints, shall be admonished to inquire diligently after her Husband, his Friends and Relations shall be summoned to give what account they know of him. The said Wife shall wait for him a full Year, and if she cannot hear any thing of him, she shall make her Address to the Consistory, which having well considered the Matter, if it is found that she has good reasons for being married again, after an Exhortation, she shall be directed to the civil Magistrate ; she shall be put upon her Oath, that she knows not whether her Husband is gone, nor what is become of him. The same Oath shall be tendered to his Friends and Relations, and then the Magistrate shall proceed to cause the three Proclamations above-mentioned to be read publickly, and the Woman shall be at liberty to marry again ; and if it happens that the Absentee should return again, he shall receive the deserved Punishment.

If a Woman elopes from her Husband, and lives elsewhere from him, and the said Husband desires to be divorced from her, and be at liberty to marry another, let it be first considered, whether she is in such a place where a Warrant might be served on her, or at least whether Notice could be given her to appear and answer to her Husband's Suit, and the said Warrants and Letters shall be delivered to her Husband for that purpose. Then the abovesaid Proclamations shall be read, her Friends and Relations having been first called, and charged to admonish her to return. If she appears within the Term, and her Husband refuses to receive her, suspecting that she has been unfaithful to him during her Absence, tho' it is a very scandalous thing for a Woman to elope from her Husband, yet Endeavours shall be made to engage her Husband to forgive her Folly: But if he withstands all Intreaties, then Inquiries shall be made in the places she has haunted, and how she has behaved herself; and if there is no Proof or Indication of any ill Behaviour, and Unfaithfulness to her Husband's bed, then the Husband shall be compelled to receive her, and be reconciled to her: But if on the contrary there is some Suspicion well grounded, that she has not been faithful, if she has been found in lewd Companies, or been heard talking without any regard to Modesty, then her Husband's Suit shall be granted, as it is but just and reasonable. But if she do not appear within the prescribed time, then it shall be proceeded against her in the same manner as it has been directed in the foregoing Articles, against a Husband guilty of the like fault.

If a Man, having made a Promise of Marriage unto a Maid or a Widow, goes into another Country, and the Maid or Widow complains of it, craving to be discharged from her Promise because of his Disloyalty, it shall be inquired upon what Occasion he has left the place, whether it be for a lawful Subject, whether he had done it with the consent of his Betrothed; or whether out of Debauchery, being unwilling to perform his Promise. If it appears that he had done it without any good reason, and only out of a wicked Design, the place of his Abode must be known if possible, and how to give him Notice to return within a certain day, and perform his Promise; and if upon Notice given he does not appear, then the abovesaid Proclamations shall be read, after which the Maid or Widow shall be declared free from all Engagement with him, and he shall be banished for his Disloyalty. But if he does appear within the prescribed time, he
shall

shall be compelled to perform his Promise out of hand. But if there is any just Cause for his Absence, and he hath advised and acquainted his Betrothed with it, then the Maid or Widow shall use all possible diligence by herself and his Friends to induce him to return ; and if he does not comply within a Year, then let Proclamations be made as above directed,

And the same Course shall be followed as to Maids or Widows, who shall offend as the Men ; with this difference only, that a Man shall not be obliged to wait a full Year, altho' the Maid or Widow has absented with his Knowledge and Consent, unless he had given her leave for being so long time abroad.

If a Maid, being duly tied by Promise of Marriage, is fraudulently carried away out of the Territories of this Republick, that she might not accomplish the Marriage, it shall be inquired, whether some one or other in the City hath not assisted in this taking away, that they might be compelled to restore her, upon such a penalty as shall be judged meet ; and if she be under Guardians and Trustees, they likewise shall be enjoyned to make all possible Search, that she may be found again.

If a married Woman hath eloped from her Husband, and he makes no Complaint of it, or if a Woman being forsaken by her Husband, dissembles it, if this afterwards comes to the Knowledge of the Publick, they shall be both, or either of them summoned to appear before the Consistory, there to give an Account how the Matter stands, that so all Scandal might be prevented, and that no Deceit or Collusion might be tolerated, or, what is worse, winked at ; and the most proper means shall be made use of, to prevent those wilful Divorces which a Husband and a Wife would make of their own Accord,

with-

without the Authority of the Magiſtrate, and the Woman ſhall be obliged to follow her Husband at his requeſt, when and whither he ſhall be pleaſed to go and ſettle himſelf, either if it ſhould be of his own Choice, or conſtrained to it by ſome Neceſſity : provided that the Man ſhould not be a Debauchée, who will carry her away out of a Frolick into ſome foreign and unknown Country. But if he don't go into a Country too far diſtant, to follow his Calling, then his Wife ſhall be obliged to follow him.

All matrimonial Matters concerning the Union of Perſons are to be firſt tranſacted in the Conſiſtory, but not Matters concerning Eſtate and Dowry ; and in all the Tranſactions there ſhall be a friendly and ſincere Agreement between the Parties. But if there is any occaſion for a Sentence from the Judge, then let the Parties concerned direct themſelves to the Magiſtrate, who having been rightly informed by the Conſiſtory, ſhall pronounce a final Sentence.

> Done and concluded at Vertueil on the 7th of September 1567, and ſigned in the Name of all the Deputies, by

> Mr. De Lestre, Moderator.

I make no doubt but that many of my Readers will think ſomething ſtrange that the great Calvin ſhould go ſo far upon a Matter, which, for the moſt part, is of a civil Concern, and as ſuch, belongs properly to the civil Government, and that he has aſcribed ſuch a great Authority to the Conſiſtories : But what is ſtill more ſurpriſing is, that a National Synod in the Kingdom of France hath adopted his Deciſions upon that Matter to be a Rule whereby the Reformed Churches were to be governed in that reſpect.

It

It may be, that before Calvin, there were no Laws to decide many particular Cafes concerning Marriages at *Geneva*, and that it was neceffary there fhould be fome: It may be that that Great Man was defired by the Magiftracy of that City to make fome Regulations upon that Matter, which were afterwards approved of by them. But I don't fee how the Reformed Churches of France could do the fame, or to receive amongft their Canons what had been done at Geneva upon that Subject: there were Laws enough in the Kingdom, fufficient to decide the moft material Points upon Marriages, and what was added by thefe Decrees of Geneva, was only, for the moft part, an Incroachment upon People's Liberty. Therefore they were obliged in the next Synod held at *La Rochelle* about four Years after, to alter feveral things in thefe Decrees, and to fubmit them in general to the Laws of the Kingdom: But let this be faid by the way.

Now every thing tended to a Rupture in the Kingdom; the Edict of Amboife far from being obferved, had been almoft made void, by the Reftrictions, Explanations, &c. of the fubfequent Edicts: The Reformed had the greateft Injuftices, and the moft barbarous Ufages to undergo in every place where the Catholicks were the ftrongeft; their Grievances far from being redreffed, when complained of, were laughed at at Court; and oftentimes their Deputies were fent to Prifon for their Trouble: The Cardinal of Lorrain and his Houfe bore the Sway at Court, where their Credit was as great as ever: The Prince and the Admiral's Advices were fcorned by the King and his Council: The raifing of the fix thoufand Switzers, that were already entered the Kingdom, and the great Levies of Troops throughout the Provinces; Laftly, the Paffage of the

M 3 Duke

Duke of Alva with a strong Army, without any opposition; a thing so much contrary to the Rules of good Policy.   All these things were a strong Demonstration that the Court of France acted in concert with that of Spain, for working the utter Destruction of their Reformed Subjects.   I do not magnify the Objects, the Catholick Historians Castelnau, Thuanus, and D'Avila tell us, that the Court kept no measure at this time; and paid no regard at all to the Remonstrances of the Reformed; that the Queen-Mother and the Cardinal of Lorrain, had nothing else in view than to execute the Scheme laid at *Bayonne*, for the Extirpation of Hereticks (*m*).

Now should the Reformed have sat still? ought they to wait patiently till they would come and cut the Throats of about two Millions of People, who desired no better than to live quietly under their King's Protection, and the Benefit of his Edicts? No, to be sure; they could not do it without incurring the Guilt of being as so many Self-Murderers.   It is needless to alledge here, the Example of the Christians of the three first Centuries; the case is quite different, and among many other Differences I quote this only.   They had no Edicts of the Emperor's, whereby the free Possession of their Religion was granted unto them.   Therefore the Reformed in France did nothing but what they were obliged to do, in putting themselves in a posture of Defence; but they went too far, and lost the Merit of that Action by the ways and means which they had chose at first for getting their Grievances redressed, as I shall say presently.

Several

(*m*) Casteln. Mem. liv. VI. ch. II, III.   Thuan. Hist. lib. XLII.   D'Avila, Tom. I. liv. IV. Addit. aux Mem. de Casteln. Tom. II. liv. VI. ch. iii, iv, v, vi.

Several Conferences had been held since the latter end of July, first at *St. Valery*, and then at *Chatillon*, between the Prince, the Admiral D'Andelot, the Count of La Rochefoucault, and several other Lords and Gentlemen, for advising about the means of preventing their utter Ruin ; at first they all assented to the Admiral's opinion, to try every thing before they should make use of extreme Remedies, and take up Arms. But their just Jealousies were increased at several things which occasioned them, and especially because the Duke of Alva being arrived in the Low Countries, the King under several frivolous pretences delayed to dismiss the Switzers (*n*). Besides that, a Letter from a Lord of the Court, who countenanced the Reformed was exhibited, whereby he warned the Prince of Condé, that it had been resolved in the most privy Council, to seize upon him and the Admiral, to keep his Highness under a perpetual Confinement, and to put the Admiral to death ; that in the mean time two thousand Switzers were to be admitted into *Paris*, as many in Orleans, and the other two thousand to be sent to Poitiers; which done, the Edicts should be repealed, and others, quite contrary, tending to the utter Extirpation of the Reformed, be published. And what added a greater Authority to that, and obliged them to give credit to it, was, that the Switzers, instead of going back, as the Prince had desired, advanced further and further towards *Paris*.

The Lords and Gentlemen of the Prince's Council being incensed at this News, exclaimed, ,, How long shall we suffer ourselves to be abused ? ,, Shall

XLII. *The Prince and his Council resolve upon a War.*

M 4

(*n*) D'Aubigné says, that when the Constable was intreated by his Nephew to pity the fate of the Kingdom, &c. He answered, *What should we do with those Switzers, who are well paid, if we do not employ them ?* Hist. Univ. Tom. I. liv. IV. chap. vii.

„ Shall we wait till we shall be led triumphant-
„ ly, Feet and Hands bound, to Paris, and from
„ thence to the place of Execution, there to feed
„ the Cruelty of our Enemies with our own
„ Blood ? What do we stay for ? We have al-
„ ready a foreign Enemy in the Kingdom, who
„ come strait to fall upon us ; remembring of
„ the Battle of *Dreux*, they will revenge upon
„ us all the Injuries they received then from us
„ in our just Defence. Have we forgot that so
„ many thousand Men of our own have perish-
„ ed by the Wickedness and Treachery of our
„ Enemies, since the last Edict of Peace ; where-
„ of when we have complained, we have re-
„ ceived no other Satisfaction or Redress, but
„ Words and frivolous Answers, and Delays.
„ At least, if these things were done by the
„ King's Will and Command, to whom we
„ owe all Respect and Obedience, may be, we
„ shall bear with it patiently ; but whereas eve-
„ ry one knows that these things are done either
„ without his Majesty's Knowledge or Will (*o*),
„ by those who abusing the King's Name, hin-
„ der us from a free access to his Majesty, where-
„ by, being deprived of his Royal Protection,
„ we are delivered, as it were, to be a Prey to
„ our Enemies ; shall we bear with such Injuries
„ at their Hands, and invite them by our Pa-
„ tience to be more audacious and cruel towards
„ us ? Our Fathers have patiently suffered for
„ above forty Years the bitterest Pains, the most
„ exquisite Torments, for Christ's sake, and the
„ Defence of the Gospel ; which same Cause
„ we defend likewise. And now that not only
„ Families, and Boroughs, but whole Cities,
                                              „ have

(*o*) They mistook, Charles had openly declared himself
against them, and followed in every thing his Mother's direction.

,, have made an open Confeſſion of their Faith
,, under the Authority and Protection of two
,, Royal Edicts, we ſhould be unworthy of the
,, glorious Titles of Chriſtians and Gentlemen,
,, ſhould we by our Neglect, or Puiſillanimity,
,, let periſh ſuch a vaſt number of People in
,, periſhing ourſelves. Therefore we do be-
,, ſeech ye, my Lords, you, who have taken
,, upon yourſelves the Defence of the Common
,, Cauſe, to take ſpeedily a good Reſolution ;
,, for that Affair cannot admit of any delay *(p)*."

All the Aſſiſtants were moved at this Speech,
leſs by the Vivacity of the Expreſſions than by
the Truth of the Matter. However, ſome were
of opinion to delay ſtill, but the Lord D'Andelot carried it for War.

The next Query was how to begin ? Some
were for ſeizing in every Province upon as many
Cities as poſſible, but that Scheme was eaſily refuted by the Inconveniencies wherewith it was
attended, as it had been experienced in the firſt
Civil War ; for having not Forces enough to
keep theſe Cities, they had loſt them almoſt as
ſoon as they had been Maſters of them. Others
were for ſeizing upon Orleans, and then to ſend
to the King their Remonſtrances. But that
Scheme was eaſily refuted by the Impoſſibility of
putting it into Execution, becauſe of the Fortreſs
lately built with a Garriſon in it.

At laſt they reſolved to take up Arms, and
to obſerve four things at the beginning. Firſt,
to ſeize upon few, but important Cities. Secondly, to raiſe a brisk Army. Thirdly, to cut to-
pieces the Switzers, by whoſe help the Catholicks
would

(p) Thuan. lib. XLII. La Noüe Diſcours polit. & milit.
p. 867, &c. This laſt Gentleman ſpeaks of three Conferences between the Prince and his Adherents ; and of intercepted Letters from Rome and Spain, concerning the Plot
againſt the Proteſtants.

would be always Masters of the Field.   Fourthly, to endeavour by all means the Expulsion of the Cardinal of Lorrain out of Court, because he was thought to be the Man who sollicited the King to destroy his Reformed Subjects.

Very great Difficulties were found in the Execution of the two last Articles.   Because the Cardinal and the Switzers were always with the King, and if they attacked these, and endeavoured to frighten the first, it would be said, that they attempted against his Majesty's Person, and not against others.   But it was answered, that the Event would show the Truth of their Intention, as it happened in the time of Charles VII, when he was only Dauphine, and had armed not against his Father or the Kingdom, but against the Duke of *Burgundy* the common Enemy of both :   That it was very well known that the French Nation had never attempted against their King's Person. Lastly, that if they were successful in this first attempt, it would be the properest means of putting a stop to the civil Divisions and Wars, because they would have an opportunity of declaring unto his Majesty several things which were industriously concealed from him ; and thereby obtain the Confirmation of the former Edicts, when those who endeavoured to surprize them should be surprized the first.

La Noue, who was present at these Consultations, and out of whose Memoirs I have extracted what I have just now related, observes, that that attempt upon the Court served only to exasperate the King against the Reformed to such a degree, that he never forgave them afterwards. And Montluc says, that it occasioned the Massacre of Bartholomew's-day. And indeed it cannot be denied that having no certainty at all of the Success, they made themselves obnoxious to
what-

whatever bad Judgment their Enemies would make concerning their Intention. And being not in a condition to juftify that, they minded no Evil againft his Majefty or his Mother, for want of Succefs, whereby they could have fatisfied the Publick as to the Sincerity and Uprightnefs of their faid Intention, that want of Succefs was enough to make them appear guilty of High Treafon. And it is needlefs to fay, that they intended only to deprive a Party of the King's Perfon, the Name and Authority whereof they abufed to the Deftruction of the State ; for tho' that be certainly true, their mifcarrying in the Attempt was enough to make them guilty, for the fame reafon, and becaufe of the bad confequences of fuch Attempts (*q*).

To be fure they were in the right by all the Laws Divine and Human, to defend themfelves againft the Violence of their Enemies, and had they feized upon fome of the beft Cities for that purpofe, they could not have been blamed for it. But to affault his own King, to make an attempt upon his facred Perfon, a young King ! and in the manner as they did, for they could not anfwer, but that he might have been killed by Chance and againft their own Will in the Fray : Indeed we muft fincerely acknowledge, that fuch a rafh and defperate Attempt cannot be warranted by any Law either Divine or Human.

But God forbid, that we fhould charge the Prince, the Admiral or his Brothers, the Count of La Rochefoucault, La Noüe, and the other Chiefs that were prefent at that Confultation, with any Defign of murdering the King or the Queen-Mother, and feizing upon the Kingdom,

as

(*q*) La Noüe Difcours polit. & milit. ch. xxvi. p. 867, &c. Than. lib. XLII. Mem. de Caftelnau, liv. VI. ch. iii.

as Montluc pretends, and that upon very flight Arguments; such as a little Note, inclosed in a Letter without Name, wherein these words were written. *From the 28th to the 30th of September, the King is taken, the Queen murdered, La Rochelle is taken, Montauban is taken, Lectoure is taken, and Montluc is dead.* Very likely this last Article put him in a greater fright than all the rest, especially because of what he had dreamed some Nights before, whereby he says himself, that he was put into such Agonies that his Bed Was all soaked with Sweat. He pretends, and that may be true, that he kept Spies even in the Consistories, who sent him Notice of every thing. But the strongest Argument is the Confession of about a hundred and more Witnesses, most of whom were Hugonots, that deposed before the Parliament of *Toulouse*, that the Design of their Chiefs was to murder the Queen-Mother, the King and his Brethren. But he did not care to let us know that these Confessions were extorted amidst the most cruel Tortures (r). And it is what D'Avila has revealed unto us. *Several,* says he, *have published*, (AND THAT WAS DECLARED AMIDST THE CRUEL TORTURES BY SOME GASCOONS, WHOM THE SIEUR MONTLUC CAUSED TO BE TAKEN AND PUT TO DEATH AT SUNDRY TIMES:) *that the principal view of that Attempt was to murder the King, the Queen, and the rest of her Children; that the Prince of Condé might ascend the Throne.* BUT SUCH A GREAT INHUMANITY WAS NOT BELIEVED BY EVERY ONE. It is true, that in another place, D'Avila relating a Speech which the Constable made to the Princes, the Knights of the Order, the Captains of Horse, and the Colonels of Foot, assembled in the King's Council, he makes him

to

(r) Comment. de Montluc, lib. VI. fol. 433——444.

to fay, *that they ought to employ themselves for the Defence of their own King, against those, who, in order to make one after their own fancy,* ENDEAVOUR TO DESTROY THE ROYAL FAMILY. Suppose that these laft words could amount to a Charge of High Treafon againft the Prince and his Adherents, the main point remains always undecided, viz. whether thefe words have been really uttered by the Conftable? Nay, whether the Conftable had ever made any fuch Speech, or any at all in this Occurrence? D'Avila quotes no Authority in his whole Hiftory for what he writes; and neverthelefs, being arrived at France only under the Reign of Henry the IIId, he could not have been a Witnefs of what he relates of the foregoing Reigns, therefore he ought to have quoted his Authorities, and as he don't do it, we may judge of this Speech as we have judged in our firft Volume of thofe of the Admiral, which being to be found only in his Book, took, very likely, their Origin in his own Head (s).

Notwithftanding this Juftification of the Prince of Condé, as to his Defigns in this Attempt, we have feen in our days the JESUIT DANIEL magnifying the Objects above what Montluc has faid; and fpeaking of this Attempt as if it was a Matter of Fact. But how doth he prove it? by thefe moft convincing Arguments.

XLIII. Daniel cenfured.

1. That it was not the firft time that the Hugonots had framed fuch an execrable Plot. Several Inftances are to be feen in the Duke of Never's Memoirs.

2. By a Book which was publifhed about that time, and was afcribed to one ROSIERES, Minifter of *Tierache*, wherein, among other damnable Errors, he had afferted, That it was lawful

to

(s) D'Avila, Tom. I. lib. IV. p. 168 & 175.

to murder a King or a Queen, who oppose themselves to the Reformation of the Church.

3. By a long Letter without Name, which
the Queen-Mother found in her way, one day,
as she was going to Mass, wherein she was threatened, that *she would be served with the same turn
as the Guisard, if she did not alter her Manners,
and if she did not grant a full Liberty of Conscience to the Reformed.*.

4. By Brantome's Testimony, who says, (but
without warranting the Truth of it) that the
Prince of Condé caused a piece of Silver Money
to be coined, with this Inscription ; *Lewis* XIII.
King of France, and that the Constable shewed
it in the Louvre in full Council on the 7th of
October 1567. NOTA BENE.

Lastly, ,, A new Proof of this Fact, says the
,, Jesuit, has been found in our days, which
,, seems unquestionable. *The Author of the Hi-
,, storical Treatise of the French Coins*, affirms,
,, that being in *London* he saw at a Goldsmith's
,, Shop, a Golden Piece, representing on one
,, side the Prince of Condé's Head, and on
,, the other a French 'Scutcheon, with this
,, Inscription, Ludovicus XIII. Dei Gratia
,, Francorum Rex primus Christianus.
,, That Prince willing to denote by that Title
,, of the first Christian King which he assumed,
,, that he was the first of the French Kings,
,, who had professed the pure Gospel, and the
,, Christianity purified of the Roman Church's
,, Superstitions : But very likely, adds he, they
,, thought proper at Court to feign as if they
,, were ignorant of such an Attempt ; for it is
,, certain that in the Manifesto's or Writs pub-
,, lished by the King's Orders, no mention was
,, made of it, at least distinctly, and which could

,, give

„ give to underſtand, that the Prince of Condé
„ had carried things to ſuch an Extremity (*t*)."

Two or three Reflections will be ſufficient to
confound the Calumniator, and to begin with the
Remark whereby he ends his Charge ; Can any
one in his right Senſes imagine, that if there had
been the leaſt likelihood that the Prince or his
Party had framed ſuch a Plot, the Court would
have been ſilent ? what more proper means could
the Queen-Mother have found for ruining the
Prince and his Party in the Minds of all the foreign Princes, and bereaving them of their Protection and Affiſtance, than this ? And indeed,
what Prince, what State, what Society in Europe would have undertaken their Defence, or
afforded them any Relief ? Was it the Queen of
England ? But Queen Elizabeth's Wiſdom and
Politicks did not allow her to countenance ſuch
a wicked Attempt, ſuppoſing that her Moral and
Chriſtian Virtues and Graces had not filled up her
Royal and Heroic Soul with a juſt Abhorrence
for ſuch heinous Crimes; ſhe had too much to do
at home for preſerving herſelf from the wicked
and deviliſh Attempts of the Jeſuits and their
Diſciples, to be ſure ſhe would not have encou-
couraged any ſuch thing abroad. Was it the
Emperor ? But Maximilian II. filled up the
Imperial Throne at that time : The Proteſtant
Princes of Germany were too great Lovers of
Juſtice and Probity ; they would have united
themſelves with the Catholicks of France, for
puniſhing ſeverely ſuch a wicked Act, rather than
for countenancing it. All the Reformed States
of Europe have always expreſſed the utmoſt Abhorrence for ſuch Deeds ; and ſome of them began at that time to feel the noiſome Influence
of the Jeſuitical Spirit. No other Society but
that

(*t*) Daniel Hiſt. de France, Charles IX. 1567, p. 852.

that of the Jefuits, could have afforded any Help or Relief for executing, or after the Execution of that execrable Crime, had they been fo much afraid of Charles IX. and his Mother, as they were of Henry III. and Henry IV. Therefore fince it was the true Intereft of the Queen-Mother to publifh in the moft folemn manner that Attempt of the Prince, or of his Party; fince having refolved with the King of Spain the utter Deftruction of the whole Reformed Body in France, nothing could be more conduceive to the Accomplifhment of her Defigns than to render them odious to all the Potentates of Europe; and fince nothing could be more efficacious for that purpofe, and deprive them of all afliftance, than the publifhing of that execrable Plot of the Prince and of his Party; we muft infer from the Silence of that Princefs, at a time when fo many ftrong Reafons obliged her to fpeak, either that fhe heard nothing of that Plot, or that having heard of it, fhe found it attended with fo many Inconfiftencies, that not only fhe judged it improbable, but even that it would caft a Blemifh upon her own Reputation, if fhe opened her Mouth to fpeak of it. Therefore the Queen's filence muft be taken as a moral Demonftration of the falfehood of this Imputation.

As to the other Reafons, wherewith Daniel endeavours to corroborate his Charge, they cannot ferve as Ground to entertain as much as a bare Sufpicion; he fays, that this was not the firft Attempt of that kind done by the Reformed: But where is the firft? We have feen in the firft Vol. when fpeaking of the Plot of Amboife, that notwithftanding his Falfifications in quoting Caftelnau's Memoirs, and Thuanus, he has not been able to make good his Accufation againft the Hugonots. I did not fee the Duke of Never's

Me-

Memoirs, but if I might judge of this Quotation of Father Daniel, by those of Castelnau, Thuanus and Daubigné, which he has not only misrepresented, but falsified too ; I dare say, that this Prince has never charged the Prince of Condé his Grand Uncle, with any such base Intent as that of murdering the King and his Brethren in order to ascend the Throne.

As to the Book whereof he speaks, and which, he says, was ascribed to Rosieres, a Minister, such a Doctrine as that which he quotes, smells so much of Jesuitism, that one cannot help being tempted to ascribe it to Father GUIGNARD, or VARADE, or JAMES COMMOLE', or to some other of the same Tribe, inasmuch, that every one knows that this darling Doctrine of the Jesuits, uttered at sundry times and in several manners with Approbation of their Society, has been universally rejected with the utmost Abhorrence by all the Reformed Churches of *France, England, Holland, Germany* and *Switzerland.* Therefore suppose for a moment that an Enthusiast amongst the Reformed of France, let him be of what rank or condition soever, had asserted such a Devilish Proposition ; for God's sake what way of arguing is this? Such a one, a Reformed, a Minister, had advanced such a Proposition; That it was lawful to murder a King, &c. The Prince of Condé, Admiral de Coligny, and others, were Reformed ; then they have attempted to murder the King. I might with as much reason argue thus against the Jesuits. Such a one, a Jesuit, named GIRARD, abused his Penitent Miss GA-DIERE in the most scandalous manner ; Father Daniel and others are Jesuits ; then they have abused their Penitents in the most scandalous manner. Shall I not be censured as a wicked Calumniator, if before I draw such an Inference

I do not evince this Premise, that the Principles of the Jesuits have a natural tendency to indulge their Disciples in all manner of Lewdness and Wickedness? It is the same thing in our case.

As to the pieces of Gold and Silver Coin, whereof one was exhibited in the King's Council in October 1567, and t'other was seen at *London* by Monsieur *Le Blanc* ; we must observe that Brantome does not affirm the Fact as to the first : but let it be true as well as the second, what can this prove against the Prince ? Those pieces, had they been coined by his Orders, or only his Consent, nay, with his Knowledge ; this ought to have been made out, before we charge him with the Crime of High Treason ; but not a word of it. We have said in our second Vol. that his Highness had been obliged to erect a Mint at Orleans during the first civil War, that he coined Money there, but with the King's Stamp and Effigy. Now is it improbable that some of the Workmen, either of their own Accord, or bribed by some other inconsiderate Man, or blinded with a false Zeal, had coined a certain number of such Pieces in secret ? This is certainly more likely than that the Prince had any hand in it, and that the King and the whole Council had overlook'd it, so far, as not to make any Complaint of it. In a word, we must not judge by the Appearances only, but we must join all the Circumstances together to frame a right Judgment, especially in such Cases as this, wherein the Reputation of a Prince of the Blood, and of a Million of People, his Adherents, lies at stake.

The Prince and his Confederates being resolved to follow the abovesaid Scheme, they prepared every thing necessary for the Execution. It had been thought proper to seize all at the same
time

time upon *Lyons*, *Thoulouse*, and *Troyes*. But those who had taken upon them the Execution, miscarried, either by their own Fault, or by Misfortune, as well as almost all their other Designs whereupon they had resolved after so many Consultations and Deliberations. And on the contrary, several others succeeded against their Expectations whereof they had very little thought, and which were very useful and advantageous unto them. Whereby it is evident, that Men conspicuous for their Sagacity, Prudence and Experience, very often consult, and propose to execute; but that it is God Almighty who disposes of every thing as he thinks meet.

The Prince had appointed the 29th of September for to meet together on Horseback, at a place called *Rozay* in the Province of *Brie*. There many of the neighbouring Nobility and Gentry came to his Highness, who was attended by the Admiral, D'Andelot, the Count of La Rochefoucault. They were already assembled, to the number of four hundred Horse, before the Court had any Notice of it, or at least before the Queen would give any Credit to the Advices sent by Montluc some Weeks before, nor even to those of Castelnau, which he had given several days before. But at last the News being confirmed by too many Witnesses for doubting any longer of it, the Court removed from *Monceaux* to *Meaux*; from whence, in order to give time to the Switzers to come to the King's assistance, the Queen sent the Marshal of Montmorency unto the Prince, to amuse him by a Parley. He asked him what was the matter, and spinned out the time until he could guess that the Switzers were arrived; his Message was to the following purport. To inquire about their Business; to blame the Confederates. For if they had a mind

to

to petition the King for something, why did they not come to him in a peaceable rather than in a warlike manner. Where is your Fealty, says he, where your Allegiance? What will your Enemies say? To what Hatred does not your Highness expose himself, seeing that being one of the first Princes of the Blood you have alienated so many Noblemen from the King's Affections, inciting them by your Example to come to the King in such a disrespectful manner. Lay down your Arms quickly, and come to his Majesty like humble Petitioners: This is the friendly Advice which I give you. To this the Prince replied; That these Names of Faith and Allegiance were become obsolete long ago, seeing that those who boasted of them had violated the Sacredness of them, and were become, by their Ambition, the King's real Enemies: That they had armed themselves for a just Cause, having been forced unto it in their own Defence. As for the rest, the Sincerity of their Designs and Intentions will be made manifest by the Event, if they did but succeed in their Undertaking, and will put an end to all civil Commotions.

While they were disputing together, a Messenger came to the Marshal of Montmorency to let him know that the Switzers were very near, and marched with full Speed to *Meaux*. Whereupon the said Marshal returned to Court, and the Prince of Condé continued his March with the Confederates, in order to join the Auxiliaries, if they came soon enough; but they arrived too late for executing the intended Scheme, because the Switzers had already joined with the King.

When the Marshal of Montmorency was arrived with the Petition he had received of the Prince and the Confederates, and had related what he had done and heard amongst them, a
Council

Council was held at the Conftable of Montmorency's Houfe, to confider what was to be done
in fuch an Emergency : The Conftable voted
for ftaying at Meaux, and infifted upon it with
fo great ftrength of Arguments that the Queen-
Mother affented to it for that time.

But either out of levity, or having been ftrongly follicited by the Cardinal of Lorrain, (who
could not fee without the greateft Spite fo fair an
opportunity of gratifying his Ambition, and of
ingratiating his Nephews, who were of Age, into the People's Affections, elapfing without improving it) (*u*) fhe altered her Mind the very
fame day upon a very flight pretence ; fhe called
again the Council in the Duke of Nemours's
Houfe, becaufe he was lame with the Gout ; there
it was reprefented that the number of the Confederates increafed every moment ; that it was
to be feared left the King fhould be befieged in a
place without Defence, tho' he had with him fix
thoufand Switzers ; therefore the Cardinal's Party prevailing (*v*), it was refolved to fet out that
N 3 very

(*u*) Thuan. lib. XLII. p. 468.
(*v*) It feems to me, that Reafon as well as the Spirit of
Party prevailed together in this Deliberation. And indeed
if Caftelnau is to be credited, he was the firft who gave Notice of the Plot to the Court ; he difcovered it by chance as
he returned from Flanders, where he had been to compliment, in the King's Name, the Duke of Alva, upon his arrival in that Country. He was not credited at Court, nay
he was chid for it by the Conftable and the Chancellor,
neverthelefs, his Report was confirmed by fome Couriers
coming from Lyons the next day ; but the Court was ftill
incredulous, and even refufed to give Credit to one of Caftelnau's Brethren fent by the Queen on purpofe to *reconnoitre* ;
but at laft they opened their Eyes upon the relation of *Titus*
de Caftelnau. Now what better Courfe could the Court
take, than to leave a place without Defence, before the Confederates fhould be ftrengthened by the Increafe of their Number, and avoid by that means a fhedding of Blood, which
inevitably would be fpilt in the fury of the firft Onfet ; that
and

very Night for *Paris*, notwithstanding whatever the Chancellor could say to the contrary, and his Exclamations, that it was to expose the King to the greatest Danger ; that it was to betray the Kingdom ; to deprive themselves of all means of Peace ; to involve themselves in a fatal Necessity of entering into a cruel War, for gratifying the Inclinations of some ambitious Men, who could not abide with Quietness and Peace ; and that those who being suborned had spread industriously these Rumours, deserved to be hanged. But all this availed nothing more than to encrease the Suspicions against the Chancellor, who was obliged the next Year to resign his Office, and to retire from Court.

The Resolution being taken, the Switzers were ordered to be ready at Midnight ; which Order was chearfully obey'd, for having rested but three Hours at most, they came to their Posts and marched, Colours flying, in good Order ; the King with his Nobility, to the number of nine hun-

and several other Reasons, which the Reader can easily discover, makes me to say with Reverence due to the respectable Name of THUANUS, that he is not in the right to blame the Resolution the Court took on this Occasion. I have said that Castelnau discovered the Plot by chance ; it was as follows : As he came from *Bruxelles* in his way to France, he was met by some French Gentlemen with whom he had been formerly acquainted ; they had been sent into the *Low Countries* to exhort the Reformed to oppose the Duke of Alva's coming in : They desired Castelnau to give them leave to improve his Company ; which being granted, they talk'd with him concerning the Suspicions and Mistrusts of the Prince of Condé, the Admiral, and the Hugonots of France : They told him, that in order to be rid of them, they were all prepared to rise in Arms, and to begin a War the first : That for that end, they intended to seize upon the King, the Queen his Mother, and his Brethren, and their Council, to punish those who endeavoured to destroy their Religion, and the Defenders thereof, and to hinder their Enemies and Ill-wishers from doing them any further harm. See Memoirs de Castelnau, liv. VI. ch. iv.

hundred, almoſt unarmed, and riding for the moſt part very ſorry Horſes, being in the Centre. When they had marched about four Leagues, they met with the Confederate Troops, conſiſting of four hundred Horſe or thereabouts, armed only with Piſtols, Swords, and Cuiraſſes: then the Conſtable ſeeing that he could go no further without fighting, ordered the Switzers to halt, that they might withſtand the Confederates. The Prince of Condé, with a few of his Attendants, came out of the Ranks, and deſired to ſpeak with the King, which being refuſed, ſeveral Skirmiſhes enſued between his Troop and the Switzers. The Conſtable thinking that the Matter might come to a general Battle, and ſeeing that the number of Skirmiſhers increaſed apace, thought proper to ſend the King by ſome By-ways, known only to the Natives of that Country, to Paris; where he arrived ſafely with few Attendants. Mean while the Confederates diſcontinued not their Skirmiſhes, and the Switzers, according to cuſtom in ſuch caſes, having kiſſed the Ground, and devoted their Bodies and Souls to the King's Service, diſpoſed themſelves to fight. They bravely withſtood all the Onſets of their Enemies, and continuing their March, they repulſed them for twelve Miles together; they arrived ſafe at Bourget, four Miles diſtant from Paris, having loſt only thirty Men, which were killed out of their Rank (x).

The Confederates ſeeing that the King had been ſent away, deſiſted from their Purſuit, and arrived at *Clayes* on the 30th of September; there they ſtayed five days waiting for the coming of the Auxiliaries that came from *Picardy, Champaign,*

N 4

(x) Thuan. ibid. Dinoth. Hiſt. lib. III. pag. 188. Caſtelnau. lib. VI. ch. v. he ſays, that the Confederates were five or ſix hundred in number.

I

paign, *Burgundy*, and the adjacent Countries, as well as for an Anſwer from the King to the Petition which the Marſhal of Montmorency had tendered in their Name to his Majeſty.

When the Court was arrived at Paris on the 29th of September, according to Thuanus, the Cardinal of Lorrain thought proper to go to *Rheims* ; but being near *Chateau-Thierry*, he fell in with a Party that went to join the Confederates, and tho' he rode a very ſwift Spaniſh Horſe, he eſcaped very narrowly from being taken ; he loſt all his Plate and Baggage, which was divided amongſt the Soldiers.

XLV.
The ſecond civil War.

The Prince and his Confederates doubting not but that the King would deny all their Demands, ſent Orders to their Agents in Poitou, Guienne, Languedoc, Dauphiné and Auvergne, to haſten the March of the Troops that were ſent from theſe Provinces ; and having received thoſe that were come from the neighbouring Provinces, they thought proper to hinder the Proviſions from coming into Paris : for that end they ſeized upon *Montereau-Faut-Yonne* above, and *St. Denis* below that City, near the borders of the Seine, which commands all the Country on that ſide. They put a Garriſon in the firſt ; and the Prince took his Quarters at St. Denis. As he paſſed he burnt all the Mills between the Gates of the *Temple* and of *St. Honoré*, which ſerved only to increaſe the King's Anger, and the Hatred of the *Pariſians*.

Before this, Orleans had been ſeized on the 28th of September for the Reformed. La Noue having been ſent by the Prince for that purpoſe with only 15 Horſes, according to D'Aubigné, executed bravely, but very cunningly, his Commiſſion, with the Help of the Reformed Inhabitants, with whom he kept Correſpondence, and

obliged

obliged Captain Caban to capitulate for the
Castle wherein he lodged, with his Garrison.
Then having settled every thing for the Preser-
vation of that place, he set out to raise Troops ;
and having conferred with the Vidame of
Chartres, the Count of Montgomery, the
Count of Suze, Charles de Beaumanoir
Lavardin, and some others, each of them took
their Division, and travelled with an incredible
Diligence through *Britany, Anjou, Touraine, High
Normandy, Perche,* and *Beauffe* ; they assembled
together a Body of Troops of a thousand Horse
and three thousand Foot, wherewith they took
Janville, Eftampes, Dourdens, where they left
Garrisons ; then by the Prince's Orders the rest
continued their March without any further delay, and having overcome several Difficulties,
they crossed the *Seine* at *St. Clou,* with Boats
prepared for that purpose, and came to *St. Ouyn,*
where they were covered by the Admiral ; and
having joined all their Troops together, they
made a Body of two thousand Horse and four
thousand Foot (*y*).

The more we consider this Step of the Prince
and his Confederate, the more we find their
boldness very surprizing : With a handful of
Troops they pretend to besiege a City of such large
extent as Paris was, full of People, with the King,
his whole Court, the most experienced Officers,
and six thousand Switzers, besides his own Guards.
Nothing but Despair could engage the Prince to
attempt such a thing. It is what La Noue observes in his political and military Discourses.

,, When Men, says he, are spurred on by Ne-
,, cessity, their Courage increases double, and
,, their

(*y*) Amirault vie du Seig. de la Noüe, corrected and improved in this place, with the help of Thuanus and others.
Thuan. lib. XLII. pag. 473.

,, their firſt Fears loſe their Grounds, they are
,, leſs afraid to run into the moſt difficult and
,, hazardous Attempts.   It was then the caſe of
,, the Reformed.   For ſeeing the Sword already
,, drawn, and hanging over their Heads, they
,, reſolved to eſcape rather with their Arms than
,, with their Legs; and overlooking ſeveral Con-
,, ſiderations, they thought that it behoved them
,, to be magnanimouſly the firſt with their Ene-
,, mies. (*And three things rendered this beginning*
awful, wherewith the Catholicks were confounded
at firſt).   1. The univerſal Inſurrection all over
,, the Kingdom, all on one and the ſame time.
,, Many Reformed, that were not in the Secret,
,, were ſurprized at it, and many Catholicks that
,, did not expect it were frightened by it; had
,, theſe begun the firſt, they would, perhaps,
,, have been more ſevere to the Reformed, than
,, the Reformed were to them.   However, they
,, were mighty ſorry to ſee ſo many Cities ſeiz-
,, ed upon all at once by the Reformed; and
,, ſome of them ſaid, The Brethren have
,, ſurprized us unawares, but, one time or an-
,, other, we ſhall requite them for it.   And they
,, were as good as their word——Some thought
,, that ſo many Notices ſent throughout the Pro-
,, vinces would diſcover the Enterprize.   But
,, this happened only in few places (*eſpecially in*
Languedoc and Guienn) who were, however, the
,, moſt important (z).   2. Their boldneſs in aſ-
,, ſaulting ſix thouſand Switzers, and obliging
,, them to give ground with leſs than five hun-
,, dred Horſe.   True it is, that according to the
,, Scheme laid, they were to be a greater number,
,, eſpe-

(z) This ſhows that the Conſtable and Chancellor's opinion above-mentioned, that the Court ſhould ſtay at Meaux,
and come to a Parley with the Prince, was not the beſt;
ſince the Inſurrection was general all over the Provinces, it
was impoſſible to quell ſo ſoon the Tumult, and a War was
unavoidable.

,, efpecially fome Harquebufiers on horfeback :
,, however they failed not to take the Field, but
,, to be time enough at the appointed place ; and
,, becaufe they were fo few, the Chiefs of the
,, Reformed durft not venture a general Charge
,, with that thick Body, much like a Foreft.
,, Befides that their Horfes were half fpent with
,, the long March they had done. Neverthelefs I
,, heard them fay, that had the Troops of Pi-
,, cardy, of 150 Horfe ftrong, been arrived, they
,, would have tried their Fortune, caufing the
,, Harquebufiers to alight, and charging with
,, their Squadrons on three Sides. But tho'
,, they had done fo, the Succefs would have
,, been ftill very dubious. 3. The feizing upon
,, the Town of *St. Denis,* where the Prince
,, of Condé took his Quarters with all his Forces,
,, and in two neighbouring Villages, which he
,, caufed to be retrenched, to befiege Paris on
,, that fide. All thefe things being confidered
,, even by the beft Captains among the Catho-
,, licks, they wondered at it, and thought that
,, the faid Prince expected fpeedily fome great
,, Forces, and had fome good Intelligence, both
,, in the City and at Court; for otherwife, faid
,, they, he would not have been fo bold, being
,, fo weak, to come and take his Quarters fo
,, near us. And the Admiral, a wife and great
,, Captain, would not have advifed this, had he
,, not fome fecret help. Therefore they pro-
,, longed the time till they had gathered all their
,, Forces. Several others were much offended at
,, their Chiefs, becaufe they fuffered fuch a hand-
,, ful of Men to come and dare them every day
,, by continual Skirmifhes ; feeing that they had
,, in the City near ten thoufand Men ready to
,, fight them, and that it was a great fhame to
,, fee an Ant befieging an Elephant. But me-
,, thinks the Confiderations of others were more
                                            ,, wife,

,, wife, who affirmed, that it would be notori-
,, oufly imprudent to hazard the whole Body of
,, the State, which is, as it were, inclofed in the
,, Walls of Paris, by a Battle even againft Mad-
,, men, fay they, who have now no other Counfel-
,, lor but their Defpair, nor any other Riches than
,, their Arms and Horfes. And that having in
,, their Poffeffion fuch a facred thing as the King's
,, Perfon, it behoved them to do every thing
,, with Security, and that in a fhort time the
,, good effects of fo wife a Refolution would be
,, felt. So there was between the Wifdom of
,, the one and the Temerity of others a difcord-
,, ing Agreement, if I may fay fo, for fome days."
So far the great La Noüe (*a*).

XLVI.
*Several
Parleys be-
tween the
Court and
the Prince.*

Paris being blocked up, and Provifions beginning to grow fcarce in the City, the Court fent
feveral Meffages to the Prince, feigning a great
Inclination to bring Matters to fome Agreement,
and to give all reafonable Satisfaction to the Prince
and his Adherents.

In one of the Petitions fent by the Prince to
the King, he required, 1. That the King fhould
disband the foreign Troops that were in his Service. 2. That he would be pleafed to receive
kindly, the Prince, and the Lords his Adherents,
when having laid down their Arms, they would
go and tender their Remonftrances to his Majefty, concerning the many Vexations and Injuftices done to the Reformed, and to redrefs
kindly their Grievances. 3. To punifh feverely
their Calumniators. 4. To reftore to their full
Force the Edicts granted in behalf of the Reformed, which had been enervated by fubfequent
Interpretations, and Declarations. 5. To prefer
to Dignities, Honours and Offices, thofe of his
Majefty's Subjects, of what Religion foever,
who,

(*a*) La Noüe Difc. pol. & mil. pag. 879, 880, 881, &c.

who, by their perfoual Qualifications, fhould deferve them. 6. To eafe the People from thofe Taxes and Impofts whereby they were overloaded through the Suggeftion and Avarice of the *Italians*, and other Blood-fuckers, who bore fway with the Court. 7. To affemble the General States of the Kingdom, who might, with a full freedom, frame fome wholefome Laws for reforming the ill Adminiftration of the Government.

That Petition having been brought to Court by Lignerolles, the Queen-Mother was extremely incenfed at it, being a Princefs of a lavifh Temper ; the new Taxes every day invented and loaded upon the People, were fcarce fufficient for gratifying her Inclinations. Therefore taking for herfelf what the Prince faid of the Italians, and thinking that he had a mind to frighten her with the threatning of the General States, and to deprive her of the Adminiftration of the Government ; fhe provoked the whole Court againft the Reformed, and that the more eafily, inafmuch that it was reported at Court, that the Prince had caufed a Proclamation to be fet up, in his own Name, at *Montereau-faut-yonne*, and feveral other places, which was to the fame Purport with the faid Petition : So inftead of an Anfwer, fhe fent on the 7th of October an Herald, in the King's Name, to fummon the Prince and his Adherents, to lay down their Arms, and to come to pay their Homage and Duty to the King, as their lawful Sovereign, conftituted by God over them to govern them : Or to declare in Writing, that thefe Troops were affembled with their Approbation, fo that the King might decree what he fhould think proper.

The Prince, and the Lords his Adherents were fomewhat confounded at this Summons, and moft part of them were of opinion to moderate

rate

rate their Demands. They were sensible that they should expose themselves to the Hatred of foreign Princes, especially those of Germany, was it made publick that they mixed together Political Affairs with those of Religion ; and that the Zeal of their Friends and Allies would quite grow cool, as soon as they should be acquainted that they undertook to prescribe Rules to their King for the Civil Government of the State. Therefore they unanimously agreed to send another Petition to his Majesty, wherein they demanded nothing else but Liberty of Conscience, and the free and publick Profession of their Religion throughout the Kingdom ; as to the rest, they most humbly besought his Majesty to forgive them for having interfered with such things: They intreated him, not to put any bad Construction upon their Meaning, but to look upon what they had said concerning Taxes, and the convening of the General States, only as Counsels proceeding from the sincere Heart of his most faithful Subjects, who truly concerned themselves in his own Glory, the Prosperity of his Reign, and the Welfare of the whole Kingdom, but not for prescribing any thing upon that Subject to his Majesty, &c.

This Petition being brought to Court, caused great Alterations in their Minds ; the Wisest and most Moderate thought, that since the Confederates desired nothing else but Liberty of Conscience and Freedom of Religion, there were yet some Hopes of bringing Matters to an Agreement. The Queen at first exclaimed against it ; being quite altered by the Increase of her Authority since the Duke of Guise's Death, and the decay of that great Power *(which she had so much dreaded)* and by the Cardinal of Lorrain's Adulations, she endeavoured to sow discord between the Constable

and

and the Colignies, his Nephews, whose Union and Concord during the Peace, was suspicious unto her. However, the Constable's Interest prevailed on this Occasion, and notwithstanding her Opposition, it was resolved to try another Conference.

The Constable himself, the Marshals of Montmorency and Cossé, Biron, the Secretary L'Aubespine, came to *la Chapelle*, a Place lying halfway from Paris to St. Denis, where the Prince, the Colignies, the Vidame of Chartres, the Count of Saulx and de Cany, repaired. But whereas, these last insisted upon the free publick Profession of the Reformed Religion throughout the Kingdom, without any Distinction of Places or Persons ; and that the Constable answered that the King would never consent to any thing like, and said that the Edicts granted unto them, were not perpetual ; that the last was only for a time ; that the King intended not to suffer two Religions in his Dominions, but rather to endeavour by all means to reunite the Reformed with the Catholick Church ; and that he chose to be at War with them, rather than be exposed to the Hatred or Suspicions of the neighbouring Princes, upon that account ; the Conferences broke up, and they parted without doing any thing, and both Parties disposed themselves for War. *(b)*

All this while Castelnau had been sent to Bruxelles to ask aid of the Duke of Alva; for tho' the Levies of Troops had been ordered throughout the Kingdom, before the Insurrection of the Reformed, as D'Avila observes *(c)*, nevertheless these Forces, being dispersed in the Provinces, could not be so soon ready to come to Paris ; therefore it was agreed to send Castelnau
with

(b) Thuanus, lib. 42. pag. 471, 72, 73.   *(c)* D'Avila, Tom. 1. liv. 4. pag. 171.

with all speed to desire the Governour of the Low Countries, to assist the King in this Occurrence, and to send him three or four Regiments of Spaniards and Italian Foot, with the thousand Light Spanish Horse, and the thousand Italian which he had brought along with him. But the crafty Spaniard, who desired no better than to see the Civil War kindled in the Kingdom, amused maliciously for several Weeks the French Ambassador, and at last denied such a Succour as was desired ; instead of which, he offered four or five thousand Lanskenets, and fifteen or sixteen hundred Horse of the Gendarmery of the Low-Countries. Castelnau accepted of the Gendarmery, which was led by the Count of AREMBERG, which however arrived at Paris but one or two days after the Battel of St. Denis.

The News of the coming of these Troops being brought to the Confederates Camp, Montgomery and D'Andelot went with a Detachment of the Prince's Army, the first to Pontoise, t'other to Poissy, to oppose their Passage *(d)*. But the Constable (offended at the Murmurings of the Parisians, who complained loudly that he juggled with his Nephews the Colignies) improved this Opportunity to fight the Confederates. Few days before, he had drove the Reformed out of several Villages and Places which they occupied along the *Seine*, and by that means had opened a free Passage for Provisions to come into the City ; but for all that the People were not satisfied, they required that the Confederates, who made incursions every day to the very Gates of Paris, should be intirely drove out. Therefore the Constable having sent out of the City, on the 9th of November, some Troops of Horse to *reconnoitre* the Strength of the Confederates and their

*(d)*Mem. de Castelnau, liv. vi. ch. 6, 7.

their Situation, and for harraffing them by frequent Skirmifhes, underftanding that D'Andelot
and Montgomery were gone as above faid, came
out from Paris on the 10th, with the whole
Army, confifting of fixteen Thoufand Foot of
the old Bands, and three Thoufand Horfe, befides the Trained Bands of Paris, and fourteen
Cannon ; the Prince had no more than fifteen
Hundred Horfes, and twelve Hundred Foot,
without any Cannon or Field-Piece, and even
the Horfe were very ill armed, moft part of the
Lanciers having only fome Poles of St. Denis's
Fair inftead of Lances. The Conftable thought
that the Prince would never venture to fight upon
fuch a great Inequality, and that it would be an
eafy matter for himfelf to cut his fmall Troop to
pieces, or to diflodge him from St. Denis and
other neighbouring Places occupied by him, or
at leaft to inclofe them in that Town, and have
them at his mercy. But he miftook in his Conjectures, for the Prince was no lefs eager for
fighting than his Aggreffors.

I fhall not enter into the Particulars of that
moft renowned Day, called of St. Denis, from the
Place wherein the Battel was fought, and wherein
an Ant was feen engaging an Elephant with fuch
Superiority of Courage as to make him all over
bloody, without being crufhed under its Feet.
None but Frenchmen, in the Heat of a Party,
would venture fo far as the Confederates did on
this Occafion ; to engage their Enemies, without
Cannon, with fo fmall a number of Foot, to cope
with a Royal Army compofed of the beft Troops,
rather than to diflodge out of a Place which they
could not keep long ; the Wifdom of the Prince,
the Admiral, and other Chiefs might be called in
queftion, was it not for other Confiderations :
and the firft is, that having ftayed fo long in

XLVII.
*The Battel
of St. Denis.*

thofe

those Quarters, their Enemies had time to strengthen themselves to that degree, that it was almost impossible for them to escape without flying. Secondly, their main Forces consisted chiefly of Nobility gathered from several Parts of the Kingdom, which ought to be employed, left they should disband without doing any thing, for want of Furniture, and of what was necessary for their Subsistence. Thirdly, it was much for their Credit amongst the Foreigners, to take such a Resolution, for had they suffered themselves to be shut up in St. Denis, or had they fled without fighting, their Reputation would have sunk abroad, they would have been looked upon as a Party, quite despicable for its Weakness. Fourthly, they were not without Hopes that they should get the day, by some unforeseen Accident, either because their Enemies, despising their small Number, would be less cautious, or because they would be frightned at their stout Countenance, not expecting that they would have ever been bold enough to wait for them and withstand them ; besides that, they considered that the Days were then very short and dark ; that it would take a long time before the whole Army could be marched out of Paris, and be drawn up in Battalia, and before the Guns could be ready to play ; that therefore, suppose they should be worsted, it would be easy for them to retreat by means of the Darkness ; in a word, that it was better to die with Honour, than to live with Reproach ; and several things happened as they had foreseen.

The Royal Army could not be drawn up in Battalia, nor the Guns be ready, till late in the Evening ; they were surprised to find the Confederates resolve to withstand them ; their Artillery was not well levelled, and fired over their Enemies head ; and the Confederates assaulted

with

with such a Bravery, that their Enemies were surprised at it, and suffered much from their first Onset. D'Aubigní relates, that a Turkish Ambassador having been brought to Montmartre to see the Fight, exclaimed several times, *O, had my Master only two Thousand Men like those White Coats,* (the Confederates) *at the Head of each of his Armies, the whole World would not stand before him for two Years together!* The Battle lasted but three quarters of an Hour; the Confederates being overpowered by Numbers, retreated in good Order to St. Denis, being pursued only for half a quarter of an Hour. The Prince of Condé had a Horse killed under him, and was very near being taken : The Admiral was carried amidst the Enemies by his hard-mouthed Horse, and was not to be seen for some time, insomuch that the News was brought to Court that he had been taken Prisoner, brought to Paris, and concealed in some House ; the Queen giving credit to that Report, caused a search to be made; and whereas she suspected Christophorus de la Chapelle aux Ursins, because of some Affinity between him and the Admiral, she ordered his House to be thoroughly searched from the top to the bottom. The Constable was desperately wounded by Stuart, some say by another Scotchman, and was carried half dead out of the Field, to Paris, which occasioned great Confusions in his Army. The Royalists Loss amounted to above three Hundred Horse, and two or three Hundred Foot, but no Persons of great Note, the Count of Chaulnes excepted, and forty-four Officers ; many were wounded, some of whom died of their Wounds a few days after, amongst whom, the most considerable were, the Constable, and his Nephew Claude de Battarnay, Baron of Anton, a very promising Youth. On the Re-

O 3   formed

Charles
IX.
1567.
Pope Pius
V.

formed Side they loſt above three Hundred Horſe, and a few Foot, and about 50 of the Prime Nobility, amongſt whom were the Counts of Saulx and de la Suze, and the Vidame of Amiens *(e)*.

D'Andelot who had been ſent for in all haſte, arrived at Midnight, and the next day the Troops being reinforced by his coming, they came again into the Field of Battel, and endeavoured to provoke their Enemies to come out again and renew the Fight ; but it was in vain, and that for three Reaſons, 1. Becauſe of the Condition the Conſtable was in ; for not being able to ſtir, there was no body to command the Army. 2. The general Conſternation of the Pariſians ; for tho' the Royaliſts might boaſt themſelves that they had got the day, ſince they had been Maſters of the Field of Battel, nevertheleſs that ſmall Advantage coſt them ſo dear, that it was to them a matter of Sorrow rather than Joy. 3. They were afraid in the City leſt the Aſſaſſins and the ſtarving Mob, which were in great Numbers, having raiſed ſome tumult, ſhould plunder the Houſes and murder the People ; and likewiſe leſt thoſe who countenanced the Confederates, ſhould ſeize upon ſome of the Gates and introduce them into the City. Therefore the Confederates ſeeing that the Royal Army could not be provoked to fight again, they went back to their former Quarters, after having burnt La Chapelle and ſome Windmills at the Gates of Paris.

XLVIII.
The Conſta-
ble's Death.
The next day, the 12th of November, died Annas of Montmorency, Great Conſtable of France, in the 74th Year of his Age, and not

near

(e) La Nouë Diſc. Pol. & Mil. pag. 884—892. Caſtelnau Mem. liv. vi. ch. 8. Addit. aux Mem. de Caſtelnau, liv. vi. ch. 7. pag. 458. Thuan. Hiſt. lib. xlii. pag. 477. 8, 9. Dinothi Hiſt. lib. iii pag. 194—198. This laſt ſays that the Battel laſted for two Hours, but he is oppoſed by all the former. D'Aubigné, tom. I. liv. iv. ch. 9 & 10.

near 80, as some have said, much less an hundred, as Voltaire says. He was a Man conspicuous for his Sagacity, and for his great Experience in Military Affairs, caring but very little what the People said; he had done great Services to the Kingdom under Francis I, and Henry II. and would have been still very serviceable under Francis II, and Charles IX, had he endeavoured to reconcile the Heads of the two Parties, rather than adhere to any. He had been present at eight Battles, in four whereof he had commanded in Chief, but generally he had been unsuccessful. His Bigotry went so far, that it carried him to do Things much unbecoming his Character and high Station, whereby he got the Nick-name of Captain Burning-Pews, as above said in our 2d Vol. It is said, that as he came out of Paris at the Head of the Army, he told those that were there present, *This Day will evince my Innocence, and deliver me from the Reproaches of the People, and the Jealousies of my Enemies; for either I shall come back Vanquisher, or a dead Man.* And as he was on his Death-bed, a Fryar being come to comfort him, he desired him to let him alone, for, says he, *it would be a very shameful thing, should I have lived so long without learning how to die a quarter of an Hour.* D'Avila admires this, but, if it is true that the Constable had ever uttered such Words, which I question much, they shew, methinks, either that the Fryar had nothing but some of his old Tales of Purgatory to tell him, or that the Constable was very sorry to die; for a truely honest Man in his Condition never refuses Counsels and Comforts to support him, unless, by the Violence of the Sickness, he should be out of his Wits *(f).* However, he was buried

O 3

(f) What makes me to question this Account of D'Avila, is, that he makes the Constable say that he had lived 80
Years;

ried with a funeral Pomp almoſt Royal, by the
Queen Mother's Orders, his Effigy being carried
in the Proceſſion. Her Majeſty paid the Charges
of it very willingly ; ſhe looked upon the Death
of her Critick as a great Bleſſing to her. She was
very cautious not to fill up the Vacancy but by a
Perſon intirely in her Dependance, and upon
whom ſhe might ſafely rely ; therefore ſhe engaged the King by her Intreaties, to name the
Duke of Anjou his Brother for his Lieutenant-
General, which ſhe obtained at laſt with great reluctancy, for the King ſaw, not without Jealouſy,
the Preference which his Mother gave to his Brother in her Affections, and he was afraid to in-
veſt him with ſuch great Power and Authority,
which he might abuſe to his prejudice. However, having complied, the Queen named for
his Council, whereby he ought to govern himſelf,
the Dukes of Nemours and of Longueville, and
the Marſhals of Coſſé and Tavanes, and ſome
others.

XLIX.
*The King's
Forces in-
creaſe eve-
ry day.*

Every day arrived at Paris ſome new Re-in-
forcements from the Provinces, and I do not
know where D'Avila has read that Montluc excuſed himſelf to ſend any, on pretence that he
wanted all his Forces to oppoſe the Huguenots in
Guienn and Languedoc ; ſeeing that Montluc
affirms poſitively in his Memoirs, that tho' the
King, (who had acquainted him by his Letters of
the Attempt of the Huguenots, to ſurprife him
at Meaux) did not command him to ſend any
Succours, thinking that he could hardly keep all
the Countries of his own Government with the
Troops he had ; nevertheleſs he gave notice to
his Majeſty of the Succours which he intended to
ſend,

Years ; now it is certain that he was but 74, according to
his Epitaph, and he could not miſtake himſelf ſo far in the
reckoning of his Age. D'Avila, liv. iv. pag. 178.

send, and that the Succour was not even incon- Charles
siderable, since it consisted of twelve Hundred IX.
Horse or thereabout, and thirty Companies of 1567.
Foot, which marched out from *Limoges* at the Pope Pius V.
latter end of October or the beginning of November, and took their way thro' *Moulins*, under
the Command of Terride (g).

    The Confederates having got notice of the L.
March of their Auxiliaries from Germany, were *The Prince*
very glad of that Opportunity to dislodge from *marches out of St. De-*
St. Denis, under pretence of going to meet the *nis.*
Germans in Lorrain ; they began to be afraid lest
the Royal Forces increasing every day, they
should be besieged in that little Town, or at least
hindred from joining the said Auxiliaries ; therefore they marched out on the 15th or 16th of
November, and went to Montereau-faut-
Yonne, where they left Rance with seven Companies of Foot, and proceeded into Lorrain to
receive the Auxiliaries. The Prince had sent his
Orders to all the Provinces to hasten the March
of the Troops that were raised in *Poitou, Angoumois*, and *Xaintonge*.

    Several Cities had been already seized for the LI.
Prince ; Soissons, in Picardy ; Auxerre and Ma- *Several*
con, in Burgundy ; Valence, in Dauphiné ; Nimes, *Provinces*
and Montpellier, in Languedoc ; Dieppe, in *and Towns declare for*
Normandy, and several others in other Provinces, *the Prince,*
either had been seized, or had declared themselves
of their own accord for the Confederates.

    The Troops of Guienn being in readiness, *And send*
marched, to the number of three Regiments of *Troops to his*
Foot, each Regiment composed of nine Ensigns, *Assistance.*
commanded by very experienced Officers, such
as Pardaillan, Piles, and Champagnac,
who had been formerly a Monk, but was turned

O 4 to

(g) D'Avila, tom. i. liv. iv. pag. 174.   Commentaires
de Blaise de Montluc. liv. vi. 446, 47, 48.

to the Reformed, and fourteen Troops of Horse commanded by PUY-GREFFIER, SAINT CYRE, LANGUILLIER, LANDERAU, PLUVIAUT, and St. MARTIN DE LA COUDRE; having provided themselves with some Field-Pieces at *Confolens,* they stormed *Dorat* and came to *Poitou*; they took *Lufignan* by Composition, then they stayed some days before *Poitiers,* thinking to take it by means of their Intelligence with the Reformed Inhabitants; but the Count of LUDE having hastened with the Nobility of the Country, they were obliged to desist, and proceeded to Orleans, where having taken along with them two great Guns and a Culverine, a good stock of Gunpowder, and other Ammunitions, they came by the latter end of November to *Pont-fur-Yonne,* kept by St. Martin and St. Loup, with three Companies of Foot; they forced their way by storming the Place, and were happily joined by the Admiral, who proceeded to *Sens* with the rest of the Confederates, in order to seize upon that Town, but they were prevented by the Duke of Aumale, whom the Court had sent that way to hinder, if possible, the junction of the Auxiliaries coming from Germany to the Confederates (*b*).

LII.
The Court sends Ambassadors to Germany.

The Court doubting not but that the Prince would treat with the German Princes for Troops, had sent unto them BOCHETEL Bishop of Rennes, and

(*b*) Thuanus mistakes, when he says that the said Duke had been sent to Lorrain to receive three thousand Horse, led by the Duke John William of Saxony, &c. for Castelnau, who had been sent to the said Duke on purpose to manage those Succours, contradicts him as to the time, and as to the Person sent to receive them. As to the time, Castelnau says positively that himself was Ambassador to the Saxon Prince after the junction of the Confederates with their Auxiliaries of Germany, that is, in January next; as to the Person who received them, he himself had led them into France; as to their Number, they were 5000 Reisters. See Mem. de Casteln. liv. vi. ch. 9. and Thuan. lib. xlii. p. 481.

and after him Lanfac, with orders to reprefent to
the faid Princes, that the Reformed had took up
Arms, not for the Defence of their Religion,
fince they enjoyed a full Liberty of Confcience,
and every thing granted unto them by the former
Edicts, which they pretended to make out by
fome fuppofititious Letters from fome of the Reformed of France to their Friends abroad. But
that they carried their Views further, with an
intent to deprive his Majefty and his Brethren of
their Eftate ; for that Reafon they had attacked
them when they had not thought to make war,
and had attempted to feize upon their Majefties
and the King's Brethren, the Princes, Lords and
Counfellors that followed the Court, and that
their Intention had been made very plain, by
their befieging *Paris*, and fighting a Battle at the
very Gates. Thefe Inftructions of the two Am-
baffadors above named, and which I have tranflated out of Thuanus, and corrected by Caftelnau's Memoirs, are a Demonftration of the Falfhood of the Charge laid by Father Daniel upon
the Prince of Condé and his Adherents ; for had
they plotted to murder the King and his Brethren,
and to place the firft Prince of the Blood upon the
Throne, had they coined fuch Medals with the faid
Infcription, how came it to pafs, that the Queen,
far from infifting upon that, faid not a word of it
in thefe Inftructions ?

However, tho' the Cafes were thus mifrepre-
fented to the Princes of Germany, the Ambaffa-
dors prevailed fo far with the Landgrave of
Heffia, the Electors Auguftus of Saxony, and Jo-
achim of Brandenburgh, that they refolved to
give no Affiftance to the Prince of Condé ; but
the Elector Palatine was more cautious, he could
not give credit intirely to Lanfac the King's Am-
baffador, nor to Chaftelier de la Porte, and Barbier

de

Charles
IX.
1567.
Pope Pius
V.

They repre-
fent againſt
the Prince
and his Ad-
herents.

They pre-
vail with
several
Princes.

de Francour the Prince's Envoys, who intreated him to grant some Auxiliaries to the Confederates; therefore, in order to be rid of his Scruples, he resolved to send Venceflaus de Zuleger, whom our French Historians call de Soulegres, one of his State Counsellors, to the Court of France with Lanfac; having obtained promise from the French Ambaſſador that he would bring him back safe with him. This Gentleman was not long at the Court of France, and in the Prince's Camp, without being fully convinced of the Falfity of Lanfac, and the Biſhop of Rennes's Aſſertions as to the Condition the Reformed had been in before the War, and were ſtill in, and as to the Reaſons which had forced them to riſe in arms; and being gone back to his Maſter, he gave him a true Relation of the Caſe, and how the Matter ſtood in the Kingdom, and adviſed his Electoral Highneſs not to delay any longer the promiſed Auxiliaries, but to grant liberty to Prince CASIMIR, his own Son, to march directly: and he took upon himſelf the Commiſſion of going to the Electors of Saxony and Brandenbourg to tell them the Truth of the Matter, to the end that they ſhould not take it ill, that the Elector Palatine ſhould lend his help to the Prince of Condé. As ſoon as the Prince got notice of this Succeſs, and that the Auxiliaries had began their March, he marched to meet them (*j*).

LIII.
*The Royal
Army
marches a-
gainſt the
Prince.*

The Duke of Anjou had marched out of Paris at the Head of the King's Army, to fight the Prince while he was at Montereau; but he was gone when the Duke arrived there. However, as he had Orders to engage them at any rate before the junction of the Germans, he followed them, and met with a fair Opportunity at *Our Lady of Thorn*, near *Châlons*, in *Champaign*, but he

(*j*) Thuan. lib. xlii. p. 481.

he let it flip, by the neglect, as it was said, of the Marshall of Cossé ; and not being pursued, they entered into Lorrain by long Journeys : The Duke went with his Army to *Vitry,* and the Confederates to *Senne,* waiting for the Germans.

The Queen-Mother came to visit her dear Son, and to consider of the best means either of engaging the Confederates, or of coming to some feigned Agreement with them. Before that time, and while the Reformed were still in Champaign, she had desired a Conference with the Confederates, which the Vidame of Chartres had much opposed, but the Prince's Advice prevailed, and having agreed with Combault the Queen's Deputy, that he would be himself at Montereau upon such a Day, to confer there with the King's Deputies, his Highness found, to his great Surprize, that he had been deceived, and that the Court had no other View but to amuse him, and delay his March.

They had agreed upon a Truce for three Days between the two Parties ; but that Facility of the Confederates was very near to cost them very dear : for the Prince of Condé having took his Quarters in very bad Places while the King's Army followed him, he would very likely have been engaged, had it not been for the Count of Brissac's Hastiness ; he surprised some Troops of Horse led by Captain Blosset and some others in the Confederates Party, and cut them to pieces during the Truce, which News being brought to the Prince, he dislodged quickly.

For all that the Treaty was always upon the Carpet, Combauld was sent again by the King with some Articles, whereby he consented that the Cardinal of Chatillon, the Count of La Rochefoucaut and Bouchavanes should be named Com-

I

Charles
IX.
1568.
Pope Pius
V.

LVI.
*Conferen-
ces that
come to no-
thing.*

Commiffaries for the Prince, and fent to them a Safe-Conduct for coming to him.

Accordingly the Cardinal of Chatillon, with fome of the Nobility (for it was not thought proper to fend the Count of La Rochefoucaut nor Bouchavanes, their Prefence being neceffary in the Army) fet out for *Ambert*, and from thence for Châlons, where the Queen arrived the next day, with the Cardinals of Bourbon, Lorrain and Guife. The Cardinal of Chatillon having told her Majefty that the Confederates were ready to fubmit themfelves to the Terms tendered by the King, only they defired to be plainly refolved as to fome obfcure and ambiguous Words that were in them ; he befought her Majefty to confider that all manner of Delays were very prejudicial to the Kingdom, that the Expences for the Maintenance of the Army amounted to above an hundred thoufand Crowns a day, befides the Murders, Plunders, and other dreadful Inconveniences, wherewith a Civil War is always attended, and that half an hour's time was enough for clearing all the Difficulties, did both Parties proceed but fincerely.

The Queen anfwered, that the Matter was of fuch a Moment, that the King, who was at age, ought to take cognizance of it, and deliberate with his Council upon it, and that it could not be refolved but before him, and by him. Therefore fhe defired the faid Cardinal to come himfelf to *Vincennes*, and having given all the Securities required, fhe commanded Bloffet Lord of Torcy, Knight of the Golden Fleece, with twenty Yeomen of the Guard, to attend his Eminency to *Vincennes* ; there he received the King's Orders not to confer or keep any Intelligence with any Parifian foever.

The

The Queen, having taken another Road, arrived at *Paris* ; and the Cardinals of Lorrain and Guise at *Rheims*. Morvilliers and Lansac were sent to confer with the Cardinal of Chatillon, who at first declined the Conference, becaufe he had been promifed that it fhould be before the King. But being told, that when the Matters fhould have been debated, then the King would conclude with him, he confented to it, and the Conference began : He required that the Edict of Amboife fhould be fully reftored to all its Purport and Intent, without any Reftriction or Limitation ; and whatever had been done to the contrary fhould be repealed ; that an Edict for that Purpofe fhould be publifhed and regiftred in all the Parliaments of the Realm, at the Inftances of the King's Attorney-General, and fhould be in force till the Determination of a free General Council.

That being agreed upon, it remained to refolve fome Articles of the faid Amboifian Edict ; and the Cardinal thought that would be done before the King. But on the next day, Chriftophle de Thou, and René Baillet were fent unto him, but judging rightly that fuch Mutation of Perfons was done on purpofe to prolong the time, he refufed to enter into any Conference with them, and fo three days were fpinned out. At laft the Queen fent for him to the Convent of the Minimes, not far from Paris ; where the Conference had no better Succefs than the firft. On the 20th of January, Morvilliers was fent again to him with a Meffage from the King, wherein he charged the Prince and his Confederates with a Breach of Faith, becaufe they had attempted to furprife the Court unawares at Meaux, whereby they had difcovered that they aimed at his Royal Perfon ; therefore
he

he required a juft Satisfaction on that Account, before he proceeded any further.

The Cardinal anfwered in Writing, and affirmed that the Confederates Meaning had never been to attempt any thing hurtful or prejudicial to his Majefty's Perfon or Service, but only to fecure themfelves againft their Enemies, who had plotted their Deftruction, and were ready to execute their wicked Defigns againft them, had they not been prevented, &c. &c. That Anfwer was publifhed afterwards; fo ended the Conferences (*i*).

LVII.
The Confederates join the Germans.

The Confederates being arrived in Lorrain, they found not the Germans, as they expected, neither could they hear of them for fome days, which caufed many to murmur againft their Chiefs, and feveral had a mind to disband, had it not been for the merry Humour of the Prince, and the grave Speeches of the Admiral.

But at laft, they heard that Prince Cafimir Son to the Elector Palatine was not far off, whereby their Sorrows were turned into Joy.

But the Anxiety of the Chiefs increafed, for the Prince's Agents had promifed unto the Germans to pay down an hundred thoufand Crowns, as foon as they fhould have joined with the Confederates, and they had fcarce Money enough to difcharge their own daily Expence.

LVIII.
Great Generofity of the Prince's Army.

Reduced to this Strait, the Prince and the Admiral refolved to engage their own Army to contribute towards the Payment of that Sum, or at leaft, part of it; their Words, but above all, their Example, were fo perfuafive, that what had never been feen before, was done at this time, viz. that a part of an Army deprived themfelves of their neceffary Subfiftence, in order to gratify the other: and indeed not only the Prince, the Admiral,

(*i*) Thuan. lib. xlii. pag. 486, 87.

Admiral, (who delivered all their Plate and Jewels for that purpose) and the Commanding Officers and Subalterns, but even the Centinels, nay, the Servants and Black-guards themselves, incited by the Example of one another, and by the Ministers Exhortations, contributed what they could towards it.

The Collection amounted to thirty thousand Crowns, wherewith the Germans were satisfied for that time, especially at the Intreaties of Prince Casimir, who wrote to the King from *Pont à Mousson*, declaring to his Majesty, that what had moved him to come, was not a sordid Interest, but for the Defence of those who professed the same Religion with himself, and that he was ready to go back with his Troops, as soon as his Majesty would be pleased to grant unto them Liberty of Conscience, and the free Profession of their Religion, and that they might be sufficiently secured, as to their Life, Liberty, Goods and Honours (*k*).

Another good Fortune happened to the Confederates at this time; La Rochelle declared it self for their Party.

That City, one of the richest in the Kingdom by its Commerce, had much increased by the great Privileges which it enjoyed at that time. Lewis VIII had taken it from the English in the Year 1224. SAVARY DE MAULEON, Governour of Acquitain for the King of England, having been so basely treated by his Master's Ministers, who had sent to him full Chests of old Iron instead of Money, for paying his Garrison, was obliged to surrender it on the 28th of July (*l*). That City fell again into the hands of the English,

(*k*) Thuan. lib. xlii. pag. 487—88—89.   (*l*) Paulus Æmilius fol. 299, says that Mauleon was forced to stand his Tryal in England, being charged with having betrayed the Nation; he was acquitted.

lifh, in 1360, by the Treaty of *Bretigny* (*m*). But in the Year 1372, they thought proper to change their Mafter, and fubmitted themfelves to Charles V. King of France : They had premeditated the Expulfion of the Englifh, and for that purpofe, the Spanifh Fleet was at the Bar. There was but the Caftle that hindred them from executing their Defign. The Mayor bethought of a Device : He invited to a Dinner the Captain of the Caftle, and while he fat at Table, he delivered to him fome Letters fealed up with King Edward's Seal, wherein the faid Mayor feigned to read that his Majefty ordered them to mufter the Garrifon of the Caftle and the Militia of the City. There was no fuch thing in the Letters, but, as the Captain could not read, he believed whatever the Mayor faid, and commanded the Garrifon to come out. The Mayor had laid fome Ambufhes behind fome Ruins, that came out in good time and ftopt the Garrifon's way, and hindred them from coming again into the Caftle. Twelve or fifteen Wretches that had remained in it, were very glad to capitulate. Then the wife Rochellefe, before admitting the French into their City, made their Treaty with the King, and obtained the demolifhing of the Caftle. Befides that, they obtained fo many Privileges, and fuch advantageous Terms, that all of them tended as much to fet the City at liberty, as to make them change their Mafter (*n*). Now fince that time the City remained under the Kings of France's Obedience ; tho' in King Lewis XI's Reign, he gave it to Charles Duke of Berry, his Brother, as part of his Apennage, but he did not keep it long, for that Prince was wickedly poifoned by JOHN FAURE VERSOIS,

(*m*) Thuan. lib. xlii. pag. 480. (*n*) Mezeray, 1.Partie
Tom. II. pag. 704. 2d Part. Tom. III. pag. 60, 88, 89.
Edit. d'Amft. 1673.

VERSOIS, a Benedictine, Abbot of *St. John d'An-*
gely, at the Inftigation of Lewis XI, this happened in the Year 1471.

Amongft the Privileges of that City, this was
of very great Moment, viz. to be governed by
Magiftrates of their own Choice ; there was a
Council of an hundred Citizens called PAIRS and
ESCHEVINS, by whom it was governed ; out of
that Council a Mayor was elected every Year,
after Eafter Holy-days ; that Mayor was the firft
Magiftrate after the Governor, or his Deputy,
and had a great Authority in the City, for which
reafon he was changed every Year. Now it was
the Cuftom, that the Citizens nominated three of
the Council of the Hundred, to be prefented to
the Governor or to the King, who chofe one of
them to be Mayor for the enfuing Year. At
this time the Lord of JARNAC was Governor of
the City, and AMATEUR BLANDIN Mayor of it ;
this laft gave notice to the King, that if he had a
mind to preferve the City, he ought to take care
left TRUCHARD, who afpired to that Charge
fhould not be admitted, becaufe he was intimate
with St. ERMINE, who adhered to the Prince,
and was in his Army. Neverthelefs it happened,
that by Truchard's Shrewdnefs, and at Jarnac's
and other Courtiers Recommendation, the faid
Truchard was elected Mayor, and a little after,
having held fecret Correfpondence with the Prince,
and St. Ermine being arrived, the City declared
itfelf for the Prince, and on the 10th of February
the Citizens promifed upon their Oath to affift
his Highnefs with all their Power. Since that
time, to Lewis XIII. that City had been always
confidered as the ftrongeft Bulwark of the Reformed in France. (*o*)

(*o*) Thuan. lib. xlii. pag. 480, 81.

Charles
IX.
1568.
Pope Pius
V.

LX.
*How the
Matters
stood in the
Southern
Provin-
ces.*

I shall not enter much further into the Particulars of this War, which was but of a very short Duration: I shall only observe that, generally speaking, the Confederates had better Success almost every where than their Adversaries. In *Dauphiné, Provence,* and *Languedoc,* Troops were raised by the Prince's Orders; that Commission had been given to D'Assier, Brother to the Count of Crussol, who having travelled thro' the *Bourbonese, Auvergne, Vivarais,* &c. exhorted them to be at their Ensigns on the appointed Day.

Sipierre, Son to the Count of Tendes, Governor of Provence, assembled his Troops near *Cisteron,* which Place Mouvans had seized upon by his Orders.

Montbrun assembled Troops in Dauphiné, and the Dauphinese with the Provençals were already assembled, in order to go by long Marches to the Prince's Assistance; when being desired by D'Assier, who had resolved to make himself Master of the Citadels of Nimes and Montpelier, they stayed till the said Lord had accomplished his Designs.

Nimes and Montpelier being secured, Sipierre came back with his Troops to Cisteron, because he understood that Des Gordes and Maugiron were in arms in the Neighbourhood.

Mean while the Viscounts Burniquet, Montclair, Paulin, Rapin, Caumont, Serignan and Montagut, were raising Troops in the Countries of *Rouërgue, Quercy, Foix, Albigeois* and *Lauragais,* and having assembled seven thousand Men, they led them to *St. Fronton,* kept by the Royalists (who annoyed all the Country thereabout) and stormed the Place. From thence they joined with D'Assier, who having been desired by those of Dauphiné to assist them, went to *St. Marcellin* besieged by Des Gordes and
Maugiron,

Maugiron, and forced in their way thofe of *Avignon* to forfake the Bridge of the *Holy Ghoſt*; they ſtormed St. Marcellin and put the Garriſon to the Sword, and obliged Des Gordes and Maugiron to fly into Grenoble.

Poncenac and De Verbelais raiſed likewiſe three thouſand Foot and 5 hundred Horfe for the Prince's Service, in the Bourboneſe, Maconneſe, Auvergne, Forets and Baujeolleſe; and gave them Rendezvous for the Month of October. When they were aſſembled, they debated whether they ſhould go directly and join the Prince, or whether they ſhould wait to be joined by the Troops of Provence, Languedoc aud Guienn. They reſolved to ſtay; but left they ſhould disband, it was thought proper to lead them into the Maçonneſe and the Principality of Dombes. The Abby of *Clugny* redeemed it ſelf for a Sum of Money, and the Liberty of ſome Reformed that were detained Priſoners. Then they came to *St. John*, which was kept by Charongeraux, and took it.

Poncenac being come back to *Pacaudiere* with the Troops, they adviſed what to do, and agreed to go into Dauphiné, and join their Forces with D'Aſſier; but Lovefe, a covetous Man, who had made himſelf Maſter of Macon, could not be perſuaded to follow ſo good a Counfel, and paid very dear for his Obſtinacy, being routed afterwards by the Duke of Nevers.

Poncenac marching thro' the Forez with feven hundred Foot and an hundred Horfe, and de Verbelay with three hundred Horfe and fix hundred Foot, was routed by Terride at Champouilly, as he went to the Royal Camp with the Troops put under his Command by Montluc, and loſt in that day three hundred Men; the reſt capitulated for their Life, upon Promiſe that they would not take up Arms during this War, and

Poncenac

Poncenac escaped very narrowly; Verbelay was not present.

The Duke of Nevers having joined all his Troops, (the famous Baron Des Adrets was with him) had an Army of thirteen thousand Men; he came to Lyons, where having taken some Ammunition he proceeded to Mâcon, which was surrendred by Composition, from thence he went to Champaign and joined his Army with that of the Duke of Anjou.

As to Poncenac and Verbelay, having joined D'Assier, after the Fight of *Champouilly*, with the Remainder of their small Troop, he insisted much upon the necessity of marching without delay to join the Prince of Condé; but D'Assier being earnestly desired by the People of that Country not to forsake them, thought that it was not convenient for the Prince's Service to leave these Countries (*Dauphiné*) without Troops. Therefore he put a Garrison in *St. Andrew*, a Borough not far from *Vienne* in *Dauphiné*, of three hundred Arquebusiers to oppose the Excursions of the Enemies on that side; but being gone, Des Adrets having assembled two thousand Foot and some light Horse, hastened to that Place, and battered it with his Artillery till he had made a large Breach; the Commander of the Place, expecting no Succour, and being acquainted with the violent Temper of his Aggressor, questioning not but that he would treat the Reformed as he had treated the Catholicks in the first Civil War, took a generous Resolution to open his way thro' his Enemies Camp Sword in hand, which he bravely executed at Midnight, with his Garrison and some of the Inhabitants, and made a great Slaughter of the Adressians, and with a very inconsiderable Loss of his own, he retreated to the nearest Garrison.

Mean

Mean while the Viscounts, with Mouvans and Poncenac, having obtained leave of D'Assier, led their Troops to the Prince of Condé. They were then six thousand Men, Horse and Foot, but they were reduced to four thousand, by the Desertion of the Gascoons, especially of those who being used to rob upon the Pyrenean Mountains, chose that loose way of living rather than another more strict.

The Viscounts having crossed the *Loire* at *St. Rambert*, came to *Ganat*, on the Frontiers of *Auvergne*. As they proceeded, and Poncenac being come to *Pont de Vic*, not far from *Cognac*, they discovered a Body of Royal Troops, consisting most part of Horse; then the Viscounts set their Army in array, and caused the Bridge of *Vic* to be broken, to the end that their Troops should put their Safety in their Hands rather than in their Legs. The two Armies ingaged very soon, the Viscounts got the better and routed the Enemy, who lost above an hundred Horse; the Foot ran away, many were wounded, and several taken Prisoners; amongst whom La Forest de Beullon, an Officer; who, because he bragged of his Enormities, and the many shameful Abuses he had put upon all the Reformed Women that had fell in his hands, was most outragiously treated, and then put to death. But a thing happened which decreased the Joy of the Reformed; for as they returned to Cognac, where they had left their Baggage with a sufficient Guard to keep it, being not able to distinguish their Colours because the Night was very dark, they fell suddenly a fighting one against another, and fired their Pieces, whereby Sudaret, Provost of Forez, and Poncenac himself were unhappily killed; the Corpse of this last was decently buried in the Castle of *Changy*, not far off. But a little after, as Chau-

mont

Charles
IX.
1568.
Pope Pius
V.

mont and Urfé, two Royalifts, retreated, and paffed that way, they caufed the Corpfe to be digged out of the Ground, and expofed it to the Outrages of their Soldiers; then they mangled it in the moft inhuman manner.

LXI.
Orleans
relieved.

After that, Mouvans and other Chiefs marched into Berry, where they arrived with great Difficulties, there having received Letters from the Princefs of Condé, who defired their Affiftance at Orleans, which was befieged by Martinengue, and where fhe, the Countefs of Coligny, and many other Ladies of the Confederates were fhut up with their Families; they haftened to their Relief, and at their approach, Martinengue raifed the Siege, and retreated to Baugency, and from thence to Blois.

LXII.
Blois taken
by Mou-
vans.

Mouvans having refrefhed his Troops for fome days at Orleans, feeing that they had increafed in the way, to the number of five thoufand Foot and four hundred Horfe, thought himfelf in a Condition to make fome confiderable enterprize, therefore having took at *Orleans* two Guns and the neceffary Ammunition, he went to befiege *Blois*; in his way thither he took *Baugency* without Refiftance. Blois withftood not a long time, Mouvans having ftormed one of the Suburbs and made a large Breach in the Walll; Richelieu was fummoned to furrender the Place, which having refufed, the Befiegers made another large Breach on another Side, then the Governor thought proper to come to a Parley, where, after many Altercations it was agreed, that the City fhould not be expofed to Plunder, and that the Garrifon fhould come out with their Arms and Baggage. Thefe Articles were ill obferved; but then it was the Catholicks fault, who never thought themfelves obliged to keep their Treaty
with

with the Reformed, whenever they could break it with Impunity.

Blois being taken, Mouvans having left a Garrison in the City, proceeded to *Mont-richard*, but while he endeavoured to force that Place, he received Orders from the Prince to march directly to him (*p*).

In Guienn, Montluc with an ncredible Diligence, seized upon *Lectoure*, from whence he drove Fontrailles, Governor thereof, who sided with the Prince ; then in less than twenty nine days, having assembled an Army of about six thousand Men, Horse and Foot, he sent it to the King, as above said, under the Command of Terride. Then having received the King's Orders to besiege La Rochelle, tho' he was not in a Condition to execute that for want of Money, and other things necessary for such an Undertaking, nevertheless being come to *St. Macaire*, he exhorted the neighbouring Nobility not to be wanting to themselves, but to chearfully undertake something that might be serviceable to their King, and redound to their own Glory ; he made all the necessary Dispositions for preventing or stopping the Progress of the Confederates Party in all the Provinces under his Government ; then he sent Madaillan in all haste to *Saintes*, with Orders to attack those of *Maran*, if they were still at *St. Sernin*, and to kill them all, to one, without Mercy, if he got the better of them ; which Orders, Madaillan obeyed very faithfully. Then he himself came to *Marennes*, where he met with Antony of Pons, Lord of that Place, and they made themselves Masters of the Islands adjacent, *Oleron*, *Allevert*, and *Ré* ; where they used great Cruelties, sparing no body of what Age, Quality, or Sex soever. These were his Exploits in his

P 4   Govern-

(*p*) Thuan. lib. xlii. pag. 484, &c.   pag. 493, &c.

LXIV.
*The
Prince's
Army's
Progress.*

Government, related more at large, and with great Encomiums by himself, in the 6th Book of his Memoirs.

The Reisters being joined with the Prince's Army, as abovesaid, it was unanimously agreed to carry the War to the Neighbourhood of Paris, because there was no better means than that to oblige their Enemies to come to some reasonable Agreement. The Prince and the Admiral were likewise very sensible that, in order to continue the War, they ought to be provided with Artillery, Powder, Money, and other Necessaries, which could not be got but from the Merchants and Tradesmen, and that they would be deprived of all these Things, unless they should come near Orleans, their Nurse; therefore they went back, being sure that the Royal Army would follow them by the side, as well for hindring them from seizing upon several Towns ill provided, or putting them under Contribution, as for observing and improving the Opportunity of surprising some of their Troops (*q*).

*His Me-
thod for
subsisting
his Army.*

At that time the Kingdom abounded with all manner of Provisions, nevertheless it was not easy to feed an Army of above twenty thousand Men, not paid, having but a few Carts to carry their Necessaries, marching in an Enemies Country, and in the midst of the Winter: But by the Wisdom and Prudence of their Chiefs, all these Difficulties were overcome. The Admiral was above all, very cautious to have the most expert Commissaries, and to find Waggons for carrying the Provisions. He was used to say that, *for forming such a Monster,* so he called an Army in the Civil Wars, *it was absolutely requisite to begin by the Belly.* Each Cornet had a Baker, and two Horses of Burden; and every day as soon as they were
arrived

(*q*) La Noue Disc. Pol. & Militaires, pag. 893.

arrived at their Quarters, they baked a certain
quantity of Bread to be diftributed amongft the
Regiments of Foot: When they feized upon
any Town or Borough which abounded with
Victuals, they fet apart the faid Provifions and
delivered them to the Commiffaries: The Cities
that had no Garrifon, redeemed themfelves for
a certain quantity of Provifions which they carried to the Army, and delivered them into the
hands of the faid Commiffaries. Befides that,
the Prizes and Booty made by the Troops,
either of Horfe or Foot, ferved for the private
Ufes of thofe who got them. As to their Quarters, the Prince and the Admiral ordered them
in fuch a manner that the Army was equally fhel-
tered againft the bad Weather, and the Surprizes
of the Enemy. As to their March, the feveral
Bodies of the Army were appointed to be in fuch
a Place at fuch an Hour, and dividing themfelves
into feveral Columns they marched thro' feveral
Roads, whereby they went very far in a fhort
time; and tho' that Method was not the beft,
becaufe of the Dangers wherewith it might be
attended, as La Nouë obferves, neverthelefs it
was the moft expedient at that time. The firft
Column that fronted the Enemy was of fix hundred Light Horfe, and fix hundred Arquebufiers
ftrong. Marching in that order between *Joinville*
and *Chaumont*, after having been oftentimes annoyed by the Garifons, they croffed the *Marne*
at *Langres*, and came through *Burgundy* at the
Fountain of the *Seine*. There they met with
the Italians led by the Duke of Nevers, which
he had put in feveral Places to oppofe the Paffage
of the Confederates, or to retard their March,
for which purpofe they bethought themfelves of
this Device; they put a quantity of Galtrops and
fharp Nails in the bottom of the River, at the
Place

Place whereby they suppofed that the Confederates were to crofs; that the Horfes being hurted,
might tumble, and the Rider fall into the Water. But that Device had not the defired Succefs, for the firft that came in to try the Ford,
having at their own Peril difcovered the Cheat,
cleanfed the River with proper Engines before the
others croffed, and being much fuperior in number, they very eafily executed their Defign, notwithftanding all Oppofitions of the Italians, which
were purfued by the Prince's Orders, and many
were killed, while the reft were routed. From
thence they proceeded to *Auxerre*; and thofe of
Irancy having killed one of the Cornets of the
Prince, and refufed Satisfaction, their Town was
forced, and a moft barbarous and inhuman Slaughter of almoft all the Inhabitants enfued. Then
having croffed the *Yonne* and *La Cure*, they came
to *Bleneau, Chatillon* and *Montargis*; they croffed again the *Loin*, and entered into *Beauffe*,
from whence the Prince was to go to *Orleans* to
receive the Troops that were come from *Guienn,
Languedoc*, and *Dauphiné*, fome Guns and Ammunition neceffary for the Siege of *Chartres*; but
underftanding that Mouvans had led them to
Mont-richard, he fent thither for them, and their
Forces being joined together, they befieged
Chartres (r).

That City could not withftand long, and its
lofs was of a very great Prejudice to Paris, and
indeed to the whole Royal Party. Therefore the
Court renewed the Propofitions of Peace. It is
to be obferved, that in all the Civil Wars of
France, tho' the two Parties warred one againft
another, there was always fome Treaty or other
upon the Carpet to bring Matters to an Agreement.

(r) La Noue pag. 900, &c. Thuan. lib. xlii. pag. 490.
495, &c.

ment. So the Cardinal of Chatillon was then
fent with fome other Gentlemen to meet with
the King's Deputies at *Lonjumeau* ; thefe were
Gontault de Biron, afterwards Marfhal of
France, and Henry de Memme, Lord of Ma-
lafife, Mafter of the Requefts ; the Articles having been debated between them ; and the Lord
Thomas Sacville, Baron of Buckhurst, Embaffador of *England*, and Guy Cavalcanti of
Florence, being Mediators, at laft the Articles
were agreed upon.

Thefe Articles may be all reduced to thefe
four. 1. An intire *Oblivion* of whatever had
been done on account of the laft Troubles, the
Prince and all his Adherents acknowledged for
good and faithful Subjects to the King, &c.
2. The full Reftoration of the Ambofian Edict
to all its Intents and Purport, and the repealing of every thing under what Denomination
foever, that had been publifhed to the contrary, by way of Explanation, Refervation, Limitation, &c. 3. That all the Cities, Towns,
Strong-holds, &c. feized upon by the Reformed
during the laft Troubles, fhould be reftored to
the King without any delay, &c. 4. That all
foreign Troops, on both fides, fhould be difmiffed, and all their Arrears and other things due
unto them paid at the King's Charge.

Had the Reformed had more Patience they
would have obtained better terms, at leaft fome
better Securities for the performance of this Treaty, than the bare word of a Prince who durft not
do any thing but by the Advice of his Mother,
who was intirely devoted to the Cardinal of Lorrain, whofe cruel and ambitious Spirit was ftiffly
bent on the utter Deftruction of the Reformed,
tho' he knew very well that he could not compafs his ends without expofing the whole Kingdom

dom to the very brink of its utter ruin. But moſt part of the Prince's Army longed after a Peace, and they behaved themſelves in this juncture juſt as if the bare name of PEACE would have ſerved the ſame Turn as the Reality of it.

And indeed, tho' it muſt be owned, that Peace is the moſt deſirable thing in the World, that it was much neceſſary at this time, yet very few cared to be at the trouble of conſidering the nature of this, but the greateſt number were for accepting of it. This obliged the Prince and the Admiral to condeſcend; it was, as it were, a Whirling wherewith they were carried off. True it is that the Prince had ſome Inclination to it, but the wiſe and prudent Admiral foreſaw that the Treaty would never be kept, queſtioning not but the Court would take her Revenge for the Affront put upon her at Meaux. And even at that very time they had Intelligence enough by ſome Catholicks, great Babblers, by one of the Negociators of the Peace, and by ſome Ladies at Court, to be upon their guard, left they ſhould be deceived by falſe Appearances, becauſe no good was intended for them. But for all that, it was impoſſible to ſtem the Tide. One will think it very ſtrange, that the Prince and the Admiral, who had ſo great an Aſcendant over their Party, were not able to perſuade them to what was beſt for them! But then, we muſt conſider, what it is to have to deal with Voluntiers, what an earneſt Deſire to ſee again a Family, after an Abſence of ſeveral Months ſpent amidſt the greateſt Dangers. Beſides that, they ſaw their Army weakening itſelf every day by frequent Deſertion: The Troops of *Poitou* and *Xaintonge* were already gone without asking leave, and the reſt were upon the point of following that example. How then could the Prince

keep

keep the Field, or do any thing that might redound to the Advantage of his Party, either as to War or as to Peace? The Articles being signed on both sides, the Peace was proclaimed at Paris, and the Edict regiftred by the Parliament on the 27th of March 1568.

According to the Articles Prince Casimir with his Reifters were dismissed ; but whereas there was no Money in the Exchequer to pay them, they would not go out of the Kingdom without it ; and it was but after many Debates, big Words, Threatnings and Promifes, that Castelnau obliged them to march out of France. The fame Gentleman had been fent before to the Duke of Alva to give him Notice of the Conclusion of the Peace, and to thank him in the King's name for his Auxiliaries ; but he was very coldly received by the Duke upon that account, that bloody Man thinking that the Court was in earneft, could not like to fee the Kingdom in peace. *Soiffons, Auxerre, Orleans, Blois, La Charité,* and feveral other places were reftored to the King, and the Prince having difbanded his Army, every one went to his own home, where they lived not long without having juft reafons to repent their Haftinefs.

Rapin, one of the Prince's Gentlemen, was fent by the King at Thoulouze to have the Edict publifhed and regiftered ; but the Parliament, far from obeying the King's Orders, caufed the Envoy to be put in Prifon, tried, and publickly beheaded, upon fome falfe pretence, but really out of Hatred againft his Religion, whereof he had been a ftrenuous Defender in Languedoc. Upon the Prince's Complaints, the King feigned to be very angry at this unprecedented Impudence, and fummoned the Parliament to fend their Deputies to fhow Caufe ; but by length of time, tinie, and especially the third civil War breaking out soon after, put an end to the Pursuits of the one, and the Perplexities of others. That Parliament could not be brought to comply till after the 4th Session.

On the King's side, not a tittle of the Articles agreed upon by the Treaty was fulfilled, besides the payment of the Reisters. He kept most part of the Troops he had at his Service; most part of them were kept on foot, and quartered in the Neighbourhood of Paris, strong Garrisons were sent to Orleans, Tours, Amiens, &c. and others were sent to shut the passages of the Rivers. The Edict was no better observed, as to the Article of the free Profession of the Reformed Religion. But before we proceed any further, let us see how Matters stood in the Low Countries, and the Expedition of Gourgues in the *West Indies* (s).

LXVIII.
Continuation of the Affairs of the Low Countries.
The Prince of Orange was too wise to wait the arrival of Alva; he knew too well the Temper of the Man to be willing to trust himself in his Hands, as the Counts of Egmont and Horn, who could not be persuaded by the Prince to provide for their own Security by flight, or to raise Troops for opposing his Entrance into the Low Countries; but chose rather to stay for his coming, and to do whatever was in their power to please the King. As to the Prince of Orange he went into Germany, and declared at his parting, That he would never attempt any thing against the King, unless he should be first attacked either in his Goods and Estates, or in his Honour; he made no mention of Religion, because, at that time, he was not resolved as to that point.

That

(s) Castelnau's Mem. liv. VI. ch. ii. Thuan. lib. XLII.

That great Prince's Abfence caufed a general Confternation amongft the Oppofers to the Spanifh Tyranny. *Antwerp* received a Garrifon. The Reformed of *Holland* confented to be deprived of their Affemblies; provided that their Cities fhould be freed from Troops. B R E D E R O D E came out of *Amfterdam*, and the Perfecution began to rage more fiercely than before.

A prodigious number of Families forfook their Countries. The Gibbets were full of Corpfe, and *Germany* of Refugees. In the City of *Tournay* only, all the Goods of a hundred Merchants and feveral other wealthy Families, were feized upon. Many Minifters were put to death, and the Anabaptifts were not lefs feverely handled.

The Refugees in Germany publifhed an Apology, complaining that they were unjuftly charged with Herefy, fince they had never been convicted of it by the Holy Scriptures, the only Rule of our Faith. They were already encreafed to the number of a hundred thoufand Perfons.

Alva arrived at *Bruxelles* on the 28th of Auguft 1567, having firft quartered his Troops in the neighbouring Cities, he took his Lodging in Culemburgh's Houfe, and went to pay a Vifit to the Governefs, unto whom he delivered fome Letters written with Philip's own Hand, whereby he notified unto her, that Alva was charged with fome private Commiffions which he was to execute in the Low Countries. The Governefs defired him to let her know what were thofe Commiffions; but he fcornfully laughed at her, and told her, that he had forgot what they were, unlefs he fhould look in his Pocket-book, which he had not with him at that time.

On the 9th of September he caufed the Counts of Egmont and Horn to be arrefted, with feveral other Perfons of Diftinction, whereupon he
fent

sent word to the Governess, that this was the secret Commission wherewith she had desired to be acquainted. At this News every one was seized with a fright, and twenty thousand more Inhabitants avoided the Country; amongst whom was THOMAS TILLIUS, Abbot of *St. Bernard* near *Antwerp*, who forsook his Abbey of sixty thousand Florins per Annum, and went into the Duchy of *Cleves*, where he married, and was afterwards Minister of *Harlem*, then at *Delft*, where he died. The Governess endeavoured in vain to put a stop to these Desertions by several Placaerts; for Alva's base and cruel proceedings drew all the Attention of the People.

His base,
brutish and
cruel Pro-
ceedings.

He had erected a new Court of Justice, which he called, *The Council of Tumults*; but was more properly stiled by the Inhabitants, THE COUNCIL OF BLOOD. The fundamental Maxims whereof were, that to remonstrate against the Erection of the new Bishopricks, the Inquisition, the Penal Laws, or to consent to the Profession of any new Religion, or to say, or to believe that the Holy Office was obliged to have any regard for the Charters and Privileges of the Country, or to affirm that the King was bound to his People by Promises and Oaths; it was a Crime of High Treason in the first degree.

The Temper of the Counsellors was no less terrible than their Principles, They were all Spaniards, having for their Chief the most execrable *JOHN VARGAS*. This last Monster was used to say, *Hæretici fraxerunt Templa: Boni nihil faxerunt contra. Ergo debent patibulari.* That is in better English than his Latin, *All the Inhabitants of these Countries deserve to be hanged; the Hereticks, because they have destroyed or plundered the Churches, and the Catholicks because they have not defended them.* The Spaniards
under-

underftood very well how to depopulate Coun- Charles
ries ; they had tried their Skill in the *Weft In-* IX.
dies ; and what they intended to do in the *Low* 1568.
Countries was no more than what they had done Pope Pius
in *Peru.* V.

Vargas fpoke the Senfe of the Inquifitors of *Wicked and*
Spain, if John Petit is to be credited ; they *deteftable*
had in the Year 1556 framed the following Ar- *Articles,*
ticles. *and Decifi-*
on of the

The moft Holy Office of Inquifition fo many *Spanifh In-*
times attempted to be fet up in the Low Coun- *quifition.*
tries by his Majefty, and till now oppofed, fhall
be however fet up, and promoted by this moft
expedient Method.

1. The Emperor † going aftray, and wicked- *† Charles*
ly confederating with the Hereticks, muft be *V.*
perfuaded to refign unto his Son the Kingdoms
and other his Dominions, and the whole Adminiftration of the Low Countries.

2. Then the Emperor with his two Sifters
having refigned their Titles and Adminiftration,
fhall depart the Low Countries, and come into
Spain with us, that we might be fure, that they
would never go back to hurt us.

3. Thefe being put out of the way, we muft
likewife have the King with us, and keep him for
ever, not allowing any Flemings to come near him,
and lefs to fpeak to him.

4. The King fhall write, and bid the Clergy
and the feveral Orders of Fryars, to receive with
the Inquifition fifteen new Bifhops, which fhall be
freed from all fecular Jurifdiction even in cafes of
High Treafon.

5. The Subjects of the Low Countries by their
Malice and Petulancy, will rebel, raife Seditions
and Tumults.

6. The Princes and the Nobles, Heads and Authors of theſe Factions, and their Subjects ſhall be taken out of the way, and others brought to reaſon.

7. Some Robbers and Image-breakers ſhall be hired at our own Charge, the Crime whereof ſhall be by all charged upon the Rebels by ſome cunning or other ; and ſo we ſhall be Maſters.

8. Let all Trade, Goods or Eſtates, Liberties, and Privileges, be intirely ruined, and let all the Rebels or Hereticks be reduced to the utmoſt Poverty, whereby we ſhall reign for ever.

9. None in the Low Countries ſhall be deemed worthy to live, but thoſe who defend our Cauſe ; but all others without exception ſhall be utterly extirpated.

10. The ſtout and brave Duke of Alva in Perſon ſhall be employed in that Office, and none other not even of the Royal Blood ſhall pretend to it ; and if they are ſuſpected the leaſt in the World let them be taken out of the way.

11. No Contracts, Rights, Promiſes, Gifts, Oaths, Privileges, and ſolemn Aſſertions, of the Low Countries, ſhall avail any thing to the Inhabitants, being all guilty of High Treaſon.

12. But above all, one muſt be very careful not to proceed too haſtily or ſuddenly in things of ſo great moment, but by degrees and orderly, to the end that the Nobles and Subjects ſhould rebel, and that one ſhould perſecute the other. For in all Chriſtendom there is no Nation ſo fooliſh and imprudent, and which might be ſo eaſily abuſed as the Flemiſh, God puniſhing by theſe Means their Unfaithfulneſs.

These Articles were ſent in Latin from Spain, to James Haſſels, Attorney-General of Flanders, whom we ſhall mention hereafter ; he was one of the Council of the Tumults. They were
found

found translated into French, and written with his own Hand, amongst his Papers in the City of *Ghent*, when he was taken Prisoner, and then hanged out of the City in 1578. As to the Sentence of the Inquisition, the purport of which was, that all the Inhabitants of the Countries, those only excepted which had been recommended for their Loyalty, were all guilty of High Treason, the one for being Hereticks and Rebels, and the others for not having opposed them with all their Might, especially in the beginning; that Sentence was given at Madrid on the 16th of February 1568, and confirmed by Philip on the 26th of the same Month.

The Governess was unwilling to be Spectatrix of all the Barbarities to be used, and having obtained Philip's leave, she resigned the Government unto Alva, and set out for *Italy*. After her Departure nothing was to be seen but *Fury* and *Slaughter*, Men and Women of all Ages and Conditions were imprisoned and put to the Rack. Many were put to death only for having been once or twice at the Reformed Meeting-house; eighteen hundred Persons were executed by the common Executioner in a short time. Every day brought forth some new Object of Sorrow and Mourning.

Alva summoned the Prince of Orange, the Count Lewis of Nassau his Brother, the Counts of Hoghstrate, Bergue, and Culembourg, the Lord Brederode, and several others, and on their Non-appearance he proclaimed them Traitors to the King. They answered by a publick writing, and a few Years after the Prince published a Manifesto, wherein Philip's odious Character, and his tyrannical Government were set in their true light.

Q 2

The

Charles
IX.
1568.
Pope Pius
V.

LXX.
*The Prince
of Orange
raises an
Army.*

The People groaning under that hellish Yoke cried after a Deliverer ; they saw none other but the Prince of Orange. Unto him therefore they made their Address ; moved by their Petitions, he resolved to undertake their Defence. Having obtained leave from the Protestant Princes of Germany, he raised Troops in their Dominions ; his first care was to find Money for that purpose. Some of these Princes advanced unto him a Sum. His Brother Ludovic did the same ; and Gatherings were made in all the Churches of the Refugees in *London*, *Embden*, *Cleves*, and elsewhere. With this help the Prince delivered his Commissions, wherein he declared his Reasons for taking up Arms. The general Command of the Army was given to Count Ludovic, who took in his way, *Wedden* and *Dam* in *Guelderland* ; and carried the Day in a Battle against the Enemy.

At this Alva grew almost mad, his innate Ferocity was provoked by the Shame of his Defeat ; a great number of innocent Persons fell a Victim to his Fury. On the 28th of May he condemned to Banishment and Forfeiture of their Goods and Estates, the Prince of Orange, Ludovic his Brother, the Counts of Hoghstrate, Culembourg, and Bergue. On the first of June the two Barons of Battembourg, with sixteen other Gentlemen, were beheaded at *Bruxelles* by his Orders ; the next day the Lords Du Villers and Duy, the Bailiff of *Enguien*, and the Minister Cornelius de Meen underwent the same fate ; and on the 5th of the same Month the illustrious Counts of Egmont and Horn were likewise beheaded : the first died a Catholick, he left three Sons and eight Daughters in very low Circumstances. It *is* said that the Count of Horn

refused

refused to confess; and what Brantome relates is very observable if true, viz. That the Countess of Egmont, a very honest, wise and fair Lady, arrived that very same day at Bruffels, to condole the Countess of Aremberg, whose Husband had been killed lately, and while she was in the said Countess's Room talking with her upon that Subject, one came to tell her that her Husband was going to be beheaded. Then Alva took the Field, and having attacked the Count Ludovic at a place called *Jemmingen* in *East-Frifeland,* he routed him. That Victory cost very dear to many; Alva brought himself the News of it to *Amsterdam, Utrecht,* and *Bois-le-duc;* and every where he left the dreadful Marks of his Cruelty.

That was something less surprizing, when the News came of the lamentable death of Don Carlos, Infant of Spain, who was either strangled, or poisoned, or smothered between two Pillows; for the Historians do not agree as to the manner of his death, but they all own that the Sentence was given by the Inquisition, and executed by his own Father's Orders: and as to the Reasons, some say, that his Father suspected him to be too favourably inclined towards the pretended Rebels and Hereticks of the Low Countries, and was afraid lest he should go and put himself at their head. Others owning this Suspicion, add an inveterate Hatred of that Prince against Alva, and others of Philip's Ministers, and that even his Father's Life was threatened, because he always carried two small Pistols loaded in his Breeches Pockets. Others pretend that this was the effect of Jealousy, that this young Prince was too privy with Queen Elizabeth his Father's Consort, with whom he had been betrothed, before she was married to

Q 3

his

his Father. Few Months after the said Princess followed her Son-in-Law, she was with Child, and too many of her own French Servants certified her having been poisoned for questioning it ; the Prince was twenty-three Years old, and the Queen of the very same Age, when both were taken out of the way.

Now that News increased, as naturally it ought to do, the dread the Provinces were in ! for if Philip had not spared his own Son nor his Consort, what hopes could be left of finding any Commiseration in such an hard-hearted Man, for a People for which he had always shown the greatest Scorn ? The Governour kept no bound at all, and his Inhumanity answered perfectly well what his Master expected of him when he chose him to be the Minister of his Passions. There were no Privileges, how just soever, which were not violated ; no Pretences, how frivolous soever, which were not made use of against the most honest Men ; no Tortures, no kind of Death, how new and extraordinary soever, which were not put in use.

LXXII.
New kind of Torture.
And whereas the Martyrs suffered death with a wonderful Constancy, and that the Gaggs came out sometimes from their Mouths, they invented a dreadful Instrument to hinder them from speaking. They put the Martyr's Tongue betwixt two small Irons, and they burnt the end of it with a hot Iron. It swelled immediately, and became unmoveable, and rendered a confuse Sound near like that of the Phalarian Ox. It is impossible to put Human Patience to a greater Trial. But a Man truly persuaded that he serves God, bears patiently with it. Such a Man never fears the effects of the most dreadful Cruelty.

Mean

Mean while the Prince of Orange made all the neceffary Preparations for penetrating into the Low Countries at the Head of a numerous Army, part whereof was compofed of part of the German Auxiliaries difmiffed by the Prince of Condé after the Peace. But having croffed the Meufe, and finding every where the Enemies well intrenched, and being himfelf in great want of Provifions, he was obliged to come back.

On the other hand, Coquaville and fome other French Officers of the Reformed Religion having gathered fome Troops in *Artois* and *Flanders*, made Incurfions in the *Low Countries* in behalf of the Prince of Orange ; Alva was provoked at it, he complained of it to King Charles, by the Spanifh Embaffador ; the King fent to the Prince of Condé to know whether it was by his Orders that Coquaville and others made thofe Incurfions ; the Prince difowned them, and the King gave Orders to the Marfhal of Coffé to go and reprefs them ; which he did, and he took Coquaville and the other Captains Prifoners at *St. Valery* ; being fent to Paris, they were beheaded.

Alva being extolled by thefe Succeffes, he caufed his own Statue to be erected in the Caftle of *Antwerp*, and the Pope fent him as a Gift the Hat and the Sword which they ufed to blefs every Year at Chriftmas. The pious and charitable Bifhops of Rome made ufually fuch Gifts to the Chriftian Princes that diftinguifh'd themfelves by their Zeal for the fervice of the Church ; and if it is to ferve it to fhed a flood of Blood, we muft fincerely acknowledge that no body deferved better that token of Pius Vth's favour than Alva. In lefs time than a Year he had found the Secret to empty a hundred thoufand Houfes whofe Inhabitants were fled, and had

Q 4　　　　　　peopled

LXXV.
*Horrid
Neglect in
the Admi-
nistration
of Justice*

peopled the neighbouring Countries with the Sub-jects of his Master. No shadow of Justice could be seen in the Judges proceedings, and the Taxes increased every day.

As to the first point, it cannot be conceived how neglectful the Judges were, even in cases where Life was at stake, sometimes poor inno-cent People were condemned by Mistake, and when the Error was found out, Vargas would not allow to revise the Sentence, saying in a ban-tering manner, *that it was good for the Condem-ned to die innocent.* There was also amongst those Judges one JAMES HESSELS, a Civilian, who was always asleep while they were pleading the Causes; they were obliged to awaken him to deliver his Opinion, and that base Man, with-out knowing any thing of the Matter, voted al-ways for death, right or wrong.

As to the Taxes and Imposts, Alva himself says in one of his Letters to Philip, *That out of the produce of them, there will be enough for making a golden Bar as big as his own Arm, and long enough to reach from* BRUXELS *to Spain.* At first he asked the hundredth upon all the Stocks, then the twentieth upon the Immove-ables, and the tenth upon the Moveables, to be paid by the Seller. The States refusing to con-sent to such heavy Subsidies, were threatened to be punished for their past and present Disobe-dience; but before they came to these Extre-mities, they tried to obtain, by Craft, what they ran the hazard to lose otherwise. They pro-mised under hand to the States of *Hainaut* and *Artois,* that they should be free from these Taxes, if by their Approbation they would set an Ex-ample to others. By that Device they engaged several Provinces to consent, however with this Restriction, that if a single Province opposed that

Pro-

Propofition, the confent of the others fhould not avail. The Province of *Utrecht* being inflexible the Scheme fell to the ground for that time, and they offered only a free Gift. But that Province was feverely punifhed for its Obftinacy; they were much oppreffed by Troops quartered upon them, who lived at difcretion, and plun-dered every one, without fparing the Clergy; thefe things were done in the beginning of the Year 1569 (*v*).

And whereas for the future, the Infraction of the civil Privileges and Liberties of the Low Countries, occafioned the Troubles and Wars wherewith they were afflicted for fo many Years, as much as Religion, we fhall not dwell any longer upon that Subject, referring our Reader to the Hiftories of the Low Countries, written by Meteren, Petit, and others.

Only I fhall obferve, 1. That the Army which the Prince of Orange had levied, having muti-nied, difbanded themfelves, and of it remained on-ly 1200 Horfe, with whom the Prince and the Count Ludovic his Brother, joined the Duke of Deux-Ponts's Army, that came to the Succour of the Prince of Condé.

2. That Alva having filled up the meafure of his Cruelties, and fenfible that he was become the Object of the Hatred of all the People, and that by his late ill Succefs he was no lefs the Object of their Scorn, defired to be recalled, which his Mafter granted him, and he fet out from *Bruxelles* on the 12th of December 1573. That bloody Monfter lodging upon the Road at an Uncle's of the Prince of Orange, was not afhamed to glory himfelf, that during the time

of

(*v*) Thuan. lib. XLIII. Meteren, lib. III and IV. Petit, liv. IX and X. Abregé de l'Hift. de la Ref. écrite par Brandt, liv. VIII and IX.

of his Administration he had caused above eighteen thousand People, of all Sexes and Ranks, to
be put to death by the common Executioner's
hands, besides those who had perished in the
War. Whereupon Vargas added, *That the Low
Countries would be lost by too great a Mildness.*

3. The Case of an honest Anabaptist, *RI-
CHARD WILLIAMSON* by Name, de-
serves mostly to be recorded here: He was of
Asperen, and being pursued in Winter-time by
an Officer of Justice, he fled upon the Ice,
which being not very thick as yet, he came over
with great difficulty; but it broke under the
feet of his Pursuer. Williamson seeing the danger his Enemy was in, came back to his Assistance, helped him out of the Water, and saved
his Life at the peril of his own. The Officer
moved with Gratitude for such a piece of Generosity, was willing to let him go; but the
Burgmaster coming at that time, hindered him
from it, so that Officer fearing lest he should pay
his own Life for the escape of his Deliverer,
brought that honest Man to Goal. He was
condemned to be burnt alive on the 16th of
May 1569. When the Fire was kindled out of
the Town of *Asperen,* on the side of *Leerdam,*
an Easterly Wind drove the Flames, insomuch
that the upper part of the Body was not consumed, whereby the Martyr suffered the bitterest Pains, and was heard from afar off crying,
O Lord! O my God! The chief Magistrate present at the Execution, moved at it, ordered the
Executioner to put a speedy end to the Martyr's
Sufferings; so died Williamson, whose Honesty,
Virtue and Simplicity deserved a better fate.

4. We must lament the Frailty and Weakness
of human Nature, while the Calvinists and Lutherans were equally exposed to the Teeth of the
Wolves

Wolves who tore them to pieces, far from uni-
ting themselves together against their common
Enemy, they served as Instruments in his hands
for compassing their Ruin by their Disputes, Divisions and Heats, about no fundamental Points.
All the wise and christian Remonstrances of the
Prince of Orange, all his Intreaties availed nothing, their Pride prevailed above Reason and
Religion; the burning of Hereticks *(that is, those
who thought differently from them concerning Points
not clearly revealed in the Scripture, or even not
revealed at all)* was, it seems, the darling Doctrine of too many Divines in those days, hardly
escaped themselves from the Flames. It was the
Fashion of that Age; an Erasmus, a Melanch-
ton, a Cassander, and some other of the same
Character, were deemed Hereticks, at least Luke-
warms, and without any Zeal for the Glory of
God and the Honour of his Church, only because
they had learned of our great Master, *to be meek
and lowly in heart*; because they were careful
*not to destroy him with their Meat for whom Christ
died.*

During the Peace, one of the Admiral's chief
Cares was to increase the Navigation and Trade
of the Kingdom chiefly in the Countries of the
New Continent, and that as much for settling Colonies of Reformed in those Parts, as for
the Honour of his Charge. For that purpose he
had sent Villegagnon into Florida, as mentioned
in our first Vol. Book II. but had been deceived
by him. Some Years after, viz. in 1562, he
sent one John Ribaud, with two Ships. This
Captain landed happily at *Florida*, where he came
by another Road than the Spaniards usually kept;
when he had taken a view of the Country, made
Alliance with several petty Princes, given Names
to several Capes, Rivers and Gulphs, he built a
Fort

LXXVI.
*Gourgues's
Expedition
in the West
Indies.*

Fort at the end of the Streight of St. Helena, which he called after the King's Name, *Charles's Fort*, and leaving a Lieutenant with some Troops well armed, he put to Sail in order to come back to France, promising them to come again very soon with Recruits and a Supply of Necessaries.

But he could not be as good as his word, because of the Civil War, therefore wanting Provisions, they imbarked again. About the middle of their Voyage they were so far pestered with Famine, that they killed one of their Companions who had been sick for a long while, and fed upon him. An English Ship happily met them, relieved them in their Distress, and brought them over to England.

The Admiral, who knew not that they had left their Fort, manned three Ships at Havre de Grace, to supply their Wants. RENE LAUDONNIERE commanded that Armament; he landed at the Gulph which Ribaud had named *May*, and made Alliance with some petty Princes; but as he fell sick, part of his Men, inticed by some Factious, obliged him to give them leave to go to *New Spain* for Provisions, and having taken a large Ship, immensely rich, on board whereof was the Governour of *Havannah*; they were afterwards surrounded in an Island, and all of them sold or carried into *Spain*.

That Piracy gave a specious Pretence to the Spaniards (who were already very jealous against the French that settled themselves in that Country) to fall upon them without showing any mercy. They pretended that these Lands belonged unto them, for they affirmed that they had been the first Discoverers of them. Tho' a *Venetian*, STEPHEN GABOT by Name, had been the first Discoverer under the Protection of Henry VII. of England, in the Year 1496,

long

long before their Ponce of Leon, who gave
to that Country the Name of *Florida*, becaufe he
landed there on Palm-Sunday, which in Spanifh
is *Florida*.

As Laudonniere was upon the point of failing
back to France, he difcovered feven Ships: It was
the fame John Ribaud. At the fame time the
Spaniards had fent thither one Peter de Me-
landez, with fome Ships to hinder the fettling
of the French in thofe parts. Ribaud left the
Fort with very few People in it, and put to fail
in order to go and fight him. But he was over-
taken with an Hurricane, whereby his Ships
were fplit againft the Rocks; the Crew having
taken to their Boats came afhore, but fell into
the hands of the Spaniards; who having made
themfelves Mafters of the Fort, put them to
death in fuch a barbarous and cruel manner, that
none but Spaniards can be guilty of fo great an
Inhumanity, for they plucked out their Eyes,
and fliced their Flefh by fmall pieces, faying
that they treated them fo, not as French but
as Lutherans. Laudonniere having faved
what he could of the poor Wretches, in Barges
which he fent along the Coaft, came back to
France.

The King's Council being then almoft *Spani-
alifed*, took no care of avenging that Maffacre.
But a private Man, Dominick de Gourgues
by Name, born at *Mont de Marfan* in Gafcony,
a very generous and courageous Man, who re-
fenting the ill treatment he had received from
the Spaniards, when having taken him Prifoner
of War in Italy, had fent him to the Galleys,
undertook to revenge his own and the Kingdom's Injury; he fitted out fome Ships at his
own Charge, felling for that purpofe part of his
Eftate, and borrowing a Sum of his Brother,

President of the Generality of Guienn, and manned them with two hundred Soldiers and a hundred Sailors, and having landed at *Florida*, he joined with the Natives who groaned under the tyrannical and barbarous Yoke of the Spaniards, and took by Storm the Fort Charles, and two others which they had built in two different places. There were in them above eight hundred Men. The Natives murdered all thofe who thought to make their efcape in the Woods, and Gourgues caufed all the reft who had furrendered themfelves at difcretion, to be hanged with this Motto, NOT AS SPANIARDS, BUT AS PIRATES.

When he came back to France, the Avenger of his Country, and the Deliverer of Florida, inftead of Praifes and Recompences met with Accufers, and the utmoft peril of his Life ; the Spanifh Embaffador profecuted him with all his Might, the King's Council were very willing to give him all the Satisfaction he could defire ; therefore Gourgues was obliged to hide himfelf till the Peace was made, and then the Admiral and his Friends obtained his pardon (x).

LXXVII.
*Captain
Peyrot's
Expedition
at Madera.*

About the fame time, PETER BERTRAND, commonly called *Captain Peyrot*, Son to Blaife Montluc, acquired no lefs Glory than Gourgues in his Expedition, tho' he was not fo fuccefsful as he. He intended to build a Fort, whether the Inhabitants would or no, in the firft convenient place he could meet in the Kingdoms of *Macinengo*, or *Mozambick*, or *Melinda*, for fecuring the French Trade in *Africa* and the *Eaft Indies*, which was for the moft part in the hands of the Portuguefe. For that purpofe he fitted out, at his own Charge, three large Ships, and fome Barks, with twelve hundred Men ; his Brother

FA-

(x) Thuan. Hift. lib. XLIV. p. 530——537.

Fabian, and the youngeſt Son of the Houſe of Pompadour went along with him.

Being caſt by a Storm upon the Coaſts of *Madeira*, the Crew had a mind to land to take in Water; the Portugueſe fired their Guns at them, and ſallied in order to cut them in pieces. Bertrand provoked at this Inhumanity, whereby the Laws of Nations were violated, as well as the Alliance that was ſettled between the two Crowns of *France* and *Portugal*, landed eight hundred Men, and directly marched againſt the Portugueſe, while his Brother Fabian attacked them by the Rear, having ſurrounded them they were all killed. Then he marched directly to the Town, and having battered with his Cannon he took it by Storm, and plundered it: But as he was attacking the great Church, wherein part of the Garriſon withſtood ſtill, he was wounded in the Thigh whereby he died a few days after.

So miſcarried an attempt which would have proved no leſs uſeful than glorious. All his Followers were in great danger of their Lives when they came back to France; they were obliged for a long while to flee, or to live concealed; it was with much ado, that by Montluc's Intereſt and the Admiral's Power, who was always very zealous for whatever was conducive to the Honour and Glory of the French Nation, that they eſcaped the Sollicitations of the Portugueze Embaſſador, who proſecuted them in the King's Council as Pirates (*y*).

Thoſe who had made the Treaty of Chartres intended not to keep it, but only to take better meaſures than they had done heretofore for deſtroying the Reformed, after they had diſarmed them. Every where the Catholicks proſecuted to their utmoſt the Reformed, and far from enjoying

LXXIX.
Infraction of the laſt Edict of Peace.

(*y*) Thuan. ibid.

joying the benefit of the Peace and the Liberty of their Consciences, they were in a condition much worse than during the War. In less than three Months, more than *T E N   T H O U S A N D* of them were publickly murdered and massacred in several Cities, as *Roüen, Amiens, Auxerre, Bourges, Issoudun, Troye, Orleans, Angers, Blois, Sens, Ligny,* and some other places ; several were also condemned at *Clermont,* and burnt alive.

The People incited by the Preachers, and especially by the Jesuits, could not be kept in any Restraint, after having made Executions upon the Commons, they fell upon the Nobility. René Lord of Cipierre, Son to the Count of Tende, was inhumanly massacred at Frejus, with thirty of his Attendants, as he was coming from Nice, where he had been to pay a visit to the Duke of Savoy his Kinsman. The Lord of Amançay was murdered at his Castle-gate, where he was holding his Daughter, a young Child, in his Arms *(z).*

The News of these Violences arrived at La Rochelle just at the time that the wealthiest were resolved to open their Gates, and to receive the Marshal of Vielleville for their Governor, but then the Commons opposed that Design ; and whereas the Court had taken almost no manner of Caution for hiding their Design from publick Notice, and that far from dismissing the foreign Troops, they endeavoured to increase them ; several Cities refused to admit into them Royal Garrisons, of that Number were Montauban, Millaud, Sancerre, Alby, Castres, and some others. Besides that, they had great Reason to suspect that Pius V. one of the most zealous Sticklers for the Immunities of the Clergy, having granted a Bull to the King for alienating for

a

(z) Idem, lib. XLIV. p. 544, &c. D'Aubigné liv. V. c. i.

a hundred and fifty thousand Crowns of yearly Church-Rents, in a time of Peace, such a Concession could not be intended for any other Design but to execute the Scheme of Bayonne for extirpating the Reformed. Furthermore, the Jesuits incensed the People by their execrable Tenets which they delivered in their Sermons, viz. *That Peace ought never to be made or consented to with Sectaries ; that no body was obliged to keep Faith with them ; that it was a pious and salutary thing to lay violent hands upon them ; that all Christians ought to arm themselves against those Infidels ; and to the Decree of the Council of* Constance, *they added several particular Examples out of the Holy History, such as that of the Levites, who at Moses's Command fell upon the Worshippers of the golden Calf, and killed many of them ; that of Jehu who caused all the Priests of Baal, whom he had gathered together under the pretence of a Feast, to be murdered.* By these and other like Discourses, People, as abovesaid, were so far provoked, that they threatened the Reformed every where, bragging that they had but three Months longer to live, till the Harvest and the Vintage were over, and that after that, they would be all murdered ; that the King, tho' he would, could never hinder them from executing their Designs, and if he undertook it they would dethrone him, put him in a Cloyster, and elect another (a).

The Prince was at this time at *Noyers,* a Castle belonging to the Princess his Consort, where having certain Intelligence that the Attempt made to surprise him being miscarried, the Marshal of Tavannes, Deputy Governour of *Burgundy,* assembled his Troops to take him forcibly, he wrote to his Friends all over the Kingdom,

LXXX. *Devices of the Queen to sow Division amongst the Reformed.*

Vol. III. R dom,

(a) Thuan. lib. XLIV. p. 544.

dom, to let them know the Danger he was in, and to exhort them to watch over themselves, and to be ready in case of need. Mean while the King, (or rather the Queen) issued out his Letters-Patent, whereby he ordered that the three hundred thousand Crowns which he had paid for dismissing the Germans that were come as Auxiliaries to the Prince, should be levied immediately upon the Reformed ; however, (*in order to sow Divisions amongst them*) he declared, that he intended not that all the Reformed of his Kingdom should contribute towards the raising of that Sum, but only those who had joined themselves in Arms with the Prince.

His Highness being sensible that this was only some of his Enemies Devices, frequently complained of it by his Letters to the King, beseeching his Majesty to be moved with pity for his People, exhausted by the Civil Wars. The Admiral wrote to the same purpose to Margaret Duchess of Savoy, thinking that she had a great Interest at Court.

At the same time a Soldier having been taken as he was upon measuring the depth and breadth of the Ditches of the Castle of Noyers, the Prince sent Telligny to Court to complain of the Wrong done unto him by the abovesaid Letters, of the said Soldier's Attempt, of the many Murders and Massacres perpetrated, of the Plots laid against the Reformed, of the seditious Sermons of the Preachers, and so on ; beseeching his Majesty to cause that the late Edict should be kept in all the Provinces.

Tho' the King was moved by these Complaints, and desired his Mother oftentimes to take care left a Civil War should break out again, and that the Edicts should be religiously kept, or otherwise the Kingdom would be subverted :

verted : Nevertheless, she guessing that these Requests of the King proceeded from the Chancellour de L'Hospital, represented to his Majesty that the Rebellion of the Rochelese (for so she stiled the just Defence of their Rights and Privileges) would be a bad Example to other Cities ; and knowing that the said Chancellour was averse to all violent Designs and Resolutions, and that he had a great Influence over the King, she undertook to lessen him in his Majesty's Esteem by many false Reports, as if he countenanced in secret the Cause of the Reformed, telling him that nothing hindered him from publickly professing that Religion, but the Office he was invested with, seeing that his Wife, his Daughter, his Son-in-Law, his Grand-Children professed openly that Religion : and a thing happened at this time which gave a great weight to the Calumnies of his Enemies, viz.

The abovesaid Bull of the Pope's for alienating 150 thousand Crowns of yearly Rent of Church-Goods, declaring the Use whereof, viz. for destroying the Reformed, or obliging them to reconcile themselves with the Church of Rome, several of the King's Counsellors, at the head of whom the Chancellour was, opposed that Bull, because it supposed that a War against the Reformed had been for a long while before hatching ; and that it was better that the Pope should send another Bull, and in the mean while to make use of this only as far as the present Case required. This Opinion of the Chancellour increased much the Suspicions against him. Therefore the Queen improving all Opportunities of rendering that great Man suspicious to the King, from that time his Majesty grew every day cooler towards him, and being not able to bear patiently with the Indignities put upon him on account of

his

his Integrity and Stedfastness in whatever he thought the Duty of his Charge, he began to think of his Retreat ; and being gone to *Vignay*, a Country-house of his near Estampes, the Queen sent to him Peter Brulart one of her Secretaries to let him know that the King advised him to take rest, and deliver the Seals, which were given to John Morvilliers, Bishop of Orleans, till his Majesty should dispose of them otherwise.

The Chancellour being removed from the Helm of the Government, the Queen began to act according to her own Will without any controul at all, and took the most violent Methods ; and whereas every thing was ready for making war upon the Reformed, in order to weaken their Forces, and to disunite them, she sent throughout the several Provinces of the Kingdom a set Form of an Oath to be taken by them, whereby they swore before God and in his Name, that they acknowledged Charles IX for their Sovereign and lawful King, and promised to pay unto him all manner of Honour, Obedience and Submission, and never to take up Arms unless by his express Command, or to countenance those who should take them up against him or assist them in any wise either by their Counsels, or Supplies of Money, Men, Provisions, or Ammunitions ; and to reveal to the King or his Governors whatever they shall discover concerning any Plot or Enterprise, &c. as soon as it came to their knowledge : and that they would beseech his Majesty with all Humility, that according to his innate Goodness and Clemency he would be pleased to use them as his faithful and most obedient Subjects, and receive them under his Royal Protection, and that they would put up Prayers to God for the Welfare and Prosperity of his Majesty, his Mother,

and

and his Brethren ; that they willingly submitted
themselves to the most cruel Death, if any Di-
sturbance should happen in the City, Town, Borough, &c. (expresly named in the Act) wherein
they inhabit, by their own Fault ; and to do
whatever lies in their power for its Defence, and
for keeping a strict Correspondence and Friendship with the Catholicks of the said Place.

The Prince looking upon this as a Snare laid
for his own and the whole Reformed Body's destruction, avoided it partly by excusing himself
from swearing upon such a Form, and partly by
explaining the meaning of the Words he made
use of. But having every day some new Intelligence of the Plots laid against him, he sent notice to the Admiral, who was come to *Tanlay* for
his own and his Family's Security, and desired
him to come and meet him at *Noyers*, and then
they thought that their best way was to fly. And
indeed they saw that the thirteen Companies of
Horse and as many of Foot destined for the Siege
of *La Rochelle*, had been then recalled into *Burgundy* ; and tho' Telligny had brought very civil
Letters from Court, nevertheless he was pretty
sure that no good could be expected from the
Queen. However, the Prince not to be deficient
in any thing that could be conducive to the keeping of the Peace, desired the Marchioness of Ro-
thelin his Mother-in-law, to go to Court, in order to try whether she could divert the Storm
wherewith he was threatned.

But she was no sooner gone than the Prince
received Letters whereby he was warned to pro- *Attempts*
vide, without any further delay, for his own Se- *to seize the*
curity, and that if he did not improve the present *Prince and*
Opportunity, it would be too late in two days ; *the Admi-*
that even now, very hardly would he escape the *ral.*

R 3 threat-

threatning Danger he was in, being every where surrounded by his Enemies (b).

It is said that the Marshal de Tavanes, Deputy-Governor of Burgundy, had so great an Abhorrence of the Plot against the Prince and the Admiral, the Execution whereof had been committed to his Care, that having tried, but in vain, to dissuade the Queen from it, he resolved to discover cunningly the Intrigue to the Prince, that he might take his measures for making his escape, that for that end he ordered his Couriers to pass hard by *Noyers*, on purpose that his Letters might be intercepted by the Prince; which succeeded to his Wishes, for the Courier being stopt, these Words were found in the Packet, written with the Marshal's own Hand; THE STAG IS IN THE TOILS, THE GAME IS READY (c).

However, the Prince having conferred with the Admiral upon all these Advertisements, resolved to provide for their own Security by flight. But before they set out, he wrote to the King, and charged the Cardinal of Lorrain as the Author of all the Troubles and Miseries the Kingdom was involved in; that his turbulent and restless Spirit forced innocent People to fly from one Place to another for Safety, with their Children in the Cradle. To these Letters he added a Petition, wherein he complained of the manifold Infractions of the last Treaty, and set forth the innumerable Grievances of the Reformed; and declared that since the Cardinal was the Cause of all the Mischief, he and his Adherents were fully resolved to prosecute that Perjurer and common Enemy of the Country, with all their might. In order to conceal their Flight the better, the Prince having sent the Letters and Petition, feigned to give

(b) Thuan. Ibid. (c) Add. aux Mem. de Casteln
liv. vi. p. 529. liv. vii. p. 576.

give out that he would stay till he had received
the King's Answer.

And now let us consider a while, who has been
the Author of the third Civil War, either the
Catholicks or the Reformed.   All the Catholick
Historians of those days agree upon this, that the
Treaty of *Chartres* had never been made with an
Intent to keep it, but only to get time to prepare
themselves for the better Execution of their Plot,
which was impracticable as long as the Reformed
were in Arms.   Now, that such was their Design,
is plain by their Conduct : For they did not follow even the common Rules which Prudence required in such a Case, to oblige the Reformed to
trust themselves intirely upon their Word ; but
they acted so openly, and with so little Caution
that they forced them whether they would or not,
to be upon their Guard ; they did not allow them
time to disarm, but they began, as it were, while
the Pen was still in their hands to sign the Treaty,
to use them with the greatest Injustice and Cruelty in all Places where they were the strongest,
as above said ; they kept their Troops on foot,
they augmented them, they garrisoned the Cities
in the heart of the Kingdom, they guarded the
Passages of the Rivers.   In many Places, the Reformed, far from enjoying that Liberty of Conscience, were cruelly massacred ; in others they
were deprived of their Goods, Estates, Honours,
and Offices, far from being restored to, much
less maintained in the Possession of them.   Was
it then strange that the Reformed at *Montauban,*
Millaud, and others, understanding how their
Brethren were used in other Places, refused to
trust themselves into their Enemies Hands, much
less *La Rochelle,* which by the Privileges she enjoyed for two hundred Years, was not obliged to
admit any Garrison from the King ? Therefore it

would

would be a great piece of Injuſtice to charge the
Reformed with having been the firſt Infringers of
the Treaty of *Chartres.* But let us hear the Judgment of a Man which cannot be challenged by
the Catholicks, it is the PRIOR OF JUVIGNE',
in his Additions to the Memoirs of Caſtelnau,
Book VII. Ch. 1.

,, Since the Peace of *Chartres* the Prince of
,, Condé had retired to his Houſe at *Noyers,* in
,, *Burgundy,* to give leſs Suſpicion to the Court,
,, living in a Province quite Catholick, governed
,, by the Marſhal of Tavannes, Deputy of the
,, Duke of Aumale, and a Creature of the Houſe
,, of Lorrain. He thought that depriving him-
,, ſelf in that manner of the Opportunities and
,, Means of attempting any thing, he would be
,, free from all Suſpicions: And indeed there was
,, nothing to fear for the State; but his High-
,, neſs's Ruin being the chief Means of his Ene-
,, mies Greatneſs, and the Pretence of Religion
,, being too ſtrong and powerful for neglecting to
,, make uſe of it to the utmoſt, with the Pope's
,, Approbation, and by the Counſels of the King
,, of Spain, who backed all the Deſigns of the
,, Cardinal of Lorrain, they very eaſily came to
,, perſuade themſelves, that whatever they would
,, do under ſo fair a Pretence, would be deemed
,, a piece of PRUDENCE rather than a piece of
,, INFIDELITY, and that it was only queſtion to
,, oppreſs a Party, which had divided the King-
,, dom. To this they added that Politicks diſ-
,, penſe the Princes with keeping Faith to their
,, own Subjects, and that it was honourable to
,, avenge themſelves of a Treaty which they had
,, been ſhamefully conſtrained to. But what is ſuch
,, a Policy other than a Prudence ſo refined, that
,, it may be called, THE MALICE OF THE CHIL-
,, DREN OF DARKNESS? What is it elſe than A

I

CHAL-

,, Challenge against Honour and Fide-
,, lity ? and by what other Authority can it be
,, defended, but by the Cabinet's, where
,, every one minds his own Self-Interest,
,, where there is always some Faction
,, or other which over-rules the State's
,, true Interest ? I shall not engage my self
,, too far in that Matter, but I shall say, that few
,, Sovereigns have broken their Faith with their
,, Subjects without being blamed for it ; and shall
,, affirm again, that no such things had been seen
,, under our first Kings, who thought it not a
,, disparagement to them to treat with their Vas-
,, sals, nay, to give them Pledges and Sureties
,, for their Word, as any other private Man
,, could have done. That was a Means of paci-
,, fying the Troubles of the State, which hath
,, always succeeded well, and I might make a
,, large Book, would I relate all the Examples
,, which the Titles of the Treasury, and of the
,, Chamber of Accounts afford us upon that Sub-
,, ject. Since that Method has been altered, a
,, reciprocal Jealousy hath fomented all the Di-
,, visions, and sometimes a Party has been obliged
,, to prosecute by desperate Means the Differences
,, wherein he had at first entered by Misfortune.
,, There was another Method in Use in those
,, days, even amongst Equals, *viz.* to take some
,, Umpires for deciding, concerning any Breach
,, of a Treaty sworn upon ; but since now-a-days
,, the Royal Word is the only Security of a Trea-
,, ty, methinks it ought to be still more inviola-
,, ble : And to be sure, it ought to have been so
,, as to the Execution of the Treaty of Chartres,
,, the Violation whereof exposed once again the
,, Religion and the Kingdom to the greatest Dan-
,, ger, as well as that of the Treaty of *Angers,*
,, violated on *Bartholomew's-day,* without any o-
ther

,, ther Succefs than to have revenged, by the lofs
,, of the King's Honour, and at the State's Peril,
,, the Quarrels of a Cabal, which, by that means,
,, was put in a Condition of difputing the Crown
,, with the lawful Heir, and of continuing the
,, War till the latter end of the laft Century (*d*).

Such are the Reflections of the moft judicious
Agricola, to which every fober Man will find
himfelf obliged to fubfcribe whenever he fhall
have examined the Cafe impartially. It is evident by this, and by two or three other paffages
of the fame Author, that while the Court was
wholly intent to devife ways and means for fur-
prifing and deftroying the Reformed, with their
Chief, in defiance of the moft folemn Treaties
fworn upon, the Prince was wholly intent to execute the Articles of it, and to fee that his Adherents fhould do the fame ; that for that very
purpofe, and to avoid giving any Jealoufy at
Court he had chofe to live in a Province, the Government whereof was in his mortal Enemies
hands, and the Parliament whereof was entirely
devoted to the Guifian Faction ; where the Reformed were not the moft powerful. In a word,
where he was fo clofely furrounded by thofe who
fought his Ruin, that had not God Almighty
touched fome of them with a Senfe of Pity, he
was utterly undone. Therefore this third Civil
War cannot in any wife be charged upon the
Reformed (*e*).

The

(*d*) Add. aux Mem. de Cafteln. liv. VII. ch. i. p. 575, 76.
(*e*) The fame Author fpeaking of the Marfhal of Vielleville, Book IV. ch. vii. p. 154, 155, faid, Brantome following the Court's Method, charges the faid Marfhal with a
Correfpondence with the Hugonots, and feems to blame
him for having not purfued the Prince of Condé, who retreated, all out of order, with his Family, after they had
mifcarried in the Attempt to feize him at Noyers, WHERE
HE EXECUTED SINCERELY AND CANDIDLY THE
TREATY

The Resolution being taken, and the Prince having sent the abovesaid Letter and Petition to the King, he set out on the 25th of August, with the Princess his Consort, who was with child, all his Family consisting of six Children, three whereof were in the Cradle, the Admiral with his Countess and their Children, some of whom were carried in their Nurse's Arms, D'Andelot's Lady with a Child of two Years old, and some other Ladies, all attended with 150 or 60 Gendarmes. What a sad Sight was this, a Prince and a Princess of the Blood in the condition she was in, six small Children in their swaddling Clothes, or in the Cradle, forced to run away in the dark, and through By-ways, exposed to the bad Weather, having above two hundred and fifty Leagues, and so many Rivers to cross in an Enemy's Country before they could find any place of Safety ! And all this, not for any Misdemeanour or Crime of

Charles IX. 1568. Pope Pius V.

LXXXIV. *The Prince and the Admiral's escape, and the third Civil War.*

TREATY OF PEACE, WHILE HIS ENEMIES PLOTTED HIS AND HIS HOUSE's RUIN AGAINST THE PUBLICK FAITH, and Book VI. p. 529, speaking of the Marshal of Tavannes, he says, that the Prince was unjustly prosecuted WHILE HE WAS FAITHFULLY EXECUTING THE PEACE THAT HAD BEEN SWORN WITH HIM. And Book VII. p. 551. speaking of an Enterprize of the Court upon *La Rochelle*, he says, They ought then to have been intent only upon this Affair; but to undertake at one and the same time to seize the Prince of Condé, the Admiral, and all the Chiefs of the Hugonot Party in every Province, and to spread a Net, as it were, as large as the Kingdom, THAT WAS A RASH ATTEMPT, if we will not term it AN INFIDELITY, which put the Kingdom in a worse Condition than before, and FORCED the Hugonots TO DO OUT OF DESPAIR what they would never have presumed to do with their own Strength. It was a Body full of Ears and Eyes, the first Sound or Light put it all in Motion, in an instant they received Notice, in an instant they were in a condition to join together, and especially *La Rochelle* passed from Mistrust to a Defence, &c. All these Testimonies are sufficient methinks to oblige us to cast the blame and odium of this third Civil War upon the Court and the Guisian Party.

of their own, but only for gratifying the cruel Ambition of an unworthy Prieſt, and ſatiating the Rapaciouſneſs of four or five other Wolves, that hunted after a Prey, and poſtponed the publick to their private Intereſt. But let us ſee the wonders whereby the Prince and his Company ſo narrowly eſcaped from the hands of their Enemies.

They went by long Marches, and croſſed the *Loire* at a Ford over-againſt *Sancerre.* Hardly had they croſſed, before the Troops of Burgundy, who purſued them, were diſcover'd at *St. Godon,* on the oppoſite Shore from whence they juſt came. The River was then fordable, and had their Enemies improved that Opportunity, it was impoſſible for them to eſcape ; but the next Morning the River was ſwelled up to ſuch a degree, that not only it could not be forded, but it was impoſſible to ferry over, ſo ſtrong was the Current.

At this unexpected Accident whereby they were providentially delivered, the Prince and his Company, full of the ſame Gratitude which the antient Iſraelites had felt after the croſſing of the *Red Sea,* fell on their Knees and gave their hearty thanks to God for this ſignal Protection, and ſang the 114th Pſalm.

Proceeding in their Journey, they were expoſed to a new danger, as they went through *Poitou,* the Count of Lude and Montſalez ſollicited the Marſhal of Vielleville then at *Poitiers,* to give them leave to go in purſuit of the Prince ; but the Marſhal denied them, ſaying, that he had no ſuch Command from the King, and that he waited for his Orders upon that account. The Prince had thought proper to ſend Word unto the ſaid Marſhal, to take no notice of his paſſage, that he had been forced to fly from his

Houſe,

House, where he had been upon the point of being seized by his Enemies, and that he was going to Rochelle, from whence he would send him his Case more at large, and to the King too, desiring no better than to be his Majesty's faithful Subject and Servant, and to live in Peace and Safety where he could in some corner of the Kingdom. However, either because the said Marshal had some secret Inclination for the Reformed Religion, or because he was inwardly convinced of the Prince's Innocence, he never thought of opposing his passage, as he could have done easily.

Montluc, Governour of *Guienn*, and the King's Lieutenants in *Limosin* and *Perigord*, were in Arms for opposing his Passage ; but he prevented them all, and arrived safe at *La Rochelle* on the 18th of September. The Queen of Navarr arrived at the same place a few days after, with her two Children, Henry Prince of Bearn, and Catharina. The Cardinal of Chatillon was at his Castle of *Bresse* in *Beauvoisis*, when he heard of the Prince's flight, and being in an Impossibility of going to join the Confederates, because he ought to cross several Provinces full of Enemies, he fled in a Sailor's disguise into England, where he was kindly received and entertained by Queen Elizabeth, and was very useful to the *CAUSE*.

The Prince was no sooner arrived at *La Rochelle* but many of the Reformed Nobility and Gentry came to him with Troops they had raised in their Country, and amongst their Vassals ; I shall presently give a short account of a few of them. The Queen of Navarr had brought 4000 Men, Foot or Horse, along with her. D'Andelot who was in Britany had assembled almost the same number in the Provinces of *Normandy*, *Maine*, and *Anjou*, which were joined
with

LXXXV.
*The Queen
of Navarr
with her
Children
and seve-
ral Lords
joined the
Prince at
Rochelle*.

with thofe of Montgomery, La Noüe, and fome others.

They all together, after fome Skirmifhes with the Vifcount of Martigues, croffed the *Loire;* Montgomery having found a Ford, and without being oppofed on this Occafion by the Duke of Montpenfier, who commanded the King's Forces in thofe Parts.

LXXXVI.
Both Parties publifh their Manifefto's.
Both Parties, that is, the Royalift, or rather the Guifian, and the Reformed publifhed their Manifefto's for juftifying their Conduct. The Queen of Navarr wrote to the King, to the Queen-Mother, to the Duke of Anjou, and to her Brother-in-Law the Cardinal of Bourbon; this laft fhe upbraided for Pufillanimity, and want of Senfibility for the many Affronts put upon him by the Cardinal of Lorrain, whereof, fays fhe, he was become the Drudge, not being able to refent an Attempt of that impure Prieft againft his Life and that of the Duke of Montpenfier. For it was confidently reported, that the Queen-Mother having been in danger of her Life in a late Sicknefs, the Cardinal of Lorrain had hired fome Affaffins to murder thefe two Princes as foon as the Queen would have expired, becaufe he was afraid left the King would not liften to his violent Counfels, as long as they would be alive, and that they both being dead, that would pave the way for his Nephew to the Throne; for he did not mind much the Princes of Bearn or Condé, becaufe he was pretty fure to raife againft them moft part of the Kingdom, and to be affifted by Philip of Spain and the Pope, who would never fuffer a Proteftant or Reformed Prince to afcend the Throne of France, how juft foever his Title could be (*f*).

The

(*f*) Thuanus, lib. xliv. p. 549.

The Prince drew a set Form of Oath, whereby
he and all his Adherents engaged themselves never to lay down their Arms till they had obtained a full Redress of their Grievances, especially
against the Cardinal of Lorrain, and that they
would obey the Prince in every thing conducive
to that end. He published a Manifesto to the
same purpose.

On the other hand, the King published an
Edict, whereby he declared, that he took all the
Reformed of his Kingdom under his Protection,
and promised to do them Justice for all the Injuries they had suffered ; provided they should
live peaceably in their own Houses. The Snare
was too grossly laid, very few were drawn into
it. Therefore the Queen and the Cardinal of
Lorrain, seeing that this would not serve their
Turn, they published another quite contrary to
this, whereby the publick Exercise of the Reformed Religion was expressly forbidden, and
all the Ministers were ordered to depart the Kingdom in a Fortnight's time. By a third Edict
all the Reformed who held any publick Employ-
ment or Office were ordered to resign the same
into the King's hand, and the Parliament of Paris added this Clause of their own Accord, That
from henceforward no body should be admitted
to any publick Office, but those who would swear
that they would live and die in the Roman
Church.

During the Month of October the Prince and
his Adherents made themselves Masters of all the
places in *Aulnix, Saintonge, Angoumois* and *Poitou* ;
and they would have been more successful, had
not their Troops, to the number of 25000
Men, coming from *Dauphiné, Languedoc,* and
Guienn, under the Command of D'Assier, received a check as they came out from the Country
of

of *Perigord.*   Mouvans, an experienced and courageous Captain, but too much self-conceited, had taken his Quarters a little out of the way with three thousand Men, because of some mis-understanding between him and Beaudiner, Brother to D'Assier, Count of Crussol.   The Duke of Montpensier, who had been in those Parts for opposing their junction with the Prince, gave Order to the young Count of Brissac to attack him while he himself should skirmish with D'Assier, that he might not come to his assistance.   D'Assier knowing very well what they intended to do, sent word to Mouvans not to stir out from his Quarters for that day, because he was so well retrenched, that he could not be forced : but Mouvans followed not his Orders, for Brissac feigning to retreat, he came out of his Retrenchments the very same day, and fell into an Ambuscade ready laid for him in his way, where he was killed, with a thousand of his Men; the Remnant fled into the neighbouring Woods.   D'Assier received a thousand of them on the next day, and the other thousand were either routed or killed by the Peasants.

When the Prince had joined D'Assier at *Aubeterre,* the Duke of Montpensier was obliged to retreat to *Chatelleraud.*   When the Duke of Anjou the King's Brother, and Generalissimo of all his Armies, was come into the King's Army, it was found to consist of twenty-four thousand Foot and four thousand Horse ; that of the Prince was of twenty-five thousand Foot and three thousand Horse strong, and all stout and resolute Men, who having forsaken their Families, Goods, and Estates, trusted only upon God and in the strength of their Arms.

For that reason the Prince sought after an opportunity of fighting the Duke of Anjou, and
pro-

provoked him to it; but for the very same reason the Duke of Anjou declined the Battel, however for his Honour's sake he was obliged to keep the Field. The sharpness of the Winter could not oblige either of them to go into Quarters, till their Troops, overcome by the extreme Cold, refused to fight any longer against Snow and Ice; above 8000 of both Parties died with Cold, and other Miseries they had undergone.

The Queen of Navarr was very busy in making Provisions for discharging the Expences of the War, there was no Money in the Military Chest. Plunder was a thing not only very odious, but very precarious too in itself; and what the Reformed that remained in their own Houses, could spare for the common Cause, was very inconsiderable. Therefore her Majesty, on the 15th of October, had wrote to the generous Elizabeth Queen of England, and deputed unto her Chastelier Portaut, one of the Gentlemen of her Chamber, whereby she acquainted her with the true Motives of the present War, and desired her that since they did not wage War against the King, she would be pleased to grant them her Assistance in the Defence of so just a Cause wherein all the Protestant Powers were concerned, since it was for opposing the detestable Plot laid against them all in general at Bayonne, and since that time renewed in Lorrain, and that she would be pleased to receive herself and her Children under her Royal Protection, &c.

These Intreaties, joined with those of the Cardinal Odet de Chatillon, then at the Court of England, were as efficacious as could be expected at that time, for Queen Elizabeth sent a hundred thousand gold Ducats, six large Guns, with other Ammunitions and Provisions. Castelnau says, that in order to reimburse her Majesty,

jesty,

jesty, the Prince of Condé sent to her a vast quantity of Metal, Bells, and Wool, but that is not likely ; and the other Historian does not mention any such thing. Besides that, she received and entertained very kindly the poor French Refugees that fled from *Normandy, Picardy, Britany,* and other Provinces, and took Sanctuary in England.

The Queen of Navarr borrowed also twenty-six thousand Ducats from the Rochelese ; Mezeray reckons but sixteen thousand ; and La Hode, a modern Author, in his Annals of the Kings of France, says, that the Rochelese made a Gift of sixty thousand Crowns to the Prince. However, besides all these Sums it was resolved in the Council of the Princes to sell the Church's Lands ; and whereas they were possessed of several great Provinces, they raised by that means a very large Sum of Money ; for tho' there was no great Security, nevertheless they met with many buyers, who were bold enough to venture their Money upon such a slight Foundation.

XCI.
The King sends several Embassies.

The King had already deputed the Bishop of Macon to the Pope, and Hannibal de Rucellai to the *Venetians,* and to the Dukes of *Ferrara, Mantua,* and *Florence,* to desire them to lend him a Sum of Money, and Auxiliary Troops. And at the same time he sent Anthony Fumée, Lord of Blandy, his Embassador to the Emperor, to complain of the Insolency of his own Subjects who had again taken up Arms against him, and to desire him to interpose his Authority, and not to suffer that the Prince of Condé should receive any Auxiliaries, either Foot or Horse, from Germany. Fumée had his first Audience on the 16th of October at Vienna. But the wise, prudent and good Maximilian II. dismissed him with an Answer not much to his liking ; for he told

told him, that he was vexed at his Heart to see the Kingdom of France expofed again to civil Commotions, whereby the Forces of Chriftendom, already much depreffed by the Infidels Army, exhaufted themfelves more and more every day ; therefore he thought very advifeable to find out fome ways and means for faving the Chriftian Blood, and fettling a fincere and lafting Peace between the moft Chriftian King and his Subjects, or otherwife he would find himfelf and his Kingdom involved in the greateft Inconveniences and Troubles ; the Rumour of his and his chief Counfellours Defigns being already fpread not only in Germany, but alfo in Britain, therefore he ought not to doubt the leaft in the World, but there would be feveral Princes not fo far inconfiderable as to deferve to be defpifed, who, not only out of Inclination for the Prince of Condé's Party, but even out of Self-Intereft, and for their common Prefervation would affift him with Men and Money. As to what he required of him to oppofe the inlifting and levying Troops in Germany for the Prince's Service, that could not be eafily done, and was attended with many difficulties : for if the laft Year, when the King's Caufe feem'd more juft, fuch Levies could not be hindered notwithftanding all poffible diligence and care for that purpofe, how could that be avoided now, when the Motive of the War was quite another thing, and that many thought it to be common with them and the King's Subjects *(g)* ?

Fumée having received that Anfwer, went to Altembourg to John William of Saxony upon the fame Errand as he had been to the Emperor ; but he was anfwered on the 27th of November, that he was very forry that the War

S 2 was

(g) Thuan. lib. XLIV. p. 560, 561.

was kindled again in France, and so much the more because he saw that one Party rejected the Cause of it upon Religion, and the other upon Rebellion ; and yet by the express Command of God, Divine things ought to be parted from Human. That so had judged the most Christian Emperors Constantine, Theodosius, Martian, Justinian, Charlemaign, Lewis the Good, and of late John Frederick, Elector of Saxony, his most honoured Father. Therefore he thought that the King would do rightly and prudently, if he did not suffer that his Subjects should be exposed to any danger for their Religion's sake ; for the effect of true Religion is not Sedition, but it enforces a lawful Obedience. As to the rest, the Princes of the Empire took very ill, what was publickly reported every where concerning an Alliance between the King of Spain and the Pope for the utter extirpation of the Protestants and the Reformed all over Europe, into which he heard that the King of France, by the Advice of his bad and corrupted Counsellors, was entered ; that the King ought to consider well all these things, and that he would be always ready to assist him as his Ancestors had done, as far as his Conscience and Religion could allow it. So Fumée was dismissed on both sides without being able to prevail either upon the Emperor or upon the Duke of Saxony *(b)*. Now while the two Armies are in their Winter-Quarters in France, I shall give a short Account of some of the most celebrated that had joined with the Prince.

XCII.
Of Telligny. Amongst several Lords that signalized themselves in the Reformed Party, Charles Lord of Telligny is one of those that have deserved the greatest Esteem and Veneration. He was

(b) Idem. ibidem.

was Grand-son to Lewis Lord de Telligny, de
Lierville and du Chatelier, Seneschal of *Rouërge*
and *Beaucaire*, Governor of the Milanese in the
absence of the Lord of Lautrec, and Deputy-
Governor of Therouenne in the Year 1512, and
was killed at the Siege of St. Quintin. His Son
de Telligny, &c. inherited his Virtues as well
as his Name : In his Youth he was made Standard-bearer to the Duke of Orleans, but he ran
so far in debt for the support of his Rank, that
he was obliged to depart the Kingdom, and retire to Venice, where he died. His Son, our
Charles de Telligny, was so great a Proficient
in all the Qualifications necessary for the Court
and the Army, being endowed with such a Prudence and Sagacity, speaking in so agreeable and
persuasive way, that he was, as it were, the
Mercury of the State, and the perpetual Nego-
tiator of all the Treaties of Peace. The Prince
of Condé and the Admiral, to both whom he
had the Honour to be allied by his Mother Ar-
tusia Vernon, Lady of Monstreuil-Bonin, Grand-
daughter to Philippa of Montmorency, who was
Aunt of Louisa of Montmorency, Mother to
the Admiral de Coligny, and Grand-mother to
Eleonor of Roye, the Prince's first Wife : The
Prince, I say, and the Admiral intrusted him
with all their Concerns, and the Queen-Mother
was very kind to him, and heard him with
pleasure, knowing that he was a very wise and
prudent Man, much averse to all violent Counsels. But all his great and good Qualities could
not save him on Bartholomew's-day, being singled out to be one of the first Victims that were
to be sacrificed to the furious Ambition of the
Guisians. His Crime was not only his being
firmly adherent to the Reformed Religion, but
chiefly his having married Louisa of Coligny,

S 3

Daugh-

Daughter to the Admiral, who preferred the happiness of having a Son-in-Law so virtuous, and endowed with such great parts, to all the Fortunes in the World. He had premeditated this Marriage long before it was accomplished, as it appears by his Will made in 1569, wherein he says, *Item, according to what I have told my eldest Daughter, I do advise her for the reasons she knows, to marry Mr. de Telligny, for the goods and rare Parts that I have seen in him : and if she does so, I shall deem her very happy ; however, I will not make use of my Authority on this Occasion, only I do advise her, as loving her so intirely as she knows that I do, I give that Counsel unto her, because I do really think that it will be for her Good and Satisfaction, which we must always prefer to the greatest Estates and Riches.* That Marriage was accomplished two Years after in 1571 ; and the next Year he was massacred, as abovesaid, without leaving any Issue. The Lady Telligny was married afterwards to William of Naffau, Prince of Orange, as much for the sake of her own Perfections of Body and Mind, as for the sake of the most celebrated and respectable Name of the Admiral her Father ; she had by that second Marriage Henry Frederick of Naffau Prince of Orange, Grand-father to King William of glorious and immortal Memory *(j)*.

Of the Vidame of Chartres.

JOHN of FERRIERES, Lord of Maligny, of an illustrious House in *Burgundy*, Son to the Sister of Francis of *Vendôme*, Vidame of Chartres, whereof mention had been made in our first Vol. inherited not only the Principality of Chabannois, and all other Estates, but also the Religion of his Uncle, and his Inclination and Adherence to the Reformed Party. He was
valiant

(j) Add. aux. Mem. de Casteln. liv. VII. p. 577, &c.

valiant, magnanimous, bold in his Undertakings, and zealous for his Religion as well as his Lady Francess Joubert.

CHARLES of BEAUMANOIR, Baron of LA-VARDIN, brought to the Prince for the present War four Cornets of Horse, and two Companies of Arquebusiers, which he levied in the Maine, and the adjacent Countries, where the greatness of his House made him the most considerable Chief of the Reformed in those Parts. His Name was one of the most illustrious in Britany, and his Family one of the ancientest, his Credit and Valour were such that he was one of the first Proscripts on Bartholomew's-day. His Son John of Beaumanoir, Baron of Lavardin, abjured the Religion of his Father, and served King Charles and King Henry the IIId, in the Civil Wars; but whereas this last did not recompence him as he thought he deserved, he forsook him and adhered to the King of Navarr, whom he followed in all his Wars, and obtained from him when King of France the Marshal's Staff, and the Governments of *Maine*, and of the Counties of *Laval* and *Perche* (l).

Of Baron de Lavardin.

JAMES of CRUSSOL, Baron of Assier, afterwards Duke of *Uzes*, Count of *Crussol*, Knight of the King's Orders, Lieutenant-General of his Armies in *Languedoc*, made himself so famous in his time under the two Names of Crussol, Baron of *Assier*; and Duke of *Uzés*, and in the two Parties which he followed, that he deserves to be taken notice of.

Of the Count of Crussol, Duke of Uzes.

As Baron of *Assier*, and a Reformed, he was one of the most considerable Lords of that Party; and as Duke of *Uzés*, and a Catholick, he was the King's General in Languedoc.

There is a very notable Particularity in his House, which is scarce to be found in any other

S 4   of

(l) All this is extracted out of Agricola, Book VII. c. i.

of the Kingdom of France, and that is that from the Year eleven hundred to the middle of the 17th Century, which contains eighteen degrees of Generation, tho' it had been very teeming with Males; nevertheless it is not known that it had ever been divided in Branches. For which reason that illustrious Name was in great danger of being extinct in this James, Baron of Assier, who was so often exposed in the Civil Wars. He was the third of six Brethren, whereof only one left a Daughter, which died unmarried. His Father Charles, Viscount of *Uzés*, Lord of *Crussol*, of *Levis* and *Florensac*, Counsellor and Chambellan to the King, and Great Pantler of France, had married Jane of *Genouillac*, only Daughter of James Galiot, Lord of *Assier*, Great Master of the Artillery, and Great Standard-Bearer of France, Knight of the King's Order; who ordered by his last Will that the Male Issue of his Daughter, as Lords of *Assier*, should, in remembrance of him, take the Arms of *Galiot* and *Genouillac*, with those of their own House.

James of Crussol married Françess of *Clermont*, Daughter of Anthony, Viscount of *Tallard*, &c. and Niece of Louisa of *Clermont*, first Wife of Anthony of Crussol, first Duke of Uzés, his eldest Brother, who being dead without Male Issue, James succeeded to his Titles and Estate. As to his Religion he professed the Reformed till the beginning of the Reign of Henry III. I cannot tell whether he had been brought up in it from the Cradle, or whether the Example of his Brother the Duke of Uzés, and especially of his Sister-in-Law, a great Stickler for it at the Court of Francis II. and Charles IX, had any influence upon him; but if the Cardinal of St. Croix is to be credited, he was but very fickle

in

in it, and waited only to recant, till the Pope should take some Steps towards him (*m*) : And according to Agricola it is very difficult to determine whether there was no more temporal Concerns in his Change than Zeal ; for, says he, if his Conduct was thoroughly examined, most part of it must be ascribed to a necessity of Conveniency for improving the favour of Henry III. and gratifying the desire he had to obtain the Government of Languedoc. But if we judge of his Designs by the Success, the Sincerity of his Change will be the more questioned, because the Marshal of Damville, afterwards Duke of Montmorency and Constable of France, in order to maintain himself in that Government, was obliged to come to an Agreement with the Reformed, that they might together defend themselves against the said Duke, who attempted to ruin them both, that he might build his Grandeur upon their Decay. But he was mistaken in his Account, for tho' a Catholick, and supported

(*m*) Lettres du Card. de St. Croix au Cardin. Borromée Lettre 47. But this Letter is so nonsensical, that either it is spurious, or the Cardinal was misinformed : for example, he says, that the said Lord had promised him in a Conference he had with him, that far from countenancing he would oppose all those who should side against the Pope ; this he writes from Avignon the 12th of October 1564. Now it is certain, that from the Year 1560 to 1575 the said Lord has always supported with all his Might the Reformed Party every where in Provence, Dauphiné and Languedoc, without ever deviating a moment ; again, the same St. Croix makes him to say, that he had never heard any of the Hugonots Sermons, nor received the Sacrament amongst them, nor signed any thing concerning their Religion, &c. But whoever knows a little of the manners of those days, will no more believe this, than what he says in the same Letter concerning a Conversation passed between him and Smith the English Embassador, who told him that he had a mind to keep a stricter Correspondence with him than his Predecessors ; whereby it might be, that some Agreement would be found between Queen Elizabeth and the Pope.

ported by the King's Authority, tho' his Titles and Dignities were increased, yet he found himself actually weaker than when he was but Baron of Assier ; and that in the quality of Chief of the Reformed in Languedoc, Provence, and Dauphiné he had Interest enough to put on foot an Army of twenty two thousand Men picked up out of the best Militia of the Kingdom, and were very serviceable to the Cause in this present War, and at a time when the Reformed seemed so inconsiderable, that it was then asked in a banter, whether there were some Hugonots left besides those of *Rochelle?* However, this Lord was a most wise, prudent and brave Captain, but an ambitious Man ; he died in September 1584, and was succeeded in his Titles and Estates by his Son Emanuel, Count of *Crussol*, Duke of *Uzés*, Prince of *Assier*, Baron of *Levis* and *Florensac*, &c. who died in 1657.

Of Paul de Mouvans, Montbrun, and Pierre-Gourde. We have spoke already of this Gentleman in the second Book of our first Vol. as well as of the Lord of Montbrun. They both had exiled themselves from France during the latter part of the Reign of Francis II. they came back into France little before the first Civil War broke out, and acquired a great Reputation in the Reformed Party, on account of their Courage and Prudence in the management of Affairs wherewith they were intrusted. I refer to the next Book the Account of Montbrun ; and as to Mouvans and Pierre-Gourde, the first was always very zealous for his Party. Brantome says, that when the Rumour was spread, that the Duke of Alva was going to besiege Geneva, Mouvans went to that City's Assistance, with a Regiment of 7 or 800 stout Men of his own chusing, and that that News being brought to the Duke, it was thought that his Ardour was

cooled

cooled by it, and that it diverted him from his Undertaking. The same Author reckons him amongst the greatest Captains of his Age, after several great and glorious Feats of him in Provence, Dauphiné and Languedoc, he came to die at *Messignac* in *Perigord*, and it was by his fault, as abovesaid, Pierre-Gourde shared the same fate, at the same place, but Mouvans's Corpse could never be found in the Field after the Battle ; he was much bewailed by the Prince and the Admiral who had a great value for him (*n*).

The Lord Francis de la Noüe has had so great *Of Francis* a share in all the Transactions of this and Hen- *la Noüe,* ry III's Reign, and the beginning of Henry IV. *surnamed* that I think myself obliged to give here some *Iron-Arm.* Account of that Great Man. He was born in the Year 1531. His House was one of the ancientest in Britany, and of such a Nobility that William de la Noüe was chosen in the Year 1200 by the Duchess of Britany to be one of the twelve Knights Britons that were to fight against a like number of English Knights, for deciding the Quarrels subsisting between the two Nations ; and it was decided in behalf of the Britons, by la Noüe's bravery, who was the only one of the twenty-four that remained alive. His Branch was distinguished from the other of the same Name, by the surname of *Briort*, since that Estate was come into his Family by the Marriage of Francis de la Noüe, de *Chavannes* and de *Duault*, his Father, with Bonaventura l'Epervier, Daughter to Francis, Lord of *la Bouvardiere*, and of *Briort*, and Grand-daughter to Arthur l'Epervier, Lord of *la Bouvardiere*, and to Frances Landais, Daughter to Peter *Landais*, that wicked and unworthy Favourite of Francis II.

Duke

(*n*) Add. aux Mem. de Castel. liv. VII.

Duke of Britany, who while in the height of his favour settled his own Sister and two of his Daughters in the best Families of Britany, out of whom are issued some of the greatest Men in France. And this I do observe as an Instance of the Vicissitude of Fortune, which raised up a Taylor, Son to a Taylor, much over and above the Barons of Britany, and cast him down from the top of his Grandeur, and of the Gibbet, only after he had procured the most honourable Settlements to his Family; whereby he shared, as it were, the Glory of a Posterity most illustrious by their Virtues, as well as by their high Station. Another Revolution most remarkable in our la Noüe's Family, is, that his Grandfather on his Mother's side, after his Wife's death, turned a Dominican Fryar, and was a great Benefactor to his Order, but in the mean while a violent Persecutor of the Reformed, whereof his Grandson became one of their most generous Defenders.

Tho' he was born under the Reign of Francis I. the Restorer of Sciences, nevertheless he was educated like other Noblemen had been before that time, that is, he learned to read and to write, and his Exercises, to fence, to dance, and to ride; so whatever he knew in the Sciences, and in the Languages, wherein he was a great Proficient, he acquired it by his own private Application, by reading of the best Books, and the strength of his Mind, and his excellent Understanding. It must be after his coming back from his Travels, about the Year 1558, that he renounced the Roman Religion, and adhered to the Reformed, to his last breath. He made himself very conspicuous for his Courage, whereof he gave so many Instances; and for his great Experience in civil and military Affairs. His
Pru-

Prudence and Sagacity, his Moderation, and Probity, his Evenness of Temper and Impartiality were such, that both Parties had an equal Confidence in him, and was often chosen as an Umpire for deciding the Differences between them; but especially in the Reign of Henry III. when the Court and the Kingdom were divided into several Factions, la Noüe was always one of the chief Men singled out for adjusting the Differences between the King and his Brother of Alençon. He was so far Master of his Resentment, that he scorned to revenge the Affronts undeservedly put upon him, tho' he had it in his power to do it in the most solemn manner, a great Instance whereof he gave at Rochelle during the Siege. After the breaking up of a Council held for examining whether they ought to accept the Propositions of Peace tendered unto them by the Court; a Minister named LA PLACE, (one of those who waited at the Town-house Gate, to know what would be the Deliberation upon an Affair of so great Moment) understanding that la Noüe had been for accepting, followed him in the Streets as he went to his Lodgings, and upbraided him for his Counsels, with the greatest Violence, calling him *Traitor, Perfidious, Deserter,* and tho' la Noüe answered him with the greatest Mildness and Civility, that furious Madman was deaf to all manner of Arguments, and hearkening to his Passion, he came nearer to him, and was so impudent, nay, so brutish, as to give him a box on the Ear. Some Gentlemen that attended him, provoked at that Outrage, undertook to punish him for it as he deserved; but la Noüe, not moved by it, hindered them, and brought himself that unworthy Minister to his House, and recommended him strictly to his Wife. The same Man did afterwards several

other

other scandalous things, for which he was depo-
fed. He was of a ftrict Equity, and tho' he
would not have been blamed had he lived at
difcretion upon the Road, as many others of his
and even of a greater Quality did, neverthelefs he
never made any ufe of his right to the Prejudice of
the Farmers or Inn-keepers, but every where he
paid conftantly for whatever he took for him or
his Attendants ; or if the Landlord was not at
home, and had forfaken his Houfe out of fright,
he left the Money in fome corner of the Houfe,
that it might be found by him. Whereupon I
fhall relate an Inftance of his Generofity and
Equity together. He had lodged in fome place,
and as he was ready to fet out, he gave Orders to
his Steward to pay the Reckoning ; the Steward
told him, that there was no Money in his hands.
Then he bid him to fell one of his Horfes, and
to pay the Landlord out of the Money that
fhould be received. The Horfe was publickly
fold in that place, and when the Steward was
come back, la Noüe asked him, how much the
Horfe had been fold for ; a hundred Crowns,
fays he, to fuch a one, whom he named, and
who was a very honeft Man : *A hundred Crowns!*
replies la Noüe, *it is too much ; I paid but four-
fcore for him, and I have made ufe of him for a long
time ; and the Buyer being an honeft Man, does not
deferve to be cheated in that Manner ; go and return unto him twenty-five Crowns.* He was alfo
very ftrict in his Devotions ; but it happened
one Night in 1575, when the Army led by
Prince Cafimir had joined with the King of
Navarr's Army, that Du Pleffis Mornay, the
Vifcount of Turenne, and la Noüe, having
treated the Prince, with his chief Officers, at
Supper, they drank plentifully ; after Supper
thefe three Gentlemen who lodged together in
the

the fame room, before they went to bed, had
a mind to fay their Prayers, as they ufually did
every Night by turns; it was the Vifcount's turn
to do it that Night, but being kneeled down,
and having begun, he was out immediately and
could not go on, whereupon he defired la Noüe
to take his turn, which he did; but fcarce had
he uttered two Periods, that the fame thing happened to him as to the Vifcount; fo turning to
Du Pleffis he defired him to go on; but this
Gentleman who was in no better condition than
they, told them, *Gentlemen, let us go to bed, and
let every one pray for himfelf in the Bed, and another time we will follow our Order.*

Tho' wife, courageous, and experienced, yet,
generally fpeaking he was not fortunate, for he was
very often taken Prifoner of War, and in this next
Campaign he was fo terribly wounded in his left
Arm before Fontenay, that he was obliged to
have it cut off, in order to fave his Life; and
it is obfervable that the Queen of Navarr herfelf held him by that Arm, while the Surgeon
made the Operation; an expert Workman made
for him an Iron Arm, which was fo artificially
contrived, that he was able to hold the Bridle
and manage his Horfe with it. He was detained Prifoner of War by the Spaniards in *Flanders*
for five Years together, as I have faid in the
Preface of my fecond Vol. p. 24. and whereas I
fhall have occafion to fpeak oftentimes of him
in the fequel of this Hiftory, I fhall not now
infift any longer upon his Feats. As he was at
the Seige of *Lamballe*, looking in the dark over
the breach, the Enemies difcovering him, fired at
him, and a Bullet grazed upon his Forehead; and
as he was beckoning to his Troops with his right
Hand, his Iron Arm was not ftrong enough to
fupport him, fo he fell down from the Ladder and
                                        fractured

fractured his Skull; he was carried away to his Quarters almost dead, and was in a Swoon for an Hour, then he was carried to *Montcontour*, and suffered in his Head such intolerable Pains that the Surgeons were of Opinion to trepan him. But one of them, to whom la Noüe trusted much, promised with great Assurance, that he would cure him in a few days without it. At last, the 15th day after his Wound, seeing that his Pains continued, and that for want of Rest his Strength was spent, he desired one of his Friends to read by him, and three days after he died, with all the Demonstrations of a true and unfeigned Piety. He was in the 60th Year of his Age. Thuanus says of him, That he was truly a great Man, and who by his Courage, Prudence and Experience in military Affairs, was to be parallelled with the greatest Captains of his time; but that he was far above most part of them, by the Innocence of his Life, his Moderation and Equity. Witness the large Debts which he left behind him; and which he had contracted, not for gratifying Luxury, a Vice which he abhorred to the utmost, tho' naturally he was generous and bountiful, but for the Necessities of the War, wherein he employed his Life for the Defence of the State and of his Religion. He had two Sons, Odet and Theophilus de la Noüe de Telligny; by his Wife Magdalen de Telligny, Sister to Charles de Telligny, mentioned above; and the eldest sold part of his Estate to discharge all the Debts of his Father (o).

XCIII.
Propositions
of Peace.
    While the Troops were in their Winter-Quarters, the Queen being sensible that it would not be an easy matter to execute the Plot of *Bayonne*,

(o) Addit. aux Mem. de Castel. liv. VII. p. 580, 581. Amirault, vie de François de la Noüe dit Bras-de-Fer. Leyden 1661. Thuan. Hist. lib. CII. p. 176, 177.

Bayonne, as long as the Reformed were in Arms, endeavoured to raise that Obstacle which so mightily opposed his Designs, and feigned to be willing to come to some Agreement with the Prince. For that end she sent to his Highness one Portail with some Overtures for a Treaty ; but after several Debates they could not agree, and the Messenger went back with nothing else but Compliments for their Majesties ; so both Parties prepared themselves for the next Campaign.

Amongst other Provisions which the Prince had made for discharging the Expences of the War, he had fitted out a Fleet at La Rochelle, being invited to it by the Situation of the place ; it was composed of Nine Sail, and some light Ships, or Pinnaces, he manned them with a thousand either Sailors or Soldiers, and gave the Command of it to one LATOUR, youngest Brother to Chatelier du Portail ; he had put to sea on the 10th of October 1568, and had made several very rich Prizes upon the Flemings, Britons and Normans ; and having sailed beyond the Haven of *Conquest* in Britany, as all the Country People run in Arms along that Shore, he landed at *Plymouth*, from whence he went Post with some Noblemen to *Hampton-Court*, where Queen Elizabeth was at that time, and by the means of Cardinal of Chatillon he was empowered to attack, under her Majesty's Protection and Name, the French and the Flemings upon Sea ; and that whatever he could seize upon them, should be declared a lawful Prize with the Cardinal's Approbation, and what Sum should proceed from those Prizes, should be laid out for the use of the CAUSE (*p*), which was of a vast advantage to the Prince and the Reformed Party.

Vol. III.   T .   I

(*p*) Thuan. lib. XLIV. p. 562.

Charles
IX.
1569.
Pope Pius
V.

XCV.
St. Mi-
chael's Mo-
naſtery de-
ſtroyed.

I do not intend to enter into all the Particulars of this, nor of the following Wars, which
could not be done without increaſing the Vo-
lumes far beyond the Number I have propoſed ;
I ſhall ſingle out only ſome of the moſt remarkable Events for brevity ſake.

The Rocheleſe having obtained leave of the
Prince, aſſaulted the Monaſtery of St. Michael
in Poitou, which they had already aſſaulted twice
before, but at laſt it was ſtormed after many Labours ; the Plunder was ineſtimable, becauſe
many of the Nobility and Gentry in the Neighbourhood had ſent thither their beſt Moveables
for a greater Safety. The Slaughter was cruel and
barbarous, above 400 Monks or Soldiers that
defended the place were killed, and even murdered, ſeveral of them, in cool blood ; the Monaſtery itſelf was pulled down to the Ground left
the Royaliſts ſhould take poſſeſſion of it, and
annoy the adjacent Country, as the Monks had
done before (q).

XCVI.
Sancerre
beſieged in
vain.

About the ſame time Martinengue Governor of *Gien*, Entragues Governor of *Orleans*,
and de la Châtre Bailiff of Berry, beſieged Sancerre for the King, with three thouſand Foot,
ſome Horſe, and eight Cannons. That Town
was ſtrong enough by its Situation, and wholly
inhabited by Reformed ; the King had ordered
them to receive a Garriſon, but upon their Remonſtrances he asked only that the Walls and Fortifications ſhould be demoliſhed ; whereunto they
agreed, provided the Count of Sancerre would
conſent to it. So they ſpinned out the time till
the War broke out, and prepared themſelves for
their defence : Now Martinengue and the two
others knowing that Avantigny, their Governor,
was abſent, had a mind to improve that Opportunity,

(q) Thuan. lib. XLV.

tunity, and laid the Siege as abovesaid : But three
Advocates at the head of three hundred of the
Inhabitants withstood so stoutly all their Efforts,
that after above five Weeks Siege they were
forced to raise it, having lost five hundred of their
Troops, and some Officers of distinction ; amongst
whom was D'Aigueville, Son to the Baron of
Neufbourg (r).

Tho' the Emperor had refused to assist the
King of France in this War, nevertheless he
could not hinder the Catholick Princes of the
Empire from sending to him their Auxiliaries to
the number of two thousand Reisters, according
to Castelnau, under the Command of the Rhingrave, Bassompierre, and others, who arrived at
the King's Camp about the latter end of February. The Reformed made several unsuccessful
Attempts upon *Lusignan, Dieppe, Havre de Grace*,
and some other places, by the Intelligences they
had in them, the Chiefs whereof being taken
were capitally punished. The Viscounts in Languedoc, with an Army of six Thousand Foot,
and some Horse, strongly opposed the Designs
of Montluc, covered *Montauban, Puilaurens,
Millaud*, and some other places, from the Enemy's Insults, and kept in awe the City of *Thoulouse*. Piles was sent by the Prince into Guienn
and Languedoc to make Recruits for the grand
Army ; he, with twelve hundred Arquebusiers
and two hundred Horse, took *Bergerac* and *St.
Foy*, wherein having left his Foot, he, with his
Horse ran up and down the *Perigord*, burning
all the places which he suspected to be Accomplices of the Rout of Mouvans ; then having gathered all the Troops he could, he came to
Saintes. These Fights, or rather Skirmishes, decided nothing ; therefore the Duke of Anjou

T 2

having

(r) Id. ibid.

having marched thro' *Poitou*, *Limosine*, and *Angoumois*, came on the *Charente's* Banks, as if he had a mind to take *Chateau-neuf*, in order to put himself between the Prince of Condé and Piles, who was coming with Auxiliaries from the South-west Provinces. To avoid which, the Prince having crossed the *Charente* at *Coignac*, came directly to Chateau-neuf (which was kept by a Scotch Officer) just as if he had a mind to give Battle. The Duke of Anjou was not averse to it, his Army being much increased by the new Supplies he received every day ; and understanding that the Confederates intended as soon as they had joined their Forces together to march to the *Loire*, there to wait for their Auxilaries from Germany, who had begun their march on the 5th or 6th of March, he thought that it was necessary to oppose such a Design as well as he could. Therefore seeing that he could not cross the *Charente* at *Jarnac*, he crossed it beyond *Angouleme*, took *Chateau-neuf*, and the Castle, the Bridge having been broken in two pieces. The Admiral, in order to know better their Disposition, and the Passage, came himself with seven or eight hundred Horse, and as many Arquebusiers ; the River was between the Duke of Anjou and the Admiral : Some Troops of the first had crossed, and there was a Skirmish between them and the Admiral's. However it was easy to know that the Duke had a mind to come through that Passage.

The Admiral, in order to oppose it, at least for a day longer, ordered that two Regiments of Foot should lodge at a quarter of a League from the Bridge, and eight hundred Horse a little further behind the Foot, the third part whereof should be upon Guard near the Passage, to warn the Army, as well as to oppose the first
that

that fhould come.   Having given his Orders, he
went to Baffac, a League diftant from that place,
with the remainder of the Van-guard, and the
Prince came to Jarnac, a League diftant from
Baffac.

Had the Admiral's Orders been executed, the
Misfortune of the next day, the 13th of March,
might have been prevented; but fcarce was he
gone to his Quarters, than thofe whom he had
intrufted with the Guard of that Paffage, finding
their Quarters not good enough for them, forfook them to look for fome more commodious,
and very few remained, at about half a League
diftance from the place.   So the Catholick Army
having mended the Bridge in all hafte, and
made a new one with Boats, they begun at Midnight to crofs without noife.   The Reformed
Guard that were at a Mile diftance, to the number
of fifty Horfe only, knew nothing of that till
the break of day; then they fent immediate notice of it to the Admiral, who fent for the Troops
that were fcattered into feveral Villages in the
Neighbourhood, with orders to march in all
hafte to him, that they might make their Retreat together.   He ordered alfo at the fame
time, that all the Baggage, and the Infantry
fhould retreat, which was done accordingly.   And
if at that time, nay, an Hour later, all his Troops
had been affembled, it would have been very eafy
for him to make an honourable Retreat.   But
the length of the time (for they were three Hours
before they could be affembled) was the principal Occafion of their Rout.   He was willing to
fave thofe Troops, confifting of Nine Cornets of
Horfe, and feveral Companies of Foot, under
the Command of Montgomery, Affier, and Pu-
viaut.

At laſt, being all joined with him, Aſſier excepted, who took the Road of *Angouleme*, the Catholicks, who for the moſt part had already croſſed the River, were in ſuch a number, ſo near the Reformed, and they had Skirmiſhes ſo frequently, and with ſuch bravery, that the Battle was unavoidable. Therefore the Prince of Condé, who made his Retreat, and was already half a League diſtant from that place, having received a Meſſenger from the Admiral, came back with all ſpeed, and joined him ; the Catholicks ſent the choice of their Horſe under the Command of the Duke of Guiſe, the Viſcount of Martigues, and the Count of Briſſac ; at the firſt Onſet they broke four Cornets of the Reformed, who retreated, and la Noüe was one of thoſe that were taken Priſoners ; then they aſfaulted D'Andelot in a Village, who withſtood their Onſet ; then proceeding further, and diſcovering two thick Batallions of Horſe, led by the Prince and the Admiral, they came at them, the Admiral had the firſt Charge, and the Prince the ſecond, which was more briſk than the firſt, and at the beginning forced the Catholicks to turn their backs. But at laſt all the Catholick Army coming upon them, they were obliged to fly.

It is obſervable that the Catholicks were almoſt ten to one againſt the Reformed, for tho' before the Battle the Armies were almoſt equal in number, each of them conſiſting of about twenty-ſeven thouſand Men, Horſe or Foot ; neverthe-leſs, that of the Prince was quartered in ſo many different places, one, two, and even four Leagues diſtant one from another, that not above fifteen Cornets and ſix Companies of Foot could be preſent at the Battle.

There

There are three or four Miftakes in the relation
D'Avila gives us of that Battle : 1. As to the
time, which he fays was the 16th of March ; but
by all the Hiftorians, even thofe that were prefent at the Battle, fuch as Caftelnau and la Noüe,
it was the 13th of March.   2. As to the Duke
of Anjou, whom he fays had a Horfe killed under him, no body elfe befides himfelf fpeaks of
it ; and Caftelnau, who was deputed by the faid
Duke to inform the King of all the Particulars
of the Battle, would not have omitted this, which
was fo glorious to the Duke. 3. As to the death of
the Prince of Condé, he fays, that being fell from
his Horfe, killed under him, he fought upon his
Knees till he was killed by Montefquiou ; this
would extenuate the Crime of that Man, but he
is contradicted by la Noüe and Caftelnau. He
adds, that Stuart was at the fame time killed by
him ; but according to la Noüe and others, who
have mentioned his Death, he was murdered in
cool Blood in the Caftle of Jarnac, where he
had been brought Prifoner of War, and Brantome himfelf condemns that Action as cruel.
4. As to the number killed on both fides, he
fays, that the Reformed loft 700 Men, but all
of them Gentlemen, and Cavaliers of a great
Name. That is much magnified ; their Lofs, according to Thuanus, amounted to 400 Men, a-
mongft whom, according to Caftelnau, there
was above a hundred Lords or Gentlemen of
note ; on the Catholicks fide there were about
two hundred Men killed, amongft whom were
many Lords or Gentlemen of Note ; the Names
of feveral of both Parties are mentioned by
Caftelnau, liv. VII. ch. iv. La Hode, a Modern, fays, that according to the Hiftorians, the
Lofs of the Reformed amounted to the number of fourteen hundred Men, and that of the

Catholicks to two hundred ; but it is plain that he or the Printer have miſtaken four for fourteen, ſince all the Hiſtorians have not reckoned ſome more than four, others five, and D'Avila ſeven hundred. I obſerve this once for all, that D'Avila is not an Hiſtorian intirely to be depended upon ; for it appears by the many Miſrepreſentations of Matters of Fact, that either he has written upon hear-ſay, or truſting too much to his own Memory, or which is worſe, that being bent only to ſet up for a Wit, he was not very diligent after the ſearch of Truth : That is very plain in all the Speeches he aſcribes to his Actors, which certainly are of his own, and have never been ſpoken by any of them.

But to return. The greateſt Loſs was the Prince of Condé, he had one of his Arms in a Sling, and that very day one of his Legs had been broken in the Boot, by the kick of the Count of la Rochefoucault's Horſe ; therefore his own Horſe having been killed under him, he fell upon the Ground, and was unable to ſtir about. He could receive no Aſſiſtance of his own, and ſeeing D'Argences, who was of his Acquaintance, and one St. John, he called them, delivered his Sword, and ſurrendered himſelf unto them, they promiſed to ſave him, and did indeed what they could for it ; but here came a baſe Villain, MONTESQUIOU by Name, Captain of the Duke's Guards, who took his time while he was talking with D'Argences and St. John, and firing at him backwards killed him upon the ſpot.

Thus died on the 13th of March 1569, Lewis of Bourbon, Prince of Condé, being thirty-eight Years ten Months and ſix days old, for he was born at Vendome on the 7th of May 1530 ; he was the youngeſt of ſeven Sons, of

Charles of Bourbon, Duke of Vendome, and of Frances of Alençon, and the only one that was defective in his Body, but the more lovely, tho' he was short and crooked ; for he had in an ill-favoured Body all the Perfections of the Soul and Mind which can adorn such an august Birth ; Superior to the King of Navarr, in any other respect, he yielded to him only as to the Titles ; he increased the Glory of the Name of the Duke of *Enguien*, the Title whereof he joined with Prince of Condé, after the death of two of his illustrious Brethren, Francis the Conqueror at *Cerisoles*, and John killed at St. Quintin. These two Estates supplied him with nothing else but a Name and Emulation, and having no other Income but his County of *Soissons*, of about a thousand Crowns of yearly Rent, and some other small Estates, as the Viscounty of *Meaux*, and in the *Perche* ; his own Merit and his Virtue joined with the Crown's Favour, and the Wealth of the King his Brother, could only support him in his high Station. He submitted himself generously to that Necessity, and did important Services to King Henry II. as well at the Conquest of *Bologn*, as in his glorious Journey to *Germany*, and at the Defence of *Metz* ; he was so desirous to improve in the Military Art, that he accepted to be Colonel of the French Infantry in *Piedmont*, that he might have more and better Opportunities of signalizing himself, as he did chiefly at the Siege of *Ulpian*.

He was afterwards gratified by Henry II, who had a great value for him, with the Government of *Picardy*, which Province he preserved by his Prudence and Valour from the Invasion of the Spaniards, after the Battle of St. Quintin. But by King Henry's death the House of Guise, having usurped all the Power and Authority under

Francis

Francis II. this Prince was so much the more jealous of it, that besides that ambitious House divided amongst six Brethren, all the Dignities and great Preferments, they were ready to form a Party against the Royal House in order to remove it intirely from the Government. He had increased his own Patrimony with the best of the large Estate of the House of Roye, by his Marriage with LEONOR, Lady of *Roye*, *Muret*, and *Conti*. But tho' he had had enough to support his Rank, A PRINCE OUT OF THE COURT IS LIKE A STAR FALLEN FROM THE FIRMAMENT, because he borrows all his Brightness from the King's own Light. AND IT IS NO LESS CONDUCIVE TO THE KING'S OWN GLORY, TO BE SURROUNDED BY A MULTITUDE OF TRUE STARS, THAN BY COMETS, THAT RATHER STEAL THAN BORROW FROM HIM MOST PART OF HIS BRIGHTNESS. The Prince of Condé took not amiss that the King should employ the Duke of Guise and the Cardinal of Lorrain in the Administration of the Government ; they were able, if they were but willing to discharge that Office, they were besides that his first Cousins, nay they were intimate before ; but what he could not bear with was, that the haughty Cardinal should scorn as he did at first, the Princes, and the greatest Men of the Kingdom, and that he should render them despicable to the King ; that touched him to the quick. Lorrain was very sensible of it, therefore he left no Stone unturned to prevent his Resentment, by procuring his Ruin and Destruction. It was enough for that lewd Priest, that the Prince was in a Capacity to redeem the Kingdom from the miserable Thraldom under which it groaned, and was to groan as long as it should be governed by him ; the mere Suspicion

cion he had of him was sufficient to ground upon it the intire Destruction of the Royal Branch of Bourbon. We have seen that as soon as the Amboisian Plot was discovered, he charged the Prince with it ; that afterwards, whatever Motions the Reformed and others made in the Provinces, he looked always upon the Prince as the Author and Abettor of them, because at the Exhortations of the Countess of Roye, and of the Princess his Consort, he had embraced the Reformed Religion, and was firmly and sincerely adhering to it, and he never ceased till he had brought him to his Trial at Orleans, and condemned, but gnashed his Teeth when he saw that it was no longer in his power to have him executed. After his return from the Council of Trent, he ceased not till he had by his false Suggestions exasperated the Queen against the Prince, to that degree that had he not provided in good time for his own Security, he would have been clapt into a Dungeon for all his Life ; it was at his persuasion that the Queen broke the Promises she had made unto him at Orleans, that he should hold the same Rank in the Kingdom as the late King of Navarr his Brother, and be the King's Lieutenant-General ; it was at his Instigation, that the Queen engaged the Duke of Anjou to ask that place for himself, which occasioned the Quarrel he had with the Prince at St. Germain, which caused the Hatred the Duke conceived against him, which occasioned at last the base and barbarous Order he gave to Montesquiou † to go and kill him. So it is evident that the House of Guise, but especially
the

---

† There was the Chevalier de Montluc, who took the Name of Montesquiou ; but I don't say, that he is the same Man. Comm. de Montluc, liv. VI. at the Margent, pag. 486.

the Cardinal of Lorrain, has been the second
Cause of all the Mischiefs which befel the Kingdom, from the middle of the Reign of Henry II.
to the sixth Year of the Reign of Henry IV. As
to the first Cause, the Sins of the Nation had
provoked the Vengeance of God against it, and
the Guises were the Plague wherewith, in his
Wisdom, he thought proper to chastise them.
The Prince died with Reputation, even amongst
his Enemies, of having faithfully performed to
the utmost of his power, whatever he had himself ingaged to, by the Treaties of *Amboise* and
Chartres (r).   He was worthy of a better time
and of a happier Death by all the great Endow-
ments wherewith his Royal Extraction was attended.   It is said that a little before the Battle,
having had one of his Legs broken, as abovesaid, instead of retiring himself in order to have
his Leg drest, the violent Pain he felt served
only to raise up his Spirits, and he said only in
the first Motion, *French Gentlemen, know that
mettlesome Horses are more noxious than useful in
an Army, and that it is a foolish Vanity to pretend to daunt them in a Day of Battle, and to share
unavoidably ones Cares between that Object and the
Enemies, which require all our time and the greatest
presence of Mind. Here is a sad Instance of what I
say, but for all that, I will not be disabled to
fight.*   Then raising his Voice, and ready to af-
sault, he cried out, *French Nobility, know that
the Prince of Condé, with an Arm in a sling, and
a Leg broken, has Courage enough to give Battle.*
Whoever will read Agricola's Additions to the
Memoirs of Castelnau, Book VII. from p. 609
to 626, will see, that I have said nothing too
much, concerning the Plot against the King at
Meaux, and the Medal with the Inscription.
Lewis

(r) Addit. aux Mem. de Castelnau, ubi supra.

Lewis XIII, &c. which Daniel quotes as a ſtrong Argument to prove his Charge againſt the Prince of Condé, and that had he lived in Agricola's time, or Agricola in his own, he would have been handled with much more Roughneſs than I have done, had he had the Aſſurance to advance ſuch a Fact without being able to prove it by better Authorities and Reaſons.

That Prince, after his Death, was, by way of Deriſion, put a-croſs an old She-Aſs, his Legs and Arms hanging down, and in that poſture was carried to *Jarnac*, and put in a Hall, under the Chamber of the Duke of Anjou, where the ſaid Prince had lodged the day before, and was expoſed there to the publick View; the ſaid Duke was overjoyed to ſee in that condition a Prince whom he looked upon as his Enemy, and his Competitor, but is he excuſable for having ſuffered, nay commanded that a Prince of his own Blood ſhould be treated ſo baſely and ſhamefully? At laſt he gave the Corpſe to the Duke of Longueville, Brother in-law to the Prince, according to Caſtelnau preſent, and Brantome; but according to Thuanus, it was delivered to the Prince of Bearn, who cauſed him to be buried at Vendôme. But theſe Authors can be very well reconciled together, the Prince of Bearn kept no Correſpondence with the Duke of Anjou, that is certain; but underſtanding that the Duke of Longueville had obtained the Corpſe, very likely he deſired that Prince to deliver it to him, and put it in ſome place from whence he had it removed in a better time, in order to be buried at Vendôme with his Anceſtors. I ſhall inſert here ſome Verſes done by Catholicks upon this ſad Occaſion. Theſe four are an Epitaph.

L'an

Charles
IX.
1569.
Pope Pius
V.

L.'an mil cinq cens foixante neuf
Entre *Jarnac* & *Chateau-neuf*,
Fut porté fur une Aneffe
C'il qui vouloit oter la Meffe.

The famous John D'Aurat, called by the Reformed, the Limofine Frog, becaufe of feveral
Poems he wrote againft them upon all the Events
of this War, compofed two Pieces, amongft o-
thers, upon the Prince's Death ; the one for the
Cardinal of Bourbon, Brother to the Deceafed,
the other was to congratulate the Duke of Anjou ; and they are as follows :

DE BORBONIORUM NECE.

Quæritis in noftrum quid fati confcia poffint
   Aftra caput? non prifca loquor, vulgata docebit
   Borboniæ fortuna Domus tot fratribus orbæ.

* *Francis
accidental-
ly killed at
la Roche-
guyon in
1546.*

Aufonii terror Franciscus * & horror Iberi,
   Invictus bello dum ludum ludit inermem,
   Occidit injecta mediis cervicibus arca.
Quintini ad fanum, circumveniente Philippo,
   Vinclorum impatiens & nefcius vertere terga,
   (s) Innumeris Jani † virtus eft obruta telis.

† *John
killed at St.
Quintin in
1557.*

Trajectis humeris tormenti Antonius ‡ ictu
   Mœnia dum Populi premit obfidione rebellis,
   Communem hanc lucem & dotalia fceptra re-
     liquit.

‡ *Anthony
of Navarr
died in
1562.*

Dum veterum ritus convellit, & otia turbat,
   Tertia bella gerens Patriæ funefta fibique
   Diffudit vitam fractis Lodoicus ‡ in Armis.

‡ *Lewis
murdered
in 1569.*

Dimidium jufti vixerunt quatuor ævi
   Adverfis fatis rapti florente Juventa.
Cum quintus numero è fratrum nunc, Carole*,
    reftes,

* *Charles,
Cardinal
of Bourbon
furviving.*

Si tibi fata velint detractos fratribus annos
Adjicere, explebis Pelei tria fæcula Regis.

De

(s) Mr. de l'Etoile reads Theutonicis inftead of Innumeris.

De Ludovico Borbonio.

Mense tuo cecidit Cæſar, Mars, cæſus ad Idus,
Menſe tuo cecidit cæſus Condæus ad Idus,
Ambo hoſtes Patriæ, belli civilis & ambo
Authores, miſeram vìtam ſic finit uterque.
Diſſimili haud fato, ſed non fortuna duobus
Par fuit, æqua licet merita cum morte perirent ;
Armatæ namque hunc acies videre cadentem
Turba togatorum victorem, & victa cecidit
Debita ſors illum : nam quis viciſſet in armis,
Victori Henrico & quis non ceſſiſſet in armis ?

But ſome of the Reformed with greater Sincerity and Truth made the following Diſtich.

Vivit adhuc, vivetque diù, qui vindice dextrâ
Annixus Patriæ, ne cadat illa, cadit (*t*).

He had eight Children, viz. five Sons and
three Daughters by Leonora of Roye his firſt
Wife, five whereof died young, the three
others were Henry, Prince of Condé ; Francis,
Prince of Conti, this died without Iſſue in 1614 ;
and Charles, afterwards Cardinal of Bourbon and
Archbiſhop of Roüen, theſe two laſt were
brought up in the Catholick Religion. By Frances of Orleans his ſecond Wife, he had Charles
of Bourbon, Count of Soiſſons, who was likewiſe brought up in the Romiſh Religion by his
Mother.

The Prince's Death cauſed a general Conſter- XCVIII.
nation in the Reformed Army, they betook to *The Prince*
flight, the Horſe that could eſcape ran till the *his Army*
Afternoon. The Admiral with d'Andelot his *routed.*

Bro-

(*t*) Will it not be better to read, *ne cadat, ille cadit ?* however the Poet's meaning is obvious enough, the Prince zealous
for the Kingdom's Welfare has ſacrificed himſelf for it, and
thereby has endeared himſelf to Poſterity ; but the Expreſ
ſion, ne cadat illa, cadit, ſeems to me ſomething ambiguous.

Brother feeing that it was not in their power to rally their Troops, retreated to *St. John of Angely*, attended with fome of the Nobility ; they ftayed there but a Night, and came the next day to the Prince of Navarr and Condé at *Saintes.*

D'Affier, who was near *Angouleme*, underftanding that the two Parties were to engage, marched with all the hafte he could, that he might be prefent at the Battle with fix thoufand Arquebufiers, (Thuanus fays, fix hundred Companies, which would make at leaft ten thoufand) but being arrived at two Miles from *Baffac*, he judged by the Runners-away that the Prince had loft the day, therefore he made hafte to Jarnac. In his way thither he was briskly affaulted by a Party of the Catholick Army that purfued their Victory, but he withftood their Onfet with fuch bravery, that without lofing a fingle Man he arrived fafe at *Jarnac*, from whence he marched out immediately, underftanding that thofe who had efcaped at *Baffac* were gone to *Coignac* ; and to be covered from the Purfuit of the Enemy, he caufed the Bridges whereby he paffed to be cut down : thus he arrived fafe with all his Troops and Baggage to the place where he intended to go (*v*).

XCIX.
Confequences of the Battle.

The Joy which the Catholicks received by this Event was inexpreffible. The Duke of Anjou was fo far tranfported with it, that he had a mind to build a Chapel upon the very fpot of Ground where the Prince had been murdered, but was diverted from it by Carnavalet, who remonftrated unto him, that, in fo doing, he would corroborate the Rumour, that the Prince had been murdered by his Orders (*x*). He difpatched

(*v*) Concerning the Battle of Baffac, fee Cafteln. Mem. liv. VII. ch. xiii, xiv. Dinoth. lib. IV. 242, 3, 4, 5. Thuan. lib. XLV. p. 568, 69, 70. (*x*) Thuan. ibid.

patched a Courier to the King, then at Metz, the Meſſenger arrived at Midnight, and the King roſe up out of his Bed, and went to the Cathedral, and cauſed the *Te Deum* to be ſung : by his Orders, Prayers and Thankſgivings were put up all over the Kingdom, and the Virgin Mary nor the Saints were not forgotten. He diſpatched immediately his Couriers to the ſeveral Catholick Courts of Europe, to notify unto them his Victory, and he even ſent to the Pope ſome of the Standards that had been taken upon the Reformed. The Pope received them with the utmoſt Demonſtration of Joy and Satisfaction, and cauſed them to be hung in St. Peter's Church, then from that Church he went in Proceſſion to that of the Holy Ghoſt, with all the Cardinals then at Rome. The Senate of *Venice*, and Alva in *Flanders* made ſuch like Proceſſions in their reſpective Countries. They were all ſure that the Prince of Condé being dead, the Hugonots were utterly undone, whereby it appeared that the Prince's Name was very formidable unto the Catholick Powers ; for, as to the reſt, they miſtook a great deal in their Notions.

The Duke knew not how, or it may be, his Council would not improve their Victory. His Troops reſted for two or three days at Jarnac; then they marched to Coignac, which he thought that the Reformed had forſaken ; but he was much ſurpriſed to find it kept by four Regiments of Foot, commanded by Beaudiſner, Brother to D'Aſſier, Blaccons, Mirabel and du Chelar. The Duke having ſent ſome Companies to reconnoitre the Situation and Fortifications of the place, the Garriſon ſallied upon them, killed two hundred of them, and routed the reſt. So the Duke ſeeing that the place was too hot for him,

Charles
IX.
1569.
Pope Pius
V.

*Prepara-
tions on both
fides for the
Campaign.*

was diverted from befieging it, and quartered his Army in the neighbouring places.

Four days after the Battle he had fent Caftelnau to their Majefties, to acquaint them better with all the Particulars, and to haften the Levy of the Reifters which the Marquis of Baden had promifed to raife, having received a Sum of Money for that purpofe fome time ago. The King fent him into Germany for that end, and that Lord was fo diligent that in a Fortnight's time he was come back to Court with the German Auxiliaries. Then his Majefty fent him to Bruxelles, to defire Alva to fend the Auxiliaries which had been promifed by the Spanifh Embaffador at the Court of France. At this time that Governor was very glad of that Opportunity for gratifying his bloody Temper, queftioning not but all the Hugonots of France would be now deftroyed all at once, and by that means be revenged upon them for the Succours they had fent to the Prince of Orange, of twelve Cornets, and two thoufand Foot, under the Command of Genlis, Morvilliers, the Marquiffes of Renel and D'Autricour, Mouy, Renty, Feuquieres, and fome others, who all remained in *Brabant,* when the Prince had fled into *Rochelle,* daring not to venture into France, becaufe it was impoffible for them to join the Prince's Army without expofing themfelves to the moft threatning danger.

For thefe reafons, I fay, Alva, after many Compliments, promifed to the Lord of Caftelnau, to give him in ten days time two thoufand Foot, and two thoufand five hundred Reifters, under the Command of the Count of Mansfield, Governor of *Luxembourg,* advifing withal their Majefties never to make Peace with their rebellious Subjects, much lefs with the Hugonots, but to deftroy them entirely without Mercy, and to treat their Chiefs, if ever they fell into their hands, as he had treated the Counts of Egmont and Horn, tho' both were very confiderable for the greatnefs of their Houfes, as well as for their Services *.

Caftel-

* Caftelnau fhows that there was more Vanity, than any real Affection for the Service of his Prince in the bloody Execution Alva caufed to be made of thefe two unfortunate Lords, and of many others. That blood-thirfty Man, at his coming into the Low Countries, followed the Method of thofe Architects or Gardeners, who pull down old Buildings without any regard for their Beauty and Antiquity, on pretence of making new ones after a new Fafhion, but lefs durable, lefs commodious than the former, or turn upfide down a Garden planted with the beft Fruit-trees to make a Champain ground of it, and who undertake, with more Malice than Art, to make Alleys in places where the fineft Trees were; for the glory fake of having cut them down: and laftly, who put foreign Plants, fuch as Cyprefs-Trees, that bear nothing, and even afford no Shadow, but only a fad Gloominefs, inftead of thofe that bear Bloffoms, Flowers and Fruits. Hear them fpeaking about their Schemes, they promife you the greateft Wonders in the World; but they give you very uncertain Profpects for a real Good which you lofe; and fometimes the Mafter is obliged to live in fome old decayed place till his Undertaker has done, but often his Patience being tired, he frets at the faid Undertaker, who leaves him with only fome imperfect Rubbifh inftead of Caftles which he has pulled down. The Application of all this to Alva is very eafy, that Man whofe Looks and Countenance offered nothing to the Sight but what was moft terrible and frightful, endeavouring, by the moft wicked Methods, to fubvert the Government of the Low Countries, worked actually his Mafter's Expulfion out of feven of them, whom he forced, will they or not, to erect themfelves into a Republick. One of the moft flagrant Crimes of the Count of Egmont, tho', for good Reafons, it was not in the Articles exhibited againft him, was his Titles upon the Duchy of Gueldres, and the County of Zutphen, he complained too freely that the late Duke of Burgundy had wronged him; that was enough to ruin him in the King of Spain's mind; who thought that to him only it belongs to bear quarterly all the Empires and Crowns of the World, to the end that his Efcutcheon might be the perpetual Mirrour

U 2 of

Thuanus places this Voyage of the Queen three or four days after the Battle of Baffac, and before the Events which we have juſt now related; and as to the place where ſhe came, he ſays that it was at Coignae.   As to the reſt the Hiſtorians agree, that it was for ſtrengthening the diſheartened, and for taking proper meaſures to retrieve the Loſſes they had ſuſtained by the laſt Battle.   Howbeit, ſhe made a ſet Speech to the Aſſembly of the Nobles, and chief Officers of the Army, having praiſed the Valour and Virtue of the late Prince of Condé, who had ſo generouſly undertook the Defence of the *CAUSE*, and had maintained it to his laſt moment; ſhe exhorted them to follow his Example, and tread in his Steps, and to be ſtedfaſt in the Defence of their Religion, and the Liberty of their Country, which were attacked by the Violence of ſome wicked Men, to chear up, and to remember that the good *CAUSE* was not dead together with the Prince of Condé; that generous and good Men ought not to deſpair becauſe of that Accident, ſince God Almighty had ſo well taken care of his *CAUSE*, that he had permitted that the Prince had had Followers of his Zeal while he was alive, who were ready to ſucceed him now, and had Remedies eaſily to be procured, and ready at hand.   That the Prince of Bearn and the young Prince of Condé who had inherited the Virtues as well as the Name of his Father, were there preſent, beſides many other Lords, whom ſhe hoped would never forſake the good CAUSE.   Thus the Queen ſpoke to the Generals, and to the Army, and in private ſhe exhorted her Son, and told him many things proper to ſtir up his Courage.

CI.
*The Prince
of Bearn
declared
Generaliſ-
ſimo and*
PROTEC-
TOR *of the
Reformed.*

Then the Prince of Bearn, for ſo Thuanus ſtiles him, but others call him Prince of Navarr, was

declared,

declared Generalissimo of all the Armies of the Reformed, and PROTECTOR of the CAUSE. In order that the reciprocal Promises of the Princes to the Lords and Gentlemen their Adherents, and of these to the Princes should be known unto all, they were published in Print, and are to the following Purport: The Princes promised before God and his Angels, that having been elected to be chief of the Army, they would live and die (if such was their fate) for their Defence, and were resolved never to depart from their Covenant, till the Affairs of the Kingdom should be put in such a Posture that they could serve God according to his Holy Will, and till the King should be delivered out of the hands of those who besieged him as it were, kept him under Restraint, and abused his Name and Authority; so as the Reformed might enjoy the free and publick Exercise of their Religion. The Nobles, &c. promised likewise to obey the Princes and those who by them should be constituted; to submit themselves unto all military Laws; to deem those who should absent from the Army without the Princes Licence, as perfidious, and Deserters. Besides that they published a new Manifesto whereby they declared the Causes and Reasons for which they had taken Arms, to wit, for the Preservation of the Liberty of Conscience, and the free Profession of the Reformed Religion, and to defend themselves against the Tyranny of the Disturbers of the publick Peace; that they were entirely resolved to spend their Goods, their Estates and Lives for so just a Cause. They added, that they plotted nothing against the King whom they acknowledged as their supreme Lord and Prince, ordained by God, to whom they will pay all Respect, Submission and Obedience.

U 4   The

The Joy which the Army shewed upon this Occasion was inexpressible; they saw at their head the two first Princes of the Blood instead of one who was but the second, and tho' they were very young at that time, they were so hopeful and promising that they thought to have in them a sure prospect of better things for the future, than what was past: And whereas the Prince of Navarr is the first that I can find out who has received the Name and Title of PRO-TECTOR, which he hath kept even when he came to the Crown of France, except while he was kept a Captive, after the Massacre of Bartholomew's-day, till he made his escape from Court; it will not be amiss to give a Notion of the Protectorship, what it was.

*What was
the Protec-
torship a-
mongst the
Reformed.*

The Reformed having been obliged, after above forty Years Sufferings, to unite themselves for their common Defence, they put themselves at first under the Protection of the Prince of Condé (z), who had the same Interest with them. The natural Design of this Protection was to procure Security and Repose to the Reformed, to tender to the King their Complaints and Petitions, to repress, out of regard for their Protector, the attempts of the zealous or ambitious Catholicks, to have a Guarantee and a Guardian of the Treaties and Edicts. So that this Protection allowed to the Protector nothing else but the Care and Sollicitude for obtaining tolerable Conditions for the Reformed, and to watch over the Observation of the Treaties; consequently it could give no Jealousy to the King as long as he

(z) The Prince of Condé has never been a Protector at large of the Reformed; for tho' he took the Oath in the first Civil War at Orleans, nevertheless, the Reformed, far from obeying him, even in the necessary things, as Supplies are, they very often disobeyed him; the same thing happened not under the Prince of Navarr.

he stood by his Treaties, since to render the Protector useless, nothing more was required than to keep to his Promises and Treaties; the Protection fell of itself when there was no Infraction of the Treaties and Edicts. The Royal Authority was always respected, far from being restrained, the Reformed desired rather to increase it: But the cruel Zeal of the Catholicks, not satiated with so much blood they had spilt by so many exquisite Tortures, desired no less than the utter Destruction of them. Therefore if that inhuman Spirit occasioned a Party in the Kingdom, the Reformed, I hope, will not be blamed for it by any thinking Man, seeing that they had no other way left to defend themselves. It is true this Protection has oftentimes produced War under the last Kings of the House of Valois, but it has been always accidentally, always occasioned by the breach of the Edicts and the most base breach of Faith, as long as the Court was governed by a She-Wolf, who desired no better than Slaughter, was it not a Duty incumbent on the Mastifs to watch over the Flock to keep it, to defend it?

Furthermore, the Reformed have had no Protectors but what were Princes of the Blood, and even these Protectors have not been always Reformed, the Dake of Alençon, the King's Brother, was a Catholick; and as to the Prince of Navarr, afterwards King of France and Navarr, the Protection was reciprocal between him and the Reformed, for if he headed them in the War, or if the War was waged in his Name, if he supported them in time of Peace, watching over the Observation of the Edicts, and the Redress of their Grievances, he stood no less in need of the Reformed's Protection, for the Preservation of his Rights, especially since the League had begun

gun to display what was his real Intention, viz.
to deprive the lawful Heir of the Crown, under
a specious Pretence of Religion, in order to have
it set upon a GUISIAN HEAD. Whether after
Henry IV, the Protectorship ceased intirely or
was transferred over to the Kings of England,
or whether the Deputies-General of the Reformed
Churches to the Court of France had intirely the
whole management of their Concerns, under the
Guaranty of the King of England, that is a
point not very well decided in History, at least,
as far as I know of ; certain it is, that the Title
was extinct with Henry IV, that the General
Deputies approved of by the King, had the
management of the whole Concerns of the
Churches under Lewis XIII, and Lewis XIV,
and how their Affairs were managed during the
Civil Wars under Lewis XIII, that we shall see
in its proper place : we must return.

The Admiral declared Lieutenant-General of the Princes.

The Admiral was declared Lieutenant-General of the Princes Armies ; then it was considered in that Assembly what was more proper to
be done in the present Juncture, and as they had
Notice that the German Auxiliaries had begun
their March since the beginning of March,
it was resolved to go and meet them ; but before
that they resolved to secure some place upon the
Loire, to raise Contributions, to scour the Province of Poitou of the Royal Garrisons, and to
review the Army.

Accordingly the Army was reviewed, and
there was found four thousand Horse, besides
the Foot, not reckoning the Troops that were
in Garrison, or upon Party.

D'Andelot's death.

D'Andelot was sent to Poitou, but he came
back with bad Success, and the worst of all was
that he fell sick with a pestilential Fever, and
died at Saintes on the 27th of May ; the Physician

fician that opened his Body found in it the Symptoms of Poison ; but if it is so, it must have been a lingering one, for he had been attacked long ago with a quartan Ague which had wasted him by degrees, He had been of a very strong Constitution, well-bodied ; but what was more valuable in him, was his Christian, Moral, and Military Virtues, extremely conspicuous for his Integrity, Probity, Equity, and his Piety ; he was the first amongst the prime Nobility that declared for the Reformed Religion, wherein he persevered constantly till the latter end of his Life, and there can be no exception against his Sincerity in that respect, since the open Profession he made of his Faith before Henry II, exposed him to the Persecution of that Prince, and that he had at that time no other Prospect, in so doing, than a certain death, or at least a perpetual Captivity. His Experience in military Affairs, his Courage in Execution, his Care and Sollicitude for the Soldiers endeared him to them to that degree, that nothing was too hard or difficult for them, whenever he commanded, and put himself at their head, they ran chearfully after him as to a certain Victory. He had married Lady Claudia de Rieux, Heiress of the Houses of Laval and Rieux in Britany, by whom he had a Son, who took the Name and Title of Count of Laval, which Title was extinct with Guy XX, who died without Male Issue. D'Andelot's second Wife was Anna, Daughter of John Count of Salme, by whom he had two Sons, who died without Issue in 1586, and a Daughter named Anna of Colligny, Wife of James Chabot, Marquis of Mirebeau, from whom was issued the Marchioness of *Termes* and *Montespan* (a).

A

(a) Thuan. lib. XLV. p. 572, 573. Dinoth. lib. IV. p. 248. Add. aux Mem. de Castel. liv. I. ch. v. p. 374, &c.

Charles
IX.
1569.
Pope Pius
V.

Buchard's
death.

A little after D'Andelot died likewife at *Saintes*, James de BUCHARD, General of the Artillery, he was fucceeded by Yvoy, who took then the Name of Jenlis, his Brother being dead by this time at Strasbourg. D'Andelot was fucceeded in his Charge of Colonel General of the Infantry by James of Cruffol, Lord D'Affier, and the King on his part gave that Charge to PHILIP STROZZI, a near Relation to the Queen-Mother.

By this time la Noüe had been exchanged for SESSAC, a Lieutenant of the Company of Gendarmes of the Duke of Guife, and a Man of great note ; that difpleafed fo much the Brother of Montgomery, Corbuffon by Name, who was likewife Prifoner of War, and had much infifted with the Princes and the Admiral for being exchanged with Seffac, that out of fpite he deferted the Reformed Party and Religion.

The young Count of Briffac and Pompadour had been killed at the Siege of *Mucidan* a little before ; that Town was furrendered to the King by Capitulation, which was fo little regarded that the whole Garrifon was put to the Sword, and the Soldier who had killed the Count condemned to be hanged by the Royalifts, to revenge his death.

It would be too tedious to relate all the Skirmifhes, Sieges, taking and retaking of the Places which paffed between the two Parties, before the Princes had joined with their German Auxiliaries, I fhall obferve only, that they were fuccefsful in moft part of their Enterprizes.

Now I muft relate that famous Expedition of the Germans under the Command of the Duke of Deux-Ponts, who travelled above three hundred Leagues in an Enemy's Country, and joined

hap-

happily the Prince's Army after above three Months march, without any considerable Loss.

When these Troops were ready, the Elector Palatine sent to the King a kind of Manifesto, on the 21st of February, whereby he declared, that it was not against his Majesty or the Kingdom, but for his own Defence, and against the Enemies of the State, the Disturbers of the publick Peace, that he had armed, for keeping his Frontiers, and for assisting the Princes of Navarr and Condé, their Adherents, and those who professed the same Religion with him. That however if it was found that the said Princes and their Adherents mixed in their Case some other Concerns besides those of Religion and Liberty of Conscience, not only he would forsake them, but even join his Forces with his Majesty's against them : furthermore, that if at his entering into the Kingdom they were restored to their religious Privileges, and other Rights, according to the former Edicts of Amboise and Chartres, he would come back without requiring any thing for his Charges, which amounted already to a hundred thousand Crowns ; but otherwise he thought himself obliged in Honour and Conscience to undertake the Defence of the Afflicted, who desired his assistance.

The next day, part of his Troops having crossed the *Rhine*, the Duke of Deux-Ponts set out from *Reinzabern*, and arrived on the last day of February at *Hochfeldt* in the District of *Haguenau*, where he stayed till the 15th of March. There he mustered his Army, which he found to consist of seven thousand five hundred and ninety-six Horse, without reckoning those for Carriage, and six thousand Foot well armed ; they were joined, as abovesaid, by the Prince of Orange, his two Brethren, with some Troops of Horse, and

and by Morvilliers, the Marquis of Renel, and others abovementioned, with six hundred Horse, and eight hundred Arquebusiers; they came thro' *Alsace*, the Duke of Aumale being too much inferior in number was not in a condition to hinder that Army from entering the Kingdom; he followed them through the County of *Burgundy*, till they had crossed the *Saone* : on the 28th of March he fought them at *Gilly near Cistewn* *, the Loss was almost equal on both sides, and amounted to no more than two Hundred Men in all.   Then they went to *Beaune*, where they stayed for two days, till their Carts and Baggage should be arrived ; from thence they removed to *Vezelay*.   Here Aumale, despairing to hinder them, ceased to pursue them that way, and came by the *Auxerrois* to the *Loire*, in order to hinder them from crossing that River, as also to join with the Duke of *Anjou*, who was coming that way with all his Forces.   He was already arrived at *Gien*, with five thousand Horse Auxiliaries of Germany, led by the Marquis of Baden and other Chiefs, besides the French Troops. Guerchy, Standard-bearer to the Admiral, having found a Ford near *Pouilly*, in the Nivernois, the Duke of Deux-Ponts caused part of his Troops to cross the River *Loire* ; then they thought proper to seize upon *la Charité*, a Town upon the *Loire*, very convenient for crossing that River whenever they should have occasion for it, therefore they laid Siege to it, and having battered it for a few days they made a large breach in the Wall ; whereby the Commandant was so much terrify'd, that, on pretence of going to ask Succours of the Duke of Anjou, he forsook his Post.   Then the Garrison and Inhabitants being disheartened, desired to come to a Parley,

* Castelnau says at *Nuys*.

Parley, which was granted, but while they were
upon debating the Articles, some of the Inhabitants of the Reformed Religion, having given a
Signal into the Camp, let down a Rope by the
Wall, whereby the Besiegers came up one after
another into the Town, and made themselves
Masters of it on the 20th of May. But by the
Authority of the French Officers it was agreed,
That the French Troops should forbear plundering, and that the Plunder should be left to the
Germans instead of a Month's pay due unto
them. Feuquieres, one of the best Engineers
then in France, was killed at that Siege; Guerchy, with two Companies of Foot and some
Horse, was left Governour of the place; then
having left in it their Mortars and Culverins,
and taking along with them the rest of their
Artillery, the Army continued their march.

Mean while the Queen-Mother came to *Limoges*, in order to pacify the Murmurs that were
in the Duke of Anjou's Army, (for the Officers
as well as the Soldiers complained loudly of the
Hardships they were to undergo for want of Pay;)
she likewise desired to advise with her Son, and
the chief Officers of the Army, concerning what
was to be done in the present juncture of Affairs.
They were all very sensible that the junction of
the Germans with the Princes would give them
a Superiority which could be very hardly withstood. They could not but blame the Conduct
of the two Generals Aumale and Nemours, who
by their Jealousies had countenanced the Passage
of the Duke of Deux-Ponts, for so it was confidently reported, according to Castelnau. Therefore it was resolved in the Council of War, to
harrass the Enemy by frequent Assaults, and, if
possible, to hinder the junction of the two Armies.

*The Queen-
Mother
comes to her
Son's Army.*

Now

Charles
IX.
1569.
Pope Pius
V.

Now the Princes, (of Navarr and Condé) according to the Resolution taken, having marched with their Army to meet the German Auxiliaries, took by Storm *Nantrou*, and sojourned there two days : from whence they sent Montgomery into *Gascony* to command the Viscount's Army, because they could not agree amongst themselves, and for opposing the Progress of Terride in Bearn.

The Duke of Deux-Ponts's death.

On the 9th of June the Admiral with some General Officers set out, and having forded the *Vienne* at *Verthamont* went to receive the Duke of Deux-Ponts. But he found that he was dead at *Escars*. (Thuanus says at *Nesson*, but no matter). That Prince had been troubled for a long while with a quartan Ague, but by the great fatigue he had undergone, he fell into a Fever, which carried him off very soon. He exhorted all his Officers to prosecute with the same Resolution what they had so chearfully undertaken, for the Defence of so just a Cause ; he died in the 43d Year of his Age, and was succeeded by Count Mansfeld in the Command of that Army.

CIV.
Junction of the Germans with the Prince.

The Admiral presented the chief Officers of that Army with golden Chains and Medals with this Motto, CERTAIN PEACE, INTIRE VICTORY, or HONOURABLE DEATH ; and on the Reverse were the Names of the Queen and the Prince of Navarr, to show that they were fully resolved to die for the Defence of the CAUSE. The Junction of the two Armies was intirely made at *St. Yrier*, on the 23d of June, and by the Prince's Orders the Germans having mustered received their Pay (b).

The Princes Petition to the King ill received.

Few days after the Princes, by the Admiral's Advice, sent a Petition to the King in their own and

(b) Thuan. lib. XLV. p. 574, 575. Casteln. Mem. liv. VII. ch. vi.

and the whole Reformed Body in France's name, whereby they befought his Majefty to pity the fad Condition of his People, and to grant unto his Reformed Subjects the free Exercife of their Religion, with their requifite Securities, without any Reftriction or Modification : Protefting withal, that if there was any Article in the Confeffion of Faith which they had tendered to his Majefty fome Years before, contrary to the Holy Scripture of the Canonical Books, they were ready to alter it, and renounce their Error. Such was the Subftance of that Petition, which the King refufed to receive till the Princes had laid down their Arms. The Duke of Montmorency wrote to the Admiral to certify him, that as foon as they had fubmitted themfelves to this the King's Will, his Majefty would treat them as his faithful Subjects. But the Admiral anfwered with a Proteft, calling to God and all the Princes of Europe, for the Uprightnefs of his Intentions, and cafting all the Mifchief of their juft Defence upon the Obftinacy of the King's Enemies, and the Difturbers of the publick Peace (c).

The Queen-Mother reviewed the Catholick Army, and going File by File fhe encouraged the Officers and the Troops, giving them very fair Words inftead of Money. That Army was thirty thoufand Men ftrong, that of the Princes twenty-five thoufand. The Duke encamped at *la Roche-Labelie*, about a League diftant from the Princes Army, where there was a bloody Skirmifh, wherein the Catholicks loft above four hundred Men, and Stroffy, Colonel of the French Infantry, was taken Prifoner. The Admiral, unwilling to come to a decifive Battle, caufed his Troops to retreat. Two or three

Vol. III.   X   days

(c) Cafteln. liv. VII. ch. vi. & vii.

Charles
IX.
1569.
Pope Pius
V.

days after the Duke sent most part of his Army into the Garrisons of *Guienn*, there to refresh themselves, for they could not subsist in the *Limosine*, by reason of the great scarcity of Forage and Provisions.

By this time la Noüe, who had been made Governor of Poitou, Angoumois, Aulnix and the adjacent Countries, while the Princes and the Admiral were gone to meet the Germans, procured, by a Diversion, the Deliverance of *Niort*, besieged by the Count of Lude, who lost three hundred Men before that place, and retreated to *Poitiers*.

CV.
Progress of the Princes.

The Royal Army being gone into Quarters of Refreshment as abovesaid, and the Duke of Anjou having joined the Court at Tours, the Princes Army took several places in the *Limosine*, and then marched into the Lower Poitou by the latter end of June. They took *Chatelleraud* and *Lusignan* by Composition, and then

Siege of Poitiers.

the Siege of Poitiers was resolved upon, against the Opinion of the Admiral and la Noüe ; and having sat before that place above six Weeks, and lost three thousand Men, most part by Sickness, he was forced to raise the Siege, and to go to the Relief of *Chatelleraud*, besieged by the Duke of Anjou, who rais'd likewise that Siege, which he had undertaken only for Diversion's sake.

CVI.
Proclamation of the Parliament of Paris against the Admiral, &c.

By this time, that is the 10th or 11th of September, the Parliament of Paris, at the Request of the King's Attorney-General Bourdin, had issued out a Proclamation against the Admiral, the Vidame of Chartres, and the Count of Montgomery, whereby they were condemned to Death as guilty of High Treason, and a Reward of fifty thousand Crowns was offered to any one who should take the Admiral ; then on the 28th of

the

the same Month, for removing all Equivocation, the same Sum was offered to any one who should take the Admiral dead or alive, and free pardon, in case the Taker had been engaged in the same Rebellion ; and for reflecting a greater Ignominy upon them, the Parliament caused their Pictures to be drawn upon a Cart, and hung publickly on the Gallows; the Cardinal of Lorrain caused the Proclamation to be translated into Latin, English, German, Italian, Spanish, and sent it over into those several Countries. But, as Castelnau observes, what availed these Decrees ; for Men who were not afraid of an Army of thirty thousand strong, did these good Senators think to frighten them with Pen and Ink ? This was only a Fuel for entertaining the Combustion.

However, the Admiral took no notice of it at first. But at last he was obliged to be cautious for himself; for while he was at *Faye la Vineuse*, DOMINICK D'ALBE, his Valet de Chambre, was charged with Treason, and with having attempted to poison him, and being convicted thereof by his own Confession, he was condemned to be hang'd, and was executed. This Man having been charged to carry some Letters of the Princes of Navarr and Condé, and of his Master, to the Duke of Deux-Ponts, was taken upon the Frontiers, at *Brissac*, by la Riviere, one of the Guards of the Duke of Anjou ; he delivered his Letters, and declared his Commission to the Queen, the Duke, and the Cardinal of Lorrain ; they bribed him with some pieces of Gold, and the Promises of a much greater Reward ; he carried the Letters to the Duke of Deux-Ponts, and brought those he received of him to la Riviere, and told him what he knew of the Germans Affairs. Riviere questioning not but the Rogue, having already been unfaith-

His Valet de Chambre bribed to poison him.

X 2 ful

ful to his Master, would henceforward stick at nothing, loaded him with new Promises, and told him that if he would poison his Master, he might expect the greatest Rewards ; he engaged himself to do it, and having received Money and some poisoned Powders, he came back to his Master, who was then before *Poitiers*. His long stay upon his Journey rendered him suspected to the Admiral ; he caused him to be arrested, and having confessed his Crime, he was condemned and executed, as abovesaid (*d*).

CVII.
*Exploits
and Injusti-
ces of Mont-
gomery in
Bearn.*

We have said that the Count of Montgomery had been sent into *Gascony*, to take upon him the Command of the Viscount's Army and to oppose Terride's progress in the *Bearn :* Now that General was so diligent and successful, that having assembled the Forces of the Viscount's with those which he could draw from the Garrisons of *Castres, Castelnau d'Arry*, and other places, he marched into Bearn, notwithstanding the Oppositions of Damville, Montluc, and others, and forced Terride to raise the Siege of *Navarrins*, the only place remaining to the Queen of Navarr of all her Dominions in *Bearn*, and to fly into *Orez* ; he took that place by Storm, and Terride, who had shut up himself in the Castle with the chief Officers, was obliged to surrender by Composition ; which was not kept by Montgomery in all its points : for he detained Terride Prisoner of War, to exchange him for his Brother, and as to St. Colombe, Favas, Pordiac, and other Lords and Gentlemen, he had them tried, condemned and executed, as guilty of High Treason, because they were Subjects to the Queen of Navarr, and had taken Arms against her. Now what a pitiful
Pre-

(*d*) Mem. de Casteln. liv. VII. ch. viii. Thuan. liv. XLV. P 593, 594.

Pretence was this? Ay! were the Prince of
Condé, the Admiral, Montgomery himself, &c.
were they not all of them Subjects to Charles
the IXth? were they not in Arms against their
lawful Sovereign? What then! were the Reformed only allowed to arm and attack the Catholicks, and the Catholicks not allowed to do
the same against the Reformed? To what Extremes doth Passion or blind Zeal carry a Man!
What Profit did Montgomery receive from this
Act of Injustice and Cruelty? he afforded a Pretence to Montluc to behave himself like a mad
Wolf against the poor Inhabitants of the Mount
of *Marsan* ; he did cast a Blemish upon the Queen
of Navarr which can hardly be washed away by
all the lustre of her Virtues and Royal Perfections ; he whetted the Fury of the victorious Roy-
alist, against the vanquished Army of the Princes
at the Battle of Montcontour, which followed a
little after ; and passing Sentence of Death upon
those unfortunate Lords and Gentlemen, he
passed it against himself, which was executed
upon him about four Years after. Having reduced the other places of Bearn under the Queen
of Navarr's Obedience, he put strong Garrisons
in the most considerable, and retired to *Nerac*,
and from thence to *St. Mary*, where he joined
the remainder of the Princes Army, after the
Battle of *Montcontour*, whereof I am now to
speak.

The Duke of Anjou having crossed the *Vienne*
with his Army, on the 26th of September entered into *Poitou*, and encamped near *Loudun*,
where he found abundance of all sorts of Provisions, whereof he intended to deprive the Enemy ; and the better to hinder them from passing
into *Poitou*, and entering into *Guienn*, he proceeded to Mirabel. Biron, his Camp-Marshal,

CVIII.
*The Battle
of Montcon-
tour.*

X 3   told

told him, that he had met with the Van-Guard of the Princes Army going to *Montcontour*, whereupon he refolved to give Battle. The Admiral was drawn to it, not by his own Inclination, but rather by the ftrong Sollicitations of the Troops of *Provence*, *Dauphiné* and *Languedoc*, that murmured continually, being fo far from their home, expofed to fo many hardfhips, they threaten'd to defert the Army; and the Germans, for want of Pay, were no lefs troublefome : In a word, the whole Army cried aloud after a decifive Battle, which might put an end to their Troubles and Miferies. The Admiral feeing himfelf reduced into that dangerous Dilemma, either to be deferted by the Army, or expofed to a Sedition under the Enemies eye, who might improve that Opportunity for oppreffing him, feigned to be no lefs defirous of fighting than any of his Troops. Therefore being arrived, on the 30th of September, at St. Claire, two Leagues diftant from Montcontour, he put his Army in array the next Morning in a plain Field hard-by ; the Princes Forces amounted to fix thoufand Horfe, French and German, eight thoufand Arquebufiers, four thoufand Foot armed with Pikes and long Spears, three Cannons, two Culverines, and three fmall Field-pieces, and no more, becaufe the Admiral had fent the reft to *Lufignan*. But that day, and the 2d of October, there was nothing elfe but fome Skirmifhes between the two Armies ; but on the third the Battle was engaged, and tho' at firft the Victory feemed to incline on the Reformed fide, neverthelefs the Catholicks carried the day with great advantage.

Inftead of defcribing the feveral Attacks, &c. I fhall obferve four or five things on this Battle. 1. That the Mutiny of the Troops in the Princes
Army,

Army, occasioned the Battle as abovesaid, which was one of the most rash Attempts that ever was made during the War, for the Catholicks were much superior to the Reformed in number, being nine thousand Horse and eighteen thousand Foot strong, provided with seventeen good pieces of Artillery, which made a terrible havock in the Princes Army. 2. La Noüe relates, that the Night before the Battle, two Gentlemen unknown that followed the Catholick Army, came secretly near the Camp of the Reformed, and desired to speak to some body, having a Ditch between them ; *Gentlemen*, say they, *tho' we have upon us the Marks of Enemies, nevertheless we do not hate you nor your Party. Warn the Admiral, from us, to forbear by all means from a general Battle ; for our Army is wonderful strong since we have received the Reinforcements sent from all parts of the Kingdom, but let him spin out the time only for a Month, for the Nobility has declared upon Oath to the Duke, that they will not stay any longer, and that he must employ them during that time;——if they are not victorious very soon, they will be obliged to come to a Peace, for several Reasons, and they will grant it advantageous. Tell him, that we know this from very good hands, and that we have earnestly desired to give him notice of it.* The Admiral and several other chief Officers thought that the Advice was very good, and ought to be followed; but the Majority were of a contrary Opinion, and looked upon it as a trick of the Enemy, therefore he was forced to follow the Stream against his Will. 3. The new Mutiny of the German Foot, and some Regiments of Reisters, on the very day of the Battle, who refused to fight till they were paid, obliged the Admiral to spend about two Hours time before he could appease them ; and

he

he loft by that means an Opportunity of feizing upon a much better place than that where
he was, and which was occupied by the Duke of
Anjou. 4. The Admiral having been wounded
with a Musket-fhot in the Cheek, and received
another Wound in his Arm at the beginning of
the Battle, was obliged to fteal away, being not
able to bear any longer with the Acutenefs of the
Pain, and the great lofs of blood, which occafioned fome Confufion in his Army. 5. The lofs
of the Princes was very great, befides their Artillery, all the Baggage of the Germans, all the
Colours of the Foot. They loft about 4500
Foot and 350 Horfe ; befides a great number
of Servants, about 3000 were taken Prifoners of
War, amongft whom were la Noüe, and the
Count of Cruffol, but feveral of them were bar-
baroufly murdered in cool Blood, by the Soldiery, in revenge for what they had done unto
them at *la Roche-la-belie*, and for the Executions
in *Bearn*, by Montgomery ; and la Noüe would
have fhared the fame fate, had it not been for the
Duke of Anjou, who refcued him out of their
hands.

The Pope was very angry with his Nephew, the Count of Santafiore, for his having
not killed the Count of Cruffol, as he had commanded him, rather than to take him Prifoner ;
however, he was releafed by his Orders without
Ranfom, that it might appear that his Troops
fought only the Deftruction of the Sectaries, and
not prey and plunder. *What a piece of Generofity is this ! what a Chriftian means of converting
the Hereticks !* Amongft the Slain there were
four French Noblemen, viz. Puy-greffier, Au-
tricourt, Biron, Brother to the outwardly Catholick who ferved in the King's Army, and St.
Cyr, an old Gentleman of 85 Years of Age ;

I

I do not reckon the German Officers, several of whom were wounded.

On the Catholick side the Loss was inconsiderable, as to the Number, for it amounted to no more than 5 or 600 Horse, besides few of the Foot, but amongst them there was several Lords and Chief Officers, such as the Marquess of Baden, the Count Rhingrave, Scipio Piccolomini, &c. many were wounded, several of whom died in a few days after (*e*).

The Princes seeing the rout of their Army had retreated in good time to *Parthenai* ; from whence the Admiral had desired them to come to their Army in order to appease the murmurs of the Troops : The broken Remnants of the Army took the same refuge, at least most part of them; the Princes, the Admiral and their Council, questioning not but the King would magnify his Victory every where, thought proper to send Expresses to England, Scotland, Denmark, and Switzerland, to give an account of the Battle, and of the Condition wherein they where now reduced, intreating these several Powers to send a speedy supply of Necessaries to with-stand their Enemies. Then, having taken a little rest, they set out at three in the Morning on the 4th of October for *Niort*, where they arrived the next day, and the same day arrived in the same Town from *Rochelle* Henry Champernoun with a hundred English Horse ; he was very honourably received by the Princes, as he had been by the Queen of Navarr.

Retreat of the Princes.

Queen Elizabeth not only did what she could to relieve the Princes in that emergency, but sent likewise Orders to her Embassadors to the Protestant

(*e*) Thuan. lib. 46. p. 597, — 601. Casteln. liv. ch. 9. La Noüe 981, — 989. Dinoth. lib. 4 pag. 278,— 281. D'Avila has many mistakes in the relation of that Battle.

CIX
*Exploits of
the Duke
after the
Battle.*

Proteftant Princes, to exhort them to continue in the Affiftance for the Defence of a Cause which was common to them all.

On the other hand, the Duke of Anjou after his Victory, fent an Exprefs to the King his Brother, who was at *Tours*, to congratulate him upon the happy Succefs of his Arms; at the fame time he held a Council of War, and the Opinions were divided, the wifeft were for purfuing without lofs of Time the Princes and the broken remnants of their Army; had they followed that Advice, the Reformed were intirely undone; but the worft Opinion prevailed, which was to feize upon all the Places in *Poitou* and *Xaintonge* occupied by the Reformed, whereby they gave time to the Admiral to recruit his Forces, and to become more formidable to his Enemies, than ever he had been before, as we fhall fee prefently.

*Siege of
Niort.*

*Mouy
wounded by
Maurevel.*

Accordingly, the Duke marched with the Army to *Parthenay*, and the Gates were immediately opened; then he proceeded to *Niort*, from whence the Princes were gone, leaving in the Place Mouy with 500 Arquebufiers and a Cornet of Horfe, with orders to ftop the Army as long as he could, while they would reach *Rochelle*; therefore he refufed to furrender, and having made a Sally upon the Enemies, as he came back into the Town he was wounded in the Back with a Piftol Shot by De Louviers Maurevel, the fame who wounded treacheroufly the Admiral at Paris about three Years and a half after.

*Some Account of
that Man.*

That bafe Man had been brought up amongft the Pages of the Lorrain Princes, and had given very early Proofs of his vicious Inclinations, for having been very feverely chaftifed by the Governor, for fome grievous Offence by him committed,

committed, he killed him proditoriously, and fled into the Spanish Army after the Battle of *Renty*, and remained amongst them, till the Peace being made with Philip, he ingratiated himself again into the Guises Family; being allured by the great Reward promised to whoever should take the Admiral dead or alive, he undertook the Work, and having received some Money he came into the Princes Camp, and feigned a great Inclination for the Reformed Religion, and complained likewise of many wrongs done to him by the Guises, he ingratiated himself into the familiarity of some of the Chief, and especially of Mouy. Seeing that he had often attempted in vain to execute upon the Admiral what he had promised, and fearing left he should be discovered, he resolved to make amends for it, by murdering Mouy, which he executed in part as abovesaid, and fled upon a swift Horse, which Mouy himself had given him, to the Duke's Camp.

The Governor being so desperately wounded was forced to leave *Niort* to go to *La Rochelle*, where he died a few days after; *Niort* was surrendered, then *Lusignan*, *Fontenay*, *Chatelleraud*, and several others did the same, all Poitou was reduced in ten days, the Garrisons whereof retired, some to *Sancerre*, others to La Charité.

After the taking of *Niort*, the King, the Queen Mother, and the Cardinal of Lorrain came to the Camp, it was debated in the Council what was then to be done; the worst Opinion was again followed, viz. to take all the Places which held for the Reformed; accordingly they sent an Herald to St. John of Angely, wherein Piles, that brave Hero (whereof mention has been made in our second Vol.) commanded, to summon him to surrender, which he refusing to do, tho' the

Place

*It capitu-
lates.*

Place was but meanly fortified, and not ftrong by
Situation, it was attacked by the Royal *Army*,
the King's Majefty prefent ; and by the *brave*
refiftance of Piles, it held about two *Months*,
when the Walls being all down, wanting of Ammunition, and without hopes of being relieved,
he furrendered it by Capitulation ; the Articles
whereof were in Subftance as follow, that they
fhould not bear Arms for the CAUSE for four
Months together ; that they fhould march out
with their Arms, Baggage, and other things
unto them belonging, but Colours folded, and go
with fafety where-ever they pleafed ; that thofe
of the Inhabitants that would follow the Garrifon
might do it, and carry along with them whatever they would; that thofe of the Reformed Inhabitants that would remain in the Town, fhould
not be molefted on account of their Religion,
nor on any other foever for what-ever was paft,
provided they fhould forbear to meet together
for Divine Worfhip.

These Articles were figned by his Majefty, but
fo ill kept, that the Garrifon, confifting of 800,
Foot and 100 Horfe, was hardly arrived in the
Suburb, when they were robbed of their Arms
and every thing elfe, and fome were killed, thofe
that could efcape came to *Angoulême*, and thought
themfelves freed from their Engagements, fince
the Enemies had the firft violated the 2d and 3d
Article of the Capitulation.

The Befieged loft during the Siege about 100
Men, but the Befiegers, according to Caftelnau
there prefent, above 3000 Men, amongft whom
was the Vifcount of Martigues, Duke of Pon-
thievre, who was killed with a Musket-Ball; but
according to Thuanus, the number amounted to
6000, either killed or dead with Sicknefs.

The very fame day that the Garrifon marched
out,

out, that is on the 3d of December, the King
entered into that Town, and having settled every
thing the best as he could, for the keeping of
Xaintonges, he went to *Angers*.

It is to be observed, that this Siege of *St. John*
was no less prejudicial to the King's Affairs, than
that of Poitiers had been to the Princes; they
both committed the same error, in staying obstinately before a Place which could not be of great
Service unto them, and weakening thereby their
Army to no purpose, and that as the Princes Affairs began to decline by the Siege of *Poitiers*,
and those of the King to be flourishing, so the
King's Affairs fall into decay by the Siege of *St.
John*, and those of the Princes began to be restored (*f*).

After the Battle of *Montcontour*, and at the
beginning of the Siege of *St. John*, Montbrun,
and Mirabel with the Prince's leave were gone
into their own Country, as well for raising new
Recruits, as for securing *Privas* and *Aubenas* in
the *Vivaretz*; but as they went through Perigord
with Verbelet that went to command in *Aurillac*
with 300 Horse and 800 Foot, 200 of these and
more that had staid behind were routed at crossing
of *Dordogne* by the Garrisons of Sarlat, and others.

About the same time *Nimes* was surprized by
the Reformed of Languedoc; the Garrison retired into the Castle under the command of St.
Astoul, and having held out for about three
Months, were at last forced to capitulate.

Vezelay in *Burgundy* having been seized for the
Princes by Dutarot, and some other Gentlemen
of the Country, withstood all the Efforts of Sansac, who after three Assaults was obliged to raise
the Siege with the loss of above 1800 Men; he
had

(*f*) La Noue ibid. Casteln. liv, vii. ch 10. Thuan.
lib, 46.

Charles
IX.
1569.
Pope Pius
V.

*GreatCru-
elties of the
Catholicks.*

had not been more fortunate before La Charité, where Guerchy commanded.

A little before the Battle of *Montcontour*, it happened at Orleans, that the Provoſt having commanded the Reformed Inhabitants, on pretence of their own Security, to lodge in the Priſons of the City ; moſt part of them were ſo credulous to obey him, and part came into the Tower of Martinville, while the others retired into that of the four Corners. A few days after the Mob, provoked by the Preachers, ran to the Tower, and having entered into it, they murdered them all to one, without any regard for Age or Sex. Thoſe that had ran to that of the four Corners, unable to break the Gates, ſet fire to them, the Neighbours carrying great quantity of Wood, moſt part of the Reformed ſhut in it ſuffered themſelves to be burnt, the other, having thrown their Children over the Walls and ſeen them received upon the Point of the Spears, or barbarouſly murdered in another way, leaped over and were murdered in the ſame manner ; 280 Perſons periſhed in theſe two Places, Which occaſioned the flight of many Reformed of the adjacent Places to Montargis, where many had been preſerved under the Protection of the Dutcheſs of Ferrara, Grand Aunt to the King, who made a publick Profeſſion of the Reformed Religion ; neither ſhe, nor her Miniſters could approve of the Civil Wars for Religion's ſake, ſhe blamed it in ſuch a manner, that the Prince of Condé quarrelled with her upon that Subject, and it was for that very reaſon that ſhe was tolerated by the Court.

But the Preachers at Paris provoked the King againſt her on account of her receiving the poor Refugees ; he obliged her to ſend away 460 Perſons, the two Thirds thereof were Women and
Children,

Children, that could not walk ; that generous Princess provided those poor diftressed People with 150 Carts and eight Coaches with the Provisions for their Journey. But Malicorne who had brought the King's Order to that Princess, resenting some high Words which she had said to him, sent word to Villebeuf, Entragues, and some others to lie in ambush in a Wood whereby they were to pass ; but as the Men were warned by some runners, that that Troop had taken another Way, they came out of the Wood, in order to go and murder them upon the Road to *Briare.* At the sight of those Murderers that hastened Hanger in Hand, BEAUMONT, Minister of the Church of Orleans, put up Prayers to God at the Head of the whole Troop kneeling down, and exhorted them with the most pathetick Words to submit themselves to the Will of God.

,, It is enough, says he, my Brethren, going
,, out of the Way, and endeavouring to avoid
,, the Paffage unto Heaven where God calls us,
,, there is none of us but must be bodily fa-
,, tigued, and our Souls must be almost afhamed
,, with our repeated flight ; Death will cure our
,, Bodies and Souls, tired with the Roads of
,, this World, but much more with his Ways.
,, What do you think thefe Murderers will do?
,, They will deliver us from their own Wicked-
,, ness. Where were we a running ? To an Exile,
,, to Hunger, to Ignominy, and after all to
,, Death. Into what Place will thefe Murderers
,, send us ? To the Place of our Hopes, of our
,, Defires, to our Canaan fo much longed for,
,, into Eternal Glory, to the bleffed Vifion of
,, God, to that Life which only can be pro-
,, perly fo called. Let us not flee any longer
,, from that Life, let us ftretch our Hands to
,, Death, and kifs that Hand which God ftretches
,, unto

„ unto us; let us die like Lambs, for the fake
„ of the Lamb who died for us. Here our Ene-
„ mies haften to our Deliverance; it is the
„ Will of God to receive us by their Hands; let us
„ haften to come before his Presence, and to sing,
„ I commit my Spirit into thine Hands, for thou
„ haft redeemed me O Lord God of Truth."

While he was speaking, the Enemy had advanced about half a Mile, and were not half a
quarter of a Mile diftant, when an unexpected Accident happened: Some Captains coming from the
great Army of the Princes, or according to others,
from *Normandy*, with feventy Horse, were difcovered at a small diftance in that inftant. These
People took them at firft for a new Band of Enemies, and difposed themfelves to die, but one of
these Gentlemen, as they came near them, knew
a Gentlewoman of that diftreffed Troop that was
one of his Relations. Then they pulled off their
great Coats, and fhewed their white Caffocks, which
was the Colour of the Prince's Army; having been
told of the Danger they were in, and feeing the
Murderers not far off with Hangers in their hands,
they ran to them, and the whole Gang, one only
excepted, were put to the Sword. It is more
eafy to imagine than to reprefent by Words, the
Joy felt by that whole Troop at fuch wonderful
Deliverance, and the Shame and Confufion of the
Murderers. A young Woman married at Orleans
was delivered of a Child in the Cart during the
Conflict without any Pain, tho' before, while fhe
was at her eafe at home, fhe underwent great Labours, before fhe could be delivered (*g*).

It would be time now to fpeak of the Prince's
Journey with their Army from the Borders of the
Ocean, into the middle of Burgundy; but not to
be

(*g*) D'Aubigné Hift. Univ. Tom. I. liv v. ch. 13.

obliged to break the thread of that Narration, I
shall relate here in two Words, what was done
in the West Countries until the Peace.

The Civil Wars have their tides and their ebbs
like the Sea, sometimes one Party rise up, then
it falls, and again it rises; so it happened in this
War, especially in the Provinces of *Poitou, Xaintonge, Aulnix,* &c. they were taken and retaken
three or four times by the Catholicks and the
Reformed, and at last they were almost all in the
Reformed's hands, when the Peace was made:
we have seen them almost reduced to the King's
Obedience, when his Majesty set out from *St. John
of Angely* to go to *Angers*; but La Noüe having
been exchanged for Strossy General of the Infantry, at that time called Colonel of the Foot, was
no sooner at liberty, but he came to *Rochelle,*
where his Presence was much requisite and desired, and took upon him the Government of these
Provinces that had been trusted to his Care, as
above said.

That City was no less, if not more, useful to
the Reformed in this and the next Wars than
Orleans had been in the former; but besides, its
strength and the commodiousness of its Situation,
it cannot be said what Profit it brought to the
common CAUSE by the Fleet that was fitted out
in its Haven, especially a large Ship of one thousand six hundred Tons, called LA HUGUENOTTE,
whose Prizes put the Princes in a condition of
discharging most part of the Expences of the
War.

La Noüe being arrived, his first Care was to
clear the adjacent Islands of all the Royal Garrisons that annoyed the Country, he took one way
or another either by Intelligence, Composition, or
by Storm, most of the Towns, Castles, and
Strong-Holds of *Aulnix, Xaintonge,* and *Lower*

Poitou; then he experienced in his turn, that there is nothing permanent in this World, having loft moft part of his Conquefts, he faw himfelf almoft fhut up in *Rochelle.* The Baron of La Garde, alias Captain Pauiin, mentioned in our firft Vol. infefted the Seas on that fide, and hindered Provifions, and other things from coming into thatCity. Puy-gaillard and other Catholick Officers undertook to block it up by Land, and build a Fort hard by for that purpofe. La Nouë was not deficient to himfelf, he took his time, routed Puygaillard at Luçon, conquered again what he had loft, forced La Garde to flee into *Bourdeaux*, and reftored *la Rochelle, Aulnix, Xaintonge* and *Lower Poitou* into as good a Condition, as they had been from the beginning of this War; but he had the Misfortune to be wounded at the Siege of *Fontenay*, in the Month of June 1570, and loft his Arm. Several other Exploits were made in thofe Parts, which for brevity fake, I fhall omit here, obferving only that the Reformed prevailed in thefe Provinces when the Peace was made. Now we muft fpeak of the wonderful March of the Princes, from *Rochelle* to the *Pyrenean* Mountains, from thence beyond the Rhône, and from thence almoft to Paris.

I am fure, it would be as tedious to the Reader as to myfelf, fhould I undertake to give a full Defcription of all the Streights, Paffages, Mountains, Rivers, taking of the Cities, Boroughs, and of the Oppofitions they had to overcome in the Countries of *Perigord, Quercy, Languedoc, Gafcony, Dauphiné, Lyonnois, Forefts, Vivarez, Champaign, Burgundy,* and others of the Kingdom, which they croffed with a thoufand Difficulties.

It will be enough, methinks, to make fome general Obfervations upon the whole.

As to the Defign of that Journey, the Admiral himfelf

himself told Caftelnau, that it was lefs for refreſh-
ing their Army, than for paying their Reifters
with the Plunder of feveral Cities and Boroughs,
and for ftrengthning themfelves with the Troops
of Montgomery, who joined them at *St. Mary*,
and with others from *Gafcony* and Bearn, as alfo
for receiving the Forces which Montbrun, Mirabel, St. Romain, and others intended to raife in
Languedoc and Dauphiné, waiting for new Auxiliaries from Germany, which the Count Palatine
of the *Rhine* and the Prince of *Orange* had promifed to them, to the end, that all thefe Forces
being re-united together with the Germans, which
they expected to receive upon the Frontiers of
Burgundy, they might be in a Condition for coming to the very Gates of Paris, and try another
Battle; fuch was their defign.

Therefore having left the Count of La Rochefoucault at *Rochelle*, and made fuch other Regulations, they fet out from *Saintes* on the 25th of
October, with all their French and German
Horfe, and about three thoufand Foot, under the
Command of Rouvray. Eight days after they
croffed the *Dordogne* at *Argental*, paffing through
Rouergue and *Quercy*; they croffed the *Lot* at *Cadenat*, and arrived at laft at *Montauban*, there
they were joined with the Troops of the Vifcounts, and took their Winter-Quarters in thefe
Parts. At the beginning of the Spring, they fell
upon the Places round about the City of *Thoulouſe*,
wafted and burnt them all, efpecially thofe belonging to the Prefidents and Counfellors of the
Parliament of that City, in revenge for their exceeding Cruelty towards the Reformed, and for
the murder of Rapin, whom they had fo unjuftly
condemned and executed, when he came in their
City from the King, with the Edict of the Peace
of Chartres, as aforefaid. Damville was at *Thou-*

louſe with his Forces, but they were not ſufficient for oppoſing the Princes. Their Army penetrated into the County of *Rouſſillon*, which was no better ſpared than the Neighbourhood of *Thoulouſe*, as belonging to the Spaniards. From thence they marched into *Languedoc*, and having approached the *Rhône*, the Count Ludowic of Naſſau croſſed it with part of the Army, for aſſaulting ſome Places. But the main deſign of the Princes was to draw ſome Infantry from *Dauphiné*, wherein they had not ſo well ſucceeded in *Languedoc* and *Gaſcony*, becauſe the Soldiers, very willing to fight in their own Country could not bear with the thought of going ſo far as Paris, and the very heart of the Kingdom, becauſe of the great Miſeries their own Countrymen had undergone. Notwithſtanding which, three thouſand of them, ſtout and reſolute Fellows had liſted themſelves, reſolved to follow the Princes where-ever they ſhould go; and rode on horſeback becauſe of the great length and difficulties of the Road.

Though the Negociations for Peace were on foot ſince the Battle of *Montcontour*, (*for the Queen-Mother immediately after that Battle had ſent the Lord Caſtelnau to the Queen of Navarr for making the Overture of it, and Telligny and Beauvais La Nocle had been deputed by the Princes to Angers upon that account, after the taking of St. John*;) the Admiral had too great Experience not to be ſenſible, that they could not obtain a good one, unleſs they ſhould come near Paris. But the difficulty of the Roads through the Mountains of *Cevennes* and *Vivarets*, occaſioned ſome delays, and much more his great Sickneſs in *St. Stephen* of *Foretz*, where he was in great danger of his Life, which cauſed a general Conſternation in the whole Army.

Being

Being recovered, there came Biron and Malaffife by the latter end of May, to notify to the
Princes and the Admiral, as they had done in
their way to the Queen of Navarr, the final Intention and Anfwer of his Majefty to the Petitions tendered by Telligny and Beauvais la Nocle,
in the Name of the Reformed, which was in fub-
ftance, that his Majefty would grant them Liberty of Confcience, and two Places in the Kingdom where they might live as they pleafed under
the King's Authority, who would name the Governors of thefe two Places, but that he fhould not
allow the free publick Exercife of the Reformed
Religion any where elfe in his Kingdom, befides
thefe two Places.

Thefe Conditions were too hard and unrea-
fonable to be accepted. Therefore the Princes
marched out, and made fuch diligence, that they
arrived in *Burgundy* by the middle of July, and
encamped near *Arnay le Duc*, where they were
attacked by the Marfhal of Coffe, with an Army
twice fuperiour in Number to the Princes, and
well provided with Artillery, whereas the Princes
had none at all; but by the brave Refiftance of
their Troops, who ftoutly withftood their Enemies, they were repulfed. The Catholicks
feeing that it was not poffible for them to force
their Retrenchments, retreated into their Quarters, and the Reformed, wanting Powder and
other Ammunitions, went by long Marches to La
Charité, and other Places of their own Party,
where they might be provided with thefe things,
and marched to Paris. But a Truce of ten days
having been agreed upon, put an end to the Hoftilities, and the Peace was concluded at laft on
the 8th of Auguft, after ten Months, or thereabout, of Negociation; the Articles whereof are
as follow (*b*).   Y 3   EDICT

(*b*) Cafteln. liv. vii. ch. 12. Thuan. liv. 46, 17. La Noüe
Difc. Polit. & Milit. pag. 996. — 1009. Dinoth. Hift. lib.
iv. p. 306 to 315.

Charles
IX.
1570.
Pope Pius
V.

CXI.
Edict of
Peace.

EDICT of King Charles IX, about the Pacification of the Troubles.

CHARLES, by the Grace of God, King of *France,* to all those present and hereafter to come, GREETING. Considering the great Evils and Calamities occasioned by the Troubles and Wars, wherewith our Kingdom has been long, and is still afflicted; and foreseeing the Desolation that might ensue, unless, by the Grace and Mercy of God, the said Troubles were speedily pacified: We, in order to put an end to the same, to remedy the Afflictions that proceed from thence, to restore and make our Subjects live in Peace, Union, Quiet, and Tranquillity, as it has always been our Intention, to let it be known, that after having taken the good and prudent Advice of the Queen, our most dear and honoured Lady and Mother, &c. We have by their good Counsel and Advice, and for the Causes and Reasons abovesaid, and other good and great Considerations, Us thereunto moving, by this present Edict, perpetual and irrevocable, said, declar'd, and enacted, and do ordain, will and resolve what followeth.

I. That the Remembrance of all things past on both sides, from the very beginning of, and since the Troubles happen'd in our said Kingdom, and on the account of the same, shall be extinguish'd and laid aside, as of Matter that had never happen'd; and that it shall not be lawful for our Attorney-General, neither for any publick or private Persons whatever, at any time, nor on any Occasion soever to mention the same, or to commence any Process, or Suit thereof in any Court or Jurisdiction.

II. We forbid all our Subjects of what Rank, or Quality soever, to revive the Remembrance thereof;

thereof; to injure or provoke each other by Reproaches for what is paft. To difpute, conteft,
quarrel, wrong, or offend one another in word
or deed, but to forbear, and live peaceably together like Brethren, Friends, and Fellow-Citizens;
on Pain, for the Delinquents, of being punifh'd
as infractors of the Peace, and perturbators of the
publick Quiet.

III. It is our Will and Pleafure that the Roman Catholick Religion fhall be reftor'd in all
Parts and Places of this our Kingdom and Countries under our Obedience, where the Exercife
of the fame has been interrupted, there to be freely and peaceably exercifed, without the leaft trouble or hindrance, on the Penalties above mentioned. And that all thofe, who, during the
prefent War, have feized on Houfes, Goods or
Revenues belonging to Ecclefiafticks, or other Catholicks, who detain and poffefs the fame, fhall
furrender them the entire Poffeffion, and peaceable
Enjoyment thereof, with the fame freedom and
fafety they enjoy'd them before their being dif-
poffefs'd of the fame.

IV. And that there may remain no occafion of
difference or contention among our Subjects, We
have, and do allow, thofe of the faid pretended
Reformed Religion, to live and inhabit in all the
Cities and Parts of this our Kingdom, and Territories under our Obedience, without being urg'd,
vex'd, or molefted, or conftrain'd to do any thing
againft their Confcience, in point of Religion: Nor
to be examin'd in their Houfes, or Places where
they fhall inhabit upon the faid account, provided they behave themfelves according to what
is contain'd in the prefent Edict.

V. We have alfo given leave to all Gentlemen, and other Perfons, actual Inhabitants, and
others poffeffing in our Kingdom and Territories

of

of our Obedience, High Jurisdiction, or Full (a) *Fief d'Haubert*, as in Normandy, whether in proper or in usufruit, in the whole or in part, to have in such their Houses of the said High Jurisdiction, or Fief which they shall nominate for their Principal Abode to our Bailiffs or Seneschals, every one in his Precinct the Exercise of the Religion they call Reform'd, as long as they reside there; and in their Absence, their Wives or Children, whom they shall answer for; and they shall be oblig'd to name the said Houses to our Bailiffs or Seneschals, before they should enjoy the Benefit thereof: They shall also enjoy the same in their other Houses of High Jurisdiction, or of the said Fief d'Haubert, as long as they shall be actually there, and no otherwise, the whole as well for themselves as their Families, Subjects and others who shall be willing to go there.

VI. In Houses of *Fief*, where the said Reform'd shall have no High Jurisdiction, and Fief d'Haubert, they shall only be allow'd the said Exercise of Religion for their Families: Yet in case any of their Friends should chance to come there, to the Number of Ten, or some Christening happen in haste, the Company not exceeding the Number of Ten, they shall not be prosecuted, or troubled for the same.

VII. And to gratify our most dear and most belov'd Aunt, the Queen of Navarr, we have allow'd her, besides what has been above granted to the said Lords High Justices, over and above in every one of her Dutchy of Albret, Counties of Armagnac, Foix, Bigorre, in a House belonging to her, in which she shall have High Jurisdiction, which House shall be by us chosen and nominated, there to have the said Exercise perform'd for all

(a) An Inheritance held immediately and in capite of the King.

all such, as shall desire to assist thereat, even in her Absence.

VIII. Those of the said Religion shall also be allowed the Exercise thereof in the following Places, viz. For the Government of the Isle of France, in the Suburbs of Clermont in Beauvaisis, and in those of Crespi in Laonnois. For the Government of Champagne and Brie, besides the Fezelai, which they possess at this time, in the Suburbs of Villenoce. For the Government of Burgundy, in the Suburbs of Arnai-le-Duc, and in those of Mailli-la-ville. For the Government of Picardy, in the Suburbs of Mondidier, and in those of Riblemont. For the Government of Normandy, in the Suburbs of Ponteau-de-mer, and in those of Carentan. For the Government of Lyonnois, in the Suburbs of Charlieu, and in those of St. Geni-de-Laval. For the Government of Bretagne, in the Suburbs of Becherel and in those of Kerbez. For the Government of Dauphiné, in the Suburbs of Crest, and in those of Chorges. For the Government of Provence, in the Suburbs of Merindol, and in those of Forcalquier. For the Government of Languedoc, besides Aubenas, which they are in possession of, in the Suburbs of Montaignac. For the Government of Guienne, at Bergerac, besides St. Sever, which they are are also in Possession of. And for that of Orleans, Le Maine, and Le Pays Chartrain, besides Sancerre which they have, in the Town of Mailly.

IX. Moreover, we have also granted them to continue the Exercise of the said Religion in all the Cities, in which it was publickly perform'd on the first day of this present Month of August.

X. Forbidding them most expressly to make any Exercise of the said Religion, either as to the Ministry, Regulation, Discipline, or publick

Institution

Inftitution of Children, or others, in any Place befides thofe above granted and allow'd.

XI. Neither fhall any Exercife of the faid pretended Reformed Religion be perform'd in our Court, or within two Leagues round about it.

XII. Neither do we allow the Exercife of the faid Religion within the City, Provoftfhip, and Vice-county of Paris, nor within ten Leagues of the faid City ; which ten Leagues we have, and do limit to the following Places, viz. Senlis and the Suburbs ; Meaux and the Suburbs ; Melun and the Suburbs ; a League beyond Chartres, under Mount Le Hery ; Dourdan and the Suburbs ; Rambouillet-Houdan and the Suburbs ; a long League beyond Melun, Vigni, Meru, St. Leu de Serens ; in all which abovefaid Places, we do not allow any Exercife of the faid Religion : Neverthelefs, thofe of the faid Religion fhall not be difturb'd in their Houfes, provided they behave themfelves as aforefaid.

XIII. We do enjoin our Bailiffs, Senefchals or ordinary Judges, each in their Precincts, to appoint Places for them of their own, either fuch as they have heretofore acquir'd, or fuch as they fhall purchafe, there to bury their Dead ; and that at the time of their Deceafe, one of the Houfe or Family fhall go to acquaint the Captain of the Watch therewith, who fhall fend for the Grave-digger of the Parifh, and order him to go with fuch a Number of Serjeants of the Watch, as he fhall think fit to allow, to accompany him, and to prevent Scandal, to remove the Corps in the Night, and fo carry it to the Place appointed for that purpofe, only allowing ten Perfons to accompany it : And in fuch Towns as have no Captain of the Watch, the Judges of the Place fhall appoint fome other Minifters of Juftice.

XIV.

XIV. Thofe of the faid Religion fhall not be allowed to marry, in fuch degrees of Confanguinity and Affinity, as are prohibited by the Laws received in this Kingdom.

XV. All Scholars, the Sick and Poor, fhall be received in the Univerfities, Schools, Hofpitals, &c. without difference or diftinction upon the accouut of Religion.

XVI. And to the end, that no queftion may be made of the good Intention of our faid Aunt, the Queen of Navarr, of our moft dear and moft beloved Brother and Coufin, the Princes of Navarr and of Condé, Father and Son, we have faid and declar'd, do fay and declare, That we hold and repute them our good Relations, faithful Subjects and Servants.

XVII. As alfo all Lords, Knights, Gentlemen, Officers, and other Inhabitants of the Cities, Corporations, Villages and Hamlets, and other Places of our faid Kingdom and Territories under our Obedience, who have follow'd and affifted them in any Part whatever, for our good Loyal Subjects and Servants.

XVIII. And likewife the Duke of Deux-Ponts and his Children, the Prince of Orange, Count Ludovic and his Brothers, Count Wolrat of Mansfeld, and other Foreign Lords, who have aided and affifted them, for our good Neighbours, Relations and Friends.

XIX. And our faid Aunt, as our faid Brother, and Coufin, Lords, Gentlemen, Officers, Cities, Corporations, Commonalties, and others who have aided and affifted them, their Heirs, and Succeffors, fhall remain acquitted and difcharged, as we do acquit and difcharge them by thefe Prefents, for all Sums of Money by them, or their Order, taken and rais'd out of our Offices of Receipt and Treafures, whatever Sums they may amount to, as well as out of Cities, Commonalties,

or

or from particular Persons, Rents, Revenues, Plate, Sale of Goods both Ecclesiastical and others, Forests belonging to us, or others, Fines, Booties, Ransoms, or other kind of Sums taken by them, upon the account of the present, as well as precedent Wars: Neither shall they, or those by them appointed for the raising of the said Sums, or those that have given and furnish'd the same, be any ways troubled or called to an Account for the same, either now, or hereafter: And both they and the said Clerks shall be discharg'd for all the Management and Administration thereof, only producing for a full Discharge, Acquittances from our said Aunt, or from our said Borther and Cousin, or from those that shall have been appointed by them, for the examination and passing of the same. They shall also be acquitted and discharged for all Acts of Hostility, Levies, marching of Soldiers, Coining, casting and taking of Artilleries and Ammunitions, either out of our Magazines, or from particular Persons; making of Powder and Salt-Petre; taking, fortifying, dismantling, and demolishing of Cities and Towns; Enterprizes upon the same; burning and demolishing of Temples and Houses; establishing of Courts of Justice, Judgments and Executions by them; Voyages, Intelligences, Treaties, Negociations, and Contracts made with all Foreign Princes and Communities; introducing of the said Foreigners into the Cities, and other Parts of our Kingdom. And generally, for all that has been done, marag'd and negociated, during, and since the present, first and second Troubles, tho' neither particularly express'd nor specified.

XX. And those of the said pretended Reformed Religion shall depart and desist from all Associations they have made at home or abroad; and henceforwards shall raise no Money without our leave,

leave, or list any Men ; neither shall they hold Congregations or Assemblies, otherwise than above said, and without Arms ; all which we prohibit, on pain of being rigorously punish'd as Contemners and Infractors of our Commands and Ordinances.

XXI. All Places, Cities and Provinces, shall remain and enjoy the same Privileges, Immunities, Liberties, Franchises, Jurisdictions, and Seats of Justice, they had before the Troubles.

XXII. And to remove all Cause of Complaint for the future, we have declar'd, and do declare, those of the said Religion, capable to hold and exercise all Estates, Dignities, and publick Employments, both Seignorial, and of the Cities belonging to this Kingdom ; and to be admitted and received without Distinction into all Councils, Deliberations, Assemblies, Estates and Functions, depending on the things abovesaid, without being any ways rejected or hindred from enjoying the same, immediately after the Publication of this present Edict.

XXIII. Neither shall those of the pretended Reformed Religion be over-charg'd or burthen'd with any ordinary or extraordinary Taxes, more than the Catholicks, and according to their Estates and Substances. Moreover, in Consideration of the great Charges those of the said Religion take upon themselves, they shall be free from all other Taxations the Cities shall impose for the Expences past ; but they shall contribute to all such as shall be imposed by us ; as also for the future to all those of Cities, like Catholicks.

XXIV. All Prisoners that are detained either by the Authority of Justice or otherwise, even in the Gallies, on the account of the present Troubles, shall be releas'd and put at liberty on both Sides, without paying any Ransom ; but yet the

Ransoms

Ramsoms that have been paid already shall not be re-demanded or recover'd of those that have received them.

XXV. And as to the Differences that might arise upon the account of the aforesaid Sales of Lands, or other Immoveables; Bonds or Mortgages given on account of the said Ransoms; as also, for all other Disputes belonging to the case of Arms that may occur, the Parties concerned shall repair to our said most dear and most beloved Brother the Duke of Anjou, to summon the Marshals of France, and he shall decide and determine the same.

XXVI. We order, and it is our Will and Pleasure, that all those of the said Religion, as well in general as in particular, shall be restored, preserved, maintained, and kept under our Protection and Authority, into all and every their Estates, Rights, and Actions, Honours, Estates, Places, Pensions, and Dignities, of what Quality soever they be, except the Bailiffs and Seneschals of the long Gown, and their Lieutenant-General, in the room of which others have been placed by us during the present War; to whom Assignations shall be given to reimburse them the true Value of their said Offices, out of the clear Money of our Revenue; unless they had rather be Councellors in our Courts of Parliament within their Precinct, or of the great Council, at our Choice; in which case, they shall only be reimburs'd of the Overplus of the Value thereof, in case it fall out so; as they shall also pay the Surplus, if their Offices were of less Value.

XXVII. The Moveables that shall be found in being, not having been taken by way of Hostility, shall be restor'd to the Owners; however, returning the Purchasers the Price they have been sold at by Authority of Justice, or by other publick

lick Order, as well belonging to Catholicks, as to those of the said Religion. And for the Performance of the same, the Detainers of the said Moveables shall be constrained to make immediate Restitution thereof, without delay, all oppositions or exceptions notwithstanding ; and to return and to restore them to the Owners for the Price they have cost them.

XXVIII. And as for the Fruits or Revenues of the Immoveables, every one shall re-enter into his House, and reciprocally enjoy the Income of the gathering of the present Year. All Seizures or Oppositions made to the contrary, during the Troubles notwithstanding. As also every one shall enjoy the Arrears of Rent that shall not have been taken by us, or our Order, Permission, or Ordinance from us, or our Justice.

XXIX. Also the Forces and Garrisons that are, or shall be in Houses, Places, Cities, and Castles, belonging to our said Subjects of whatever Religion, immediately retire out of the same, after the Publication of the present Edict, to leave them the free and intire Possession thereof, as they enjoyed it before their being dispossess'd.

XXX. It is also our Will and Pleasure, that our dear and well-beloved Cousins, the Prince of Orange, and Count Ludovic of Nassau, his Brother, shall be actually restored and re-established into all the Lands, Lordships, and Jurisdictions they have in our said Kingdoms and Territories under our Obedience ; as also to the Principality of Orange, the Rights, Titles, Papers, Informations, and Dependancies of the same, taken by our Lieutenant-Generals, and other Ministers by us employ'd to that end ; the which shall be to the said Prince of Orange, and the Count his Brother, restor'd in the same Condition they enjoy'd them before the Troubles ; and shall enjoy

joy the fame hence-forward, according to the Letters Patent, Decrees, and Declarations granted by the late King Henry of moſt laudable Memory, our moſt honoured Lord and Father, whom God abſolve, and other Kings our Predeceſſors, as they did before the Troubles.

XXXI. We alſo will and require, that all Titles, Papers, Inſtructions, and Informations, that have been taken, be reſtor'd and return'd on both ſides to their true Owners.

XXXII. And in order to extinguiſh and lay aſide as much as can be the Remembrance of all Troubles and Diviſions paſt ; we have declared, and do declare, all Sentences, Judgments, Decrees, and Proceedings, Seizures, Sales, and Statutes made and given againſt thoſe of the ſaid pretended Reformed Religion, as well dead as alive, ſince the Death of our ſaid moſt honoured Lord and Father, King Henry, on account of the ſaid Religion, Tumults, and Troubles happened ſince, together with the Execution of the ſaid Judgments and Orders, from this Moment void, revok'd, and annull'd, and therefore order the ſame to be erazed and taken out of the Regiſters of our Courts, both Sovereign and Inferior, as alſo all Marks, Tracts, and Monuments of the ſaid Executions, defamatory Books, and Acts againſt their Perſons, Memories, and Poſterities ; and order the whole to be raz'd out. And the Places that have been demoliſh'd and raz'd on that account, reſtor'd to the Owners thereof, to be uſed and diſpos'd of according to their Pleaſure.

XXXIII. And as for the Proceedures made, Judgments and Decrees given, againſt thoſe of the ſaid Religion, upon no other accounts than the ſaid Religion and Troubles ; together with Proſcriptions, and Feodal Seizures accruing during the preſent, laſt and precedent Troubles, beginning

ginning the Year 1567, they shall be void, as never having been made, given, nor happen'd; neither shall the Parties derive any Advantages by them, but shall be put again into the same Condition, in which they were before the same.

XXXIV. We also ordain, that those of the said Religion shall keep to the Political Laws of our Kingdom, in observing Festivals, neither shall they labour, or sell in open Shops on the said Days; nor yet open their Shambles to sell Meat on such Days in which the use of Meat is prohibited by the Roman Catholick Church.

XXXV. And to the end that Justice may be render'd and ministred to all our Subjects, without Partiality, Hatred or Favour, we have and do ordain, will, and it is our pleasure, that Suits and Differences moved, or to be commenced among Parties being of contrary Religion, as well in being Plaintiffs as Defendants in any civil or criminal Causes whatever; shall be heard in the first place before the Bailiffs, Seneschals, and other our ordinary Judges, according to our Ordinances: And where Appeals shall lie in any of our Courts of Parliament, in relation to that of Paris, which is compos'd of seven Chambers, the great Chamber, La Tournelle, and five Chambers of the Inquests, it shall be lawful for those of the pretended Reformed Religion, if they please, in the Causes they shall have depending in each of the said Chambers, to demand that four, either Presidents, or Counsellors, may abstain from the Judgment of their Processes, who without alledging any Cause, shall be bound in this Case to abstain, notwithstanding the Ordinance by which the Presidents and Counsellors cannot be excepted against without just Cause. And besides that all Refusals of Rights shall be allow'd them against all others,

Vol. III.   Z   Presidents

Preſidents and Counſellors, according to the Ordinances or Statutes.

XXXVI. As for the Suits they ſhall have depending in the Parliament of Thoulouſe, if the
Parties cannot agree about another Parliament
they ſhall be returned before the Maſter of the
Requeſt of our *Hôtel*, in their Court in the Palace
at Paris; who ſhall judge their Suits impartially
and ſovereignly, without Appeal, as if they had
been judg'd in our ſaid Parliament.

XXXVII. And as to what relates to thoſe
of Roüen, Dijon, Provence, Bretagne and Grenoble, they ſhall be allowed to challenge ſix Preſidents or Counſellors to abſtain from the Judgment of their Suits, that is three out of each
Chamber; and in that of Bourdeaux, four out of
every Chamber.

XXXVIII. The Catholicks ſhall alſo be allow'd to challenge, if they think fit, all ſuch
Members of the ſaid Courts, as have been diſ-
charg'd of their Offices upon the account of Religion by the ſaid Parliaments, to abſtain from the
Judgment of their Suits, alſo peremptorily; and
they ſhall be oblig'd to abſtain from the ſame.
They ſhall alſo be allowed all uſual Recuſations
againſt all other Preſidents and Counſellors, according as they are of right allow'd by the
Statutes.

XXXIX. And whereas ſeveral Perſons have
receiv'd, and ſuffer ſuch Injuries and Damages in
their Eſtates and Perſons; that it will be difficult
for them to loſe the Remembrance thereof, ſo
ſoon as it ſhould be requiſite for the Execution
of our Intention, being deſirous to avoid all Inconveniences that might ariſe from People's being
diſturbed in their Houſes, until all Grudges and
Animoſities are allay'd, we have given in keeping
to thoſe of the ſaid Religion, the Cities of Rochelle

chelle, Montauban, Coignac, and La Charité, in
which all such as shall be unwilling to repair so
soon to their own Houses, shall be free to retire
and to inhabit. And for the surety of the same,
our said Brother and Cousin, the Princes of Navarr and Condé, together with twenty Gentlemen of the said Religion, who shall be by us nominated, shall swear and promise one and for the
whole, for themselves, and for those of their said
Religion, to preserve the said Cities for us; and
at the end of two Years, to deliver them again
into the hands of such a one as we shall think fit
to depute, in the same condition they now are in,
without innovating or altering any thing in the
same, and that without any delay or difficulty
upon any Account or Occasion whatever: At
the expiration of which Term, the Exercise of
the said Religion shall be continued there, as while
they held them. It being nevertheless our Will and
Pleasure, that in the same, all Ecclesiasticks shall
freely re-enter and perform Divine Service in all
Liberty, and enjoy their Estates, as well as all the
Catholick Inhabitants of the said Cities; which
said Ecclesiasticks and other Inhabitants shall be
taken into the Protection and Safeguard of our
said Brother and Cousin, and other Lords, to the
end that they may not be hindered from performing the said Divine Service, molested nor disturb'd
in their Persons, or in the Enjoyment of their
Estates, but on the contrary, restored and rein-
tegrated into the full Possession of the same. Willing moreover, that in the said four Cities our
Judges shall be re-establish'd and the exercise of
Justice restor'd as used to be before the Troub'es.

XL. It is also our Will and Pleasure, that immediately after the Publication of this Edict made
in the two Camps, Arms shall strait be laid down
every where; the which shall only remain in our

Z 2   hands,

hands, and those of our most dear and most beloved Brother the Duke of Anjou.

XLI. A free Commerce and Passage shall be re-establish'd through all Cities, Towns, Villages, Bridges, and Passages of our said Kingdom, in the same Condition as they were before the present and last Troubles.

XLII. And in order to avoid the Violences and Transgressions that might be committed, those who shall be by us appointed for the Execution of the present Edict, in the Absence of one another, shall make the chief Inhabitants of the said Cities of both Religions whom they shall chuse, swear to keep and observe our said Edict; shall make them guard each other, charging them respectively and by publick Act, to answer for the Transgressions that shall be made to the said Edict in the said City, by the Inhabitants thereof respectively, or else to secure and deliver up the said Transgressors into the Hands of Justice.

XLIII. And to the end that our Justices and Officers, as well as all other our Subjects, may be clearly, and with all certainty inform'd of our Will and Intention, and to remove all Doubts, and Ambiguities and Cavillings that might be made in relation to the precedent Edicts, we have declared, and do declare, all other Edicts, Letters, Declarations, Modifications, Restrictions, and Interpretations, Decrees and Registers, as well secret, as all other Deliberations heretofore made in our Courts of Parliament, and others that might hereafter be made to the prejudice of our said present Edict, concerning the Case of Religion, and the Troubles occasion'd in this our Kingdom, to be void and of no effect. To all which, and the Derogatories therein contained, we have by this our Edict derogated, and do derogate, and from this very time, as for them,

do

do cancel, revoke and annul them; declaring ex-
prefsly, that it is our Pleafure, that this our faid
Edict fhould be fure, firm, and inviolable, kept
and obferved by our faid Juftices, Officers, and
Subjects, without refpecting or having the leaft
regard to whatever might be contrary and derogating to this.

XLIV. And for the greater Affurance of the
Maintenance and Obfervation we defire of this,
it is our Will, Command, and Pleafure, that all Governors of our Provinces, our Lieutenant Generals,
Bailiffs, Senefchals, and other ordinary Judges
of the Cities of this our Kingdom, immediately
upon receipt of this our faid Edict, fhall fwear
the fame to keep and obferve, caufe to be kept,
obferv'd, and maintain'd, every one in their Precinct, as alfo the Mayors, Sheriffs, Capitouls, and
other Officers, Annual or Temporal, as well the
prefent, after the Reception of the faid Edict, as
their Succeffors, in taking the Oath they are ufed
to take when they are admitted into the faid
Places and Offices; of which Oaths, publick Acts
fhall be expedited to all fuch as fhall require it.

We alfo require our Trufty and Well-beloved,
the Perfons holding our Court of Parliament, immediately upon receipt of this prefent Edict, to
ceafe all their Proceedings, and on pain of Nullity of the Acts they fhould pafs otherwife, to
take the like Oath, and to caufe our faid Edict
to be Publifh'd and Regiftred in our faid Courts,
according to the Form, and Tenor thereof, pure-
ly and plainly, without any Modifications, Reftrictions, Declaration, or fecret Regifter, and without expecting any Mandamus, or Order from us,
and our Attorneys General to require and purfue
the immediate Publication thereof, without any
delay; the which we will have perform'd in the
two Camps and Armies, within fix Days after tho

Z 3   Publication

Charles
IX.
1570.
Pope Pius
V.

Publication made in our Parliament of Paris, in order to send back the Strangers forthwith. Injoining likewise our Lieutenants General and Governors, speedily to publish, and to cause this our Edict to be published by the Bailiffs, Seneschals, Mayors, Sheriffs, Capitouls, and other ordinary Judges of the Cities of their said Government, where-ever it will be necessary : As also the same to keep, observe and maintain, every one in his Precinct, in order to put a speedy Stop to all Acts of Hostility, and to all Impositions made, or to be made upon the Account of the said Troubles after the Publication of our present Edict ; which from the Moment of the said Publication we declare liable to Punishment and Reparation, viz. against such as shall use Arms, Force and Violence, in the Transgression and Infraction of this our present Edict, hindering the Effect, Execution, or the Injoyment thereof, with Death without hope of Pardon or Remission. And as for the other Infractions that shall not be made by way of Arms, Force, or Violence, they shall be punished by other Corporal Inflictions, as Banishments, Amende Honourable, or Pecuniary Punishments, according to the Nature and Exigency of the Offences, at the will and pleasure of the Judges to whom we have assigned the Cognizance thereof; engaging their Honours and Consciences to proceed therein, with all the Justice and Equity the Cause shall require, without respect or exceptions of Persons or Religion.

Therefore we command the said Persons holding our Courts of Parliament, Chambers of Accounts, Courts of Aids, Bailiffs, Seneschals, Provosts, and other our Justices, and Officers, whom it may concern, or their Lieutenant, this our present Edict to cause to be read, published and registered in their Courts and Jurisdictions, and
the

the fame to maintain, keep, and obferve in all points, and all whom it may concern, the fame fully and peaceably to ufe and enjoy, ceafing and caufing all Troubles and Hindrances thereto contrary to ceafe. For fuch is our Pleafure. In Witnefs whereof we have figned thefe Prefents with our own hand ; and to the fame, to the end that it may be firm and lafting for ever, we have caufed our Seal to be affixed.

Given at St. Germain en Laye, in the Month of Auguft the eighth Day, in the Year of our Lord 1570. and of our Reign the Tenth. Signed

CHARLES.

And beneath by the King being in his Council.

Signed, DE NEUFVILLE.

And on the fide *Vifa*, and fealed with the great Seal with green Wax, upon Knots of red and green Silk.

Read, publifhed and regiftered at the requeft and defire of the King's Attorney-General at Paris in Parliament, on the eleventh Day of Auguft 1570.

DU TILLET.

What is more obfervable upon this Edict, is, 1. that the Places wherein the Reformed could meet together for Divine Worfhip were fpecified. But, 2. what was the more confiderable amongft all the Articles granted, is the four Places of Security, which were to be delivered unto the Princes of Navarr and Condé, and which they were allowed to keep for two Years, together, thefe four Places were of very great advantage to the Reformed by their fituation ; LA ROCHELLE was a fafe Haven for receiving the Succours from England, in cafe of Need ; LA CHARITE' opened a free Paffage upon the

CXII.
Some General Obfervation upon this Edict.

Z 4 Loire,

Loire, whereby the Reformed of the Provinces beyond that River might have a free communication with those inhabiting on the other side; Montauban is upon the Frontiers of *Languedoc*, and *Quercy*; and Cognac is in *Angoumois*, a Province wherein the Reformed were much superior to the Catholicks at that time.

3. Another great advantage the Reformed reaped outwardly by that Edict, was the liberty of challenging a certain number of Judges in all the Courts of the Kingdom, either superior or inferior; nay, they might challenge the whole Parliament of *Thoulouse*, if they had a mind; and if the Parties could not agree upon another Parliament, they might appeal to the King's Privy Council, and the Masters of the Requests, there the matter was to be finally decided.

In a word, nothing was wanting in that Edict for the full satisfaction of the Reformed, but sincerity and honesty in their Enemies side, for performing faithfully whatever was promised unto them. And whereas the Princes and the Admiral were not able to dive into the most secret recesses of Catharine's Heart, they received these Articles of Peace with so much the more Joy, that they saw themselves out of condition of continuing War: for the Germans had lately mutinied, and the Count Volrad of Mansfeld had threatned the Admiral to retire into their own Country, if they were not paid off their Arrears by a certain time. Their French Troops were exhausted, and for want of Subsistence could not be kept under any restraint; no military Discipline could be observed in the Army, whereby the great Admiral was grieved to his heart, because of the plunders and depredations committed by the Troops, without being able to remedy these disorders; and said more than once unto his most intimate,

intimate, *that, rather than to take up again Arms
for a Civil War, he would suffer himself to be
deprived of all his Estate, Titles and Dignities,
and to be dragged along the Streets, and die in the
most ignominious manner.* And indeed he was so
constant in that Opinion, that he could never be
deterred from it hence-forward.

Besides the utmost Misery whereto the Kingdom was reduced, the Queen had another Reafon which moved her to conclude a Peace with
the Princes and the Admiral, and that is what
I have insinuated already, that being not able to
compass her ends by open force, she was resolved
to do it by treachery. But I believe Thuanus to be
in the right, when he says, that the King was
not as yet complice with her in that most detestable Plot, but only the Cardinal of Lorrain, Bi-
RAGUE, unto whom Morvilliers had wilfully resigned the Seals of late, and the three Brethren
Albert, Peter, and Charles de Gondy, to whom
afterwards some others were adjoined (*b*).

However the Court of Spain was much dif-
pleased at this Treaty, guessing not the true intentions of the Queen, and she being unwilling
to explain herself, left she should miscarry, her
Secret being discovered; all the intreaties, large
promises, and other endeavours of the Spanish
Minister were needless, the King and the Queen,
tho' by very different Motives, could not be diverted from their Resolution, Peace was solemnly proclaimed, with all the usual Formalities at
La Rochelle, where the Queen of Navarr was,
at *Paris,* and elsewhere; and the Edict was read
and registered in all the Parliaments of the
Kingdom.

Then the Princes with the Admiral, the Count
Lewis of Naffau, Telligny, Beauvais la Nocle,
went

(*b*) Thuan. lib. 47. p. 660.

went so far as *Langres*, where having took their leave of the Count Volrad of Mansfeld, and dismissed the Germans, whom they loaded with fair Promises more than with Money, the Marquess of Renel led them to the Frontiers, and the Princes, &c. proceeded to *Rochelle*, where they arrived about the beginning of October.

While the Treaty of Peace had been on foot, some hints had been given of a Match between the Princess Margaret, the King's Sister, and the Prince of Navarr, as a proper means for restoring, settling, and confirming a mutual Love amongst all the Subjects, or rather for the better concealing the most abominable Plot against the Reformed. However, the King taking notice of the too privy conversation of the Princess his Sister with the Duke of Guise, who carried his Ambition so far as to pretend to marry her, and was already sure of her consent, whereof he had even received the earnest ; the King, I say, was so much provoked at it, and fell into such a passion, that he commanded Henry of Angouleme his Bastard Brother, and Great Prior of France, to pick a quarrel with the Duke of Guise at a hunting Match, and to kill him one way or another, threatning him with terrible Curses and Oaths, that if he missed him, he would not miss him. But the Great Prior, tho' very willing, had not Courage enough for executing his Commission ; and the Duke of Guise understanding what the King hatched against him, avoided for a time to be present at any hunting Match, and then, by his Mother's advice, he married Catharine of *Cleves*, Widow of the late Prince of Porcian. That Lord was dead about six Years before with a Surfeit, having eat three dishes of green Almonds at his supper ; and tho' he had earnestly intreated his Consort not to mar-

ry

ry with the Duke of Guife, neverthelefs, his Charms were fo powerful, that fhe forgot her late Husband's intreaties and her own promifes. Few Months before Lewis of Bourbon, Duke of Montpenfier, Prince of the Blood, had married Catharine, Sifter to the Duke of Guife, whereby the Cardinal of Lorrain intended to win that Prince into his Party.

But the greateft Match was that of the King with Elizabeth, Daughter of Maximilian II. Emperor of Germany ; the Treaty of that Marriage had been on foot for nine Years together ; Philip II. had oppofed it with all his might, but at laft it had been agreed upon, and on the 24th of November the King fent the Dukes of Anjou and of Alençon, his Brethren, attended with a great number of Princes and of the firft Nobility, with about 300 Horfe, to meet that Princefs at *Sedan*, where fhe was received by the Duke of Bouillon, with all the Honours due to her Rank ; from thence fhe proceeded to *Mezieres*, where the King was come to meet her, with the Queen his Mother, the Dutchefs of Lorrain, his Aunt, and the Princefs Margaret, his Sifter ; fhe was delivered into the King's hands by the Archbifhop, Elector of *Treves*. On the 26th of the fame Month the Ceremony of the Marriage was performed by the Cardinal of Bourbon, in prefence of the Princes, the Officers of the Crown, and almoft all the great Lords of the Kingdom, there was above feventy Princeffes and Ladies of the firft Quality, all richly dreft ; the Feafts and every thing elfe anfwered perfectly well to the Genius of the Queen-Mother, who had ordered them. The King was then 20 Years and 5 Months old, and the Princefs but 16.

From Mezieres the King came to *Villiers Cofte de Rets*, where on the 23d of December, he gave
Audience

Charles
IX.
1570.
Pope Pius
V.

Audience to the Embassadors of the Protestant Princes of Germany, that were sent to congratulate him on account of his Marriage, and to exhort him to a thorough performance of the Articles of his last Edict, of *St. Germain.* They were very graciously received, entertained, and answered, and then dismissed, loaded with very rich Gifts *(i)*.

CXIV.
Complaints of the Catholicks and the Reformed about the Edict.

While the Court was at that Place, complaints were brought to the King from the Catholicks and the Reformed, about the infractions of the Edict. In order to redress the Grievances, the Marshal of Cossé and De la Proutiere, Master of the Requests, were sent to *Rochelle*, to agree with the Deputies of the Reformed about the Interpretation and Execution of the Edict.

1571.

Being arrived into that City, the affair of the Marriage of the Prince of Navarr with the Princess Margaret, was again proposed by them, and in order to insnare the Admiral, present at their Conferences, whom they knew to be much averse from the Civil Wars, and much inclined to a War against *Spain*; they talk'd of assisting the Prince of *Orange* in the *Low Countries.* After several Debates about the controverted Points of the Edict, the Marshal of Cossé told the Deputies, that he would make his Report to the King. Then the said Deputies made many Complaints against the Power which their Enemies enjoyed at Court, tho' it *was certain that they were the only Disturbers of* the publick Peace; they rehearsed whatever had been done since the Peace of *Orleans*, their manifold Plots and Attempts against the Reformed and their Chief; they complained that even now, many Restrictions and false Constructions were put to the Edict lately granted, quite contrary to the obvious meaning

of

(i) Thuau. ibid.

of the Words; that the Count of Villars, one of their bitterest Enemies had been named by the King, Lieutenant of the Prince of Navarr, in the Government of Guienn, and was coming into that Province with a Body of Troops. That the Prince of Condé was refused the Re-stitution of the Castle of St. Valery, given to his Father by the Widow of the Marshal of St. Andrew; that the Bastard Son of Sansac was preferred to the Bishoprick of *Cominges*, to the prejudice of Charles, Natural Son of the late King of Navarr, who had been invested with it; that Morvilliers, Lord Keeper of the Seals, had refused to read, publish and seal the Secret Articles of the Edict, tho' they made a Part thereof; that Chancellor de L' Hospital, the worthiest Man of his Age, had been deprived of his Office, out of hatred for the Reformed Religion, because his Enemies charged him with countenancing it in secret; that in all the Pro-vinces they were plotting against the Queen of Navarr, the Prince her Son, and all the Reformed in general, and were sending Emissaries to *Spain* and *Portugal*, for raising Troops and Money; that Blaise of Montluc inraged by the Wound he received of late at the Siege of *Rabasteins*, was not satisfied with the Slaughter he caused then to be made of so many innocent Persons, but continued now, and publickly to vent out his rage against the Reformed in his Province. They inferred from the Premisses, that it was not to be wondered at, if they were afraid, left by the impulsion, or violence of the same Persons that bore the sway at Court, and every where in the Kingdom, the publick Peace should be again dif-turbed, even against the King's Will.

To these the Marshal of Cossé answered, that a part of these Grievances were already past and
ought

ought to have been forgotten, since by the last Edict it was enacted, that they should be buried in a perpetual oblivion, and the other part were of such a nature, that they could not be renewed without renewing the former Causes of Jealousies, therefore they ought to be quite forgotten and forgiven, by all those who desired sincerely to see a solid and lasting Peace settled in the Kingdom, lest they should afford to the timorous, or to the turbulent, a pretence for raising new Commotions; that the King had always earnestly desired Peace and Tranquillity, and that he would keep and maintain that he had made of late: But, adds he, since you have been free with me, give me leave to be the same with you, and to tell you, that you do afford the King a just Occasion of questioning your own sincerity and good will, for to what purpose do the Queen Navarr, the Princes of Navarr and Condé, and so many Noblemen make so long a stay at *Rochelle*, far from their home, exposed to many inconveniences? His Majesty wonders at it, and can but suspect that there is some Snake in the Grass; and what increases his Jealousy is, that he had been told, that they kept still their Troops on foot, that they raised new ones at a great charge, that their Ships committed every day new Acts of Hostility against the Spanish and Portuguese Ships upon the Coasts of *Guienne* and *Xaintonge*, whereof frequent Complaints were brought to his Majesty, &c.

To this it was replied, that their stay at Rochelle was occasioned only by the long delays of several Noblemen, whom they waited for, for advising about means to discharge the Debts contracted with their Auxiliaries of Germany; that as soon as Peace had been proclaimed, they had dismissed all the foreign Troops in their Service,

and

and if there remained fome of the Natives in the Neighbourhood of *Rochelle*, it had been oc-cafioned by the coming of the Count of Vil-lars, whom they fufpected, as abovefaid, and be-caufe the neighbouring Garrifons had been dou-bled by the King's Orders. That was the Sub-ftance of their Conferences.

The Marfhal fet out for Paris, where Tellig-ny, Briquemaut and Cavagnes had been depu-ted by the Princes to follicit the execution of the Edict. That Winter was very fevere in France, the *Seine*, *Loire*, and even the *Rhône*, were quite frozen, infomuch that Carts loaded went a-crofs upon the Ice, and in *Provence* and *Languedoc* the Fruit-Trees were deftroyed by the Froft. (*j*)

Though the Reformed trufting to the King's Promifes, were every where very fubmiffive and obedient to the Magiftrates Orders, endeavour-ing as much as they could to entertain Peace and Concord; it was not the fame with the Catholicks, they infulted them in many Places, and threatened them with utter Ruin. Thofe who were lefs turbulent, told them, that they fhould enjoy the Benefit of Peace for two Years only, at which time they were obliged to reftore to the King the Cities of Security, wherewith they had been invefted. But the Seditious, far from waiting for thefe two Years, endeavoured to difturb the publick Peace, a few Months after the Publication of the Edict.

At *Orange*, at the beginning of February, the Catholicks headed by Mignoni and La Baume, having plotted againft the Reformed, committed many Outrages upon them in the Night-time, breaking their Windows, beating and wounding thofe they could meet; the Magiftrates being

not

(*j*) Thuan. lib. 50.

not able to repress these Violences, and the Reformed being not provoked by them as they expected they would have been, the Seditious forced into their Houses, and fell upon the Dwellers therein, without sparing either Sex or Age; they threw the wounded out of the Windows, who falling upon the Pavement shattered their Limbs, and died with the most exquisite Pains; some they choaked with Smoak at their own Chimneys, and lest any thing should be wanting to their Cruelty, they gave the Corps to be devoured by Dogs. Those who could escape, were murdered upon the Bridges, or in the Ports of the *Venaissine County*; some who had fled to *Montelimar*, were expelled out of the Town. That Fury lasted for three days, and would have lasted longer, had it not been for Montmejan, whom Damville had left Governor of the Citadel, who received in it those who could flee thither, and who with the Garrison repressed the fury of the Seditious. Count Ludovic of Nassau who was at *Rochelle*, understanding what had been done, wrote to the King in his Brother's Name, and required, that according to the Edict, the Prince of Orange should be allowed to name a Governor of his own, whereby the Inhabitants should be kept in the bounds of their Duty: That Request being granted, Berchon was sent by the Prince, who having strenghtened the Citadel with a good Garrison, he invited the Seditious, who had exiled themselves to come back, and few Months after a diligent, but very secret Search, having been made of the most Guilty, he caused them to be arrested, and with the King's Consent, they were tried by Judges sent from *Dauphiné* and *Languedoc*, some of them were executed, some other condemned to Penalties, and the Absentees proscribed *(l)*.   A

(*l*) Thuan. Ibid. Dinoth. lib. 5.

At *Roüen* on the 4th of March the Catholicks fell upon the Reformed, as they came out from Church ; they wounded many of them, and killed above 40. The King's Officers, understanding what they were about, came with some of the Citizens in Arms to the Gate, where that Maſſacre was perpetrated, and took some of the Seditious, which they brought to the Priſons ; but they were reſcued by their Accomplices, who without any regard for the Magiſtrates, broke open the Priſons-Gates. The Magiſtrates were so much frightened at this Licentiouſneſs of the Mob, that they abſtained for some days from the Duties of their Charge, and kept to their own Houſes. Thoſe of *Dieppe* willing to follow the example, fell upon the Reformed, but they were repreſſed by the Governor. The King having had notice of this, was extremely provoked at it, either becauſe he took it as an Injury done to his Authority, or becauſe he thought, that such things might occaſion some delays in the execution of his ſecret Deſigns : However, he ſent the Marſhal Duke of Montmorency to *Roüen* with some Troops, and some Counſellors of the Parliament of Paris, conſpicuous for their Probity, who having tried some of the Seditious that could be apprehended, condemned a few of them to death, others to Baniſhment and large Fines ; they pronounced Sentence of Death againſt three hundred that could not be taken, and their Goods and Eſtates were forfeited (*m*).

Now the King being, as it were, free from the former Diſturbances and Cares, after the Ceremonies and Feaſts of his Marriage were over, willing to procure his Conſort some new Diverſions, had ordered great Preparations to be made

CXVI. *The King's Publick Entry into Paris.*

(*m*) Eid. Ibid. D'Aubigné liv. ch.

made towards his publick and joyful Entry into his Capital ; and every thing being ready for that purpose, he came to the Gates of *St. Denis* on the 6th of March, where he received the Compliments of all the Corporations of the City, and of all the Courts of Justice, superiour and inferiour. Then proceeding, he entered into the City with all the Pomp and Magnificence possible, and went to *Our Lady's* Church, where the *Te Deum* having been sung, he came to the Louvre. Six days after he went to the Parliament, where in a set Speech he extolled the great advantages he and the Kingdom had reaped, and would still reap from the good Management and prudent Counsels of the Queen his Mother ; then he bewailed the sad Condition of the Kingdom, proceeding from the Male-administration of Justice, and upbraided several Senators with Vices, that rendered them unworthy of their Office ; he exhorted them all in the most pressing manner, to a thorough and sincere reform and amendment of Life, and to an impartial Administration of Justice. He was answered by the first President, Christopher Thuanus.

The Queen's Coronation. On the 25th or 26th of the same Month, Queen Elizabeth was crowned at St. Denis with the usual Ceremonies, and four days after she made her publick and joyful Entry into Paris, with a Magnificence so much the greater, as more Ornaments and Formalities are generally used in the Pomps of Princesses than in those of Princes. When that Ceremony was over, the Court removed from one Royal House to another, where we shall leave them for a while.

CXVII.
The 7th National Synod. On the 2d day of April, began the Sessions of the Seventh National Synod at *Rochel*, present the Queen of Navarr, the Princes of Navarr and Condé, the Admiral, and the Count
Lewis

Lewis of Naſſah, and ſeveral other Lords and
Gentlemen, beſides the Miniſters, Elders, and
other Deputies to the Synod: Theodorus de
Beze was elected Moderator (*).   Several Obſer-
vations were made upon the Confeſſion of Faith,
notice was taken of David, Gentil, Blan-
drata, Socinus, and other Hereticks of *Poland* and *Tranſylvania*, and their Tenets condemned and deteſted; thoſe of Cozain were likewiſe condemned, and the Biſhops of *England*
deſired to ſuppreſs the Books of the ſaid Hereticks, which began to be in vogue in this Kingdom.   When the Canons of the Diſcipline were
read, notice was taken of a Book publiſhed by
a Phyſician of Bourdeaux, wherein he aſſerted
the Supremacy of the Magiſtrates, as Head
of the Church, rejected the Church-Diſcipline,
and confounded it with the Civil Government
of the Magiſtrate; the Synod condemned the
Book, and deſired Beza to anſwer it.

A Form of Ordination of Miniſters was drawn,
which is as follows, ,, The Miniſter who pre-
,, ſenteth to the People the Perſon to be ordain-
,, ed, ſhall briefly treat of the Inſtitution and
,, Excellency of the Miniſtry, quoting for that
,, purpoſe, theſe or the like Texts of Holy
,, Scripture, viz. *Eph.* iv. 11. *Luke* x. 16. *John*
,, xx. 22. *2 Cor.* v. 19, 20. *1 Cor.* iv. 1.   Ex-
,, horting every one to take ſpecial heed, that
,, both Miniſter and People diſcharge their re-
,, ſpective Duties.   The Miniſter ſhall acquit
,, himſelf with the greateſt care and diligence

A a 2   poſſible

(*) I do not know where Thuanus has found that Beza, the' Moderator Elect, and notwithſtanding the Letters
of the Queen of Navarr to the Magiſtrates of Geneva upon
that Subject, could not be preſent in the Synod, and that
de Chandieu was elected in his place; ſince according to
Quick and Aymon, he propoſed ſeveral things, made
ſeveral Reports, and ſigned the Acts as Moderator.

,, poffible of all the Duties of his Charge, be-
,, caufe of its Excellency ; and the People fhall
,, with all Reverence receive the Meffage of
,, God brought unto them by this his Em-
,, baffador. Then fhall be read 1 *Tim*. iii.
,, and *Titus* i. where the Apoftle treats of the
,, Character and Qualifications of a true Mini-
,, fter. And to the end, that the Elect Perfon
,, might be enabled by Divine Grace, faithful-
,, ly and confcientioufly to perform the Duties
,, of this holy and honourable Office, a fervent
,, Prayer, fuitable to the Occafion, fhall be put
,, up to God for him, at the end of which,
,, the Minifter fhall lay his hands on the head
,, of the Elect Perfon, befeeching God, that as
,, he is confecrated unto his Service, fo he might
,, be replenifhed with the Graces of his Holy
,, Spirit, and that he would be pleafed to blefs
,, his Miniftry, and pious Labours, unto the
,, Glory of his Holy Name, the Edification of
,, the Church, and the Salvation of this elected
,, Minifter." It is to be obferved, that the form
of Prayer at the Ordination, was firft fettled
at the Synod of *St. Maixant*, in the Year
1609, fo that for 50 Years together there was
no ftated Form, to which the Minifter ordain-
ing was tied up unvariably. It is further to be
obferved, that the above Form of Ordination
had place only when the Minifter fo ordained,
was inducted into fome Church to deferve it ;
and that very feldom, and upon very weighty
Confiderations, no body was admitted into the holy Miniftry, without being prefented to fome
Church or other.

It was agreed in that Synod, that, without
any Additions, there fhould be three Copies fairly
written in Vellum of the Confeffion of Faith,
whereof one fhould be kept at *Rochelle*, ano-

ther at Bearn, and the third at Geneva; and that all three fhould be fubfcribed by the Queen of Navarr, the Princes, the Admiral, and other Lords there prefent, befides the Minifters, Elders, and other Deputies of the Churches to that Synod.

Several other alterations and additions were made to the Articles of Church-Difcipline; efpecially in the Articles of Marriage, fome Modifications and Corrections were made to the Articles of the precedent Synod, but not fo far as they ought to have done. They gave likewife fome Advices unto the Queen of Navarr about the Officers of her Houfhold, and defired her not to fell the Offices of Judicature, nor to beftow them but upon Perfons, whofe Character and good Qualifications, fhe was perfectly well acquainted with. They made feveral other good Regulations, and ended their Seffions on the 11th of April. Thuanus obferves, that this Synod was convened by the King's Authority, and his fpecial Warrant; however with this Provifo, that they fhould admit into it, whoever his Majefty fhould depute in his Name (*m*). But I don't find that Deputy's Name in the Acts of that Synod, nor any mention made of him; it may be that the King fatisfied with the fubmiffion of the Churches to his Will, went no further, and did not think proper to fend any Deputy to that Synod.

It is further to be obferved, that a few days before the Meeting of the Synod, the Queen of Navarr, the Princes, the Admiral, and other Lords and Gentlemen of that Party, had been confulting together about the means of difcharging their Debts contracted with their Auxiliaries of Germany. Some voted for petitioning the King to difcharge them of that burden, feeing that thefe Debts had been contracted for re-

A a 3   ftoring

(*m*) Thuan. lib. 50. p. 757.

Charles
IX.
1571.
Pope Pius.
V.

storing Peace and Tranquillity in the Kingdom
But others thought that it would be unjust to
require such thing from the King, seeing that,
though not obliged to it, he had already given
of his own accord, some Months Pay to their
Reifters, for engaging them to quit the Kingdom ; therefore it was thought more proper to
raise that Sum upon all the Churches in the Kingdom, and for that end, to assess each of them, according to their power and faculties, which af-
sessment was regulated and agreed upon in the
Synod ; and whereas they had no sufficient Authority for constraining them to pay, the King
granted unto them a Warrant of Distress against
that, or those, that should refuse to pay its, or their
Quota (*n*).

CXVIII.
Great Tu-
mults at
Paris.

While the Court was absent, a great Tumult
happened at Paris, the Occasion whereof was as
follows:

About three Years before Philip Gastines, a
rich Merchant of Paris, and a very honest Man,
having been charged with having lent his House
for nightly Meetings, (notwithstanding the King's
Edicts, whereby all Meetings in the day or
night for any Religious Performance were forbidden) and that the Lord's Supper had been
celebrated in it ; for that Cause, the Civil War
being kindled, he had been condemned to death
with his Brother Richard : Nicholas Croquet, a
rich Merchant, his Brother-in-Law, was likewise
condemned to death, for having been present at
these Assemblies ; all their Goods were forfeited.
Now, as Gastines, that venerable old Man,
who, (*his Religion set aside*) was so much beloved by all his Neighbours, nay, by all the
City, of which he had so well deserved by his
Services ; as, I say, he was carried to the place of
Execution

(*n*)   Idem. ibid D'Aubigné Tom. 2. liv. 1. ch. 1. p. 52

Execution, this fight moved the pity of many, and all honest people were full of indignation against the Facticus, because by their follicitation to the Judges, and by their suborning the Rabble, who followed with terrible threats and curses, the Presidents and Counsellors as they came out of the Parliament, they had prevailed so far upon them, that a fault that was heretofore punished with a Fine or with Banishment, was made a capital Crime in Gastines, a Man in all other respects conspicuous for his great probity and integrity. And for the greater Severity, his House in the Suburb of *St. Denis,* was condemned to be pulled down, the Ground to be levelled, the Court-yard to be made a publick Place, wherein a Pillar should be erected, with a Copper-plate affixed upon it, and his Sentence engraved thereon.

Now, whereas by the last Edict, it had been enacted, that whatever Sentences, Decrees, Judgments had been given against the Reformed on account of their Religion during the Civil Wars should be reversed, and that the condemned, or their Heirs, should be restored to their Estates, Goods, Honours, and good Fame, and that all Monuments or Instruments tending to their dishonour should be abolished and rescinded ; the Deputies of the Reformed required, that the Judgment against Gastines and Croquet should be reversed, and that the Monument erected in his Court-yard, commonly called Gastines's Cross, should be pulled down. That petition seemed very just and reasonable unto the King ; but those who countenanced the seditious Faction, said, that it was to be feared lest, if such a thing sacred and religious was taken away for gratifying the Reformed, the Mob would look upon it as an injury and prejudice done to the Catholick Religion. Therefore a middle-way was agreed upon,

A a 4

on, whereby the Reformed were satisfied without giving offence, as it seemed, to the Catholicks ; and that was, that the Monument should be removed from that place into St. Innocent's Church-yard, that the Copper-plate should be taken away, and another put in its stead, with an Inscription to the praise of the Cross ; all this was to be done in the Night-time, for avoiding Tumults ; and Marcel, Provost of the Merchants, was charged to execute that resolution. But it could not be kept so secret, that the Mob having some hint of it gathered together in arms to oppose the execution, and running early in the Morning along the Streets, they forced, entered and plundered several Houses of the Reformed. But the Duke of Montmorency, Governour of Paris, having notice of this, came with a great force to the assistance of the Provost, killed all he met in his way, dispersed the rest, caused one of them to be hang'd upon the spot at the Windows of the next House, and so the Provost went upon the execution of his Commission. This is the Account given by Thuanus. D'Aubigné agrees with him as to the most material Circumstances, he differs only as to Richard, whom he says, was a Son to Philip Gastines, whereas Thuanus says, that he was his Brother. D'Aubigné adds, that he was a very learned Youth, &c. See D'Aubigné Tom. 2, livre 1. ch. 1.

On the 12th of May the King issued out a Proclamation, forbidding under pain of Death and forfeiture of Goods, to carry any sort of Musket, Guns, or Pistols in the Streets.

CXIX.
The Depu-
ties of the
Princes re-
turn to Ro-
chelle.

Mean while Telligny, Briquemaut and Cavagnes were come back from Court to *Rochelle,* with the King's Commission to certify the Queen of *Navarr,* the Princes, and the Admiral, of his

his tender affection towards them, and of his earneft defire of maintaining to all its intents and purpofes the laft Edict of Peace ; that he had a good mind to carry the War into the Low Countries, and that the Peace might be more folidly eftablifhed, he intended to marry his own Sifter to the Prince of *Navarr.*

Armand Gontault de Biron arrived foon after thefe Deputies, in order to treat of the faid Marriage in the King's Name, with the Queen of Navarr, and ingaging the Princes upon that account to come to Court. Biron having difcharged his Commiffion, reprefented to the Queen, as if it were of his own accord, how advantageous fuch an Alliance would be for her Houfe and the whole Reformed Party ; that if fuch an opportunity was neglected, it was to be feared left the King fhould refent it very ill ; that the Guifes, who were ready to retire from Court, would be more potent in it than ever ; that the King, in order to remove the difficulties proceeding from the Confanguinity and the difference of Religion, had already treated with the Nuncio Salviati, and though till now the Pope had refufed his Confent, neverthelefs he was in hopes, that all the other Articles being agreed upon, he would be able to bring his Holinefs to a Compliance. So that they ought to come to Court, without any further delay, left they fhould increafe the King's Jealoufies by their refufal.

To this the Queen replied, that that affair was of fuch importance that it required fome time for confidering of it ; for though fhe was very fenfible of the great honour and advantage redounding to her and her own Houfe by fuch an Alliance, neverthelefs fhe queftioned whether the very difficulties mentioned above, the confanguinity sanguinity and the difference of Religion, were not such, that she could not with a safe Conscience desire to see that Alliance accomplished; therefore, if her Divines thought that she could do it, she would very chearfully concur to whatever might tend to the Glory of God, and the Welfare of the Kingdom, neither would she refuse any condition whereby she might show her intire submission and obedience to their Majesties will and command, which might serve to settle a lasting Tranquillity and Peace in the Kingdom, for which she was ready to shed the last drop of her Blood (*o*).

CXX.
*Several
Occurrences
to the latter
end of this
Year.*

The Prince of Navarr, with his Cousin of Condé, attended by many of the Nobility, was gone at that time into Bearn; from whence being come back, the Prince of Condé was betrothed with Mary of Cleves, Marchioness of L'Isle, Sister-in-Law to the Dukes of Nevers and Guise; she had been trained up at the Court of the Queen of Navarr, and in the Principles of the Reformed Religion, and the Marriage-Ceremony was celebrated some Months after.

*Second
Marriage
of the Admiral.*

The Admiral, having lost his Lady Charlotte de Laval four Years before, and thinking of marrying again, a Match was proposed to him with Lady Jaqueline d'Entremont, Relict of Claude de Baftarnay, Baron of *Anton*, killed at the Battle of *St. Denis*, Heiress of a noble and rich Family in *Savoy*, who professed in secret the Reformed Religion. This Proposition being come to the notice of Philibert Emanuel Duke of Savoy, he had published an Edict, forbidding under Penalty of forfeiting Estates and Goods to any of his Subjects, of what Quality soever, to marry any Foreigner without his Consent; and though the King had written several times to the said Duke in behalf of the said Lady d'Entremont, nevertheless

(*o*) Thuan. lib. 50. p. 759, 760.

theless he had been constantly refused. But the Lady who loved the Admiral for the sake of his great Name and of his Virtues (*for she did not know him personally*) set out *incognito* from *Savoy*, and arrived about this time at *Rochelle*, and was married with the Admiral.

The same day, Telligny was married with Eloyse, Daughter to the Admiral. *That of Telligny.*

But amidst all these Rejoicings, came the bad News of the Death of Cardinal Odet de Chatillon, Brother to the Admiral. He was come over into *England* at the beginning of the last War, and had been very useful to the Cause, because of the great value Queen Elizabeth had for him, as much for his Virtue and rare Integrity, as for the Greatness of his House; after the last Edict of Peace, the Admiral, his Brother, had desired him to come back into *France*, and he was going to *Hampton-Court*, for to take his leave of the Queen, when he was suddenly taken with a fit of Sickness, whereof he died on the 14th of February in the 50th Year of his Age, and was buried at *Canterbury*; his Death was hastened or rather occasioned by Poison, which his *Valet de Chambre* gave unto him, as the Villain confessed, when taken and put to the torture at *Rochelle* some time after. He was much regretted by every one, especially by the Reformed. The greatness of his Soul, his probity, equity, and faithfulness, his sagacity in the management of Affairs, endeared his Memory to the then present Age, (*the Pope and his Slaves excepted*) and to Posterity. While he was at the Court of England, he treated with Queen Elizabeth, by the command of the King and the Queen-Mother, about her Majesty's Marriage with the Duke of Anjou, but without any success; Queen Elizabeth refused not openly the

Death of Cardinal de Chatillon.

Match

Charles
IX.
1571.
Pope Pius
V.

Macth, but she was naturally averse from marrying at all. And even it was confidently said amongst the Courtiers of France, that the King was not in earnest, but that he intended only to deceive the Reformed by that sham Proposition of so strict an Alliance with a Protestant Power, that he might also by that means have a pretence for breaking the Treaty of Marriage which was on foot between the Princess his Sister and the Prince of Navarr.

The Court comes to Blois.

The King, at the latter end of the Summer went to *Blois*, there to receive the Queen and the Prince of Navarr, the Prince of Condé and the Admiral, whom he had intreated, by frequent Messengers to come to Court. From thence he had taken a turn to *Bourgueil* in *Touraine,* where, because of its delightful situation, the Queen had caused a Pleasure-House to be built, as she did in several other places, at a very extravagant charge.

Lignerolles murdered.

While the Court was there, the Viscount of La Guierche assaulted Lignerolles, and killed him on the spot. We shall see when we shall make our Observations upon Bartholomew's-Day, by whose order, and upon what account, that Gentleman was murdered.

The Count of Nassau comes to Court incognito.

Now, whereas mention had been frequently made of carrying on of the War into the *Low Countries,* which the Count of Nassau insisted much upon by his Letters and Messengers to the King, and that an affair of that nature could not be well treated, but in some private Conference; the said Count, feigning to go by Sea into the said Countries, arrived *incognito* at Court, with La Noüe, Telligny and Hangest d'Argenlieu, and conferred often in secret for six days with the King, then at *Lumigny* in *Brie,* where he was gone upon a Hunting-match,

concerning

concerning the Utility, Neceffity, and Means
of carrying on that War; whereat the King
feemed to be well pleafed, but he ftarted pur-
pofely fome Difficulties, whereupon, he faid,
he wanted much the Admiral's advice in order
to clear them, and that he intended to give him
the general Direction of that War.

He perfuaded fo well the faid Count, that
being gone back to *Rochelle* in the fame dif-
guife as he came in, he prevailed at laft, with
the King's Deputies, upon the Admiral, who
prepared himfelf to fet out for Court.

The Marfhal of Coffé had been lately fent
to him with Letters from the King, and a fpecial
Licence figned with the King's own hand, for
having, even at Court, fifty Noblemen of his
own choofing for his Guard. To all this the
Duke of Montmorency, his firft Coufin and intimate Friend, joined his Letters to certify him
of the King's fingular affection towards him,
and to intreat him to come to Court without
any further delay.

Being not able to withftand any longer fuch
ftrong Sollicitations, the Admiral fet out for Court,
where he was received by the King with the
greateft marks of joy, honour, and love. As
that venerable Man was falling down upon his
Knees before the King, his Majefty would not fuffer it, but taking him by the hand, he embraced
him, calling him his Father, faying loudly, that
never a more defirable day had fhone than that,
wherein he faw by his prefence (*the Admiral's*)
a final end put to the War, and a lafting Peace
fettled in the Kingdom. Whereto he fubjoined
with a fmiling Face, Now we hold you, and
you are with us, it shall be no longer in your power to depart from us
when you will. He was received by the

*The Admi-
ral comes
to Court.*

Queen-Mother, and what was more surprizing, by the Duke of Anjou, with the same serenity of Countenance, and familiarity of Speech. More sincerity appeared in the Duke of Alençon's behaviour towards him, though he shewed unto him no less civility and affability than the Queen Mother and his Brethren had done, for which that Prince began to be suspected by their Majesties, and his Brother of Anjou. The King added something more real than bare words, for he gave to the Admiral one hundred thousand Livres, for repairing the Losses he had sustained in the late Wars, and one Year's Income of all the Benefices his Brother Cardinal Odet had enjoyed, with part of those Benefices, and at the same time he gave strict order to redeem the rich Furniture and Plate of the said Cardinal, which had been plundered, wherever it could be found; then he restored him to his Place in the Council. At the Admiral's recommendation, his Majesty was likewise pleased to gratify Telligny for whom he had shewed a great regard, Cavagnes Counsellor of the Parliament of Thouloufe, and several other Lords and Gentlemen of the Reformed Religion; and that the Admiral might be insnared the better by all the outward signs of a thorough and sincere reconciliation, the King proposed to renew the Alliance with the Queen of England, and with the Protestant Princes of Germany, as soon as the ways and means for waging War with Spain should have been regulated and settled.

He goes to Chatillon.

Then the Admiral, having obtained leave of the King, went to visit his own Estate at Chatillon, from whence he was recalled soon after by the King, for clearing some new Difficulties that occurred in the intended War against Spain, and again he went to Chatillon; so ended the Month of September.

The

The Deputies of the Reformed Churches having had several Audiences of the King about the Articles ambiguous, or controverted of the late Edict; at last his Majesty caused their Petitions to be read unto him by Henry de Mesmes, Lord of Malaffife, whereto he was pleased to give a very favourable answer on the ——— of October, and immediately Deputies were sent into the Provinces to cause the Edict to be executed according to these last Intrepretations.

1572.
CXXI.
*Several
Occurren-
ces from
the begin-
ning of this
Year to the
Massacre.*

All this while the Queen-Mother, the Duke of Anjou, the Cardinal of Lorrain, the Duke of Aumale, the Duke of Guise, the Vice-Chancellor Birague, and Gondy Count of Retz, were consulting together about the means how to surprize the Admiral, and the other Reformed Lords; and it is said, that they held their Council in the same Room where the Duke of Guise was murdered by the King's order about 17 Years after; and it was observed likewise, that Henry III. was also murdered in the same Room at *St. Clou*, where the bloody Council of the Massacre was held a few Months after. However, they agreed at first upon this Scheme, viz. That amongst other shows which should be represented in the Nuptials, a wooden Tower should be built next to the *Louvre* in the Isle, which should be defended by the Duke of Anjou, and attacked in a sham warlike manner by the Prince of Navarr, the Admiral, and other Lords of the Reformed Religion, with Guns, which should be fired on both sides without Balls: It was agreed, that during the attack, some quarrel or other should be picked out, and that at a certain sign the Assailed should fire upon the Assailers, with Balls in their Muskets, that thereby the Plot would be covered with the specious pretence of that quarrel; and indeed the
Tower

Tower was built in the Isle, but the most prudent suspected something in it, and that after
mature Consideration, it was thought that the
Reformed Party would not be easily persuaded to venture upon such dangerous play, their
Jealousies being not quite worn out from their
minds, that Fort or Tower was pulled down
in the Night-time by the King's orders, before
the suspicions raised from it should have made
a deeper impression in their minds, and the materials were carried elsewhere.

*The Princess of
Montpenfier's escape.*

About this time Charlotte of Bourbon, Daughter to the Duke of Montpensier, fled into *Germany*, and retired to the Court of Frederick
Elector of Palatine. She had been brought up
secretly in the Reformed Religion by her Mother,
as said in our first Vol. Afterwards, her Family, though of the Royal Blood, being in very
narrow Circumstances, she was sent to the Abbey of *Joüarre*, whereof she was afterwads appointed Abbess ; and in her retreat, she preserved
the same Opinions about Religion wherein she
had been brought up, at the persuasion (it is
said) of Joanna Chabot a near Relation to her,
and Abbess of the *Paraclete* ; who, though she
professed openly the Reformed Religion, nevertheless she would never have forsaken her Convent had she not been forced to it, during the
Civil Wars, but she never quitted the Habit of
a Nun all his Life-time. The Court was extremely moved at this News, and by the King's
Command, the first President de Thou went to
Joüarre, for making more particular Informations. The Duke of Montpensier was then at
Aigue-perse in *Auvergne*. The Elector wrote
unto him, to excuse the flight of his Daughter, who, says he, could bear no longer with
the violence done to her own Conscience ; and
he

he endeavoured to mollify his heart towards her; the Letter bore date the 15th of March. But the Duke, one of the moſt violent ſticklers for the Religion of his Fore-fathers, anſwered on the 28th of March, expreſſing the deepeſt Sorrow and Affliction he was in, for what his Daughter had done, exhorting her to come back immediately and ſubmit herſelf to the King and her own Father's Will, and intreating, in the moſt preſſing Words, the Elector to ſend her back into *France* without delay, and not to ſuffer his Court to be a Refuge for Children eloped from their own Fathers Houſe. But the Elector, a Man of rare probity and intregrity, and who knew as well as the Duke, the Duties of Children towards their Parents, replied, that he was ready to ſend back the Princeſs, as ſoon as the King would have entered his guaranty, that no violence ſhould be offered to her Conſcience, and he wrote upon that account to the King. But the Duke, though he deſired earneſtly to have his Daughter in his power, could never be prevailed to conſent to theſe terms, and at laſt he declared, that ſince his Daughter was willing to perſevere in the damned Profeſſion of the Reformed Religion, it was better for him that ſhe ſhould live in Germany than in France under his eyes; ſo that Princeſs ſtaid at the Elector Palatine's Court till ſhe was married to the Prince of Orange.

The Guiſes left the Court at this time, with a feigned diſcontent, becauſe, ſaid they, the King forgetting the many Services the Crown had received from their Houſe, and accounting for nothing the baſe and cruel murder of the Duke of Guiſe, had no eyes, attention and affection, but for their Enemies. The Queen-Mother and the Duke of Anjou feigned likewiſe to be much

The Guiſes leave the Court, feigning to be contented.

displeased at that preference, and affected to be thought averse from the King's Opinion and Will. The Admiral and most of his Friends were deceived by these outward appearances; thinking that the King, notwithstanding the oppositions of his Mother and Brother, was really and sincerely resolved to maintain the Peace, as useful and necessary to himself and to the Kingdom; that for that reason he desired the Marriage of his Sister with the Prince of Navarr, and so to wage War against the Spaniards in the *Low Countries*.

The Legate Alexandrine arrives at Court.

While the Queen of Navarr was on the Road in her way to Court, the Cardinal Alexandrine Legate of the Pope to the King of *Spain* and that of *Portugal*, received orders to come to *France*. He set out immediately, and having met with the Queen of Navarr upon the Road, he went without paying any Compliment to her Majesty, and arrived at *Blois*, where he had a private Audience of the King, and required of his Majesty, in the Pope's Name, to renounce his Alliance with the *Porte*; to enter into the League against the Turks; to marry his Sister with the King of *Portugal*, and not with the Prince of Navarr; and to forbear, as much as possible, from any familiarity and conference with Sectaries.

The Italian Writers say, that the Legate obtained nothing as to the Alliance against the Turks, and that the said Legate was satisfied with the reason the King gave for it, viz. that the affairs of the Kingdom were not in that condition, that he could meddle with the affairs of others, being scarce master of his own; that he could not assist the Christians with Money, his Treasury being almost exhausted by the vast expences of the late Wars, much less could he send abroad

abroad any Troops; for the Reformed would not go, left they fhould be forbidden to come again; and as to the Catholicks, it would not be prudent in the prefent juncture to fend them abroad, left being deprived of their affiftance, the Sectaries fhould attempt fomething againft his Government. As to the Marriage of his Sifter Margaret with the King of Portugal, the Legate infifted much upon it; but the King told him, that the Tranquillity of his Kingdom depended much upon the Marriage of that Princefs with the Prince of Navarr, and it was not poffible for the Legate to make him alter his Opinion. They add, that the King being preffed, he told him with an Exclamation, *Oh! that I might tell ye every thing, certainly you and the Pope would be fatisfied, that there is no better means for reftoring the Religion in this Kingdom, and for utterly deftroying the Enemies of God and of France than thefe Nuptials. As to the reft, I hope that the Pope, convinced by the Event, will extol my Defign, my Piety, and my fervent Zeal for Religion.* To this Hieronymus Catena, Biographer of Pius V. quoted by Thuanus, adds (according to this laft Hiftorian) that the King fqueezing the Legate's Hand, offered him a Diamond of great value, which he took off his own Finger, and told him, *There is a pledge of my Word, that I will never depart from the Obedience I have vowed to the Holy See, and that without delay I will execute the Advices I have received, and follow the means prefcribed to me for extirpating thefe impious Sectaries.* But the Legate declined the accepting of the Diamond, faying, that the Word of a moft Chriftian King was fufficient to the Pope, and to himfelf; that he defired no greater or more certain pledge, and that he could not carry any better to the Pope.

But Dr Avila, who fpeaks of that offer, makes the Legate anfwer in a quite different ftrain ; *The moſt precious and valuable of all your Jewels*, fays he, according to this Hiftorian, *is no more than Dirt in the Judgment of all the Faithful, fince your Zeal for the Catholick Religion is quite worn out, and that you have fuddenly forfaken it.* But I fhall repeat it, that D'Avila is no more to be credited, when he fpeaks of things tranfacted in France before his coming into that Kingdom, and contrary to what other Hiftorians of thofe days have related, than a Tale-teller ; he was a witty man, he has written very elegantly in his own Language, but if Veracity is the firft Character of an Hiftorian, certainly D'Avila is a very bad one, as any Reader may be convinced, who will compare his Relations with thofe of the Hiftorians contemporary.

However the Legate, having received the King's anfwer, either in fuch plain words, or, what is more likely, in more obfcure, being loaded with many fair promifes of the Queen-Mother, and the Duke of Anjou, fet out poft for *Rome*, having received news of the Pope growing worfe and worfe every day, who died at length on the firft of May, a few days after the arrival of his Nephew, in the 68th Year of his Age, and the 7th of his Pontificate.

The Cardinal of Lorrain having received that news, fet out with Cardinal de Pellevé Archbifhop of *Sens*, in order to affift in the Conclave for the Election of the new Pope. But it happened, that on the 2d day after the Sacred College had been affembled, Hugo Buoncompagno of Bologn was unanimoufly elected, and took the Name of Gregory XIII. Tho' Lorrain received that news upon the Road, neverthelefs he continued his rout, looking for an honeſt

honeſt pretence for abſenting from Court, and willing to confer with the new Pontiff concerning the Queen's-Mother's deſigns.

After the Legate was gone, the Queen of Navarr with the Count Lewis of Naſſau arrived at Court, attended with a great Retinue ; and the Nuptials of Princeſs Margaret with the Prince of Navarr were regulated, as well as the Articles of the Marriage-contract. The Dowry of the Princeſs ſettled by the King amounted to three hundred thouſand Crowns of Gold, the Crown being worth 54 Pence, French Money of that time.

By the latter end of April the Treaty of Alliance with Queen Elizabeth was concluded at Blois, by the Duke of Montmorency, Birague, L'Aubeſpin Biſhop of *Limoges*, and Paul de Foix on the King's part, and Thomas Smith and Francis Walſingham, the Queen's Embaſſadors. That Alliance was defenſive againſt any Power whatſoever who ſhould attack one of the Parties ; they were obliged to ſend one to the other in caſe of need eight Men of War, manned with twelve hundred Soldiers, and Proviſions for two Months ; Item, ſix thouſand Men, in lieu whereof the Queen of England could require from France three thouſand Horſe ; free Commerce between the two Nations ; the Engliſh were to enjoy in France the ſame privileges and immunities as they did at *Bruges, Antwerp, Berghen* in *Norway* ; no Engliſhman ſhould be moleſted in France on account of his Religion ; the French and Engliſh ſhould unite together, for reſtoring and ſettling Peace in *Scotland* ; whatever had been taken by the Engliſh ſhould be reſtored in 40 days time. Theſe Articles the King ſwore to, in preſence of Admiral Clinton, ſent by the Queen for that purpoſe, and her Majeſty did the ſame at *Weſt-*

minſter

minster the 16th of May, in presence of the Duke of Montmorency, Paul de Foix, and La Mothe Fenelon; and the next day she gave the Order of the Garter to the Duke of Montmorency.

The eighth National Synod of the Reformed Churches in France.

The eighth National Synod of the Reformed Churches in France opened its Sessions this Year on the 6th day of May at *Nismes* in Languedoc, and lasted but three days; De La Place was elected Moderator and Secretary to that Synod. Thuanus mistakes again, when he says, that De Beze was Moderator; it is true, he assisted in it, only as any other Minister and a Deputy of the Church of *Geneva*, but not as Moderator, since De La Place proposed and signed. They made several Regulations, with a great deal of discretion and moderation concerning the Doctrine and Discipline of the Church, whereupon I shall not insist here; only I shall observe, that by this Synod it was enacted, that a Professor in Divinity might keep his Wife, though convicted of Adultery, but the same liberty was not allowed to a Minister, because of the Consequences, his Character being much more publick than that of a Professor, and he being obliged to be an Example. The Admiral wrote to this Synod, and it appears, by the deliberation and resolution of that Assembly, that his Letters were full of large encomiums of the King's good intentions and will towards the Reformed Churches of this Kingdom.

The Admiral unmoveable in his Resolution.

All this while the said Admiral was the more and more confirmed in the good opinion he had conceived of the King's sincerity, and tho' he received every day, and from several places, new warnings to take care of himself, and provide for his own security, and that of so many who depended upon him; that good upright

right Man, judging of the King's Character by his own, could never be diverted from his first resolution to trust intirely to the King ; nay, he went so far, as to blame those, who being not so credulous as himself, regarded for their own preservation.

Philip Strozzi, the Baron de la Garde, and Landeray, being sent to *Xaintonge*, under pretence of sailing with a Fleet into the *Low Countries*, and from thence into the *Indies*, against the Spaniards ; the Rochellese suspecting the truth of the matter, sent several Messengers to the Admiral, intreating him not to trust so far to the promises of the Court. But his heart being void of all suspicion, he answered, that every thing ought to be interpreted in the most favourable sense, and that things were come to such a pass, that he had more to expect from the King's favour, than he had to fear from his anger. That these were some artful devices of their Enemies, who endeavoured by these false Rumours to fill the Reformed with jealousies and suspicions, that by their continual mistrusts, they might incur the King's Indignation, and render themselves unworthy of his Favours. Therefore he exhorted them to be deaf to these sinistrous suspicions, and to trust themselves and their All unto the Providence of Almighty God, and the Goodness of their King. And willing to join deeds to words, he advised the Chiefs of his Party to restore unto the King the places he had granted unto them by his Edict of *St. Germain* for their own security, though the time was not yet expired ; but in that respect, his advice was not regarded, at least as to *Rochelle*, *La Charité*, and *Montauban*; since *La Charité* was surprised by the King's Troops a few Months after, and during the Massacre, and that the Reformed kept

their

Charles
IX.
1571.
Pope Gregory XIII.

their ground at *Rochelle* and *Montauban* : and I do not know from whence Thuanus has learned, that this the Admiral's advice was followed and executed ; for which reason the King, out of gratitude, sent orders to all the Parliaments of the Kingdom, to watch narrowly over the strict Observation of his Edict.

The Queen of Navarr goes to Paris.

On the 15th of May the Queen of Navarr set out from *Blois* for *Paris*, there to make the necessary preparations for the approaching Nuptials; she took an apartment at the House of *Charles Guillart* Bishop of Chartres, who then professed publickly the Reformed Religion, and had been heretofore cited to Rome upon suspicion. The Queen having been much hurried with Business, was taken ill with a Fever on the

She dies there.

4th of June, and died on the 5th day, that is, the 9th of the same Month, in the 44th Year of her Age.

A Princess endowed with all the Virtues and other Qualifications that can adorn a Throne, sincere and stedfast in the Reformed Religion which she had embraced, and which she constantly followed, notwithstanding the many dangers she was exposed to, but she perferred Religion before all the Riches and Dignities in the World ; in all her Distresses she relied intirely upon God rather than upon Men; she was extraordinary curious of the Education of her Children, and was not without anxiety, when she thought of the danger the Prince her Son would be exposed to, as to his Religion and Morals, by the Alliance he was to contract, in the most dissolute Court that had ever been in the World, but that she could not avoid. She was poisoned with a Pair of Gloves, but the Poison having offended only the Head, which was not opened, no signs of it were perceived in the Body : Happy

was

was fhe, to die at that time, not to be an eye-witnefs of the cruel Butchery of fo many of her Friends, Relations and Servants, who pro-feffed the fame Religion with her.

She made her laft Will two or three days before fhe died, whereby, after having recom-mended her Soul to the mercy of God, fhe de-fired to be buried without any Funeral Pomp, hard by her Father Henry, King of Navarr. She earneftly intreated the Prince her Son, to be above all things Pious and Religious, according to the Principles wherein he had been brought up, and not fuffer himfelf to be diverted from it by the fumes, vain pleafures, and other allure-ments of the World, nor by any inducement of Vices; to take care that the Laws and Con-ftitutions fhe had made about Religion, in her own Dominions of *Bearn*, and *Lower Navarr*, fhould be exactly obferved; to remove intirely from his Houfhold, all bad Coünfellors, and thofe given to Impiety and Profanenefs, or other-wife vicious and diffolute; to admit none into his Council, but what were thoroughly pious, honeft, and good Men, amongft whom fhe na-med DE BEAUVOIR, DE FRANCOUR, and DE BETHUT. She recommended unto him the prin-cipal care of his Sifter the Princefs Catherine, and to treat her in a gentle and loving manner, without any roughnefs, and to take care that fhe might be brought up in the fame Reform-ed Religion in *Bearn*, and when fhe fhould be at Age to marry her with fome Proteftant Prince of the fame Rank with her, to love as Brethren his two firft Coufins, Henry Prince of Condé, and Francis Marquefs of Conti, and to entertain a-bove all a good concord and union with the Admiral to the glory of God; laftly, fhe infti-tuted him her fole Heir, and befought the King,

the

the Queen-Mother, the Dukes of Anjou and
Alençon to receive the Prince and the Princeſs
her Children under their Protection, and to grant
unto them the free Profeſſion of their Religion ;
ſhe named Charles Cardinal of Bourbon her Brother-in-Law, and Admiral de Coligny, Executors
of this laſt Will.

The Letter ſhe wrote from Blois to the Prince
her Son, doth expreſs ſo well the real Sentiments of her great Soul, and gives us ſo full
a Deſcription of the diſſolute Lives of the Court
and the Courtiers, that it would be almoſt an
injury done to her Memory, ſhould I conceal
it from the Publick ; it is as follows.

*Her Letter
to the
Prince her
Son.*

,, My Son,

,, I Am in labour, and in ſuch an extremity,
,, that was it not for the proviſion I had
,, made, I ſhould have been extremely tormen-
,, ted. The hurry wherein I am for diſpatch-
,, ing this Bearer, hinders me from enlarging
,, myſelf ſo much as I did in my former. I
,, have only given unto him ſome minutes and
,, heads, as memorandums of what he ſhall
,, tell you. I would have ſent back *Richardiere,*
,, but he is too much fatigued ; and beſides
,, that, he will go ſoon after this Bearer to let
,, you know how affairs ſtand : I ſend this
,, expreſs to let you know one thing, viz. That
,, I am obliged to negociate in a way quite
,, contrary to what I had expected, and been
,, promiſed ; for I am not at liberty to talk with
,, the King, nor with Madam, but only with the
,, Queen Mother ; who deals with me very
,, ſcurvily, as this Bearer will tell you. As to
,, Monſieur (*) he is very privy with me, but half
,, in banter, as you know him, and half in diſ-
,, ſembling. As to Madam, I ſaw her only in
,, the

*(*) The
Duke of
Anjou.*

,, the Queen-Mother's Apartment, a very unfit
,, place, from whence she does not stir, and she
,, goes into her own Apartment, only at such hours
,, that are very troublesome to me, and Madam
,, de Curton never goes from her, so I cannot
,, speak to that Princess but her Governess hears
,, whatever I say. I have not as yet shew'd your
,, Letter unto her, but I will. I have told her
,, of it, she is much reserved, and she answers
,, me always in general expressions of obedience
,, and reverence towards you and me, if she
,, becomes your Wife.

,, Seeing then, my Son, that nothing is done,
,, and that they will force me to hurry on
,, affairs, and not to digest them with or-
,, der; I have complained of it three times to
,, the Queen, but she laugh'd at me, and behind
,, my back makes me say quite the reverse to
,, what I have said : In so much that I am bla-
,, med for it by my Friends, and I do not know
,, how to give the lye to the Queen ; for when
,, I told her, MADAM, People say that I have
,, spoken unto you such and such things, tho'
,, these Reports came from herself, nevertheless
,, she denies it, as she would a Murder, and laughs
,, in my face, and uses me in such a manner,
,, that you may say that my patience exceeds
,, *Griselidis.* Do I think to show her by good
,, reasons, that I am very far from the hope
,, she had given me, to be privy with her, and to
,, treat with her in the best manner ? She denies
,, all that, and whereas this Bearer knows her
,, Words, which he will tell ye, you will be bet-
,, ter enabled to judge of my situation. Have I
,, done with her ? I have to deal with a croud of
,, Reformed, that come to talk with me, rather
,, for diving into my thoughts and spying my
,, actions, than for assisting me ; and these are

,, even

„ even some of the chief, and such that I am
„ obliged to speak with them, and say many
„ things, or else I must quarrel with them.
„ There are some others who are no less trou-
„ blesome, they are HERMAPHRODITES in Re-
„ ligion, but I keep myself from them, the best
„ I can. I cannot say that I am without Coun-
„ sel, for every one gives me his own, but not
„ two agree together.

„ Seeing then, that I am always wavering, the
„ Queen has told me, that she could not agree
„ with me, and that some of your own Coun-
„ sellors ought to meet together for adjusting
„ matters. She has named those which you
„ shall see on both sides. Every thing is done
„ by her, which has obliged me to send this
„ Bearer in all haste, to require you, my Son,
„ that you would send me my Chancellor :
„ For I have here no body so able to advise
„ me, and to dispatch business, as he is ; other-
„ wise I do forsake all, for I have been
„ brought here upon promise, that the Queen
„ and I should agree together, and not that I
„ should be treated as I am. She is always
„ bantering, and will not abate a tittle, as to
„ the MASS, whereof she had never spoken be-
„ fore, as she doth now. The King on the
„ other side requires of me, that I write unto
„ him. They have given me leave to send
„ for some Ministers, not for disputing, but
„ advising with them. I have sent for Mes-
„ sieurs D'Espina, Merlin, and will send for
„ some others ; I desire you to observe, that
„ they have nothing else in view, but to
„ catch you, therefore take care of yourself,
„ for if the King takes it once into his head,
„ as it is said, nothing vexes me more. I send
„ this Bearer upon two accounts, 1st, to ac-
„ quaint

,, quaint you, how they have altered the ways
,, of treating with me, contrary to what had
,, been promised; therefore it is absolutely ne-
,, cessary that Mr. De Francourt should come as I
,, wrote to him; desiring you, my Son, that, in
,, case he should make any difficulty, you would
,, persuade him, nay command him; for, I am
,, sure, if you knew the trouble I am in, you
,, would pity me; I am treated with the utmost
,, rigour, vain talking, and banters, it is what
,, I hear, instead of being treated with gravity, ac-
,, cording to the merit of the case: Therefore
,, I burst, because I have resolved not to put
,, myself in passion, it is a wonder to see my
,, patience. And if I have had any for the time
,, past, I shall have still more need of it for the
,, future, and that I shall resolve upon more
,, than ever. I am much afraid of falling sick,
,, for I am not very well now.

,, Your Letter is much to my liking, I
,, will show it to Madam if I can; as to her
,, Picture, I shall send for it to Paris. She is
,, very fair, well-advised and genteel; but
,, brought up in the cursedst and most dissolute
,, Company that ever was; and there is no
,, body here, but has a touch of it. Your Cou-
,, sin the Marchioness is so much altered by
,, it, that there is no sign of Religion in her,
,, only this, that she does not go to Mass; for
,, as to the way of living, Idolatry excepted,
,, she lives like the Papists, and my Sister, the
,, Princess (of Condé) is still worse. I do write
,, this to you in private. This Bearer will tell
,, you how much the King grows licentious,
,, it is a shame. I would not for any thing in
,, the world, that you should make your abode
,, here. Therefore I do desire to marry you,
,, and that you and your Wife should flee from
,, that

,, that Corruption ; for though I thought that
,, it was great, neverthelefs it is much greater
,, than I could imagine. It is not the Men
,, that make the firft fteps, but the Women that
,, court Men. Was you here, you could not
,, efcape the peril, without the fpecial Grace of
,, God. I fend you a Knot to wear on the
,, ear's fide, fince you are to fell, and fome
,, buttons for a cap. Men wear a vaft quan-
,, tity of Jewels, but we have bought already
,, for a hundred thoufand Crowns, and every
,, day more are bought. It is faid, that the
,, Queen goes to *Paris* with MONSIEUR. If
,, I ftay here, I will take a turn into *Vendomois.*
,, I defire you, my Son, to fend back this Bearer
,, immediately, and when you fhall write to
,, me, infert in your Letter, *That you dare not*
,, *to write to* MADAM, *left you fhould difoblige*
,, *her, knowing not how fhe has been pleafed with*
,, *the firft.* Your Sifter is very well.
She fpeaks of fome Letters of Mr. de la Cafe,
then fhe goes on thus ; ,, I defire you again, that
,, fince I have been deprived of the way of treat-
,, ing which I expected, and that I am obliged
,, to fpeak by advice and counfel, that you would
,, fend to me Mr. De Francourt. I am ftill of
,, the fame mind, that you muft return into
,, *Bearn.* My Son, you have rightly judged by
,, my firft Letters, that they endeavour only to
,, feparate you from God and from me, you
,, will judge the fame by this laft, and of the
,, trouble I am in for your fake. I defire you
,, to put up earneft Prayers to God, for you
,, want much his affiftance at any time, but ef-
,, peciall at this ; and I befeech him to affift you,
,, and that he would grant to you my Son what-
,, ever you defire. From your good Mother
and beft Friend,   JOHANNA.
   Blois, the 8th of March.   Poftfcript.

Poftfcript,

,, My Son, fince I wrote my Letter, having as
,, yet no opportunity for fhewing yours to Ma-
,, dam, I told her the contents of it. She an-
,, fwered, that when that Marriage had been
,, propofed at firft, they knew very well of what
,, Religion fhe was, and that fhe had a great at-
,, tachment for it. I replied, that thofe who
,, had begun that work did not fay fo, and that
,, they had made the Article of Religion fo eafy,
,, faying even that fhe had fome affection for
,, ours ; that otherwife, I would not have gone
,, fo far, and that I intreated her to think
,, of it. At other times, when I did talk with
,, her upon that Subject, fhe had never anfwer-
,, ed in fo abfolute and rough a manner. I do
,, think that fhe fpeaks, juft as fhe is bid, and alfo
,, that what we had been told concerning her
,, Inclination to our Religion, was but a fnare to
,, entrap us. I lofe no opportunity of making
,, her to talk in a way a little fatisfactory unto
,, me. I asked her laft Night, whether fhe had
,, any thing to let you know, but fhe anfwered
., not ; I infifted, but fhe faid, that fhe could
,, fend nothing without leave, however fhe bid
,, me to pay her Compliments to you, and that
,, you muft come. But I fay the contrary.
The Superfcription of the Letter, was,

TO MY SON.

It appears, by that Letter related by Le
Laboureur, in his Additions to the Memoirs
of Caftelnau, Book III. ch. 13. pag. 856, 60,
61. that the Queen of Navarr had much trouble
and difficulties to go through, before fhe could
bring that Negotiation to a conclufion, that made
her to ufe thefe Words, *I am in labour* ; befides that, we muft obferve, that fhe does not
magnify

magnify the Objects, when she represents the monstrous enormities of the Court, which were but too crying to justify the designs of Providence against the remainders of the House of Valois, which she would utterly destroy by the Civil Wars, and restore by that means the State of that Kingdom wretchedly torn in pieces by the ambition of the Factious, deformed by the hypocrisy of the Great, and become ridiculous and intolerable together, by its being exposed to the petulancy of an unruly Youth, to the lavishness, debaucheries and fury of those who were at the Helm, under whose protection Treasons and Murders became very rife, and the Traitors and Murderers Persons, were sacred.

Joanna, according to her orders, was buried at *Lescar* in *Bearn*. Many Epitaphs were made to her honour ; amongst which, these two were some of the best.

Miraris cur quæ jacet hic Regina Navarræ,
    Cum bona tum prudens, tum pia siqua fuit,
In Cœlum vix quinque dies ægrota volarit ?
    Quod mortale habuit sic fuit exiguum.

It was translated in French after this way.

S'esbahit on pourquoy la Reine de Navarre,
En sagesse, en bonté, en pieté si rare,
N'a langui que cinq jours à s'envoler au ciel ?
C'est le peu quelle avoit en elle de mortel.

The meaning is, Do you wonder at the Queen of Navarr, so wise, good and pious, having been but five days sick, fled away into Heaven ? She had but very little of Mortality in her.

Another,

Dum mens continuò cœlestia spirat, anhelum
Deficiens corpus, cessit, & humi jacet.

That

That is, While her Soul is forthwith breathing heavenly things, her Body for want of breath falls into the Ground (g).

The King feigned to be much concerned at her Death, and went into mourning, and the whole Court followed his example, left their wicked defigns fhould mifcarry by that event (h).

By this time the Count Ludovic was gone for Flanders, attended with Saucourt, La Noüe and Genlis, three Gentlemen for whom the Admiral had a great value; the King had commanded them to endeavour, by fome fpeedy means, to feize upon fome frontier Town. That order was only a device of the King, for he intended, if the Count's enterprize fucceeded well, to improve it to his own advantage, in cafe his Plot in France fhould not fucceed to his Wifhes; and he queftioned not, but that they would be cut in pieces by the Duke of Alva, if they mifcarried. So they fet out chearfully for Flanders, without giving any previous notice to the Admiral, who took it very ill, and wrote to them accordingly, upbraiding them with rafhnefs, fince they knew very well, that he could not affemble fufficient Forces to fend to their relief before fix Weeks.

However Count Ludovic, zealous for the Liberty of his own Country, and fearing left the King fhould alter his mind, attacked at firft *Valenciennes,* but being repulfed by the Spanifh Garrifon in the Caftle, he marched away fuddenly and furprifed *Mons,* which was ftrong by its fituation, and provided with every thing neceffary

Vol. III.   C c

(g) Etat de la France fous Charles IX. Vol. 1. Fol. 238. 2d Edit. Middelbourgh 1578. (h) Thuan. liv. 51. p. 792. and all what I have faid from the Article 118, the Queen of Navarr's Letter excepted, is extracted out of the Book 49, 50, 51. of the fame Hiftorian, and D'Aubigné Tom. 2. liv. 1. D'Avila. liv. v.

cessary for a Siege. That exploit was immediately published in *Flanders*, *France* and *Germany*, whereupon the Reformed began to conceive better hopes, and to think that now the King had declared himself openly. Alva incensed at this, though he had received Letters upon that Subject, of the Queen-Mother and her Secret Council, told to *Montdoucet* the French Embassador, *that the Queen-Mother had served him with some Flowers of Florence, but that he would sent unto her some Thistles of Spain.* The secret Council, and especially those of Guise, understanding how that Man was discontented, endeavoured to appease him, and warned him to be ready with his Forces for intercepting those that were going to relieve *Mons*, for Genlis was come back to *Paris*, and had obtained the King's leave for raising some Companies of Foot and some Troops of Horse for that purpose.

The King of Navarr sollicited to come to Court.

After the Queen of Navarr's Death, the King sent frequent Messages to the Prince of Navarr (*whom henceforward we shall stile King of Navarr*) to sollicit him to come without any delay; for accomplishing his Marriage with the Princess Margaret of Valois at *Paris*, as it had been agreed upon with the deceased Queen his Mother.

And the Admiral too.

The Admiral was then at *Châtillon* upon *Loing*, where he received likewise frequent Messages from the King; and because he did not stir, his Majesty sent unto him Cavagnes, and after him Briquemaut the old, in order to hasten his coming to *Paris*, for furthering and finishing the Scheme of the pretended War in Flanders. At the same time, he sent very positive orders to the Provost of the Merchants, and other Magistrates at Paris, to be careful, lest any tumult or sedition should be raised in that Capital at the coming in of the Admiral. Being

Being follicited by fo many Perfons, and defirous to carry the War out of France, and judging of the King by himfelf, he fet out for Paris, without any regard for the prefling Remonftrances of his Friends within and without the Kingdom, who intreated him, that if he could not conceive any bad opinion or miftruft of the King, at leaft he would be pleafed to confider into what place he was going to fhut up himfelf among fo vaft a croud of fworn E-nemies. But trufting too far upon his good Confcience, and upon the Providence of God, he fet out as abovefaid, with a fmall Retinue, and arrived at Paris to the great furprife of the whole City, which expected not that he would have been fo imprudent, or felf-conceited, as to expofe himfelf to fo threatning a danger ; he was received by the King, his Brethren, the Queen-Mother, and others, with all the outward demonftrations of efteem and reverence.

On the 7th of July, the King iffued out a Proclamation, forbidding all quarrelling or riotings in the City of *Paris,* and commanding all Foreigners and Vagabonds to depart from it in twenty four Hours.

The Admiral, always too open with the King, told him, that he knew three thoufand Gentlemen that would ferve his Majefty at their own charge in the War of *Flanders.* The King feigned to be very well pleafed with the News, and did not forget to enquire where they lived, and whom they were. The Admiral named feveral of them, and the King defired him to give him a lift of the chiefs and the moft notable amongft them ; which being done, and defiring further to know a greater number of them, afked him whither feveral of thofe, whofe names he faw not in that lift, were gone, and defired

him

Charles
IX.
1572.
Pope Gre-
gory XIII.

him to ſend for ſuch and ſuch ones, naming and praiſing them for good Captains and honeſt Men ; which the Admiral promiſed to do, and increaſed his liſt, to the great ſatisfaction of the King : for theſe poor Gentlemen, who otherwiſe would have ſtaid at their home, having received the King's orders, came to Paris

The King of
Navarr's
Arrival at
Paris.

about the ſame time as the King of Navarr and the Prince of Condé ; the Marriage of this laſt with the Princeſs of Cleves, had been accompliſhed at *Blandi* in *Brie*, at the beginning of Auguſt, and almoſt the whole Court went to meet them out of *Paris*.

After their Arrival the Queen's ſecret Council thought proper to delay the Ceremony of the Marriage ſome days longer, as well becauſe all their Butchers were not come as yet, as becauſe Genlis, who had with him four thouſand foot and five hundred horſe, was ſtill in France ; therefore they thought proper to raiſe ſome ſcruples in the mind of the Cardinal of Bourbon ; who was to perform the Ceremony, and accordingly he flatly refuſed to do it without a ſpecial Licence of the Pope, who feigned to be very ſtiff upon that account, but at laſt, he granted it : but the Cardinal finding it defective in ſome reſpects, they were obliged to ſend again to *Rome* to have another.

Genlis
routed.

Mean while they waited with great impatience for the News of Genlis's expedition, who was gone to relieve Count Ludovic and La Noüe who were beſieged in *Mons* by Alva. But this General having been warned by the ſecret Council, as aboveſaid, of the Forces of Genlis, of the day of his marching, of the rout he was to take, and of every thing elſe, it was eaſy for him to ſurpriſe theſe Troops, and to rout them, cutting moſt part of them to pieces, and

taking

taking the reft Prifoners : he dealt with them, not as Prifoners of War, though they went into *Flanders* by the King's command, but as with Highwaymen, hanging them and torturing them in a thoufand other cruel ways, and all that at the fecret Council's inftigation, as much as by the barbarous and natural difpofitions of the mad Cannibalian, I mean ALVA. Very few efcaped death, amongft whom was La Noüe taken in *Mons*, and fent back into France after the Maffacre. It would be too tedious to relate all the feigned Contorfions, Anger, Paffion, Oaths, Swearing and Curfes of Charles IX. at the reception of this News ; the promifes he made to the Admiral, to revenge the Blood of his Subjects, the order he gave him to raife new Forces for that purpofe, the part which Queen Catherine play'd in this Tragi-comedy, her feigned difcontent of the King, as if he had fent thefe Troops without her Knowledge, her Inftances for leaving the Court, and retiring into *Auvergne*, and fo many other treacherous Grimaces, put on on purpofe to deceive more and more the Admiral and his Friends. Let us make hafte to the unravelling of that bafe Plot.

The Admiral lull'd by the great regard which the King feigned to have for him, became almoft fenfelefs, the repeated Warnings he received from abroad, the Intreaties of his Friends, the Letters of the *Rochellefe*, who gave him a very particular account of the many infults they received from Stroffy and Captain Paulin, alias Baron de la Garde, who commanded the King's Fleet in thofe parts, and of the threatnings they heard of a fpeedy change, ferved only to exafperate him againft them ; in a word, he was angry with all thofe who were not fo credulous

The Admiral more and more deceived.

Cc 3 as

Charles
IX.
1572.
Pope Gre-
goryXIII.

as himself, and could not bear to see a Distrust in any body. Whereupon I shall relate here the Answer of Captain *Langoiran,* who being come to take his Leave of the Admiral, being asked the reason of his going away, said, *because you are too much caress'd here, and that I chuse rather to run away with the mad, than to stay with the fools, because there are Remedies for the first, but not for the others.* But what blinded him up entirely and stopp'd his Ears more and more, was the Embassy of the Bishop of Valence to the Republick of *Poland,* for solliciting the Estates of that Country to chuse for their King the Duke of Anjou, who was indeed one of the greatest Enemies the Reformed had at Court. The Admiral doubted not but that the King desired earnestly to bring every thing to a sure and lasting Peace, since the Duke of Anjou who had a great Interest throughout the whole Kingdom, being once confined in *Poland,* his Adherents being deprived of such a Support would grow milder; the House of Guise would be careful not to be so busy; for he took for a reality the feigned frownings which the King shewed oftentimes to the Chief of that House; and lastly, that the Queen-Mother would be forced to resign the whole Government to the King her Son, who feigned likewise to be much displeased at her (*i*).

Upon such fickle foundation was it, that the Admiral grounded his certain hopes of a lasting Peace, and that he looked upon those who endeavoured to dissuade him as so many Disturbers of the publick Peace, Enemies to the King and to their own Country. I shall relate more at large that Negociation of *Poland,* when I shall give

(*i*) Thuan. lib. 51. Aubigné tom. z.liv. 1. ch. 2, 3. Recueil des choses mem. arrivées en France sous Charles 9. p. 419—423.

give an Account of the principal Events of next
Year. But I cannot omit here the good Advice
given by the Bishop of Valence to the Count of
La Rochefoucault and some other Reformed
Lords a few days before he set out for *Poland*, that is before the 17th of August, not to
meddle themselves with that Chimerick War of
Flanders, but rather to return speedily to their
home; *for*, says he, *you have no great reason to
rely so much upon the fair Shews of the Court, neither to stay any longer here, considering the Jealousy,
Hatred and Malice which most of the Greatest, and
generally the whole City bear unto you.* But God
would not permit them to hearken to this good
Counsel.

*Wholesome
warning
of the Bi-
shop of Va-
lence.*

The Pope's Dispensation, either real or fictitious,
but such as it was desired, being come from
Rome, the King appointed the 18th of August
for the Wedding-Day. On the 17th the King of
Navarr and the Princess were betrothed in the *Louvre*, and the next day they were married, and the
Ceremony was performed by the Cardinal of
Bourbon in *Our Lady's Church.* It is to be observed, that the said Ceremony was performed upon a great Scaffold erected before the Gate of the
Church; which done, the Princess went into the
Church to hear Mass, and the King of Navarr
stayed in the Cloyster. I shall not describe here
the Pomp and Magnificence of the Feasts given
on this account for several days, which were
as extravagant as Catharine could imagine, because they portended nothing but what happened a few days after.

While they were a feasting, those who had
been sent for by the King, his Mother, and the
Guises, arrived every day. The Resolution
which had been taken some days before was then
fully ratified at *Paris* and at *St. Cloud*, not to let

the

the Admiral escape, but to murder him in Paris with all those who should offer to defend him. The Queen Mother, with few of her most secret and trusty Confidants, designed not only to murder the Admiral, but also to engage the two Parties of Guise and Chatillon, in order to destroy the one by the other. Those of Guise's pretended to murder the Admiral, and to have the Reformed destroyed by the Mob in the King's Name, and to favour and save as many as they could, in order to cast the odium of the Massacre upon the King, his Mother, and the Duke of Anjou, and to forward by that means by little and little their own Interest.

Maurevel that base Murderer mentioned before, had been pick'd out by the Guises for murdering the Admiral; the Duke of Anjou himself and then the Count of Retz had been two or three Weeks before to talk with him, and make sure of him: he arrived at *Paris* on the 20th, and took lodging in a House hard by the Louvre where he remain'd concealed till the 22d.

On the 20th the King took apart the Admiral, and feigning to be much uneasy about the great Company that attended the Duke of Guise, he told him, that he thought that the properest means for avoiding all disorder would be to set his Arquebusiers at some convenient places under the Command of such Officers which he named. The Admiral mistrusting of nothing, and making very little account of the Duke of Guise, as long as the King should be stedfast in the Resolution he seemed to be in, told his Majesty, that he was Master, and might dispose of every thing just as he pleased. Therefore the King ordered five or six hundred Arquebusiers to be lodged at certain Places about the *Louvre*, and many more in other quarters more distant. The Marshal of

Mont-

Montmorancy confidering all thefe Confufions, and dreading the Ambufhes of the Houfe of Guife mortal Enemies to his own, retired into his own Houfe at *Chantilly*, on pretence of a hunting Match, and efcaped thereby the danger; for he and his Brethren were particularly noted in the Lift of thofe that were to be murdered, but his Abfence hindered the Murderers from attempting any thing againft his Brethren, not to provoke an Enemy fo powerful. Now every thing was ready for beginning the Tragedy: And

—Here you might fee the moft bloody Rage
That ever did religious Fiends engage;
A Reconcilement, with a Wedding Feaft,
While Murder was the Treat of ev'ry Gueft:
Which well may prove, to Ages yet to come,
The Faith of FRANCE, the Charity of
    ROME.
FRANCE, by the moft detefted Perjury,
Enflaved its Subjects, who by Laws were free,
No Sacrament can this *great Hero* bind,
Oaths are weak Shackles for his *mighty Mind*,
And worfe than Heathens does he perfecute.
His Priefts want Senfe and Learning to difpute;
But weak Divines by ftrong Dragoons confute:
And whoe'er doubts of any Prieftly Maggot,
Th'Heretick Dog muft be convinc'd by Faggot.
With ROME's Religion and FRENCH
    Government,
What Slave fo abject as to be content?
Now, idle, difaffected, what is't you'd have?
Would you be an Idolater or a Slave?
What do you murmur for, becaufe you're free,
And this blefs'd Ifle enjoys its Liberty?
Crofs but the Narrow Seas, and you will find
Slav'ry and Superftition to your mind (*k*).

On

(*k*) Maffacre of Paris, a Tragedy by Nath. Lee.

The Admiral wounded, and the Transactions of the two days before the Massacre.

On Friday the 22d of August as the Admiral came out from the *Louvre*, where he had been all the Morning with the Marshals of Cossé and Tavannes for adjusting some quarrel betwixt two Gentlemen, and was walking home to dinner attended with about 15 Gentlemen, and reading a Petition, Maurevel fired at him an Arquebuss loaded with three bullets, from a Window in a Parlour, about 15 Yards distant from the *Louvre*; one of the Bullets shot off part of the 2d Finger of his right Hand, and he was wounded with another in his left Arm. Guerchy, Des Pruneau, and other Gentlemen that were with him, were amazed and frighted at it; as to the Admiral, he was not much moved, he shewed the Window from whence he had been shot, and the Places where he had been wounded; then he spoke very calmly to Yolet, Gentleman of his Horse, to go and tell his Majesty what had befallen him. He was brought to his House which was not very far off, and as he went a Gentleman told him, that it was to be feared lest the Bullets were poisoned; to which he replied, *Nothing will befall me but what will please God.*

Though the House from whence Maurevel had fired was forced and searched, the Villain could not be found, he was gone by a back door where a swift Spanish Horse was kept ready for him. The King understanding that the Admiral was wounded, fell into a violent Passion, he was at the Tennis, he flung his Racket upon the Ground, and cursing, as usual to him, he exclaim'd, *shall I never enjoy Quietness!*

The Admiral's wound disappointed the whole Secret Council, for they expected that he would have been killed; they saw themselves obliged to take a little time, for considering what was to be done in the present Juncture.

The

The King of Navarr, the Prince of Condé, the Count of Rochefoucault and several other Lords and Gentlemen of the Reformed Religion came to visit the Admiral, as well as several Lords and Gentlemen, his Friends of the Catholick Religion, all of them expressed the greatest Concern for what had happened.

His Wounds were dressed by Ambrosius Paré first Surgeon to the King, tho' of the Reformed Religion, he begun with the Finger which he was obliged to cut off, and the Admiral could not but suffer the most exquisite Pains in the Operation, for his Scissars being not sharp enough, he was forced to open and shut them three times, but the Patient bore it with a true Christian Constancy and an Heroick Resolution, comforting himself, and even the Ministers that were come to comfort him; *My Friends* says he, *to the Company, what do you cry for? I deem my self very happy,* that I have been so wounded for the sake of Christ. Then speaking to his Chaplain Mr. Merlin: *Lo!* says he, *my Friend, some of God's Mercies; indeed I am desperately wounded, but I know that it is the Will of the Lord our God, and I thank his sacred Majesty that he had vouchsafed me the Honour of suffering something for his most holy Name. Let us pray that he will be pleased to grant me the Gift of Perseverance, that I may glorify him to the last.* Then he desired Merlin, who was deeply concerned, to comfort him; many other pious Conversations passed between him and the Company, which he concluded with a fervent Prayer to God of his own; he declared that he forgave his Murderer and those who had abetted him; then Merlin made a Prayer suitable to the melancholy Occasion.

The King of Navarr and the Prince of Condé made their Complaints to the King, and besought

sought his Majesty to grant them leave to depart the City, seeing that there was no Security for them in it. But the King composed so well his Countenance, that with a thousand Oaths and Curses against the Murderer and his Abettors, that he would punish them exemplarily, he allayed their fears: The Queen-Mother was present, and failed not to amplify whatever the King her Son had said promising to do such Justice that the Admiral and his Friends would be fully satisfy'd, they both desired the two Princes not to stir out from Court, and to rely upon them. The King commanded the Gates of Paris to be shut up, two excepted, *left*, says he, *any of the Accomplices should escape*, and he caused a Search of them to be made. Then he commanded the Provost of the Merchants to obey whatever orders the Duke of Anjou should give him; in a word, he and his Mother dissembled so well, that the two Princes, being imposed upon by the fair Shews, thought no more of removing.

Catherine and her Secret Council seeing themselves disappointed, and that the Reformed did not stir for revenging the Admiral, upon the Duke of Guise, as they had supposed they would do, they were obliged to alter their Course, and resolved to fall only upon the Admiral and the Reformed, seeing that they could not compass their end, which was at first, as abovesaid, to engage the two Parties of the Guises and Chatillons, and to destroy them both, one by the other.

All the Enquiries made after the Murderer and Chailly one of his Accomplices were needless, and indeed they were not made in earnest, but only for a Shew; Maurevel had had time enough for making his Escape, and Chailly found a Sanctuary in the Duke of Guise's Apartment in the *Louvre*.

Mean

Mean while the Admiral fent Telligny his Son in Law, to the King, befeeching his Majefty that he might have the Honour to talk with him and impart unto him fome things of great moment which he could not intruft any body with. Whereupon the King came to vifit him at two in the Afternoon; he was attended by the Queen his Mother, his two Brothers, the Duke of Montpenfier, the Cardinal of Bourbon, the Marfhals of Damville, Tavannes, and Coffé, the Count of Retz, the Lords of Thoré, Meru; and after them came the Duke of Nevers. At firft by the King's Orders all the Admiral's Servants went out of the Room; Telligny only with his Lady, and another who efcaped providentially from the Maffacre, ftayed by him, after fome Compliments, the Admiral fpoke to the King to the following Purport.

,, SIR, I am fure that after my Death, many
,, will endeavour to afperfe my Reputation by
,, their calumnies. But God, before whom I
,, am going to appear, is witnefs unto me, that I
,, have been always a faithful and affectionate
,, Servant to your Majefty, and that I never
,, had any thing more at heart than the Welfare
,, of my Country and the Increafe of your Great-
,, nefs. And tho' many have endeavoured to
,, charge me with the Crime of Felony and
,, High Treafon, neverthelefs my Actions fhew
,, forth fufficiently, to whom all the paft and
,, prefent Miferies are to be afcribed. I call
,, God to be witnefs of my Innocency, and I
,, befeech him to be Judge between me and my
,, Accufers, and I am fure that he will be fo
,, and judge me in that refpect, according to his
,, own Righteoufnefs. As to me I am ready to
,, account for my Actions before his moft Sacred
,, Majefty,

,, Majesty, if such is his Will, that I must die
,, with this Wound. But without dwelling any
,, longer upon that Subject; your Majesty's
,, Royal Progenitor had conferred upon me several
,, Offices and Dignities, which you have been
,, pleased to confirm unto me, and as I am most
,, zealous for the increase of your own Glory,
,, I cannot forbear saying, that you do overlook
,, too inconsiderately the means of forwarding
,, it. You have now a very fair Opportunity
,, in your hands, and such a one as your Royal
,, Predecessors have never had the like. If you do
,, neglect it intirely, besides that you will be sorry
,, for it afterwards, I am afraid lest your King-
,, dom should be deeply wounded by it. Nay,
,, that it will be in great danger of being in-
,, tirely ruined. Is it not a Shame, SIR, that
,, the least thing in the World cannot be done
,, in your Privy Council, but immediately a
,, *Courier* is sent express to the Duke of Alva,
,, for acquainting him with it? What a base
,, thing is it, that that Duke has caused some
,, French Noblemen and Gentlemen, so many
,, brave Captains and stout Soldiers, your own
,, Subjects taken prisoners at the rout of Genlis,
,, to be hang'd? of which Indignity I received
,, News last night. But in your Court, SIR, they
,, do not regard that, they laugh at it. Such is
,, the Love and good Affection that the French
,, bear to their own Countrymen, such their
,, Pity for the base and cruel Usage they have re-
,, ceived. The second thing whereof I think pro-
,, per to put your Majesty in mind, is the open
,, violation of your Edicts, and especially the
,, late Edict of Peace, you have sworn it so
,, many times and so solemnly, that all the foreign
,, Nations and Princes are witnesses thereof;
,, you have sworn to observe the Treaty made
,, with

,, with your Reformed Subjects. But it is not
,, possible to tell, in how many Places of the
,, Kingdom that Promise is basely violated, not
,, only by some private Men, but even by your
,, Governors and Officers. SIR, many times I
,, have proposed these things unto your Majesty's
,, Consideration, and besought that you would
,, acknowledge that the keeping of your Faith
,, and publick Promises is the only true means
,, of restoring your Kingdom into its antient
,, Glory. I have said sometimes the same thing
,, unto you, MADAM, (*speaking to the Queen-*
,, *Mother*) but for all that every day we receive
,, new Complaints of Murders, Plunders, and
,, Seditions committed and exercised every where.
,, Not long ago the Catholicks of a Place near
,, *Troyes* in *Champaign*, having understood that
,, a Child was carried from Church where he
,, had been baptized, they assaulted the Com-
,, pany, and murdered the Baby in the Arms of
,, his Nurse. SIR, I beseech your Majesty not
,, to let such Murders go unpunished, and to
,, have regard for the Quiet and the Welfare of
,, your Kingdom, and to the Faith you have
,, promised them.,,

To that the King answered, MY LORD AD-
MIRAL, *I know very well that you are a thorough*
good Man, true Frenchman, and that you desire
earnestly my Welfare and Glory; I take you to be a
valiant Man and an excellent Captain, had I had
any other Notion of you, I never would have done
for you what I have done: I have always endea-
voured to have my Edicts faithfully kept, and even
now I desire that the last should be exactly observed,
for which purpose I have sent proper Commissaries
throughout the several Provinces of my Kingdom.
My Mother may assure you of it. The Queen said
thereupon, *That is very true, my Lord Admiral,*
and

and you know it very well. Yes, says the Admiral, but I know too that amongst those Commiffaries there are some who have condemned me to be hanged, and have offered fifty thousand Crowns reward to any one who shall bring my Head to your Majesty. *Then,* says the King, *we must send some others who shall not be suspected. But I see that you move yourself a little too much in speaking, which may prove of great prejudice to your health. Indeed you are much wounded, but I feel the pain of your Wound. And G—— d——n I will take such a Revenge of that Offence, that it shall be remembered for ever.* Several other things were said on both sides, not worth the mentioning; the King and the Queen were curious to fee the Bullet which had been drawn out of the Admiral's Arm, it was of Copper. While he was speaking with him, the Count of Retz proposed to Telligny to remove the Admiral into the *Louvre* for his greater Security; but the Phyficians being confulted, they thought that he was not in a Condition to be removed without danger.

A little after the King was gone, there was a Council held in the Admiral's Apartment, present the King of Navarr, the Prince of Condé, the Vidame of Chartres, Telligny and several other Lords and Gentlemen, to advife about what was to be done in the present Juncture. The Vidame of Chartres infifted warmly upon the neceffity of removing the Admiral from Paris; but the Obftinacy of Telligny was such, that the worft Opinion was followed, and they refolved only to petition the King for fpeedy Juftice and an exemplary Punifhment of the Guilty.

That fame day the King wrote to all the Governours of Provinces, and of the chief Cities of the Kingdom, and likewife to his Embaffadors

dors in the several Courts of Europe, to acquaint them with what had happen'd, and commanding them to let every one know how much he was displeased with that base Action; the Queen-Mother did the same, and all that was only a Deceit in order to suprize *La Rochelle*, if they could.

In the Evening, about Midnight, the Duke of Anjou sent for the Duke of Guise, with whom it was resolved, that the next Night they would begin the Work with the Admiral, and the said Duke was charged to prepare every thing for the Execution; the Queen-Mother and her Council were not asleep, no more than the King, they waited all for the next Day, with an equal Impatience.

That day being come, a false Rumour was industriously spread in the City, that the Admiral's Friends threatned much those of Guise. Whereupon the Dukes of Guise and Aumale waited upon the King, and told him before several Courtiers, that since it seemed unto them, that their Services were no longer agreeable to his Majesty from some time ago, they were ready to depart from the Court, if his Majesty so pleased. To which the King, feigning a great Discontent against them, told them with a frowning Face, *Go where you will, I shall easily find you, if you are in any wise Accessaries to what has been done to the Admiral.* Whereat they took their leave of the King, and about mid-day they feigned to set out from Paris with a great Retinue, but they went no farther than St. Anthony's Gate, and stayed there.

The Aldermen of the Wards went, according to their Orders, and visited all the Inns and Houses, writing down the Names of the Reformed that were lodged there, and brought their Lists unto those who had set them to work. After Dinner, the Queen went with the King; the

Duke of Anjou, the Duke of Nevers, Tavannes, and the Count of Retz, into the Gardens of *Thuilleries*. There she represented to the Company, that those whom they had so many times hunted after, were now in the Nets: that the Admiral was in Bed, deprived of the use of his Arms, and unable to stir: that the King of Navarr and the Prince of Condé were lodged in the *Louvre*, whose Gates were shut up at Night, and the Watch set upon them, and that they could not escape: that being once rid of the Chiefs, the Reformed would not be in a condition to wage War: that they had the fairest Opportunity in the world of doing a piece of great Policy: that all their Captains were disarmed, and that the Catholicks in Paris were above an hundred to one Reformed: that the City could afford sixty thousand Men well armed: that in less than an hour they could utterly destroy the Huguenots all to one, and abolish the very Name of those wicked profligate Men: that if the King did not improve that Opportunity, he might be sure that the Admiral being cured, a fourth Civil War would break out throughout the Kingdom.

The Queen's Opinion was approved of; then it was agreed to spare the King of Navarr, because of his Youth, and of the Alliance newly contracted with him; but as to the Prince of Condé, it was not without much-ado that his Life was granted to the Duke of Nevers, his Brother-in-law, upon promise that he would turn a Catholick. It was farther agreed, that the next Night, before break of Day, the Plot should be executed, and that the Charge of it should be given to the Duke of Guise. In the Evening, the King ordered the 1200 Harquebusiers to be set, Part along the River, Part in the Streets, and another Part by the Admiral's House.

The

The Admiral's Friends taking notice of these
Stirrings, and of the carriage of Arms in several
Places, suspected that something was hatching a-
gainst them, and having consulted together at the
Admiral's House, they sent Cornaton to the King
to acquaint him of these Motions of the People,
and desire his Majesty to send some Archers of his
Guards, to keep the Gates of the said Admiral's
House ; and that he would be pleased to allow
them some Arms in the said House. At this the
King feigned to be much moved, and asked him,
who had made such a Report, and by what means
the Admiral was come to have notice of the
Noise ? Then he bid the Count of Retz to call
for his Mother, who being come, he ask'd her,
*What is the matter? for this Man tells me, that
the People mutiny, and rise up in Arms. The Mob
does neither*, says she ; *but if you remember, you
have commanded early this Morning, that every
one should be in his Quarters for fear of some Tumult.* 'Tis true, quoth he, *nevertheless I have
forbidden to take up Arms.* Then the Duke of
Anjou, who was come with his Mother, answering
to what Cornaton had said concerning the Archers
of the Guard, said, *take Cosseins with fifty Harquebusiers :* but Cornaton replying, that only six
Archers of the Guards would be sufficient to repress, by their Authority, the Fury of the Mob ;
No, no, says the King, *but take Cosseins, you cannot
chuse a better one to do the business.* Tho' Cornaton knew that Cosseins was one of the Admiral's
mortal Enemies, nevertheless, after such a Command, he durst not reply any more.

A few hours after, Cosseins came to the Admiral's House with fifty Harquebusiers, whom
he lodged in two Shops of the Neighbourhood ;
a little after, Rambouillet a Quarter-Master, came,
and in the King's Name commanded all the

Gen-

Gentlemen of the Catholick Religion that were
lodged in that Street, to go elsewhere, and lodged
in their room as many Lords and Gentlemen of
the Reformed Religion as he could, but especially
the Admiral's Friends.

Many other things happened that very Evening, which gave great occasion of Suspicion, such
as the expelling of a Page that carried two Spears
into the Admiral's House, and was forbid the Entrance by Cosseins, he did the same to another
who carried in the Cuirasses of Telligny and Guerchy, Standard-Bearer to the Admiral. Six Por-
ters loaded with Arms, were seen entering into the
Louvre. Another Council was held in the Admiral's Apartment, the Vidame of Chartres insisted again vehemently upon the absolute Necessity of removing the Admiral, *(who was in a fair
way of recovering)* out of Paris, and to leave that
City themselves, without any further delay; but
he was almost alone of that Opinion, that of Telligny prevailed again, the King of Navarr and the
Prince of Condé followed the Stream. Guerchy
and several others, having desired to lie that Night
in the Admiral's House, Telligny thank'd them
for their Kindness, but told them that there was
no occasion to give themselves so much Trouble;
so, no other besides Cornaton, Labonne, Yolet,
Merlin the Chaplain, Paré the King's Surgeon,
and five Servants, stayed with him that Night;
Telligny himself retired to his own Lodging,
next to the Admiral's House, with his Lady at
Midnight.

Mean while, the King having told his Brother-
in-law the King of Navarr, that he would do well
if he advised his most faithful Servants and Adherents to come and lodge in the *Louvre,* for their
greater Security, because of the Audaciousness of
the Faction of Guise; that Prince, deceived by
these

thefe Out-fhews of Kindnefs, fent indeed for fome of the Gentlemen for whom he had the greateft regard, to lodge that Night in the *Louvre.*

The Night being come, the Duke of Guife, by the King's Command, fent firft for the Captains of the Switzers, and of the new Companies that were come into the City, and told them that the time was come, wherein, by the King's Command, they were to deftroy thofe defperate Men who had caufed fo many Diforders and Miferies in the Kingdom ; that they ought to take care left any one of them fhonld efcape ; that not only the Admiral, but all his Affociates and Adherents ought to be utterly undone that very Night, and encouraged them to an exact Performance, by the hopes of the Plunder. The Switzers were ordered to guard the *Louvre* with fome French Troops, and to take care left any body of the King of Navarr's and the Prince of Condé's Houf-hold fhould come out. Coffeins, Captain of the King's Guards, who guarded the Admiral's Houfe, was charged to furround it on all fides, and to lodge fome Harquebufiers from place to place, that no body could efcape.

Every thing being ready, the Duke of Guife fent for Marcel, formerly Provoft of the Mer-chants, and commanded him to give proper Or-ders, that the Captains and Tithing-Men fhould meet together in the Guildhall at Midnight, that they might receive the King's Commands. Which being done accordingly, the new Provoft, Prefi-dent Charron by name, acquainted them with the King's Refolution, to exterminate all thofe Se-ditious, who had rifen in Arms againft him in the late Years : that it was a very convenient Time, becaufe their Princes and chief Leaders were as it were fhut up in the City-Walls, and that it was with them that they fhould begin the

Work

Work that Night. As to the other, the King would send Orders throughout the Provinces to have them murdered after the same way: that the striking of the Palace-Clock was the Signal, and that the distinguishing Mark amongst themselves, was a white Linnen tied to their left Arm, and a white Cross to their Hat: as to the rest, they ought to be well armed, to have good Courage, and to put Candles and Links in their Windows before the Signal should be given, for avoiding Confusion.

That was enough for inciting Men who desired no better than to have such an Opportunity for gratifying either their bloody Zeal, or their Covetousness, or any other Passion. They took up Arms immediately, and they were set in the Cross Streets, with as little noise as possible, while the Duke of Guise and the Chevalier d'Angouleme made all the haste they could to assemble as many Men armed as they could, and to lodge them in different Places of the City.

At the beginning of the Night, the Queen-Mother came to the King's Apartment with the Duke of Anjou, who sent immediately for the Duke of Guise; the Duke of Nevers, the Marshal of Tavanes, and the Count of Retz, were present. After several Debates about the means of executing their Plot, the Conclusion was, that they must begin the Work without any further delay; the Dukes of Guise and Aumale, and the Chevalier of Angouleme were confirmed in the most honourable Charge of Chief Butchers, and they being attended by Cosseins and Goas, with many Harquebusiers of the King's Guards, went near to the Admiral's House, to be ready when the Signal should be given.

Very happily for the Count of Montgomery, the Vidame of Chartres, and several other Lords and

and Gentlemen, the King would not give leave to the Duke of Nevers to go with a Party to the Suburb of St. Germain, where they lodged; for HIS MOST AUGUST AND COURAGIOUS MAJESTY (as it happens to all Cowards whenever they are upon perpetrating some base Deed) was not secure in his *Louvre*, tho' surrounded with ten thousand Men that guarded him, and sixty thousand Men of the Militia, that were in Arms in the City; he was still afraid left the Admiral, desperately wounded, and in his Bed, should put himself at the head of about twelve or thirteen thousand Men, unarmed, Women and Children.

That secret Council lasted for above an Hour; and tho' the time appointed was very near, nevertheless Catharine was very impatient, fearing left Charles, considering the Heinousness of such Deeds, should alter his Mind, or at least some part of their detestable Scheme, she was willing to begin without any farther delay; and upon some Commotions that happened between the Guards and some Gentlemen that inquired about the occasion of so many Links and armed Men in the Streets, at an unusual Hour, she told Charles, that it was no longer possible to refrain the Fury of the Soldiery, and ordered to ring the Bell of *St. Germain L'Auxerrois*'s *Church*.

The Admiral being now certain of the Tumult, and hearing the Clashing of Arms, was not affrighted, tho' he had no body else with him than those above named, still trusting upon the King's Promises. Besides that, he thought if the *Parisians* knew once that the King disallowed them, they would sit still and quiet when they should see Cosseins and his Company. He called too to his mind the many repeated Oaths of the King, of his Mother, and of the Duke of Anjou, the Alliance made of late with the Queen of England, *Massacre of the Admiral.*

the Treaties made with the Prince of Orange, and the Proteftant Princes of Germany, and feveral other things of the fame Nature, which feemed to him to be fo many Iron Bars, but ferved only to deceive himfelf, being for Charles, not even fo ftrong as a bit of Straw.

Coffeins then, to whom the Guard of the Admiral's Houfe had been committed, perceiving the Duke of Guife, and the Chevalier of Angouleme, coming to him, after he had difpofed his Men, in order that no body could efcape, knocked at the Gate, between two and three in the Morning of the 24th day of Auguft, which was Bartholomew's Day. Labonne came to the Gate, and having opened it, was ftabbed by Coffeins, the fecond Door going up the Stairs was broken open, and one of the Switzers flain with an Harquebufs Shot. While Coffeins was jumbling at that Door, Cornaton ran up, and being afk'd by the Admiral, (who had caufed his Servants to lift him out of his Bed, and in his Night-gown, had affifted his Chaplain's fervent Prayer, and humbly commended his Soul to the Mercy of God) what meant that great Noife? My Lord, fays he, it is God that calls for us; the Houfe has been forc'd, and there is no means of refifting. To which the Admiral anfwered, Long ago I have prepared myfelf to die; as to you all, fave yourfelves the beft you can; for you cannot fave my Life, I do commend my Soul to God's Mercy. He was not at all frightened. Prefently all of them, NICHOLAS MUSS, one of his faithful Servants, excepted, (*he was his Interpreter for the German Tongue*) got up into the top of the Houfe; but moft of them were flain in the next Houfe, Cornaton, Merlin, and two or three others, were providentially preferv'd. Coffeins being come
up

up to the Admiral's Apartment, broke open the Door, and entered with one B E S M E, a Servant to the Duke of Guife, A T T I N, belonging to the Duke of Aumale, Sarlaboux, and fome others, being all armed, and with their Targets. Befme afked the Admiral, whether he was not fuch a one? *I am*, fays he with a fure Countenance, and this the Murderers themfelves have own'd; then looking upon him, *Young Man*, fays he, *you ought to refpeÉt my grey Hairs, and my Wounds; but no matter, you fhall not fhorten my Life.* Then Befme, with a thoufand Curfes and Blafphemies, thruft his Sword into the Admiral's Breaft, and redoubling the blows upon his Head, every one of the others gave his Blow in fuch fort, that he fell upon the Floor, and fo lay gafping.

The Duke of Guife and others, ftaying below in the Court, hearing the Blows, afk'd if they had done, and commanded the Body to be thrown out of the Window, which was prefently done by Befme and Sarlaboux: the Blows he had upon the Head, and the Blood befmearing his Face, the Duke of Guife, willing to fee his Features, wiped his Face with a Handkerchief, then he faid, *Now I know him, it is he himfelf;* and therewith he gave a Kick to that venerable Face, dreadful unto all the Murderers in France, when alive. Then he went, with his Company, crying aloud about the Streets, Courage, Fellowfoldiers, we have begun well, let us now to the reft; the King commands, it is his Will and Pleafure.

Thereupon the Palace-Clock ftruck; and then a Rumour was fpread about the Streets, that the Hugonots were in Arms, (*tho' they were quietly in their Beds*) and had confpired to murder the King.

The

The Admiral's Head having been sever'd, was presented to the King and Queen-Mother, and then imbalmed and sent to *Rome*, to the Pope and the Cardinal of Lorrain. The Mob ran into the Admiral's House, where they cut off his Hands, and his Privy-parts, and dragged the Corpse about the Streets for three Days together; they cast it into the River, then they took it out, and dragged it to the Gibbet of Montfaucon, and there hanged it by the Feet, then they kindled a Fire under it, and roasted it. It remained for two days, or thereabout, in that Condition; then the Duke of Montmorency caused it to be taken away secretly, in the Night-time, by some of his Servants, and carried to *Chantilly*, where it was put into Lime, and then the Bones were deposited in a Coffin in the Chapel, till the Year 1582, when they were brought to *Montauban*, then delivered to his Daughter, Widow of Telligny, and at that time married to the Prince of Orange, who kept them in Holland, till the Year 1608; when he was brought to *Châtillon upon Loing*, there to be buried amongst his Ancestors. Scaliger made his Epitaph, which was ingraved upon a large Copper-Plate.

So died the Admiral in the 56th Year of his Age, being born on the 16th of Feb. 1517. He was bubbled by his own Probity; not thinking, that a King of France would ever have been so base and cowardly, as to break his Oath in so proditorious a manner: But he did not consider, that Charles was indeed King of France, but not a French King, being born of a Florentine, of a Pope's Niece, and having been formed and fashioned after her own way. His Memory was odiously charged by several mercenary Scribblers; they supposed impudently, that having been

     wounded,

wounded, he and his Adherents had plotted to murder the King, his Mother, his Brethren, the King of Navarr, and the Prince of Condé. The Absurdity of such a Charge was so obvious to every one, that no body would believe it, no not even those, who wanted such a Pretence for justifying the barbarous Act. Nevertheless the bloody Charles had that Charge brought before the Parliament, where the Memory of the Deceas'd was tried, condemned, and Sentence executed against his Effigy, his Memory, Children, Coat of Arms, &c. without the least Evidence; and the first President, Christophorus Thuanus, was so weak, that he consented to every thing which Charles required of him. But some contemporary Authors, such as Jam. Aug. Thuanus, Montluc, Brantome, and La Noüe, have intirely cleared his Memory of any such Plot; and few Years after, the Parliament itself, convinced of the Falshood of that Imputation, restored his Memory and his Children, and unanimously repealed whatever had been decreed against him, his Honour, his Estate, and Posterity. Brantome speaks of him as of an honest, upright Man, his Religion set aside, a great Captain, a Man of vast Experience, who would have been very serviceable to the Kingdom, had Charles but employ'd him against the common Enemies of his State and Crown; and followed the Scheme he proposed unto him for increasing his Dominions. by the Conquest of the *Low-Countries*. „ He proposes upon that Subject the
„ Example of Eudon, Duke of *Aquitain*, who
„ having rebelled against Charles Martel, and
„ called the Saracens to his assistance, having
„ been pardoned by Charles, and his Assistance
„ desired against the said Saracens, was so serviceable, that he was the chief Instrument of
                                               „ the

,, the Rout and utter Destruction of these Miscreants in the Kingdom ; and so wiped off intirely the Faults he had committed in calling them to his assistance.   So would it have been (*so the Author goes on*) with the Admiral, had Charles improved the fair Opportunities he offered unto him, of conquering no less than *Flanders* and the *Low-Countries*.   Which he would have performed, for I know it certainly as well as any Man in the world, because of the great Intelligence he had in that Country,—and so he would have made amends for his past Faults in the Civil Wars.   Charles ought to have intirely forgiven the Admiral, or never to forgive him at all by any authentick Act ; but having forgiven him, he ought to have kept his Faith to him, especially, seeing that he was ready to make amends.——Had the King known the History of that Eudon above mentioned, may be, he would have followed that example, and have opposed those fine bewrayed Counsellors, &c.,,   So Brantome (*l*).

Montluc says, that Catharine wrote unto him, to acquaint him of the Admiral's execrable Plot against the King and all the Royal Family; then he adds, *I know very well what I thought of it then. It is a bad thing to offend one's Master. The King never forgot that the Admiral had obliged him to run away from Meaux. We lose our Senses —— and do not consider, that Kings forget sooner the Services than the Offences done unto them.   But no more of this* (*m*).

Thuanus, the Historian, far from looking upon the Admiral as an Author of Seditions, or as having plotted against the King and the Royal Family, gives him one of the greatest Characters,

(*l*) Brant. Eloge de Charles IX. in Agricola, tom. 3. pag. 5. 6.   (*m*) Comment. de Montluc, Liv. VII. fol. 618.

ters, as every one might fee in perufing his Hiftory, but efpecially Books 51, 52, 53.

Therefore I think, that we might fafely depend upon La Nouë's Teftimony, who gives us the following Character of the Admiral : „ If „ any one, fays he, has taken much trouble in „ the three firft Civil Wars, the Admiral has „ taken more than any body elfe ; for he „ did bear the moft heavy Part of the civil and „ military Affairs, with a great deal of Conftan„ cy, he behaved himfelf reverently towards the „ Princes, and modeftly to his Inferiors. He „ has always ftrictly adhered to the Religion he „ had embraced, and a great Lover of Juftice, „ for which he was very much efteemed and „ honoured by thofe of his Party ; far from „ feeking ambitioufly the Command, he decli„ ned it, and never took it upon him but with „ great Reluctancy, and being forced by the „ ftrong Inftances of the Party, who were con„ vinced of his Prudence and great Capacity. „ As long as he had any Command in the Ar„ mies, he always behaved himfelf like a great „ and experienced Captain, (*this is to be under*„ *ftood only of what he did, when he was Mafter of* „ *his Refolutions, and not forced to follow the Stream*) „ and has never been frightened by the Danger „ when it was unavoidable. He fhewed him„ felf magnanimous in the greateft Adverfities, „ and had a Mind always ready to find means „ for extricating himfelf out of the greateft Dif„ ficulties. In a word, he was a Man fit for to „ reftore and reform a State weakened and cor„ rupted.„ Such is the Teftimony of a Man, who, for his great Wifdom and Integrity, was equally loved and refpected by Friends and Enemies, by the Churches, and by the Court, by Beza, and by Catherine of Medicis. Therefore
that

that single Testimony which he gives of a Man, with whom he was so perfectly acquainted, and intimately united, deserves better Credit than a thousand others of one D'Avila, or Papyrius Masso, Pibrac, Pasquier, Bafin, and others like them, who, for lucre-sake, will turn black into white, and white into black (n). For compleating the Character of that inestimable Man, of blessed and immortal Memory, I shall insert here two further Demonstrations of his unfeigned Zeal for the King, and the Kingdom's Welfare.

The Plunder of his House was given to the Soldiers and the Mob ; his Papers excepted. By Catherine's Orders, and Morvillier's Diligence, they were all seized, and strictly searched and examined, in hopes to find something in them, that might serve their turn, and justify the wicked and barbarous Act perpetrated against him. Amongst his Memoirs, which he kept very exact, writing down every day whatever passed, and which were destroyed by Charles's Mother's Orders, an Article was found, that he had advised the King to settle a certain Appanage upon his Brethren, and not suffer them to have so great Authority amongst the People ; that Article being read on purpose before the Duke of Alençon, who regretted the Admiral's loss, *There is,* says his Mother Catherine, *the Counsels, which the Man so much beloved by you, and who feigned to love you, and be your Friend, gave to the King.* To which the Duke replied, *I do not know how far he loved me ; but this I know for certain, that such a Counsel could not proceed but from a Man faithful to the King, and zealous for the Increase of his Glory and Prosperity.* Walsingham, the English Ambassador, gave almost the same Answer to that Catherine. Amongst the

(n) La Noüe Discours polit. & milit. p. 1008—9.

the Admiral's loose Papers, one was found,
wherein, amongst the Arguments he made use
of in his Discourse, for proving the necessity of
the War against *Spain* in the *Low-Countries,*
which he had delivered to the King, this which
had been omitted was set down in writing, in
order to impart it to the King in secret, viz.
That if the King declined the Conditions, tendered to him by the Inhabitants of these Countries, they would make their Address to the
Queen of England, who would accept of them ;
and that it would happen, that tho' they were
Friends now, becoming so near Neighbours of
France, if they did set once their foot into the
Low-Countries, they would become their mortal Enemies, and renew their ancient Pretension
and Jealousy upon and against the Crown. That
Article having been read before the English Embassador ; and Catherine saying unto him, *See
what Regard the Admiral had for the Queen your
Mistress, tho' she had loaded him with so many
Marks of Friendship :* Walsingham answered, *I
do not know how the Admiral stood affected towards
the Queen my Mistress ; but this I know certainly,
that such an Advice cannot proceed but from a
Man faithful to the King, and extreamly zealous
for the Honour and Welfare of his own Country,
and who deserves to be bewailed, his Death being
the greatest Loss that the Kingdom could possibly
sustain.* And so was CATHERINE put to
shame (o).

　Immediately after the Admiral's Murder, Telligny, who endeavour'd to fly upon the top of the
House, was slain with an Arquebuz shot ; the
Count of La Rochefoucault, whom Charles had
a mind to save, was stabb'd in his own Apartment ; the Marquis of Renel, Guerchy, Pluviaut,

Beau-

(o) Thaan. lib. 52, at the End. D'Aubigné. Tom. 11. liv 1.

Beaudifner, Brother to the Count of Cruffol, Lavardin, Briou, Governour of the Mar-
ques of Conty, De Quellenec, Baron of *Pont*
in *Britany*, Nompar de Caumont de la Force,
and his eldeft Son, Loviers, Montamar, Mont-
albert de Rouvray, Le Vaffeur de Coigneé, La
Roche, Colombier, Valavoyre, De Francour,
Chancellor of *Navarr*, Groflot, Bailiff of *Orleans*, Garrault Callifte, Des Prunes, Denis Per-
rot ; befides all thofe, whom the King of *Navarr*, at Charles's inftigation, had perfuaded
to lodge in the *Louvre*, and who were brought
down into the Court-yard, and then led out
Sword in hand, fome of whom were flain in the
Porch, and the reft juft out of the Palace ; a-
mongft whom were Pardaillan, St. Martin de
Bourfe, and the brave and gallant Piles, who
had withftood for fo many Weeks the King's
Army at the Siege of *St. John of Angely*, as a-
bovefaid.

I cannot, without being too tedious, relate
the Names of above ten thoufand Perfons of all
Ranks, Sex, and Age, that were deftroyed in
different manners, more cruel one than another,
only in the City of *Paris*, in a Fortnight's time
or thereabout. My Pen falls from my Hand, my
Heart achs, my Soul is full of Horror, my Spirits are quite confounded, when I think of the
Abominations of thofe dreadful Days. —— How
could I keep to any Order in my Narration, a-
midft the Curfes and Blafphemies of thofe Sons
of Belial ? Alas ! who can comprehend the
Fears, Terrors, Anguifh, Bitternefs and Perplexity, which feized upon the poor Reformed,
finding themfelves fo fuddenly furprized without
Remedy, and involved in all kind of outward
Miferies, which could poffibly, by Man, be inflicted upon human Creatures ? What Sighs,
and

and Groans, Trembling and Aftonifhment ; what Shrieks, Cries, and bitter Lamentations of Wives, Husbands, Children, Servants and Friends, howling and weeping, finding themfelves without all hope of Deliverance from their prefent Miferies! How inexorable were their barbarous Tormentors, who compaffed them in on every fide, without any Bowels of Compaffion, or the leaft Commiferation or Pity! Yea, they boafted of their Cruelties. I muft beg to be excufed from entering into the Particulars of the Barbarities ; and that the Reader would be contented with fome general Obfervations upon the whole.

I°. If we look for the firft Caufe of that dreadful Calamity, which befel at firft the Reformed Churches of France, and affected afterwards the whole Kingdom, certainly it was God juftly provoked by the enormous Sins of the whole Nation. Let us hear Thuanus concerning the Catholicks : That Fury, fays he, (Book LIII. at the beginning) that Fury and Blindnefs of Mind of the French was fent by God, becaufe of their frequent Blafphemies againft his moft holy Name, to which the King himfelf was addicted, havving received but a very bad Education of his Mother, and of his Tutors chofe by herfelf, the Example of the Court influenced whole Cities, and from them fpread itfelf into the Villages, and among the Peafants, fo far, that they could fcarce utter three words together, but the third was a Curfe againft God's Head, Death, Blood and Belly. God's Patience was likewife worn out, by the Licentioufnefs of their Lives, their Whoredoms, Adulteries and fomething worfe —— infomuch, that the French Land could not bear any longer with their Iniquities. For, whatever was alledged againft the

E e

Ad-

Charles
XI.
1572
Pope Gre-
gory XIII.

Admiral, was such stuff, so ill-contrived, that even Children themselves could not think that there was any truth in it; how much less could it be evinced to convince any Man in his right Senses? *&c.* So Thuanus. But on the other hand, let us say, that God was no less provoked by the Sins of our own Forefathers, *Who knowing the Judgment of God, that they who commit such things* (as the Court and Courtiers committed) *are worthy of death, not only did the*

Rom.i 32. *same, but had pleasure in those that did them.*
We have seen the Queen of Navarr's Complaints in her Letter to her Son; let us hear now one of our Historians of those very days (*a*). Having spoke before of the great Corruption of the Court, he adds, ,, The Reformed came so
,, near the Infection, that they could not miss
,, to be Partakers thereof. *Furthermore*, they
,, were very far from being unanimous, as to
,, the Preservation of their Discipline, as they
,, ought to have been. In the Year 1571, cer-
,, tain fluttering Spirits had attempted to alter,
,, or even to subvert it. They had been repres-
,, sed by the national Synod held at *Rochelle*;
,, but having been incouraged, they attempted
,, again the same thing, with a greater Audacious-
,, ness, in the Months of February and March
,, 1572, and nothing better could be expected,
,, but a greater Division in the Churches. But
,, God Almighty was preparing Scourges for
,, them.——The Licentiousness of many was such,
,, that no other difference was to be found be-
,, tween the Reformed and the Catholicks in se-
,, veral Provinces, only that the first went not
,, to Mass, and the others went not to hear a
,, Minister's Sermon. In all other respects,
,, Wantonness, Pride, Luxury, and all other

(*a*) Mem. de l'Etat de France sous Charles IX. Tom.1. p.216.

,, Vices, were as rife amongst the Reformed, as
,, amongst the Catholicks.,,

Whoever shall consider this dreadful Calamity
with a sedate Mind, will find in it some particular Marks of God's Vengeance against his People. For very often he punishes their Sins in
their Chiefs, and for that end he sent unto them,
as it were, a Spirit of Delusion, that they might
not believe the Truth, and that they might give
credit to a Lye. And indeed who can believe otherwise? when he considers, that notwithstanding all the threatning of their Enemies, their Preparations made before their very Eyes for their
utter Destruction, their Stupidity was such, *that*
hearing, they heard, and did not understand, and
seeing, they saw, and did not perceive. Therefore we cannot admit of any other first Cause of
that sad Event, but God; and God provoked by
the Sins of our Forefathers, which however can
by no means apologize for *Assur the Rod of the*
Anger, and the Staff of the Indignation of the
Lord.

II. Another thing to be observed is the Time
and Place, when and where that abominable Plot
was contrived, and the Persons concerned in it.
As to the Time, it is certain that the Design of
destroying the Reformed in France and the Low
Countries, was laid in June 1565, in the Conference held at *Bayonne* between Catharine
and Alva; but as to the manner of executing
it, nothing was settled, only she endeavoured
to ensnare the Princes and the great Lords of
that Party, according to the Directions of Alva,
who had told her, *That it was needless to lose*
time in catching the little Frogs, as long as the Sal-
mons and other great Fishes were suffered to live.

Accordingly, we have seen her leaving no
Stone unturned for surprizing the Prince of

Condé,

the Admiral and other Lords ; and having miſcarried in the Attempt, either becauſe ſhe was
prevented, or becauſe every thing was not ready
for the Execution, as at *Moulins* in 1566, at
laſt ſhe reſolved upon that foul Device of the
Marriage of her Daughter with the King of Navarr, which ſucceeded too well to her own
wiſhes. Whoever ſhall conſider the whole Conduct of Catherine, ſince that Conference, to the
time of the Execution of her Plot, will eaſily be
convinced, that ſhe had always that Object in
view, and that the Delay proceeded not from
want of a ſettled Reſolution, but from want of a
proper Opportunity to put it in execution.

We have already ſaid, that it was at *Bayonne*
that the Plot was laid at firſt in 1565: as to the
Method, it was altered ſeveral times ; at firſt it
had been reſolved at *Bayonne*, to murder the Chiefs
of the Reformed in the Aſſembly of the No-
TABLES, that were to be convened at *Moulins*
in the beginning of the Year 1566 ; and then
they thought that the Chiefs being undone, it
would be an eaſy matter either to oblige the Reformed to recant, or to deſtroy them ; but that
Scheme was not executed for the Reaſons aboveſaid. Then they made a pretence of Alva's Paſſage through the *Frontiers*, in his way to the
Low-Countries, for raiſing ſix thouſand Switzers,
and bringing them, without any occaſion, into
the very Heart of the Kingdom, and of making
ſeveral other Preparations, in order to fall upon
the Reformed unawares ; but by the Admiral's,
and eſpecially D'Andelot's Vigilance, they were
prevented, and this occaſioned the ſecond Civil
War in 1567. After the ſecond Peace, they
plotted to ſurprize the Prince and the Admiral at
Noyers, and the other Lords in the reſpective
Places of their Abode ; the Plot was ſo well contrived,

trived, and Catharine fo fure of the Succefs
thereof, that fhe had already, as it were, prepared a Prifon for the Prince, and a Scaffold for
the Admiral, when both efcaped providentially
at the very nick of time, when their Enemies had
their hands lifted up over their Necks in 1568.
Then when fhe faw herfelf difappointed, and
that fhe had not been able to compafs her ends,
neither by open force, nor by bribing Murderers
or Poifoners, as long as the Admiral ftood upon
his guard, fhe alter'd her courfe, and by a frau-
dulent Treaty, attended with an unexpected
Propofition of Marriage, fhe queftioned not but
that fhe fhould over-reach and trap them ; when
fhe had catch'd them, fhe confider'd with her
fecret Council at *Blois* in 1571, what Method
fhe ought to follow for undoing them. Birague contrived one, which was agreed upon,
viz. to build a wooden Tower next the Louvre
as above-mention'd ; but that Scheme was again
altered, either becaufe the Duke of Anjou difcovered it to Lignerolles, or becaufe the Admiral
being fallen fick at that time, the Confpi-
rators thought that being too weak, he would
not venture upon fo hard an Exercife, or that
being too wife, he would fufpect fome Snake in
the Grafs ; therefore it was refolved at St. Cloud
to murder the Admiral, not queftioning, but that
the Lords, Gentlemen, and other Reformed,
would fall upon the Houfe of Guife and their
Adherents, for revenging his Death, whereby
they would afford fome pretence or other for deftroying them ; and Maurevel was pitched upon
for the Execution. But having miffed his aim,
the Admiral being only wounded, and the Reformed not ftirring, the fecret Council refolved
then upon the Method, which was followed.
So, after having thoroughly examined whatever

E e 3
the

the Hiftorians have faid concerning that bloody Tragedy, I find, that tho' it had been refolved upon feven Years before, yet the Method was fettled only about thirty hours before the Execution.

As to the Perfons concerned in the Plot, there is fome Diverfity of opinion among the Hiftorians. Thuanus, for inftance, fuppofes, that Charles had no notice of it, but few hours before the Execution : but the Majority of Votes is againft him ; and indeed I muft own, that his Arguments are very weak. He pretends that Charles was too young to be capable of fo great a Diffimulation, as that which was required on that occafion. But let it be faid, with Reverence due to that noble Hiftorian, it feems to me, that he was not in earneft when he fpoke fo, nor indeed could he be ignorant of the School wherein, and under what Mafters, and in what Principles, Charles had been trained up. It is true, that the Violence of his Temper feemed not to allow him to be fo long a Diffembler and an Hypocrite ; but that very Violence of his Temper, which prompted him to revenge upon the fpot, the Affronts which he thought had been put upon him, at leaft never to forgive them, obliged him alfo to conceal his real Sentiments, as long as it was requifite, when he thought that by that Diffemblance and Hypocrify, he fhould at laft obtain his ends, and be fully revenged upon thofe whom he took to be his Enemies. But for all that, I do not think, that Charles was acquainted with the Plot, fo foon as many Hiftorians, Catholicks and Reformed, will have it ; nor that, when he was made privy to it by his Mother, fhe told him all the Particulars of it.

Therefore

Therefore I take this for certain, that he be- Charles
came acquainted with the Plot, only after his IX.
Marriage with Elizabeth of *Auftria*; and that 1572.
his Mother told him but part of it, and conceal'd Pope Gre-
the reft; whereupon he readily confented to the goryXIII.
intended Marriage of his Sifter with the Prince
of Navarr, for which he had fhewn fome Reluctancy at firft.

The Murder of Lignerolles perpetrated fome
Months after at Blois, by Charles's Command,
is another Argument of that Prince's Knowledge
of a Plot, at leaft againft the Princes, the Admiral, and other Heads of the Reformed Party,
long before the Maffacre. I know that fome
Hiftorians of great name, efpecially Thuanus,
for invalidating this Evidence, afcribe this Anger of Charles againft Lignerolles to another
Caufe, than that which other Hiftorians, contemporary to that Event, do afcribe it. But
there is none that goes fo far as Father Daniel
does, who pretends, that this Murder was perpetrated long after the Maffacre. How fo? becaufe, fays he, that was done when the Duke
of Anjou was King of Poland, and quotes for
his Voucher the Duke of Alençon's Declaration,
when he was arrefted Prifoner in 1574. But he
hath miferably wrefted that Paffage; befides that
he hath not obferved, that in that Declaration
the Duke of Alençon never ftiles his Brother
Duke of Anjou, but always King of Poland;
tho' he fpeaks of things paffed above three Years
before he came to that Crown. 2. That he
fpeaks of a thing happened at Blois, while he
was in that City; for he fays, *at that very time*,
and Daniel ought to know, that the Court never
went to Blois, after the Maffacre, during Charles's
Life. 3. That the Duke of Alençon does not
explain what were thefe ill Offices Lignerolles

com-

'complained of as done him, near the Duke of Anjou his Master, and consequently he could infer nothing from that Declaration for invalidating the Relation of D'Avila, and so many others. I find in an Historian contemporary, that Lignerolles having been refused the Lieutenancy in the Duke of Anjou's Guards, which he expected, threatned to discover what he knew concerning the Plot. That feigning to be sick, he kept to his Bed, that Catharine came to visit him, in order to engage him not to divulge the Secret, and promised him very fine things. That she having imparted that Affair unto her secret Council, it was resolved to put him to death, lest he should execute his Threatnings. That the Charge was given to Villequier, Viscount of La Guerche, by Charles's Orders, which the said Viscount executed, when Charles was gone to *Bourgueil* in *Anjou,* upon a Hunting-match (o). Other Historians relate that Event in the same manner as D'Avila, and after him Agricola have done ; but in general most part of the Historians of those Days agree, that Lignerolles was killed by Charles's Orders, because he had revealed a Secret concerning the Plot, which had been imparted to him by the Duke of Anjou his Master.

However, since Charles himself owned in his Parliament of Paris, that he had designed long ago to undo the Enemies of his Crown and State, and had endeavoured to bring them into that Precipice wherein they were fallen, since he was so well pleased with the Compliment paid unto him by the first President, on account of his

(o) Mem. de l'Etat de France sous Charles IX. fol. 62—65. See D'Avila, Tom. I. Liv. V. pag. 260—61. Le Laboureur Addit. aux Mem. de Casteln. Vol. 2. Liv. VI. pag. 357. & Tom. I. Liv. III. ch. 9. p. 775—6. Daniel. Hist. de France, sous Charles IX. pag. 975—6.

his great Ability in diffembling ; why fhould we belye him ?

But we muft obferve, that tho' there were three feveral fecret Councils, viz. that of Guife, compofed of Catharine, the Dukes of Anjou and Guife, of Nevers and Aumale, the Cardinal of Lorrain, the Count of Retz, the Marfhal of Tavannes, Birague, Chiverny, and fome others ; Charles's fecret Council, wherein he was affifted by his Mother, his Brother of Anjou, the Count of Retz and Birague ; and Catharine's Council, which was the moft fecret, wherein was admitted only the Count of Rets her moft trufty Confident, and fometimes Birague made a third, but not always ; and tho' the Heads of thefe three Councils propofed to themfelves very different Views, as obferved already, neverthelefs they agreed in the means of obtaining them, viz. the Deftruction of the Admiral, and of the Chief of the Reformed Party.

III. If Charles had difcovered at firft fome Reluctancy againft fo barbarous a Deed, he made afterwards ample amends for it, he carried his Fury further than any Tyrant before ; he took a Carabine and fired out of his Window at the poor Wretches who endeavoured to fave themfelves by croffing the River: The Remnant of the Admiral's Corps having been hang'd at Montfaucon, Charles went to fee it, with feveral of his Courtiers ; who being offended with the Stench, fhut clofe their Nofes and Mouths with their Handkerchiefs, which being perceived by Charles, he rebuked them for it, and told them, *That there was no better pleafing Smell, than the Stench of a dead Enemy.* A Sentence indeed, worthy of Charles! Meffieurs Cavagnes and Briquemaut, the firft a Counfellor of the Parliament of Thouloufe, and who had been gratified by Charles with a Place of

Mafter

Master of the Requests, and the second was an old reputable Nobleman of about 70 Years of age, and a brave experienced Officer, were condemned, for the pretended Conspiracy, and for refusing (tho' miserably tortured) to charge the Admiral with being guilty thereof. They were drawn in Hurdles to the Place of Execution, and having by the way endured, with admirable Patience, the Reproaches and Dirt cast on them by the Rabble, they were hanged (together with the noble Admiral's Effigy) by Candle-light, having asserted both his Innocence and their own, to their last Breath. After this unjust Execution, their Bodies were barbarously mangled by the accursed Multitude ; and Charles (who delighted in such bloody Spectacles) did not only behold it himself, with his Mother, and their whole Court, but forced the King of Navarr and the Prince to be present at it.

The Ladies of the Court, following the Example of Catharine their Mistress, shewed what great regard they had for Modesty and Humanity, when they came down to look upon the Corps of the Lords and Gentlemen that had been slain, and which were put stark naked in a File before the Palace, upon the Pavement, and especially, they sat upon the Body of the Lord of Soubize, to search whether they could find out any mark of Impotency in it, because he was at Law with his Lady upon that account. Lady LA CHASTEGNERAYE was so inhuman, that she granted leave to l'Archan who courted her, to cause her own Father-in-law Nompar Caumont de la Force, and her two Half-Brothers to be murdered, the youngest whereof having providentially escaped, as I shall say presently, she went herself to the Arsenal, where she knew he had been received by Gontault de Biron, Great-Master of the Artillery,

and

and defired that Lord to put her Brother into her hands, that she might drefs his Wounds and take care of him; but Biron, who knew what care she had taken of her Father and Brother, told her, *that indeed he would be very glad to find out the young Caumont's Sifter to truft him in her hands, but not his Heirefs, who took too great care of him yefterday Morning:* and fo he fent her away with Scorn. Another Maid of Honour, De Royan by Name, underftanding that one of her own Relations, and another Gentleman Reformed, with whom she had been in love of late, were concealed in her own Houfe, she rode thither in a Man's Drefs, bringing fome Murderers along with her, and delivered thefe unfortunate Gentlemen into their hands, without any Pity; then she came back to the *Louvre*, and boafted of it before her Miftrefs Catharine.

IV. No wonder if Charles having violated his Promifes and moft facred Engagements with his Subjects in fo bafe and treacherous a manner, was not more faithful to his Brother-in-law and Coufin, the King of Navarr and the Prince of Condé. He fent for them to his Clofet the very Morning of St. Bartholomew's Day, and after many Reproaches, Oaths and Blafphemies, he told them, that they muft turn Roman-Catholicks, or they should be ferved as their Fellow-Hereticks. Whereupon the King of Navarr, in a great furprize, moft humbly befought the King to remember his Promifes, and the Alliance lately contracted; that as for himfelf, he would do every thing to fatisfy his Majefty, tho' it would be a very hard task for him to renounce a Religion wherein he had been trained up from his Childhood. But the Prince of Condé shewed a greater Refolution and Magnanimity: He told Charles, *that he had engaged his Faith with him and the*

His Breach of Faith to the Princes.

Fol-

*Followers of the same Religion in his Dominions,
in so solemn a manner, that he could not believe that
he would break his Oaths. As to the Obedience he
required of him, he had before, and would be always
ready to pay it. But as to his Religion, God alone
was him to whom he was obliged to account for it ;
that his Life, Goods, and Estate were in the King's
power, to do with them according to his Will, but
that he would persevere in his Religion, to the peril
of his Life.*

Charles grew furious at that Answer, he called
the Prince a *Rebel*, a *seditious Son of a Seditious*,
and threatned him to have him beheaded, if he
did not comply in three days time. A few days
after, Charles sent for the Captains of his Guards,
and for his own Armour, to go himself and make
an end of what had escaped the hands of the
Murderers, beginning with the Prince of Condé.
But Queen Elizabeth his Consort, one of the best
Princesses in the world, came and fell down upon
her Knees before him, and hindered him by her
Intreaties, from executing his barbarous Design.
On the next day, he sent for the Prince of Condé,
and bid him chuse one of these three things, MASS,
DEATH, or the BASTILE. *God forbid,* says
the Prince, *my King and my Liege Lord, that I
should chuse the first ; as to the two others, I am at
your own Disposal and Will, which may God Almighty be pleased in his Mercy to mollify.* Charles
was moved with that Answer, and sent him
away.

But it happened at this time that HUGH SOREL
DES ROSIERS, Minister of *Orleans*, having been
arrested, as he endeavoured to make his escape out
of the Kingdom, and being struck by the Terrours
of Death, turned Roman Catholick, *(outwardly
only, for a few Months after, having met with a
favourable Opportunity of quitting the Kingdom, he*
                                                    went

went to Heidelberg, where he did publick Penance for his Apostacy, and was restored to the Communion of the Church, tho' not to the Ministry). Charles sent for him to Court, and made use of him as a Tool for perverting the King of Navarr, his Sister Catharine of Navarr, the Prince of Condé and the Princess Mary of *Cleves* his Consort, and the Princess Dowager of Condé. They feigned all to be convinced, rather out of Fear, than out of any thing else; the Prince of Condé only declared that he was not satisfied at all with Des Rosiers's Arguments, and desired to have a private Conference with him; which being granted, *Is it so,* says the Prince unto him, *as you say in Publick? Do you speak out of Fear, or out of Conviction?* Whereto Des Rosiers answered, *That it was his Opinion, and he was convinced that he was in the Right.* Then, says the Prince, *if it had been so, as I have been taught from my Childhood in your School, I would have asserted the Truth at the Peril of my Life; but if I have been deceived, and my Opinions are wrong, forsaking Error, I must yield to Truth when it is found out.*

From that day the Prince of Condé wavered, and at last, overcome by the fright of a perpetual Prison, (for an Apartment in the *Bastile* had been prepared for him by Charles's Orders) he yielded to whatever was required of him. He and his Cousin the King of Navarr, and the Princesses of Bearn and Condé, made their publick Recantation, and heard Mass, the Cardinal of Bourbon officiating; they wrote to the Pope, who granted to them Absolution. The King of Navarr by Charles's Orders, sent a Decree into *Bearn* and to his other Dominions, whereby he forbad the Profession of any other Religion besides the Catholick, but very little Regard was paid to it, as coming from a Captive Prince.

V.

*Charles
charges the
Guifes
with the
Maffacre.*

V. The very fame day of the Maffacre, Charles, out of a deep Policy, or, knowing not as yet what courfe to take to avoid the Heinoufnefs of it, wrote to the Governours of the Provinces and of the chief Cities, and to his Embaffadors in *England, Germany,* and *Switzerland,* to notify unto them what had happened in *Paris,* and to his Coufin the Admiral; and pretended that thefe things had been perpetrated without his previous Knowledge and Confent, by the Guifes and their Faction, who had raifed a Commotion amongft the People. Catharine wrote unto the fame, to the fame purport, in order to render the Houfe of Guife odious to all the Nations of Europe. Neverthelefs, the fame Hand that fubfcrib'd thofe Letters, was all the while firing at the poor innocent People; this I fay as to Charles.

*The Guifes
prevail a-
gainft him,
and he
owns the
Fact in
Parlia-
ment.*

VI. The Guifes gueffing at what Charles and Catharine aimed at, oppofed their Defign with all their Might, and were fo well ferved in the fecret Council, even by Catharine herfelf, that Charles was at laft prevailed upon to own the Fact, and to take the whole upon him. Therefore, on Tuefday the 26th of Auguft, after having caufed the *Te Deum* to be fung, for Thankfgiving unto God for that glorious Exploit, he went to the Parliament, attended with his Mother, his Brethren, and the Princes of the Blood, and there declared, *that whatever had been done at Paris, had been done not only with his Confent, but likewife by fpecial Command, and of his own Accord.* He charged the Admiral with a Confpiracy to murder him, his Mother, his Brothers, and the King of Navarr, and to fet the young Prince of Condé upon the Throne, whom he had likewife refolved to deftroy afterwards, and to ufurp the Crown for himfelf. Therefore he had thought proper, being not able to do otherwie, wife, to cure a Plague by another, that he might root that Corruption out of the very Bowels of his Kingdom.

He was answered by the first President Christopher Thuanus, who serving to the Times, was so weak as to extol with great Encomiums the King's Prudence, who had dissembled so many Injuries, and prevented the threatning Danger he was in, and so restored again the Peace to his Kingdom; running upon that Topick of Lewis XI, Qui nescit dissimulare, nescit regnare : *Who knows not how to dissemble, knows not how to reign.* He was much unlike, in this respect, to the first President, John de la Vaquerie, under Lewis XI. That Prince, according to Bodin de Republica, Lib. III. ch. IV. having commanded his Parliament, on pain of Death, to register all his Edicts without any controul, La Vaquerie went to the King, attended by all the Members of that august Body in their Formalities, *non ut culpam deprecaretur, sed ut mortem precaretur,* saying that he and his Collegues chose to die, rather than to register an Edict so unjust as that proposed to them. Whereby Lewis XI was appeased, and cancelled himself his Edict. Far from following that Example, Thuanus agreeing against his Conscience with Morvilliers, formerly Bishop of Orleans, to arraign the Memory of the Admiral, and having found him guilty upon the Evidence of suborned Witnesses, the above named Sentence was passed, and executed against him, his Memory, Posterity, &c.

Two days after, Charles issued out a Proclamation, whereby, pretending always that a Conspiracy against his Person, the Royal Family, and his Government, having been discovered just at the time when it was upon the point of being executed, he had thought proper to prevent the
evil

evil Defigns of the Admiral and his Complices, and that whatever had been done, was by his fpecial Command, not out of Hatred againft the Reformed Religion, nor out of a defire of breaking his former Edict, which, on the contrary, he commanded to be ftrictly obferved, but out of a Principle of Juftice againft the Difturbers of the publick Peace, and that he willed that all his Subjects fhould live peaceably, and in full Security in their own Houfes, without being injured either in their Life, Goods, or Eftate, and that it will be death for whofoever fhould offend them in any of thefe Points : adding however this particular Claufe, that, for good Reafons, the Reformed ought to abftain from any Meeting, either publick or private, upon what account foever, till the King had ordered otherwife ; and it would be Death and Forfeiture of their Goods, for whomfoever fhould offend againft that Decree. But this was only a Device to enfnare the Reformed, and too many, that were too credulous, felt the fad Effects of it. For

Charles
fent Orders
for the
Maffacres
in the Pro-
vinces.

VII. Charles fent fecret Orders to all his Governours and Lieutenants, throughout all the Provinces and chief Cities of the Kingdom, enjoining them to follow the Example of Paris. Thefe Orders were more or lefs obeyed, according to the Temper of the Governours, and the Party which they followed, for the Montmorencians refufed to obey, pretending that thefe Orders were fictitious, being quite contrary to thofe they had received from Court, two or three days before ; fo, the Count of Tendes in *Provence*, Gordes in *Dauphiné*, St. Eran in *Auvergne*, tho' they were Roman Catholicks, and had been very fevere to the Reformed during the Wars, feigned to believe thefe Orders to be fuppofititious, and refufed to execute them. Some refufed their

Sub-

Submiſſion out of a Principle of Honour ; ſuch was the Viſcount of *Ortez* Governour of *Bayonne* and of the *Frontiers of Spain*, tho' he was extremely violent againſt the Reformed in all other reſpects, nevertheleſs he ſent this Anſwer to the King's Letters.

SIR, *I have imparted your Majeſty's Commands unto his faithful Inhabitants of this City, and the Soldiers of the Garriſon. I have found none amongſt them but what are good Citizens and brave Soldiers, but not one Executioner or Hangman. Therefore they and I moſt humbly beſeech your Majeſty, to make uſe of our Lives and Arms in any thing elſe poſſible, how dangerous ſoever it be, as being, as long as they ſhall laſt,* SIR, *yours,* &c.

He and the Count of Tendes were very ſoon after diſpatched by Poiſon, as it was rumoured. Count of Charni Deputy-Governour of *Burgundy*, either out of Compaſſion, or by an Effect of the refined Policy of the Houſe of Guiſe, preſerved the Reformed of his Government, for only a ſingle Gentleman was killed at *Dijon*, and at *Maſcon* the Priſons were a ſure Refuge for them, where they remained unmoleſted, till the Letters Patent were ſent all over the Kingdom, whereby the King declared, that he took his Reformed Subjects under his Protection, and whoſoever ſhould take up Arms, or uſe any Violence againſt them, ſhould be proſecuted with the utmoſt Severity. But theſe Letters had their Effects only two Months or thereabout, after the beginning of the Maſſacre.

In ſome other Places, tho' the Governours and the Chief Magiſtrates were well intentioned, nevertheleſs, being overpower'd by the Factious and the Rabble, they were forced to yield to their Fury. It was the Caſe of *Rouen*, tho' Carrouge

Governour thereof, and the Parliament, endeavoured to refrain the Seditious, they were forced at laſt to yield to their Madneſs, and above 700 Reformed, of all Ages, Sex and Condition, were unmercifully murdered. The ſame happened at *Bourdeaux*, where all the Endeavours of Montferrant Governour thereof, of the Attorney-General, and the firſt Jurate, (or *Alderman*) proved ineffectual ; for at the Inſtigation of the Jeſuits, eſpecially of EDMOND AUGER, who by their ſeditious Sermons excited the People, they were forced to yield to MONTPEZAT, and a greater number of the Reformed than at Rouën periſhed. The ſame happened at *Lyons*, where Mandelot, willing to ſave the Reformed Inhabitants, ordered them to retire into the Priſons of the City ; ſome went thither of their own accord, but ſeveral of thoſe that were led, were ſlain by the way. DU PERAT having brought to Mandelot the King's Order for murdering the Reformed, he was ſtruck with the Horror of the Fact, and reſolved to wait for another Command, which being brought poſt by D'AUXERRE, the King's Attorney, *Friend,* ſays Mandelot unto him, *whatever thou bindeſt, let it be bound.* Then the Executioner was ſent for, with his Servants, but he refuſed to perform, ſaying, *That his Hands worked only according to Law.* Whereupon, the Soldiers of the Citadel were called to do the Work ; but they, full of Indignation, anſwered, *Go and look for other Executioners than we.* So they gave that Office to three hundred Harquebuſiers of the Militia, who executed it with all the Inhumanity that can be imagined, without ſparing either their Kindred or Neighbours ; they began by the Priſons of the *Cordeliers,* then they went to that of the *Celeſtines* ; from thence to that of the *Archbiſhoprick,* wherein Mandelot had ſhut

up

up three hundred of the wealthiest Citizens, thinking them to be more safe there; the Murderers bid them prepare themselves for Death, and having seized what Money they had with them, they cut the Children to pieces, and slew the rest all to one. In the Evening they came to *Rouane*, which was the Common-Goal, and wherein the greater number of the Reformed were shut up, they dragged them out, and threw them into the Rhône, most part being half strangled: However, they granted life to those who promised to turn Roman Catholicks. The next Night, the plunder and murder was as frightful as in any other City, wherein the Women, Maids and Children, were not spared at all. In *St. John's Place* there was such a prodigious and horrid heap of Corpses, that two Women, frightened at that sight, miscarried. The Governor endeavoured to have them buried, but it was impossible for him to overcome the ill-nature of the Monks and Priests; and the Mob, at their persuasion, dragged them into the River. Of that number were Messrs. Dalus and other rich Merchants who traded in *Asia*, and *Africa*, and who having escaped for some days, at last were stabbed. One Capt. La Mente with his Soldiers saved two out of the three Ministers, and several others. It is reckoned that the number of the Slain amounted to 800, besides those that were drowned, whose number was as great as of the Slain; the Rhône being full of Blood and of Corpses, occasioned heavy Complaints amongst the Inhabitants of the Towns and Cities lying on that River, down to the *Mediterranean*, that they cursed those of *Lyons*, because their Water was quite spoiled, and they durst not venture to eat River-Fish. At *Arles* especially, where there is

no

no Well or Spring, they ſuffered as much for want of Water as if they had been beſieged, becauſe the River was quite bloody.

If ſuch was the Fury of the Murderers in Places where the Governors and Magiſtrates oppoſed them as much as they could, let the Reader judge what was the condition of the Reformed in thoſe Places, the Governors and Magiſtrates whereof, not only connived at, but commanded, and helped the Murderers in their bloody Executions. For two Months together that dreadful Hurricane ran throughout all the Provinces of *France*, the Effects whereof were more ſenſibly felt at *Meaux, Troyes, Orleans, Nevers, Bourges, la Charité, Poitiers, Thoulouſe,* where five Counſellors of the Parliament were hanged in their Formalities in the Palace-yard, *Dacqs, Cahors, Caſtres,* and five hundred other Places; for it is a great deal more eaſy to name thoſe that were free from that Barbarity, than thoſe that were ſtained with it, ſince the whole Kingdom became, as it were, a *Rama, wherein was a Voice heard, lamentation and weeping, and great mourning, Rachel weeping for Jacob, Jacob for Rachel, both for their Children, their Children for them, and would not be comforted, becauſe they were not.*

Matt. 11. 18. but with ſome Addition.

VIII. The Number of the Slain at Paris and in the Provinces cannot be exactly told, the Hiſtorians don't agree upon that point; ſome ſay more, ſome leſs, ſome 100000 in the whole, as Perefixe, Tutor to Lewis XIV. and Archbiſhop of *Paris;* ſome 60000, as *Natalis Comes,* but he is not to be credited when he ſpeaks of the Affairs of France; ſome 40000, as ―― and ſome 30000 only, as Thuanus: but really· he cannot be credited in this, for ſince the Waters of the *Seine, Loire, Marne,* and *Rhône,* were

actually

actually turned into Blood, for several days, there
must be certainly a greater quantity spilt than
what can be afforded by the Slaughter of thirty
thousand Men, good part whereof were slain
in places not lying upon the Banks of those
Rivers. D'Avila says, that at Paris only, there
were above ten thousand Persons in the two first
days, amongst whom were five hundred and more
Lords and Gentlemen, that answer the Description of the *Seine* turned into Blood, for the
Massacre lasted six days longer. For my part,
I am inclined to believe, that the number of
the slain was rather greater than what the Prelate abovenamed says, than less. It is true, that
that Flood of Blood carried away many Catholicks, by the Sovereign's Orders, or at the Instigation of some private Men: to be rich, or
possessed of some profitable Office, or to have
some mortal Enemy, or some hungry Heir,
was to be a Hugonot. Some called that Massacre, the *Parisian Mattins*, as the Massacre of
the French in *Sicily* in 1281 had been called
the *Sicilian Vespers*.

IX. However, many escaped from that Desolation, some by the King's Will, or their Friend's
Protection, or the Guise's Policy, some providentially, and the rest by flight. Montgomery, the Vidame of Chartres, and several others
that were lodged in the Suburb of *St. Germain*,
escaped very narrowly; for hearing the Noise
in the City, they thought that the King was
forced in the *Louvre*, and had already taken a
Boat to come to his assistance ; but as they were
ferrying, they perceived a Boat full of Soldiers,
who cried Murder, Murder! Whereupon they
went back and took to their Horses some without Boots, others without Saddles, and ran as
fast as they could: nevertheless they would not

Those esca-ped from the Massacres.

have

have escaped the Danger, had it not been that the Keeper of the Gate of *Nesle* mistook one Key for another ; for the Duke of Guise being come to that Gate, the Keeper was obliged to go home for the Keys, whereby Montgomery and others had more time ; and the Duke of Guise, &c. who pursued them for twenty four Miles together, was forced to desist. Montgomery and part of his Company came over into *England.*

The Viscount of Leiran having been wounded in the *Louvre*, ran into the young Queen of Navarr's Apartment, came up into her Bedchamber, being pursued by the Archers : the Princess got up, and he with her, and took hold of her ; whereupon Nancey, Captain of the Guards, coming, he obliged the Archers to desist, and the Princess obtained Leiran's Life of the King her Brother.

Charles granted Life to Grammont, Duras, Gamaches, and Bouchavanes, who having no Religion at all, made no scruple to adhere to the Roman Catholicks. The Marshal of Cossé was spared in behalf of the fair De Chateauneuf his Cousin, and Mistress to the Duke of Anjou ; Biron was preserved, because he took care to shut up himself in the Arsenal, and to level two Culverins against the Street. Those who could reach that Place were received and preserved, especially the young Caumont, who was providentially preserved, in his Father's Bed ; the Murderers having slain him with his eldest Son, this young Gentleman, of about eleven or twelve Years old, who lay in the same Bed with them, and had received some Wounds, feigned to be dead, and lay still by his Father, as the Blood ran abundantly upon the Floor, the Murderers took him for dead, and went away ; then came
some

some other Persons, who talking together, some lamented the Fate of that noble Family, while others approved of it. The Company being gone all but one, this man continued to bewail with himself, and detested the Tragick Act, which being heard by young La Force, he told him, that he was not dead, and that if he would lead him safe to the Arsenal, he should be handsomely recompensed for his Trouble. The Man having granted that Request, the young La Force was preserved, and became the head of a rich and potent Family in Guienn, the Lord of Biron having refused to deliver him into the hands of his Half-Sister, as abovesaid.

Many were likewise preserved by the Duke of Guise's Protection, amongst whom was the Count of Crussol, who was so grateful towards his Benefactor, that to please him he turned Roman Catholick.

Many were preserved by their Flight ; those of *Burgundy*, *Lyonnese*, *Dauphiné*, *Provence*, who took that Course, retired into *Switzerland* and *Geneva* ; amongst whom were the Lady D'Entramont, Dowager of Chatillon, with the eldest Son of the Admiral, and Guy de Laval, eldest Son to D'Andelot ; they came first to *Geneva*, and for the greater Security, they went to *Berna*, destitute of every thing. As to the other Children of the Admiral, Charles having sent on the second and third day of the Massacre for to seize the whole Family at Chatillon upon Loing, as the Lady Dowager, the eldest Son, and the Nephew had made their Escape, the rest were brought to Paris, and as a further addition to the Cruelty of those days, they affected to make them go through Montfaucon, where the Admiral's Corps was still hanging. Those of *Champaign*, *Isle of France*, and adjacent

jacent

jacent Provinces, retired into *Germany*, where they were kindly received and entertained by the Proteftant Princes, efpecially by the Electot Palatine. Thofe of *Picardy, Normandy, Britany* retired into *England.* And thofe of the middle Provinces, who had no means for efcaping, yielding for the moft part to the fury of the times, turned Roman Catholicks; but the Storm was no fooner over, but the greateft part fincerely repenting their Fault, did Penance, and were received again into the Reformed Church. A vaft number took refuge in the Country of *Cevennes*, at *Montauban*, *Sancerre*, and at *La Rochelle*; in this laft City fifty Minifters, a great number of the Nobility and Gentry, and above nine hundred Soldiers which were very ufeful during the Siege. As to the Lady of Telligny, I find fhe retired into Switzerland.

Amongft thofe who efcaped I muft not omit one who was preferved by an Act of Generofity not to be expected from an Enemy: Refnier, a Gentleman of *Quercy*, was his Name. He had commanded in that Country under the Princes in the former Wars againft Vezins, Deputy Governor of that Province; befides that general quarrel, there were fome private ones between them, becaufe Vezins, one of the moft rough and cruel Men of that time, had committed many Barbarities in that Country, killing, hanging, burning whatever came in his way, even upon Refnier's Lands; and this Gentleman, though of a milder temper, had paid him with the fame coin. The Peace being made, their common Friends had not been able to prevail upon them to come to an agreement, but they perfifted in their hatred one againft another. Now being both at *Paris* at this time, as Refnier was preparing himfelf for Death, which

he

he thought was unavoidable; Vezins came thither, (*who had received the King's Orders to go to Quercy, and execute there the same things which he saw executed at Paris*) who having broke open the Doors, entered Sword in hand, with two Men armed; he found Refnier waiting for nothing elfe but Death, lying upon the Ground, imploring God's Mercy. Vezins with a frightful Voice bid him get up to follow him, and mount a Spanifh Jenet, which was ready for that purpofe in the Yard; fo he brought Refnier out of the City, and having received his Word that he would follow him, they both continued their Rout into *Guienn*, without any ftay, only for refrefhing themfelves, and travelled Day and Night, without fpeaking a Word one to another. Vezins, however, had ordered fome of his Servants to go before to have fome Victuals ready dreft, as they came into the Inns. At laft they arrived in *Quercy*, at Refnier's Caftle. There Vezins turning to Refnier, fpoke unto him, to the following purport: *You know how eafy it had been to me to gratify my Revenge, had I had a mind to it; but my Honour did not allow me to improve that opportunity, and I have had always fuch a value for your great Courage, that I thought it deferving that I fhould try it without any advantage. Enjoy then that Life which had been preferved by my Kindnefs, and be perfuaded that you will find me always ready to determine our Quarrels in a way agreeable to our Quality, as you have found me ready on this occafion, to avert the threatning danger whereto you was expofed.* To which Refnier anfwered, *My Dear Mr. Vezins, if I had any courage, ftrength, or ill will againft you, you have radically plucked it out of my heart by this your Kindnefs to me, you have intirely*
extinguifhed

extinguished *my enmity against you by so great Generosity, the Instance whereof shall be recorded in the Annals of the World, and remain for ever fixed in my Remembrance; you having commanded me to follow, I have obeyed, though against my Will, and you have brought me here safe: Now lead me wherever you please, and I will of my own accord follow you; and be firmly persuaded that I shall be always ready to employ that Life you have preserved, and that Courage which you are pleased to praise, if there is any in me, for your Service and your own defence against any Enemy.* Which said, he ran to embrace him, but Vezins, with the same sourness in his Looks, told him, *Would you be so base as to forget what Injuries you have received from me.* To which Resnier answered, *Would not that derogate from what I owe you?* No, no, says Vezins, *Friend or Foe, they must all be brave.* And without waiting for any further reply, spurring his Horse, away he went, leaving the Spanish Jenet worth 500 Crowns to Resnier. This last coming into his Castle, found his Lady and Daughter overwhelm'd with Sorrow, who took him for a Ghost; for some of his Servants having fled as soon as they had seen Vezins entering into his Room at Paris, had reported that they had seen their Master murthered by the former. After they were come to themselves, Resnier thought of Vezins's Spanish Horse, which he had left with him, and sent it back unto him by his Steward. But Vezins sent one of his Gentlemen with it, desiring Resnier to accept of it. We shall see hereafter the fate of both these Gentlemen.

X. I have omitted purposely several Particulars, which come better under a separate Article; such as the Names of the chief Murtherers

of

of Paris, TANCHOU, PEZON, CROISET, and PERIER; Croiset boasted that he had killed for his own Share five hundred; Pezon, a Butcher by Trade, having been sent for by Charles on the 5th of September, was asked, whether there were some Hugonots still alive at Paris? his answer was, That he had drowned one hundred and twenty of them the Night before, and that he had a like number of them for the next Night's Sport; whereupon Charles fell a laughing heartily, and bid him not fail. Another Particular is, that amongst that vast Number of Slain, only two offered to make any Resistance, viz. Guerchi, Standard-Bearer to the Admiral; and Tiverni an Attorney. This last having consumed his Powder and Bullets, and melted his Pewter, when he saw that the Murtherers had got into his House, he stood behind the Door at the lower end of the Alley that went to the Hall, where he had put a large piece of Timber, whereby the said Door opened only half-way, there he waited for the Murtherers, who had a mind to come that way and killed many; but at last, seeing himself overpowered by their numbers, and that he was no longer in a condition to resist, after having taken his last leave of his Wife, and given his blessing to his Children, he took his Shield with a short Sword, and came into the Hall amongst the Murderers, who stabbed him on the spot. Another Particular was that of the White-thorn in the Church-yard of the Innocents that blossomed the Day after Bartholomew's Day; the Rumour of it being spread about the City, People of all Ranks flocked thither in so great numbers, that they were obliged to set Guards thereabouts: they began to cry out, a Miracle; and to ring the Bells in token of Joy. The Rabble excited by that, taking

king

king it for a Demonſtration of God's Approbation of their doings, grew more fierce than
before, and fell with greater fury upon the
Hugonots.　But the Reformed ſaid, that that
White-thorn had bloſſomed upon the Ground
of the Innocents murdered, not of the Murderers.　One of them publiſhed the following
Epigram upon that Subject ;

ÆTerni CHRISTVS ſoboles æterna parentis,
　In cruce pro nobis Spinea ſerta tulit,
Quæ cum PARRYSIA CÆSORVM nuper in urbe
　Chriſtiadum rurſus ſanguine ſparſa forent,
Emiſere ſuos alieno tempore flores :
　Hinc quam fœcundus ſit cruor iſte, nata ;
Qui reliquis herbis rabido morientibus æſtu,
　Germinat, & cœlo ſemina digna movet.

Floreſcant ſpinæ, caveant ſibi Lilia,　rarò
　Lilia ſub ſpinis ſurgere læta ſolent.

The Catholicks and the Reformed ſtrove to
ſhew their wit by ſeveral ſmall Poems, both
upon the Admiral, and upon the Maſſacre in
general ; a few whereof I ſhall tranſcribe here.
　Theſe two Verſes were written upon the Doors
of the Admiral's Houſe,

Qui ter Mavortem ſumptis patefecerat armis,
　Tertia pax Nudum perfidioſa necat.

Several Copies of his Picture were drawn
at his own Friends expence, and ſent to ſeveral Proteſtant Princes, eſpecially to the Elector
Palatine, who had a very great value for him,
and this Diſtich was at the bottom of it.

Talis erat quondam vultu Collignius Heros,
　Quem verè illuſtrem vitaque morſque facit.

　　　　　　　　　　　　　　　　　　The

The following Diftich is Pafquier's, who makes a frigid allufion to Colligny's Name, and his being hang'd after his Death.

> Sic fatis placuit, nomen & omen ut effet
> Igneus in vitâ, Ligneus interitu.

On Bartholomew's-day, by another Hand.

> On difoit, *dangereux comme fête d'Apotres,*
> Ce que les Huguenots eftimoient un abus,
> Mais St. Barthelemy pour luy & pour les autres
> Fit le proverbe vray, donc qu'on n'en doute plus.

On the Maffacres.

> GALLIA Maⅽtatrix, Lanius Rex, dira Macellum
> LUTETIA ; O noftri temporis opprobrium !

Unto France :

> Rex puer eft, Proceres fcelerati, Regia fallax,
> Fœdifragi Cives, urbs laniena tua eft.
> Crudelis, nec jura timens, ac fœdera rumpens.
> Eft benè de regno GALLIA Stulta tuo.

> Quæ necat Innocuos violato fœdere natos
> GALLIA, non mater, fed truculenta lupa eft.

I might add, the providential Prefervation of Merlin, Chaplain to the Admiral, who being concealed in a heap of Straw, a Hen came every day and laid an Egg in his hand ; and of another of the Admiral's Servants, who fell afleep in his Concealment for feveral days, and did not awake till Merlin, finding an opportunity, improved it and awakened his Companion. But I can't warrant the truth of neither.

XI. Charles was very careful to fend Embaffadors Extraordinary every where, and to hire fome mercenary Pens for making his Apology. His

His Embaſſadors in Ordinary were much puzzled at the new Orders they received from him, to own the Fact, ſeeing that two or three days before, they had declared in his own name to the Courts where they reſided, that what had happened at *Paris* had been done, not only without his Conſent, but even without his Knowledge, and they knew not how to recant. His Apologies met with different Succeſs, according to the different Temper and Intereſt of the Princes and States who heard or read them ; ſome approved of the Fact, others deteſted it, and others, either out of fear, or out of policy, ſeemed to be indifferent about it. In Spain, Philip II. received the news with tranſports of Joy ; Charles had charged his Embaſſadors to that Prince, to tell him, that he hoped he would forgive him whatever he had done for a Year or two, which had a ſhew of Hoſtility, ſeeing that he had been obliged to do it, in order to conceal the better his real deſigns ; which forgiveneſs was readily granted, and with great applauſe, and that Tragedy was repreſented before the King under the Title of THE TRIUMPH OF THE MILITANT CHURCH.

At Rome, the Cardinal of Lorrain received the tidings of it with ſo great a Satisfaction, that he preſented the Meſſenger with a Gift of a thouſand Crowns, and the Pope went in Proceſſion with the College of Cardinals, &c. into ſeveral Churches, eſpecially that of St. Lewis.

But the Emperor Maximilian II. Father-in-Law to Charles, received the News with the utmoſt concern, and deteſted the Fact as abominable ; he wrote upon that Subject to Lazarus Schwend, which Letter is to be found in the Abridgment of Brandt's Hiſtory of the Reformation

formation in the *Low Countries*, Vol. I. Book XI. pag. 251.

Several Proteſtant Princes of Germany, eſpecially the Elector of Palatine, ſhewed the like deteſtation ; and all the Rhetorick of Bellievre, French Embaſſador in Switzerland, nor the Libels of the baſe Carpenter, hindered not the *Proteſtant Cantons* from receiving with a ſincere and cordial affection the poor diſtreſſed that took refuge amongſt them.

The Rhetorick of Montluc, Biſhop of *Valence*, helped with Pibrac's and Bazin's, and eſpecially with the French Gold, was more perſuaſive amongſt the Polanders. The Reformed being at that time much more numerous and powerful in that Country than they have been ſince, it was to be feared, leſt the Negociations of the French Embaſſadors for having the Crown of Poland ſet upon the Duke of Anjou's Head, ſhould miſcarry ; as they would for certain, had not the Electors been bribed, or had they been thoroughly informed of the truth of the matter. Therefore Valence and his Collegues ſeeing that they could not deny the fact, neglected nothing for making it appear an Act of Juſtice, and not a perfidious Act of Cruelty.

But Queen Elizabeth (I am ſorry to be obliged to own a ſad truth) quite forgetting herſelf on this occaſion, not only ſhe did not aſſiſt the diſtreſſed at *Rochelle* and *Sancerre*, as ſhe could have done very eaſily, but ſhe did indirectly approve of the fact : for though her Embaſſador at Paris had been affronted, and forced to deliver up the good old Briquemaut, after he had been concealed for three days in his Houſe, where he had taken Sanctuary, though Charles had ſolemnly declared, that whatever had been

done

Charles
IX.
1572.
Pope Gre-
gory XIII.

done at Paris, had been done by his special Command, from whence she ought to infer, that the Violence offered to her Embassador, had been offered by his orders; nevertheless, at that very time, she accepted to stand Godmother to the young Princess, Daughter to Charles, born the very same day that Briquemaut and Cavagnes were executed. Was it out of Principle of Religion that our Queen of England took such a Step? No sure, I hope that she was too good a Protestant to approve of the superstitious Ceremonies used in the Baptism of the Roman Church, and that she had no mind at all to engage herself to take care the Princess should be trained up in the Roman Communion. Was it out of Policy? I don't think it so, no good could accrue to her from it. For my part, I believe that she was frightened out of her Wits, and that being not thoroughly informed how the matter stood, knowing not what would be the end of such a dreadful Execution, she thought that her best course was to be careful not to disoblige, at that time, the common Enemy of the Protestants. But no more of this.

HUMANUM EST ERRARE.

Effects of those Cru-elties upon Charles.

XII. However sweet and pleasant that cruel Satisfaction was to Charles's Palate for the present, it turned into a Gall in his Stomach immediately after; the Parliament of Paris's Approbation, the Pope and the King of Spain's Applauses and big Encomiums, the Medals struck in order to perpetuate the memory of it, nothing could divert that Prince from his melancholy; he was henceforward continually tormented with the horror of a guilty Conscience, which the effusion of so much innocent Blood did justly raise in him, and was frequently heard to cry; *Ah, my poor Subjects! What had you done?*

*done? And what have I done? But I was forced
to it.* He was often troubled with Visions,
and the hearing of Voices in the Air. I shall
single out two Instances related by D'Aubigné,
Tom. II. Book I. ch. VI. he quotes for his
Voucher, no less Authority than King Henry
IV. and said expressly, that that Prince had
told them many times, that he had been an
eye-witness of the fact, and that he never related it without feeling and showing unto them
his hairs bristling.

,, Eight days, says he, after the Massacre,
,, came a vast quantity of Crows, some perch-
,, ing, and others croking over the great Pa-
,, villion of the Louvre ; the great noise they
,, made excited every one's curiosity to see what
,, was the matter, and the Ladies imparted their
,, fright to the King. The same Night, two
,, hours after he was in bed, having started out
,, of his sleep, he jumped out of his Bed, caused
,, all the Gentlemen of his Bedchamber to do
,, the same, and sent for his Brother-in-Law
,, the King of Navarr, for hearing the dread-
,, ful noise that was in the Air, as it were, of
,, many Voices together crying, sighing, groan-
,, ing and howling, and amongst them some
,, furiously threatning, cursing and blaspheming,
,, just as in the first night of the Massacre. Their
,, tunes were so distinct and articulate, that the
,, King thinking that some new Massacre was
,, perpetrating upon the Montmorencians, sent
,, for his Guards, that they might go into the City
,, and hinder the murder ; but being come back,
,, they said, that every thing was quiet in the
,, City, only the Skies were in a terrible agi-
,, tation : whereupon the King was more trou-
,, bled than before, especially because that noise

„ laſted for ſeven nights, and began always at
„ the ſame hour.„

The Maſſacre was a laſting Torment for the
King to his very laſt breath, as we ſhall ſay
in its proper place, his looks and countenance
were quite altered, and he grew much more
four than before, his Mother and bloody Counſellors became to him the Objects of his utmoſt
hatred ; what added to his ſorrow was, that
he ſaw himſelf deceived in his expectation, for
he had been made to believe, that the deſtruction of the Admiral, and the chief of that Party would be the end of all diviſions, ſtruggles and
confuſions in his Kingdom, and he ſaw himſelf
much miſtaken in that reſpect, far from having
conquered that Hydra, as it was repreſented in
one of thoſe flattering Medals ſtruck upon that
Event, to keep myſelf to that alluſion, not ſeven, but a hundred heads ſprung out from that he
had ſevered.

Indeed the Conſternation was general at firſt
amongſt the Reformed in the whole Kingdom ;
many, as above ſaid, forſook their Religion to
ſave their Lives, many ſubmitted themſelves patiently to the will and barbarities of their Murderers, making a Conſcience to defend their Lives
againſt theſe Butchers. But they were ſoon recovered from their Panick, and for one that had
appeared in the former Wars, there were ſix in
the next, that thought it their Duty to defend
their Lives againſt thoſe who ſought to deſtroy
them without the leaſt provocation, whatſoever
authority they pretended for it. It is what we are
next to conſider.

*Occurrences
of the five
laſt Months
of this Year.* Among other Subjects of perplexity, the Cities of Rochelle, Montauban, Sancerre, &c:
where the Reformed had fled for refuge, cauſed
a great uneaſineſs to the King. As to *Rochelle*,
Stroſſy

Stroffy and Poulin, alias Baron de la Garde, wrote to them in a very friendly manner, the better to surprize them, on the laft day of Auguft, offering them a Garrifon to guard them, and defiring them to fend a great quantity of Stores for the King's Navy. The Rochelefe anfwered on the 2d of September, that they did not want any Garrifon, being able to guard themfelves, and refolved to maintain their Privileges; that having no more Provifions than what they wanted for themfelves, they could not fpare any for the King's Navy. Montpefat Senefchal of *Poitou*, wrote likewife a long Letter defamatory againft the Admiral, and wherein he exhorted the Rochelefe to fubmit to the King's Mercy. But the Rochelefe fcorned to anfwer him. Three days after they endeavoured to mollify Stroffy by their Letters to him; wherein they did fet forth their Innocency; whereupon it happened, that many of his Troops profeffing the Reformed Religion, feeing that the intended War againft Spain had been but a Snare to deceive the Admiral, deferted him, and retired into *Rochelle*, where two fafting days were celebrated on the 9th and the 11th of September.

The King and his Council, feeing that Stroffy, La Garde, and others were not hearkened to, fent Biron, Great Mafter of the Artillery, for Governor of *Rochelle*, with orders to engage them by all fair words and means to receive him into their City; the King himfelf fent unto them a moft gracious Declaration, and Biron wrote likewife in a very friendly manner. Audevars, Steward to the Queen of Navarr, was charged with thefe Letters, with very ample Inftructions: He arrived at *Rochelle* on the 7th of September. But all his endeavours proved

fruitlefs,

fruitlefs ; for a few days after they anfwered, that they could not believe, that fuch a command of receiving Garrifon proceeded from the King. They appealed to his former Letters, efpecially that of the 25th of Auguft, whereby he loaded the Guifes and their Faction, with the odioufnefs of whatever had been done at *Paris*, and declared, that with great ado he himfelf had efcaped the danger in his Caftle of *Louvre*, and amidft his own Guards. They added, that they thought it impoffible for the King, that of his own accord, he would have cut his own Arms, and ftain with fo much innocent Blood the facred Nuptials of his own Sifter, &c. Then they vindicated the Admiral's Innocency, and defired to enjoy freely their ancient Privileges. They made fuch others like Remonftrances to Audevars, concerning their Religion, and the Squadron of La Garde, which they defired might be ordered to withdraw from their Coafts. Mean while Biron approached, and the Baron of La Garde began to threaten them openly, which obliged them to provide more carefully for their own Security.

On the 21ft of October, Biron fent a Letter unto them by Du Vigean, but they refufed to admit him into their City ; therefore he came with a fafe-conduct to *Tadon*, a Village in the Neighbourhood, and having no better Succefs than the former Meffengers, he went the next day to *Sigongnes*, three Leagues diftant from Tadon, where he ftayed that night, and was affaulted in his Bed by fome Soldiers of St. Stevens's Company, who broke open the Inn, killed three of his Servants, wounded him, and carried away his Horfes and Baggage which they fold the next day to the beft bidder. That Breach of Faith caufed great Troubles at *Rochelle*,

Chelle, and Capt. Stevens and Guimeniere were obliged to leave the City. The Rochelese wrote to Biron for clearing themselves of the Fact, declaring that it had been done without their Knowledge, and begging that it should not be imputed unto them; they gave also Satisfaction to Du Vigean. All these submissions hindered them not from taking the necessary measures for their Preservation; having received notice, that they would soon be besieged by a strong Army; they sent new Messengers to the Count of Montgomery, the Vidame of Chartres, and other Lords Refugees in *England*, to desire their assistance.

The Deputies sailed from *Rochelle* in the night of the 25th of October. The War was almost openly declared against that City, for all those that were known to belong to it, were detained Prisoners, and put to ransom; all the Ships that were coming into their Harbour were stopped, and their Cargo belonging to the Rochelese seized and forfeited, and several other acts of Hostility made against them.

On the 7th of November, Baron de la Garde sent two Galleys on pretence of carrying some Letters to *Rochelle*, but indeed to *reconnoitre* the Haven; the next night Des Essars, elected General of the Rochelese, sent in pursuit of these two Galleys, one of whom was taken, an Engineer killed, and another taken prisoner. Not long after that a declaration of War against them was published in the King's Name.

But whereas he was still unwilling to deal with his Reformed Subjects in so open a manner, and had chose rather to catch them by some treachery, he tried another Method.

After the surrender of Mons, La Noüe knowing not what course to take, for he found no security if he went back to *France*, and he was

become

become ufelefs to the Prince of Orange in the *Low Countries*, becaufe he was ingaged by one of the Capitulation Articles, not to carry Arms againft the King of *Spain* for a Year, while he was in that perplexity, the Duke of Longueville, Governor of *Picardy*, who had a very great value for him, fent him word that he fhould be very welcome in his Government, which Offer La Noüe accepted. At the fame time, the Rochelefe thinking he was ftill in *Flanders*, fent him a Meffenger, intreating him earneftly to help them with his Counfels, in their fad circumftance for defending the Glory of God and the Remainders of his Church. But the Duke of Longueville taking him to be the fitteft Man for reducing the Rochelefe to the King's Terms, becaufe of the great Intereft he had amongft them, and the great Truft they repofed in him, brought him to *Paris*, and prefented him to the King, who received him very gracioufly. Then, by his orders, he went to the Count of Retz, where he conferred with his Majefty; who, after having praifed his Vertue and Modefty, and excufed by many bad arguments the late Maffacre, he exhorted him to imploy himfelf for pacifying the troubles that were arifing in the Kingdom, efpecially at *Rochelle*; he fpared no promifes to give them full fatisfaction if they fubmitted; and as to him, he would acknowledge that fervice by favours of all kinds, and joining Deeds to his Words, he gave him the Replevy of Telligny his Brother-in-Law's Eftate and Goods, which he reftored to his own Family.

La Noüe was much puzzled at this the King's Propofition; at firft he excufed himfelf, faying, that he was unfit for fuch a Commiffion; but at laft, feeing himfelf forced to yield to the King's Command, he told his Majesty, *that he would obey, provided he should not be made a Tool for betraying the Rochelese, and that he should not be obliged to do any thing against his Honour, which was dearer to him than his own Life*; which the King promised with many Oaths (†).

It muft be owned, that a nicer Commiffion could never be given to an honeft Man than that, whereby he was obliged to manage the Intereft of a Prince whofe hands were ftill ftained with the Blood of thofe of his own Party, Profeffors of the fame Religion, to manage, I fay, the faid Intereft with thofe whom he loved intirely, and who had fo many juft reafons of miftrufting the King's Word, yea, his moft folemn Oaths: neverthelefs, he difcharged that Commiffion with fuch circumfpection, that both Parties were generally fatisfied with his Conduct.

However, Abbot Gadagne having been joined unto him, rather for a Spy of his actions and words, than for any thing elfe, they fet out from *Paris* by the latter end of October, they conferred with the Marfhal of Biron, who was in the neighbouring of *Rochelle*, and then with a Minifter, whom La Noüe met upon the road, and whom he fent with one Tecles, to notify his coming and Commiffion to the *Rochelefe*, and to have a Pafs for himfelf and Gadagne.

The Rochelefe were much furprized at this News; and having affembled the Council, the Votes were divided, fome for receiving him, and hearing what he had to fay; and others for not receiving him, nor hearing any thing

Gg 4 from

(†). Vie de François de La Noüe, p. 70, 71, 72. Thuan. lib. liii. p. 851.

from him. At laſt, after ſeveral debates, they came to this Reſolution, to appoint a place out of the City, whither La Noüe ſhould repair with Gadagne and his Attendants, at the time he would appoint himſelf, and that their Deputies ſhould hear what he had to ſay, and make their report of it to the City's Council, without entering into any conference with him upon that Subject.

Accordingly they let him know by a Letter, that he might come to *Tadon* upon the day he would appoint himſelf, and ſhould met there their Deputies. He came on the 19th of November, and met with a very cold reception from the Deputies. After having told them in few Words, how it came to paſs that he met them then with ſuch a Character, as Deputee from the King, he ſhewed his Commiſſion, and concluded, by exhorting them to accept of the terms tendered unto them by their Majeſties, provided they ſhould have good Security for the ſtrict performance of what was promiſed and offered.

The Deputies having heard the Propoſitions, treated La Noüe in a very odd manner. They told him, *that they had been put in hopes of meeting La Noüe at Tadon, but that they had been deceived, and that they were going to make their Report to their Principals;* and feigned to take their leave of him. But La Noüe without being moved, ſaid to them, *How ſo, Gentlemen, don't you know me any more? Have you ſo ſoon forgot ſo many things that we have done together for our common preſervation?* They replied, *Yes, we do remember very well that few Years ago, a certain Nobleman, named La Noüe, did many great and glorious feats for the defence of the Truth of the Goſpel, and our own Preſerva-*
tion,

BOOK V. *Reformed Churches in* FRANCE. 457

Charles
IX.
1572.
Pope Gre-
gory XIII.

tion, the remembrance whereof will be always deeply rooted in our Hearts. But as for you, we do not take you for that La Noüe. Indeed you have some of his Features, and the same Shape as he; but your Voice and Councils are so different from his, that you cannot be the same Man. In a word, La Noüe would never have suffered himself to be bribed by the promises of the Court for perswading us to deliver ourselves into the hands of the Persecutors of Truth, and the Murderers of our Brethren. That however, they would make their Report to the City's Council. And so they went away.

How provoking soever that Speech was in it self, La Noüe suffered it patiently, without the least alteration in his Countenance; he was very glad that Gadagne had been present at it; for if the Negociation had not the desired Success, he might certify, that he could not be answerable for it.

At last, with great ado, he was admitted into the City, where the Council, after having answered his Propositions, put to his choice one of these three Conditions; either to live amongst them as a private Person, upon the publick Charge; or to take upon him the Command of their Forces, and the Direction of their Affairs; or if he had a mind to go over to England, they would fit out a Ship for him, for that purpose. He thanked them for their kindness, and having taken a little time to consider, and to consult with Gadagne, he accepted of the Command, as being more agreeable to his Quality, Courage, and former way of living, and as furnishing him with better opportunities to engage the Rochelese to hearken to the propositions of Peace, as he let it be known to his Majesty. Therefore having been elected
General,

General, by the unanimous confent of the Nobility, Troops, and Citizens, he came into the
City on the 27th of November, and took his
Seat in that quality in the Council. His Soul
was in the greatest anxieties, thinking how
difficult it was for him to behave himself in
fuch a manner, as not to afford any fufpicion
against him, either of betraying the Rochelefe,
or of not being faithful to the King. But his
Integrity was fuch, and every one had fo good
opinion of his honefty, that no body ever mif-
conftrued either his deeds or words. Therefore
as long as he ftayed at *Rochelle*, though he
never fpared himfelf, and did whatever the Rochelefe could have expected from him at any
other time, yet he was not deemed by the
King to have done any thing unworthy of himfelf, or contrary to what he had promifed him;
and though afterwards he forfook the Rochelefe, when he faw that all his endeavours for
bringing them to hearken to fome reafonable agreement, as he thought, proved needlefs, yet he was
not deemed by the Rochelefe to be a Deferter
and a Traitor, but which is almoft incredible,
and without Example, he enjoyed the good opinion of both the King and the Rochelefe (a).

The hopes of a Pacification which had been
conceived, having been vanifhed away, a general Review of the King's Forces in that Country was made on the 4th of December, and
there were no more than 18 Companies of Foot
under Strozzi's Command, and feven Cornets;
thefe having held a Council of War, they fettled the order of the attack in the following
manner. Biron named by the King Governor
of *La Rochelle*, was to draw near the City with
the Strozzians and the Cannon, while the Count

of

(a) Eidem ibidem.

Lude, Governor of Poitou, should make an attempt upon *Marans* a Strong-Hold of the Rochelese.

Capt. Norman commanded in that place with three Regiments of Foot and fifty Horse, and seeing that he could not withstand the Enemy, he marched out, in order to retreat into *La Rochelle*. But having met Biron in his way, he retired into *Grimaudiere-Castle*, strong enough by its situation to prevent a surprize. There he was summoned by a Trumpet to surrender, which having refused to do, he was attacked, and the Cannon being levelled, the Tower before the Gate was destroyed. But the night coming upon that, Norman improved that opportunity for making his retreat through the Marshes. Virolet that came with him, having refused to follow him, was taken with his Horse the next Morning; and not being able to pay his Ransom, he forsook the Rochelese's Service, and took party with the Royalists.

D'Anguilliers had been sollicited by Letters from the King about the middle of November to forsake the Rochelese and retire to his own House, there to live peaceably under the benefit of the King's Edicts. These Letters being come too late, he could not answer, till about the middle of December, which he did with a very great freedom, setting forth, that he had been forced by necessity to come into that City, to provide for his own security, and enjoy the free exercise of that Religion, the Profession whereof the King had solemnly sworn to maintain, and neverthelefs, without any regard for his Oath, he had forbidden it afterwards; therefore he desires the King not to take amiss, if he don't obey his orders, and if he stays in the City, till proper security has been

been given for their Lives, and the free Profession of their Religion.

Biron removed his Camp and came to *St. Andrew*, three Miles distant from the City, where he put sixty Cannon, and every thing else necessary for a long Siege. Strozzi advanced likewise to *Pileboreau*, a Mile off the City. Mean while, the Rochelese were very careful to get in their Provisions, and whereas the Season had been very fair, they got into the City 25000 Hogsheads of Wine, and a small quantity of Corn, because they could get no more. There was in the City at the beginning of the Siege about a thousand Soldiers, with about 1800 Inhabitants fit for Service; the most renowned amongst the Gentry of Poitou, that took refuge in it, were Roche-Esnard, Les Essarts, Champagné, Le Chaillou, and La Musse: The best Captains of the City were Norman, Sauvage, La Salle, Vaudorne, and Lis. There was nine either Cannons or Culverines, thirty-eight Field-Pieces, about eighty Fauconets, eight other Engines, twenty thousand pounds of Powder, besides that which the Mills afforded continually. Such was the condition of the City when the Inhabitants resolved to withstand a Siege: It began under the Mayoralty of James Henry, a Man of great Prudence and Sagacity in the management of Affairs, and of a stout Resolution; he was assisted by Salbert, and both found means to reconcile the disputes of the Nobles with the Commoners concerning the Command. The remaining part of December there was several Skirmishes, wherein the loss of the Rochelese was but inconsiderable, one excepted, wherein Capt. Flojeac, a Saintongese was desperately wounded, and died at *Rochelle*. Before we proceed any
further,

further, we muſt confider what was a doing at
Sancerre, and in other parts of the Kingdom.

Sancerre, a Town in the *Berry*, had belonged in the former times to one Rogers, Biſhop
of *Beauvais*, and was devolved in the Year
1004 to one Odon, Count of Champaign, as
a Compenſation for the County of Beauvais ;
and by Succeſſion, it came into the illuſtrious
Houſe of De Bueil, who became by that means
Counts of *Sancerre* (*b*).

That Town lies about half a Mile off the
Loire, and is ſtrong enough by its ſituation, its
Walls were at that time very indifferent. The
Reformed Religion had been introduced early in
that Town ; and moſt part of its Inhabitants made
a publick Profeſſion of it : It had withſtood a
Siege in the laſt War, and though it was only defended by the Inhabitants under the command of two Attorneys, yet after ſeveral Aſſaults
for ſix Weeks together, La Chaſtre was obliged to defiſt and to raiſe the Siege.

Now at the time of the Maſſacre, it became
a place of Refuge for many Reformed eſcaped
from *Bourges*, *Orleans*, and other Places, and
were very kindly received, and entertained by
the Inhabitants, which being underſtood at Court,
orders were ſent unto them on the 3d of September, to receive for their Commandant in the
Town and in the Caſtle, whomſoever La Chaſtre, Governor of *Berry* ſhould think proper to
name, with as many Troops as he would be
pleaſed to ſend ; whereto having refuſed to comply, they were ſurrounded at the beginning of
October, by ſome Garriſons in the neighbourhood which began to moleſt them ; but they
made ſuch a brave ſally upon them, that, after having forced their barricadoes, they killed
about

(*b*) Thuan. lib. lv. p. 915.

about forty-five of them, took some Prisoners; and put the rest to flight; by these means they were at rest for a few days. But it happened, that Cadaillet, one of the King's Valet de Chambre and Hunters, and a Dependant of the Count of *Sancerre*, very well known in the Town, was sent to confer with them. He behaved himself as a cunning Courtier, for he sowed division amongst those which were formerly strictly united together, from whence great Troubles and Confusions ensued in the Town, some being willing that Fontaines, sent to be their Commandant, should be admitted, and others not.

On the 9th of November, Fontaines's Brother surprized the Castle by the Intelligence of some Inhabitants, who shut themselves up in it with him; but by the stout Resolution of the other Inhabitants, especially of the Reformed, he was forced to march out of it twenty four hours after, just as Fontaines arrived with a Reinforcement, that obliged the Sancerrese to be more vigilant. They had about six hundred and fifty men of the Militia, with very few regular Troops, under the command of Martignon, Pilard, Martinat, La Fleur, Buisson, Dorival, and other Captains or Lieutenants, all of them under the Command of Andrew Johanneau, Bailiff of *Sancerre*; besides that, they had 150 Husbandmen, which were of very great service with their Slings during the Siege, as well as the Women, who carried themselves with the greatest bravery. But the Bailiff Johanneau was so self-conceited, that not believing that the Town would ever have been besieged, at least as long as *La Rochelle* subsisted, neglected all the necessary Preparations for a Siege, took no care for having a good Store of Victuals, or for repairing the Fortifications, and having the place cleaned

of

of whatever could be detrimental to it ; by which wilful neglect, the Inhabitants saw themselves exposed to the greatest inconveniences, but especially to the most dreadful Famine, scarce to be parallelled with any other mentioned in the ancient or modern History. The relation whereof comes of course amongst the events of next Year (c).

Besides *La Rochelle* and *Sancerre*, several other places in *Guienn, High and Low Languedoc,* and *Dauphiné*, came to a Resolution to repulse force by force. In *Guienn*, De Resniers above-mentioned, with Serignac, Brother to the Lord of Terride, Moulins, and some others of the prime Nobility in that Country, who had just escaped the danger, came to *Montauban*, attended with about thirty seven either Cuirassiers, or other Horsemen, on the beginning of September, in order to excite the Inhabitants to take up arms; but they did not meet with the reception they expected : for the Viscounts of Paulin and Montclair, who had been preserved by the favour of the Count de Villars, Successor to Coligny in the charge of great Admiral of France, having been persuaded by their Benefactor, were arrived before at *Montauban*, and had worked such a fright upon the minds of the Inhabitants, that they were quite dispirited, and refused to hearken to the instances of Resniers, &c. especially, when they heard that Montluc's great black Standard, and the Gendarmes of Fontenille and Sainctorens, with two Companies of Arquebusiers on horseback, were in full march. Then Resniers and his Company unwilling to remain in a City quite disheartned, took to the Fields, knowing

(c) Thuan. lib. 53 and 55. D'Aubigné Tom. II. liv. I. ch. 9. Recueil des choses Memorables arrivées en France sous Henry II. —— Henry IV. p. 444. — 452.

knowing not where to retreat. Being arrived at a place, where he was obliged to cross the Water, he saw Fontenille with his Troops coming after him. The place was so narrow, that it was impossible for him to drawback, or to avoid the fight; he resolved upon this last, and having divided his small Troop, which he encouraged by his example, as by his words, and especially by an earnest Prayer to God, which he made *ex tempore,* he assaulted the Enemy with such bravery, and wonderful success, that he took the five Standards, killed eighty Men upon the spot, took fifty Gentlemen Prisoners, and routed the rest; which done, he came back to the same place where he had offered up his Prayers to God, and gave him thanks for his Deliverance. Then with great ado, he led his Prisoners to *Montauban,* the Inhabitants whereof seeing that 390 Men had been broken and routed by 37, they were prevailed upon to defend their Estates, Liberties and Lives.

The Fame of this glorious feat being soon spread abroad, several Lords and Gentlemen joined with Resnier, and being assembled at *Montauban,* they sent for advice to *Rochelle,* and in the *High Languedoc,* and a strict union was formed between *Rochelle, Montauban* and *Nismes,* for their mutual defence. Strengthened by that union, Resnier seized upon *Villemur* upon the *Tar, Cauffade,* and *Bioulle.* Negrepelisse, and several other places in the Country of *Rouergue; Puylaurens,* and others in that of *Lauraguez; Realmont,* and others in that of *Albigeois; Mazeres,* and another in that of *Foix,* surrendered themselves. The Viscount of Gourdon took *Soillac* in *Quercy,* and *Cadenat,* then a very strong place; Serignac took *Terride,* which

was

was in debate between him and his Brother; *Buzet* near *Thoulouse* was taken by Efcalado, and the Inhabitants put to the Sword. The Reformed made fuch, and fome other exploits in *Guienn*, in a very fhort time.

Then they thought proper to fettle an order amongft themfelves; for which purpofe they held an Affembly at *Realmont*, wherein it was unanimoufly agreed to divide the Provinces in fix Parts, under fix Commanders. The Vifcount of Gourdon in *Quercy*; Serignac in the Country beyond *Garonne*; Vifcount Paulin in *Lauraguez*; Vifcount of Panat in *Rouërgue*; Vifcount of Caumont in the County of *Foix* and *Bigorre*: Villemur and other places conquered by Refnier, remained under his Command. Furthermore it was agreed, that if any one of them wanted the affiftance of any of the others, they fhould be obliged to march without delay, and with all their Forces to his relief; and for avoiding all occafion of Jealoufy, it was likewife agreed, that he, who fhould fend for fuccour, fhould command in his Diftrict, and that others fhould be obliged to obey him. After thefe Regulations, every one went to his own Diftrict, and made feveral exploits, which come under the next Year's Events (*d*).

The Confternation was fuch in Languedoc immediately after the Maffacre, that many did not think of defending themfelves, or of avoiding by flight the fame Fate as their Brethren; they declaimed againft the injuftice of their own Party, and upon the neceffity of obeying the King's, even the wickedeft, efpecially the prefent King, fince he was Major: They even feigned fome belief of the Confpiracy charged upon the late Admiral, and did not forget the

(*d*) Eid. ibid.

List of the monstrous Vices wherein the Reformed had plunged themselves, by the Licentiousness of the former Wars ; whereupon they
said, That in the First they had behaved themselves like Angels ; in the Second like Men ;
but in the Third like incarnate Devils : To all
which they added, That they were not in a
Condition to resist, being deprived of their best
Captains, and of all other Means, but especially of Money.

Such and other like Reasons as fear inspired
them, they alledged for excusing themselves
from entering into any Confederacy for their
mutual defence ; and had they been treated by
their Enemies with less Cruelty, it is not likely that they ever would have altered their first
Resolution. But when they saw themselves deceived in their expectation, and that their submission and humility, far from daunting the ferocity of their Enemies, were made use of
for ruining them with the greater ease ; when
they saw that *Castres*, and some other Places,
which had willingly received Garrisons, had been
treated as if they had been taken by Storm ;
then they thought it was high time to provide
for themselves ; and the examples of *La Rochelle*
and *Sancerre*, awakened them, and revived their
dejected Spirits.

Millaud armed at the same time as *Montauban*, *Nîmes*, and *Privats* in the *Lower Languedoc* followed that Example, having refused to
receive Garrison ; *Anduse* in the *Cevennes*, and
Le Pouzin in the *Vivaretz*, *Aubenas*, *Villeneuve*,
Mirabel, and several other small Towns, did the
same, as soon as they understood that Damville,
Governor of *Languedoc* was coming. Gremian
took *Sommieres* by Intelligence with the Inhabitants,

bitants, and made himself Master of the Castle by routing the Garrison that kept in it.

The Inhabitants of *Chelar* in *Vivaretz* seized upon their Castle, during the absence of the Governor, after an extraordinary manner. For La Mothe, the Governour, thinking that there was nothing to fear from People disheartened and unarmed, was gone for diversion sake to pay a visit to Des Gordes, Governour of Dauphiné, then at *Valence*, where he stayed for some days. It happened, that while he was bragging at Table, that the Castle of Chelar was impregnable, (and indeed it was one of the strongest and the best fortified in all the Kingdom) a Messenger came to let him know, that the Reformed had taken possession of it. How so? says he in amaze, unless they are come under the ground, or have fled over the tops of the Walls, that is impossible. Nevertheless he did guess more right and sure than he thought. For they were come from the Town into the Castle through a Passage under ground, known but by few of the Inhabitants. In the last Civil War that Town having been besieged by La Torrette, they had made that Passage, to the end, that if the Town was taken, they might retire safe into the Castle ; but whereas La Torrette had been obliged to raise the Siege, the said Passage had been of no use till now. It had its entrance in a Cellar belonging to one of the Inhabitants, and was known only to six Persons. Now, whereas the Chelarians, who for the most part professed the Reformed Religion, saw themselves exposed to the outrages of the Garrison, who used them very ill, forcing them with Cudgels to go to Mass, and that the said Garrison increased every day, and threatened them with utter Destruction, they opened that Passage in the Night-time, came into

the

Charles
IX.
1572.
Pope Gre-
goryXIII.

the Caftle, broke open the Gate, killed all thofe who had a mind to refift, made the reft Prifoners, and being intirely Mafters of the faid Caftle, they fortified it in fuch a manner, and kept it fo carefully, that it was impoffible afterwards to get it out of their hands (*e*).

Villeneuve was taken by the Reformed that came into it through the common Sewer, that went into the Town-Ditches, almoft in the fame manner as *Nimes* had been taken in the laft War, by fawing a great Iron Grate at the foot of the Wall (*f*).

Damville being arrived in Languedoc, took the field with an Army of ten thoufand Foot and fix Companies of Horfe, with fourteen Cannons. He made a vain attempt upon *Uzes*, but was received in *Calviffon* and *St. Geniers*, and judging rightly by the countenance of thofe of *Nifmes*, who had burned their Suburbs, that they had a mind to defend themfelves, he went and laid Siege to *Sommieres* ; the Succefs whereof we fhall relate in the next Year.

In *Dauphiné*, every thing was quiet enough for the remaining part of this Year, by the mild and prudent Management of Gordes, Deputy-Governour thereof ; and Montbrun remaining concealed amongft his Friends, there was no commotion in that Province, till the beginning of the next Year.

The following are fome particular Events of the four laft Months.

As foon as the Pope heard of the Maffacre, he fent in all hafte Cardinal Des Urfins to congratulate the King upon that account, and at the fame time to engage him to publifh the Council of *Trent* ; for Cardinal *de Lorraine* had given the Pope to underftand, that the Reformed had

hindered

(*e*) Dinoth. Hift. lib. 5. p. 375. (*f*) Idem, p. 376.

indered the King from receiving the said Coun- Charles
il ; which obstacle being removed by the Mas- IX.
acre of the most considerable amongst them, 1572.
nd the damp put upon every one's Spirits by Pope Gre-
> dreadful an Execution, the King would certain- gory XIII.
y comply with his Holiness's desires.

But the Legate found himself much mistaken
n his Expectations ; having stayed some time
.t *Avignon*, he was amazed when he came into
France, that what was extolled at *Rome* with the
biggest encomiums, was generally detested in
France, even by the Catholicks themselves, who
had any sense of Honour ; nay, it was consulted
at Court, whether the King should admit the
Legate, or excuse himself from conferring with
him : but having considered, that such a refusal
would avail very little with the Reformed, and
be very offensive to the Pope, it was resolved
to admit him. In the mean time, by Morvillier's advice, the Legate was desired to speak
very soberly and sparingly of what was past ;
to which request he paid very little regard : For
being arrived at *Lyons*, where he was received
with the usual Ceremonies, he highly commended the Fidelity of the Citizens, and especially
of BOYDON, that cruel and infamous Murderer,
whom he publickly absolved ; he extolled likewife, in publick and in private, the King's great
prudence, patience, and magnanimity in the management of that base and barbarous Execution.
He arrived at *Paris*, and made his publick Entry into that City on the 23d of November,
and took his Lodging in the Bishop's Palace.
In all the Audiences he had of the King, he
insisted warmly upon the reception of the Council of *Trent*, which he said was suspended in
France, to the great Scandal of all Christendom ;
then he added, that the present juncture was most

favourable for finishing that holy Work, whereby his Majesty would evince that his Zeal for
the Glory of God, and the propagating of true
Religion, and not any hatred or spirit of revenge against his Subjects, had been the only
motive of what had been done of late, &c. But
though the Court inclined much to grant his
Request, yet, for the King's Honour, it was
not thought proper to do it; for by his Letters Patents he had declared, that what had
been done at *Paris*, had been done, *not out of
hatred against the Reformed Religion*, but for preventing a Plot laid against him and the Royal
Family. Several Books and Pamphlets had been
published upon the same Topick by the Court's
Command. Therefore the Legate was dismissed
with abundance of fair Words and Promises. Then
to return the Pope his Civility, Angennes de
Rambouillet was sent Ambassador of the King
to Rome, and John de Durfort, Lord of Duras,
was sent upon the same Errand by the King of
Navarr (g).

Cardinal of Lorrain having compassed his ends,
by the destruction of his Enemies, returned from
Rome about the same time, skipping for Joy,
questioning not but he should bear the sway at
Court; but he was disappointed in that respect,
for Catherine stood in his way.

On the eighth of November was seen a new
Phenomenon in Heaven, which seemed to be
a Star, because it had the same brightness, a fixed
place, and appeared in the same altitude as the
Stars, and was moved by the same motion: It
cut the Figure of a Lozenge, with the thigh
and breast of that Constellation commonly called
Caffiopæa At the beginning it appeared to be
of

(g) Thuan. lib. 54. p. 879, 880.

f the same magnitude as Jupiter; but it decreased by degrees, and disappeared after 18 Months (b).

An Epidemical Distemper raged in France for a long while, and began to be known only in November; it went by the name of the CHOLICK OF POITOU, because it raged especially in that Country: it caused violent Contorsions to the Patient, and disjointed his Members. It is said, that the same Distemper had afflicted the City of *Rome* in the fifth Century. FRANCIS CITOIS published a Collection of Observations made upon that by several of the most learned Physicians of Poitou.

Another dreadful Massacre was upon the point of being perpetrated at *Paris*, during the King's absence; he was gone to conduct his Sister, the Duchess of *Lorrain* to the Frontiers. The Bastard of *Angoulême*, one of the most execrable Men in the Kingdom, plotted with some others of the same kidney with him, to murder whatever had escaped from the last Massacre; they appointed a day for the Execution, they set a cross, as a mark, upon the suspected Houses of the richest; every thing was ready, when some of the Conspirators bragged, that in a short time the remainder of that heretical Plague would be intirely cut off. This, joined with these unusual marks upon the Door of the Houses of the Richest, obliged the Presidents of the Parliament to wait upon the Duke of Nevers, whom the King had named Governor of the City; they told him what they had heard and seen, and desired him to provide against any new Commotion. It happened very luckily, that a little before the appointed time, two of the Conspirators, the most intimate with *Angoulême*, were so bold as to go to the Duke of Nevers, and with an unparallelled

H h 4

(b) Thuan. Ibid.

lelled Impudence, affirming, that the King had ordered them to extirpate utterly the Hugonots which were refident in *Paris.* But the Duke told them, that till he fhould be better informed of the King's Pleafure, they fhould remain Prifoners, and they were brought to Jail, whereby the Murderers were frightened, and the Execution prevented (i)

The moft part of the Year 1573, was taken up with the Sieges of *La Rochelle, Sancerre,* and fome inconfiderable Places in Languedoc, and the Ceremonies of the Duke of Anjou's Election to the Crown of *Poland,* and of his departing for that Country.

Though the Hoftilities had begun in feveral Places fome Weeks before the latter end of laft Year, neverthelefs, feeing that the Royal Armies took the Field only at the beginning of this, we fhall likewife begin with it the fourth Civil War.

It would be needlefs to juftify the taking up of arms by the Reformed on this occafion, none but dull Slaves can blame them, feeing what ufe Charles had made of late of his Treaties, Promifes and Oaths, they would have been Self-murderers, had they not endeavoured to preferve their Lives by refiftance. Therefore without dwelling any longer upon that fubject, let us confider the principal Occurrences of this Year: I don't intend to enter into all the particulars of any of the Sieges, but only to make fome general Obfervations, which may be fufficient to inform the Reader.

The King had three Armies in the Field very early this Year; one againft the *Rochelefe,* commanded by his Brother the Duke of Anjou; another againft the *Sancerrefe,* commanded by the
Marquefs

(i) Idem ibid.

Marquefs of La Chaftre, Governor of *Berry*; and a third in *Languedoc*, commanded by the Marfhal of Damville, Son to the late Conftable of Montmorancy.

La Rochelle having been invefted by Stroffy and Biron, almoft all the Forces of the Kingdom reforted thither, and the Duke of Anjou arrived in the Camp by the middle of February, attended with the greateft Lords of the Court, the Duke of Alençon his Brother, the Duke of Montpenfier, the Duke of Guife, that of Aumale, the Marquefs of Mayenne, the Duke of Nevers, and even the King of Navarr, and the Prince of Condé; this was a fad thing for thefe two Princes, to be forced, not only to behold the mifery of their beft Friends, but to contribute to it, and to fight againft thofe who had fo many times fought for them, and would have done chearfully the fame at that time, had they had an opportunity for it.

After feveral needlefs Conferences, the Place was battered with eighty Cannons. That Siege afforded a new Inftance of the great Power of Liberty and Confcience over Men's Mind, it overcomes all, and cannot be overcome by any thing.

The Siege lafted feven Months, reckoning from the time that it was invefted by Biron in the Month of November, to the raifing of the Siege in the latter end of June. That City withftood thirty-five thoufand Bullets, nine general Affaults, above twenty private ones, near feventy fpringings of the Mines, frequent Confpiracies, not only without, but even within its Walls.

The Inhabitants worked with fo great ardour, that they had raifed a double Terrace, and digged up a deep retrenchment at the batter'd places,

before

before the breach was made ; besides that, they made very frequent Sallies upon the Besiegers, Women were as courageous as Men, and extremely serviceable, some went along with Men to fight, to defend one place, or attacking another, others for carrying some refreshments, or for carrying away and dressing the wounded, or for throwing upon the Besiegers Kettles full of boiling Oil, or Water, or Tarr, Rackets, and Bavins with burning Pitch, pieces of Timber, Bricks and Stones.

Courage never failed them, though the Succours of England failed, by ——— I do not know what to say, for it is a mystery which I do not care to ravel out.

During all the Siege, the Besieged enjoyed perfect Health ; they had settled such good order for the distribution of the Victuals, that they had still enough for two Months longer when they were delivered ; for though they had no great quantity of Corn, yet they had abundance of salt Flesh and Fish : besides that, the Historians have related as a Prodigy, the vast quantity of Cockles, Winkles, and other like Shell-fish, which the Sea afforded them during the Siege, and which had never been seen before, nor have been after upon that Shore, at least in such great plenty. On the contrary, the Besiegers laboured under several inconveniences and difficulties, the want of Policy, and the devastation of the adjacent Countries, brought a great scarcity of Provisions and Forrage, and an intolerable Infection in their Camp, which produced frequent Epidemical Distempers.

But above all, the Lords, Chiefs, and Officers of the Army, were divided amongst themselves. There were three sorts of Persons in the Camp; the DISCONTENTED, almost all the Nobility were

dissatisfied

diffatisfied with the prefent Government, feeing that the Queen-Mother managed every thing by three or four Foreigners, Covetous, Proud and without Faith or Honour; the FAITHFULL, thefe were the Reformed, who had not renounced their Religion, but who, for preferving their Houfes and Eftates, or for fome Court-Intereft, had followed the Duke of Anjou; and the NEWS, thefe were thofe who out of dread of the Maffacres, went to Mafs, though they condemned it.

Out of thefe three forts of People, the Party of the *Politicians* was formed; they had agreed amongft themfelves, that without any regard to the difference of Religion, they fhould afk the Reformation of the State, and the Expulfion of the Foreigners. Amongft the Catholicks, the Montmorancians, the Marfhals of Biron and Coffé were the Ringleaders; that Party had been formed above a Year before the Maffacre; the Duke of Alençon, who from his Childhood had received fome impreffion of the Reformed Religion, and had been intimately united with the late Admiral, in hopes, that by that means he might form a Party, and be in a condition to cope with his Brother the Duke of Anjou, whereto he was ftrongly folicited by his ambitious Favourites, efpecially Boniface la Molle, and by his Sifter Margaret, Queen of Navarr, enraged at her Brother of Anjou, who fcorned her now, after having defperately loved her.

The King of Navarr and the Prince of Condé, either out of jealoufy, or miftruft, or fear, or all together, had avoided to join with them, as long as they were at Court, but thefe confiderations vanifhed away in the Camp. Henry de la Tour, Vifcount of Turenne, then ftill a Catholick, was the manager of that Affociation, though very young, but he was already very

subtle

subtle and cunning. And whereas they were all young and hot-headed, several Designs very strange and full of temerity were proposed amongst them, which cost very dear to some of their Authors, as we shall see in the next Year.

The King having got Intelligence of this, sent Secretary Pinard with orders to the Duke of Alençon not to remove from the Camp, or else he would incur his Indignation, the Duke sent back the Messenger without an answer, because he refused to show his order ; whereupon the King's Council was in a great perplexity, and the King, in order to prevent a surprize, wrote to the Duke of Anjou, to make all the haste possible for taking *La Rochelle*, because he wanted his Troops near his Person ; which occasioned so many unseasonable Assaults, and the loss of so many Men.

The brave resistance of the Rochelese, the great discouragement of the King's Toops, the extreme miseries, and more than that, the divisions that reigned in the Camp, outwitted the King, the Duke and their Councils ; when the news of the Duke's Election to the Crown of *Poland* arrived very luckily, for extricating them out of these difficulties.

Since the Year 1571, Sigismond King of *Poland*, the last of the Jagellonian House, being in a declining condition, as to his Health, and without Issue, the Council of France had thought proper to send Balagny before hand, for disposing things in behalf of the Duke of Anjou, in case the Throne became vacant, as it did by Sigismond's Death on the 7th of July 1572. Then the Bishop of Valence was sent thither ; he set out from *Paris* a few days before the Massacre, as abovesaid. The Queen-Mother and the Duke of Anjou were much afraid, lest he should have

good

good fuccefs in his Negociation, they were un-willing to part one from another ; therefore at the fame time that they feigned a great eager-nefs for it, and made ufe for that purpofe of the King's Intereft, they did obftruct it under-hand. But the Bifhop's great wit, capacity, and induftry, overcame all thefe Difficulties, and he carried his point againft Erneft, Son to the Emperor Maximilian II. John, Son to Sigifmond, King of *Sweden*, who was but eight Years old ; John, Son to Bafilides, Czar of *Mufcovy* ; and Piaftus, a Polifh Noble, all Candidates for that Crown. But whereas the Chief of two of the Factions were Calvinifts, they obliged the French Embaffadors to promife many things in behalf of their Brethren in France, efpecially that all the places then befieged fhould be releafed.

That News having been brought into the Camp, and that the Polifh Embaffadors would arrive very foon to wait upon their new King, fome new affaults were given to the City by the Duke's orders and the Conferences were renewed. On the 17th of June a Truce was agreed upon, and then the Articles of Peace were fettled on the 25th, and fent to the King, who ratified them, and they were drawn in the form of an Edict, whereby the former Edicts were extremely re-ftrained. Since Liberty of Confcience to every one was granted, but not the publick Profeffion of the Reformed Religion, except in the Cities of *Rochelle*, *Montauban*, and *Nimes*, the memory of every thing paft was to be quite blotted out of mind. So no Satisfaction was given for the former Maffacres.

Nothing could be obtained in behalf of the *Sancerrefe*, on pretence that their Town belonged to a private Lord, though the King's Troops kept it blocked up. *La Rochelle* and the other

two

Charles
IX.
1573.
Pope Gre-
goryXIII.

two Places, were reſtored to all their Rights and
Privileges, all other Decrees contrary to this were
repealed ; their reſiſtance was approved of, and the
guard of their Cities, Towers, Citadels, and For-
treſſes, were confirmed unto them, according to
their ancient Privileges, admitting however, of
Governors, provided they ſhould not be ſuſpected
by them. On the 10th of July, about ten before Noon, Biron came into the City with two
Heralds at Arms, and four of the King's Trum-
pets, being attended by the City-Lieutenant,
and M. De Villiers, the Peace was proclaimed,
then he was entertained at Dinner in the Town-
Houſe, and after Dinner he ſet out from *Rochelle.*

So ended that famous Siege, wherein periſhed
of the King's Army, either by Sickneſs, or by
the unavoidable Accidents of War, twelve thouſand Men, according to ſome ; but according to
others, twenty or twenty-five thouſand ; nay,
according to Thuanus, followed by D'Aubigné,
the number amounted to forty thouſand, either
by ſickneſs or killed ; amongſt whom, beſides
the Duke of Aumale killed with a Cannon-Shot,
Clermont Tallard, the two Goas, and COSSEINS,
the Admiral's Murderer, ſixty Captains, as many
Lieutenants, and Enſigns, ſeveral whereof were
ſome of the moſt noted Butchers of Bartholomew's-Day (*g*). The Duke of Anjou eſcaped
very narrowly, for being pointed at by a Soldier
from the Rampiers, as he was walking in the
Trenches with the King of Navarr, De Vins,
Maſter of his Horſe perceiving it, put himſelf
on a ſudden before his Maſter, and received the
Bullets, which went through and through his Body, and nevertheleſs, tho' ſo deſperately wounded, he recovered. The Duke was ſlightly wounded

(*g*) Thuan. lib. lvi. p. 927—942. Dinoth. lib. v. pag.
354—365.

ed with some small Shot in the Hand, Neck, and Knee; the Duke of Longueville died at *Blois*, and that of Usez upon the Fleet before *Rochelle*, and was succeeded by his Brother James D'Assier of Crussol; the Marshal of Tavannes died upon the road, as he came to the Siege.

The Duke of Anjou with the Princes and several Lords went by Sea to *Nantz*, from whence he proceeded through *Orleans* to Paris; where we shall leave him, till we have related the affairs of *Sancerre* and *Languedoc*.

The Siege of Sancerre.

About the latter end of January, La Chastres being arrived before *Sancerre* with an Army of five or six hundred Horse, and five thousand Foot, besides the Peasants and the Pioneers, which composed sixteen Companies; he sent a Drummer to summon the Town to surrender by Composition, which he promised should be upon reasonable terms. But the Drummer was detained and killed, and the Inhabitants sent no answer; which was taken very ill by the General, and cost them very dear afterwards. I will not undertake the description of the attacks, &c. I shall only observe, that after a furious battering, several skirmishes, and two assaults, the General seeing the obstinate resistance of the Inhabitants, turned the Siege into a Blockade, two Months after its beginning; from whence ensued one of the most dreadful Famines which ever had been recorded in any History, ancient or modern.

Dreadful Famine in that Town.

The Sancerrese being every way shut up by their Enemies, at the beginning of April they had no other Flesh but that of Asses and Mules, which were all killed and eaten in a Month's time; then they eat Horses, Cats, Rats, Moles, Mice, and Dogs; these Animals being all destroyed, they eat Hides, Calves and Sheep Skins, then Parchment, Horse-hoofs, Horns of Lanthorns,

thorns, Thongs of Leather, and Furnitures for Horses, Girdles of Leather, Herbs and wild Roots. At the latter end of June, three parts of the Inhabitants had no Bread to eat, those who could get some Linseed and other Seeds, whereof they never thought on before for eating, grounded or beaten in Mortars, and made Bread thereof, as they did also of all sorts of Herbs, mixed with a little bran, if they had any. They eat Bread of Straw-meal, the powder of Nut-shells and of Slate, nay, the dry Bones of Corps : Suet, old Ointment, and other old Grease, served to make Pottage and to fry. The very Excrements of Horses and Men, and the Filth of the Streets served for Food. And on the 29th of July, a poor Husbandman with his Wife were seized and burnt alive, for having fed upon the Head, Brains, and the Pluck of one of their Daughters, a Child of three Years old, which was starved to death, and the other parts of the Corps were found in the House, reserved for feeding upon. An old Woman who had taken her share in that dreadful Meal, died in Prison a few Hours after ; they were found guilty of some other petty Crimes, but what aggravated this, was, that the very same day they had been comforted with some little portion of Broth made with Herbs, and some Wine. Those who went or were put out of the Town, were either slain by the Centinels, or constrained with Cudgels to turn back again ; and because they could not be admitted into the Town, they lived upon Sprigs of Vines, Blackberries in Hedges, red Snails, and Herbs, and most of them died in the Trenches and the Ditches. Among other pitiful Objects, the Corps of an Husbandman and his Wife, were found lying together in a Vine, and two of their Children weeping and
crying

crying by them, the youngest whereof was but six Weeks old, which a charitable Lady of the Town sent for and took care of. If many died in the Vines, or in the Trenches and the Ditches, many more died in the Houses and in the Streets; sometimes they buried 25 and even 30 in a day, that perished for Hunger; almost all the Children under twelve Years of Age died. By the latter end of July there remained some few Horses which they had kept for Service, and six Cows, which afforded Milk for Babes, these Beasts were killed, and the Flesh sold per Pound, at a very high rate; they had also some Ears of Corn, which some of the Inhabitants went and fetch by stealth in the Night-time, and which were sold at half a Crown a Pound; but this last means held not long, because of the strict watch the Enemy kept. There were but 84 Persons killed by the War, but the Famine destroyed near 600, either within or without the Town; besides that many remained in a lingering condition after the Siege, several of whom died, while others, with much ado, recovered themselves after a long time.

All hopes in Man's Judgment failed those of *Their De-* Sancerre, the King having sworn that he would *liverance.* make them to devour each other, but the King of Kings preserved them by his Divine Providence. We have observed already that the Reformed Party of Poland had stipulated with Monthuc, several things in behalf of their Brethren of France, and especially, that all the Cities and Towns besieged at that time, should be instantly released, and they had obliged the Bishop of Valence to swear to the strict performance of these Articles. Now the Polish Embassadors had no sooner set their foot in France, but they challenged Monthuc's Promise, and he

Charles
IX.
1573.
Pope Gre-
goryXIII.

Capitula-
tion of
Sancerre.

accordingly made such efficacious Instances to the King, that his Majesty sent orders to La Chastre to grant a capitulation without any further delay on honourable terms to the Sancerrese.

Therefore after several Conferences, Hostages having been given on each side, it was agreed, That all the Inhabitants, either Citizens or Refugees of the Reformed Religion, should enjoy the Liberty of Conscience, and the Exercise of their Religion in their own Houses : That they should not be called in question for any thing past : That the Honour of their Wives and Daughters should be preserved : That all the Inhabitants should enjoy freely their Goods and Estates as before : That they should redeem their Town from being plundered for the Sum of forty thousand Livres : That what Troops they had should march out of the Town with their Arms and Goods: That those who had a mind to retire might do it with all safety, and dispose of their Goods as they thought proper, without being molested : That the King would ratify all these Articles.

A Truce being agreed, these Articles were sent to the King, who ratified them out of hand, and having been sent back to La Chastre, he entered into the Town on the last day of August, with most part of his Horse, and two Regiments of Foot. Few days after, the City's Gates were burnt down by the King's Command, the Ditches filled to the top, the Walls and the Towers pulled down, and the Bells taken away from the Churches, insomuch that the Town was made a Village only ; the Bailiff Jouanneau was murdered in the Night-time, within a hundred paces of Monsieur La Chastre's Lodging. And left any thing should be wanting to complete the Misery of the Inhabitants, they were loaded with such heavy Taxes, that many were obliged

to

to mortgage or to fell their Eftates, in order to pay them. On the 12th of September, La Chaftre fet out for *Bourges*, and left Durbois, Bailiff of Berry, for Governour of *Sancerre*, with a Company of Horfe and a Regiment of Foot, which committed many diforders and plunders upon the poor Inhabitants.

So ended the famous Siege of Sancerre, which lafted about nine Months, and coft the lofs of about thirteen hundred Men on the King's fide, and about feven hundred of the Inhabitants, above fix hundred whereof died of the Famine, as above faid, the reft were killed ; and what is very obfervable, is, that but twenty were killed by Cannon-Shot, tho' above fix thoufand Bullets were caft into the Town (b).

Now we muft relate, in few Words, the principal Tranfactions in *Guienn*, *Languedoc*, *Dauphiné*, &c. The Admiral, Count of Villars, with an Army of eight thoufand Foot and two thoufand Horfe, being entered into *Guienn*, befieged *Terrides*, and having batter'd the Caftle with two Cannons, the breach was half done, when the Garrifon obliged Farci their Captain to furrender ; Villars caufed him to be hanged at one of the Caftle-Windows. After that Conqueft, he was made Mafter of all *Gafcony* beyond the Garonne ; then having croffed that River, he laid Siege to *Cauffade*, fituated upon the *Aveyran* ; his Army, according to D'Aubigné, was then eighteen thoufand Men ftrong. That Place was but a fmall Town retrenched and fortified, but La Mothe Pujols, a brave Officer, commanded in it, and had with him fix hundred Arquebufiers : It was batter'd for twenty days, and the Enemy having been repulfed with great lofs in

The Affairs of Guienn.

I i 2 fevera̗

(b) Thuan. lib. lvi. p. 854, 914, 957, &c. Dinoth. lib. v. p. 385—391.

several Affaults, Villars was at laft obliged to raife the Siege. La Mothe the Commandant was unluckily killed by chance a little after, by one of his own Soldiers, as he was appointing the Guard.

During that Siege, the Army had been continually harraffed by the Vifcount of Gourdon's frequent Skirmifhes, wherein he was always fuccefsful; therefore after the Siege, Villars led his Troops upon Gourdon's Lands, where they made great devaftations, plundering his Houfes, and even pulling them down out of fpite to him. Then he laid fiege to *Verfeuil*, where there were but one hundred and forty Men in Garrifon, neverthelefs, he was obliged to raife that Siege; his Army, though numerous, was compofed for the moft part of thofe bafe Murderers, Bullies, and Hectors when they had to deal with Women, Maids, Babes, decrepit People, or unarmed Men, but downright Cowards when they met with refiftance: they ufed to murder when there was no danger to themfelves, they fought nothing elfe but Houfes forfaken; Merchants, Peafants, Women, and Children, that was their Game. They became fo odious to the Country People by their Plunders, Cruelty, and all kind of Wickednefs, that they raifed againft them the whole Commons, Catholicks and Reformed, who fell upon them wherever they could attack them with advantage, and killed a great number of them. The Duke of Anjou had fent to Villars fome Companies of old Soldiers, under the command of Goas, in order to reftore and fettle the Difcipline in his Army; one of which Companies was entirely routed by the Vifcount of Gourdon, at the Paffage of *Dordongne*.

John Nogaret de la Valette, who had the command of the Horfe in that Army, not ufed to fuch plunderings, pilferings, and licentioufnefs
of

of that unruly Multitude, perfuaded Villars to difband moft part of them, and to fend the reft into Garrifons. Then they both endeavoured to engage thofe of Montauban to yield to the King: by their advice it was that the Duke of Anjou wrote unto them feveral times to the fame purport, offering to be guarantee for every thing which the King would promife unto them. As long as La Mothe Pujols lived, he obftructed with all his might thefe Negociations; after his death, the Soldiery follow'd the fame Steps; but at laft, the Inhabitants were prevailed upon, and fent their Deputies conjointly with thofe of *Nimes*, to the Camp before *Rochelle*, who joining their endeavours with La Noüe's, engaged the Rochelefe to accept of the terms tendered unto them (*j*).

In *Languedoc*, Damville, Governor of that Province, being arrived as above faid, with an Army of above ten thoufand Men, and fourteen Cannons, having taken *Cauviffon* and *Monpefat*, after a vain attempt upon *Nimes*, laid Siege to *Sommieres*, on the 11th of February. St. Gremian had made himfelf Mafter of it a little before; and had but juft time enough to raife in hafte fome Works adjoining the Tower of *Caudas*, and another in the Town, and to make fome other like Preparations. The Town was but weak, and commanded from feveral Places; but the valour and fortitude of the Inhabitants fupplied the defects and weaknefs of its Fortifications. The Siege lafted about three Months, to the great detriment of the Catholicks. For the Reformed of *Languedoc*, who trembled at firft at Damville's great Preparations, took heart again, when they faw fuch a fmall Town to withftand fo long

Siege of Sommieres.

Ii 3   againft

(*j*) D'Aubigné Tom. 2. Book I. Dinoth. lib. 5.

against the efforts of his Army, and began to hope
well of the fuccefs of that War. The next
day of the Siege, the Tower of the Bridge was
beat down, and then the Walls being battered,
large breaches were made in feveral places ; feveral affaults were given, wherein the Damvillians
were almoft worfted, and forced to draw back.
Thofe of *Montauban* fent a Succour to the Befieged, under the command of Vifcount Paulin, which entered the Town ; they received
likewife Succours from *Nimes* and the *Cevennes.*
Henry of Foix, Count of Candale, Brother-in-Law
to Damville, arrived in the Camp with twenty
two Companies of Gafcoons. When they faw
fuch a fmall Town, and fo large a breach made
in the Walls, they laughed at the Damvillians,
as if they had been ignorant of the military Art,
and efpecially in the attack of Places, extolling,
with big encomiums the *Sommierians*, for their
brave refiftance againft fo great an Army ; and
trufting themfelves upon their ftrength, ability,
and courage, they intreated Candale to led them
to the affault, and that they might march in
the Van ; which Candale having obtained of Damville, they with the greateft alacrity endeavoured to make their way through the breach into
the Town : but they were fo warmly received
by the befieged, that after having loft three
hundred of their Companions, they were forced
to retreat. Candale in order to repair that affront, gave another affault the next day, but
with lefs fuccefs, for he himfelf was killed,
with a greater number of his Troops than the
day before. He was faying the day before in
a private Converfation, that he bewailed the Fate
of the Kingdom, feeing that for the Sake of
a few LEWD RASCALS, (*thefe were his Words*)
the

the Frenchmen were obliged to deftroy one another (i).

Damville was in great perplexity after fo many lofses; but while he was confidering within himfelf whether he fhould continue the Siege or raife it, St. Gremian defired him, of his own accord, to come to a parley, which was readily granted; and after feveral debates, it was agreed, That St. Gremian with his Forces fhould march out of the City with all military Honours, Drums beating, Colours flying, &c. That the Inhabitants, that would retire elfewhere, fhould carry along with them whatever they would; feven days were allowed for preparing themfelves for their departure; and Damville was obliged to fend Hoftages to *Nimes,* to remain there till all the Articles were duly performed. So on the 9th of April St. Gremian marched out of the place at the head of fix hundred Arquebufiers; and the Inhabitants retired, fome to *Nimes,* and others to the *Cevennes.* As to Damville, having loft five thoufand Men before that place, he fent the reft of his Army into feveral Garrifons.

His Conduct and Gremian's were equally cenfured by their Party; the Marfhal was charged with having defignedly confumed his Forces before a little paltry Town; and Gremian was charged with having courted Damville at the expence of the CAUSE, feeing, that if he had tarried a little longer, the Marfhal would have been forced to raife the Siege. There was fomething true in both charges, for Damville could not but be exafperated, when he confidered, that had it not been for the Duke of Montmorancy's Abfence, he and his Brethren were to fhare the fame Fate with the Admiral on Bar-

I i 4   tholomew's

(i) Thuan. lib. 55. page 910—12. Dinoth, lib. page 371, &c.

tholomew's day ; besides that, he and his Family were already very far ingaged in the Politician's Party, which broke out by the latter
end of this Year, and united themselves with the
Reformed.   As to St. Gremian, certain it is, that
Ammunition and Provisions were grown very
scarce in the Town, and had Damville been acquainted with it, very likely he would not have
granted such honourable terms ; but it is true
too, that they were not reduced to such a low
ebb, but they could hold out three or four days
longer.

However, the Reformed encouraged by that
success, which was very great considering their
Circumstances, were not satisfied with only keeping or defending of their own Towns and Cities, where they were the strongest, but now
they thought of attacking, and were so successful in their Enterprizes, that almost every day
brought the news of some new conquest of their
own, without any loss.   Amongst others, they
took *Florensac*, a very strong Place, not far from
Narbonne: Le Poufin, upon the Bank of the
Rhône: Curfol in the Diocese of Valence ; al
Places of great Importance in those times, fo
their situation and strength.   They were likewise
blest with several happy Successes in the *Vivaretz*
and the Country of Cevennes : And now f
preventing, lest any Jealousy should create som
Division amongst their Chiefs, they unanimousl
elected John St. Chaumont De St. Romain fo
their General ; he had hardly escaped from th
Slaughter of Paris, and was retired to *Geneva*
his great Qualities, his moral, civil, and milita
ry Virtues, made him justly beloved and respecte
by the Nobility and Gentry, by the Soldier
and the Inhabitants of the Country ; therefor
every one applauded his Election.   Then the
sen

sent a Deputation to Frederick Elector Palatine, craving his assistance, which he readily promised. Such was the condition of Languedoc when Peace was proclaimed at Rochelle (*l*).

In *Dauphiné*, they made at first several unsuccessful attempts, under the command of Montbrun, upon *Valence*, *Montelimar*, and *Crest* ; but they took *Or-Pierre*, *Serres*, and other Strong-Holds in the Diocese of *Die*. At this time Francis De Bonne, Lord Des Diguieres, De Morges, and Champoles, seized upon *La Mure* in the Mountains, which they fortified in all haste, while Montbrun ran up and down the Country with a handful of choice Men, spreading the terror of his Name all over the Province (*m*).

Whoever shall consider the wonderful Success the Reformed had during this short War, and the great losses their Enemies suffered, will certainly acknowledge the Finger of God, who never lets go unpunished the shedding of innocent Blood. How a handful of Men dejected, dispirited, without a Chief, without provisions, without any human support, could withstand one hundred thousand Men, under the command of the best experienced Captains, authorized by the King, intirely bent on their utter ruin, and wanting of nothing necessary for the compleating of it, unless prudence for managing their Enterprizes : That that handful of Reformed, (*for so I call about ten thousand to the utmost that were in arms during this War, either in* ROCHELLE, *or* SANCERRE, *or in* GUIENNE, *or in* LANGUEDOC *or* DAUPHINE', *and sure I am there was no more*) in the condition I have said they were in, dispersed as they were in so many different places, have been able to resist, and not only to resist,

(*l*) D'Aubigné Tom. 2. liv. 1. ch. 13. Dinoth. ibid.
(*m*) Eid. ibid.

fift, but to break the Forces of their Enemies, and reduce them, at leaft, to half their number; (*by the moft moderate computation, the King loft in this War, no lefs than fifty thoufand Men, viz. forty thoufand before* ROCHELLE, *five thoufand before* SOMMIERES, *twelve hundred before* SANCERRE, *and the reft in Skirmifhes, or the taking of Strong-Holds, Caftles, Towns, and Rencounters, I do not magnify at all the object*) while they did not lofe in the whole three thoufand of their own People, good part whereof were Women and Children. Methinks fuch an Event can't be afcribed but to God only, who fent a fpirit of blindnefs and divifion in the Catholick Army, compofed moftly of thofe execrable Executioners of Bartholomew's day, moft part whereof perifhed miferably during this War: but fuch great loffes, according to Thuanus, caufed the King to fay, *that he had got more by his Edict of Peace publifhed at Rochelle, than by Bartholomew's day Execution.* He would have got more, had he fincerely and fully reftored his Edict of 1570. But the national Sins cried for more fevere Punifhment.

Now we muft come to *Paris*, where the reception of the Polifh Embaffadors, the Feafts given on that account, and the departure of the King of *Poland*, will not ftay us very long.

The Polifh Embaffadors, to the number of 12, the chief whereof was the Bifhop of *Pofnia*, arrived at *Metz* on the 25th of July; they made their publick Entry into *Paris* on the 3d of September, and on the 10th of the fame Month, was read the Decree of Election in the Great Hall of the Palace; the King of *France* was prefent in his Regalia, attended by the Princes and Lords of his Court; the Decree being taken out of a large filver Box, fealed with an hundred

and

and ten Seals of the Prelates, Palatines, and Castellans of the Kingdom, was opened and read loudly by one of the Embassadors. The King thanked them very civilly; then he got up from his Seat, and went to embrace his Brother the King of *Poland*, the other Princes and Lords paid him likewise their compliments; he kissed the Duke of Alençon, and the King of Navarr, and treated others with more or less Honour, according to their Rank and Dignity.

I shall not speak here of the Feasts and Balls wherewith the Queen-Mother entertained them; these are but the Shrimps of Luxury and Prodigality, the memory whereof don't deserve to be kept any longer, than the smoak of Meats and the tune of musical Instruments. But I shall observe, that amongst all the Nobility, and the Lords of the Court, two only were found able to converse in Latin with the Polish Embassadors, so gross was their Ignorance at that time; these two were the Baron of Millaud, and Castelnau de Mauvissiere.

The King of *Poland* made likewise his publick Entry into Paris by St. Anthony's Gate, with an equal magnificence. It was taken as a bad Omen, that the Heralds at Arms had not rightly blazoned the Scutcheon of *Poland*.

These Ceremonies being ended, the King of France, who was intirely resolved to govern by himself, hastened his Brother's departure as much as he could, every hour that he stayed seemed to him a Year; but the more he pressed him, the more his Polish Majesty was ingenious to find out pretences for delaying his Journey; and many things contributed to make him so backward, not only the pleasures of the Court, the tenderness of his Mother, the authority almost Royal, wherewith he was invested by his charge

of

of Generalissimo of the King's Armies, the hope
of succeeding very soon to the Crown, Charles
having no male Issue ; but there was something
more poihant than all the rest, and it was his
desperate Love for the Princess of Condé. The
Duke of Guise, her Brother in-Law, flattered
him, nay, he served him in his passion, though
without success; and by that means, he was so
far in favour with that Prince, that he could not
be without him.

Seven or eight days being spent, and the
King of *Poland* not thinking of setting out,
though all his equipage was ready ; King Charles
provoked at it, and seeing that his Brother sought
only a pretence for spending the Winter in *France*,
told him in a passion, and with many repeated
Oaths, as usual to him, that he or himself must
depart the Kingdom, and swore that his Mother would not be always assistant to him.

*The
Queen's
Devices
for delay-
ing Henry
her Son's
Journey.*

The Queen Mother herself, whose darling
Henry was, was now quite altered, and as warmly and eagerly as she had sued for the Crown of
Poland for her Son, as unwilling was she now
to let him go out of her sight, and was no less
ingenious for contriving some new pretences of
delay, so far, that though King Charles had in
every other respect very great regard for her, and
was very submissive to her will, nevertheless he
was so much provoked at her on this account,
that, by his orders, she was denied admittance
into his Closet : therefore seeing, that she could
not any longer prolong the time, being quite
tired out with her former design, she set herself upon another, and imagined, that if she
could not recall him to *France*, to recall him
at least to some of the neighbouring Countries.
For that end, she charged Gaspard de Schomberg, a Man no less conspicuous for his great

prudence and sagacity in the management of Affairs, than for his military Virtues, to treat with
the Prince of Orange, upon some honourable
terms, for the Generalship of the Provinces
Forces in the *Low Countries*; for Henry her Son,
who could come easily with a Fleet fitted out
at *Dantzick*, having previously obtained leave
of the King of *Denmark*, and the consent of the
Estates of *Poland*, who should assist him, as she
thought, in that design.

Schomberg executed his Commission; and having met the Prince of Orange's Deputies at *Metz*,
they went so far as to set down the Conditions
in writing on both sides; but what happen'd
afterwards put an end to that Negociation (*n*).

Mean while, King Charles was gone to hunt
at *Villers-Coste-Retz*, designing to wait for
his Brother the King of *Poland*, who was at *King Henry sets out for Poland.*
last obliged to set out on his Journey on the
28th of September; the Queen-Mother, the Duke
of Alençon, the King and Queen of Navarr,
the Prince of Condé, and the whole Court accompanied him to the Frontiers of the Kingdom:
King Charles had resolved to do the same, not
out of love, but out of impatience, and that
he might be sure that his Brother remained not
hiden in some Corners of his Kingdom; but
he was hindered from it by a Fit of Sickness, which seized upon him at *Vitry*, from whence
he came back to *St. Germain*. King Henry
proceeded in his Journey, and the Queen-Mother, &c. went with him to *Blamont* in Lorrain, where they parted from one another, with
great sighs, and a flood of tears. Catharine seeing King Charles bent upon the departure of
his Brother, and that it was dangerous for him
to stay any longer, told him loudly, *Well my
Son,*

(*n*) Thuan. lib. 57. p. 567, 968.

Son, go, but depend upon it, you shall not stay long in that Country. Charles being taken ill, two or three days after, many inferred from these words, that his distemper was occasioned by poison. As for my part, I can't be of that opinion, but I rather believe, that the extremity which the affairs of the *Netherlands* were reduced to, would oblige the Prince of Orange to accept gladly of the abovesaid Proposition tendered unto him in her Name by Schomberg, and that by those means she would see again very soon her darling.

However, Henry proceeding, was received every where with the greatest demonstrations of respect; only the Elector Palatine, a Prince of the strictest Honour, Probity, and Virtue, was willing to improve this opportunity of shewing forth his utmost detestation for the Massacre of Bartholomew's day.

Amongst the German Princes that were come to Blamont to meet King Henry, were Christophle, Son to the Elector Palatine, the Prince of La Petite Pierre, (*or the Small Stone*) of the Palatine House, and Lewis of Nassau; they, after having conferred in secret with the Queen-Mother, concerning the expedition of the *Netherlands*, led Henry to *Saverne* or *Zabern*, where he was splendidly entertained by the Bishop of *Strasbourg*; from thence travelling through the Countries of *Spire*, *Worms* and *Mentz*, they arrived upon the Borders of the *Rhine*; which having crossed, Henry and his Council thought, that they could not commodiously and civilly proceed any further without paying a Visit to the Elector Palatine, therefore they went to *Heidelberg*. The Elector having notice of his coming, did not think proper to put all his Guards, much less his Troops, under Arms: This frightned the King of Poland and his Retinue, they

suspected

suspected that there were some ambushes laid for them : Nevertheless, that Prince received his Majesty with civility, though with a great gravity. He led the King into a Gallery of Pictures, where the first Object that offered itself to his view (*and this had been purposely done*) was the late Admiral's Picture; at this sight, there was some alteration in Henry's Countenance, which being observed by the Elector, he told him, ,, There is the Picture of the best French-
,, man that ever was born; in the death where-
,, of France hath lost much of its honour, cre-
,, dit and security : Witness the Letters that
,, were found in his Box, whereby he advised
,, his King, how he ought to behave himself
,, with his Brothers, and in the affairs concern-
,, ing the *Low Countries*, in regard to the Court
,, of *England*. We have been told, that those
,, Memoirs were read before Monsieur D'Alen-
,, çon your Brother, and the Embassador of *Eng-*
,, *land*, who were asked, whether he was such a
,, good Friend unto them, as they deemed him ;
,, and that they answered (*as we have related*
,, *above*).,, The King of *Poland* answered, that he was not guilty of what had been done, and made short upon that subject, taking for an affront what the Elector had told him; so far Thuanus and D'Aubigné his Abbreviator. But the German Historians, according to this last named, say, that in the same Gallery there was like-wise the Picture of the chief Lords and other notable Persons, who had been murdered at that dreadful time ; and that the Elector Palatine going by, had been very prolix upon that subject ; ,, We have been acquainted, Sir, *says*
,, *he to the King*, how your Embassadors have
,, disguised these Facts, by their Speeches and
,, Writings, to which none, or very few, have
,, given

,, given credit, though many feign to be per-
,, fuaded ; they quote in their own defence,
,, the Murders perpetrated by Baron des Adrets,
,, and fuch like of the Reformed's violent Actions,
,, but all that they fay, can amount to no more
,, than this, that the Reformed have fome times
,, made poor reprizals, which bear no propor-
,, tion with the many wrongs, injuries, and cru-
,, elties ufed againft them, for it is to the ut-
,, moft, no more than one Catholick for a
,, thoufand Reformed ; fo they may be confi-
,, dered rather as threatnings, in order to put
,, an end to the future inhumanities. Further-
,, more, thefe actions were but the natural ef-
,, fects of the War that was kindled, and com-
,, mitted on thofe that were armed in a con-
,, dition to refift and defend themfelves ; and
,, not on the old Men, Women, Children and
,, Babes that could not refift, and who had been
,, brought, or had retired themfelves into your
,, Prifons, into your very Bofom, as in places
,, of fafety. They bring again in their own de-
,, fence, the criminal example of others, fuch
,, as that of Mithridates, who caufed forty thou-
,, fand Romans to be flain in a day ; that of
,, Peter of *Arragon*, who procured the death
,, of eight thoufand Frenchmen in the Sicilian
,, Vefpers ; to thefe they fubjoin the Cruelties
,, of Chriftiern in *Denmark*, and ten or twelve
,, fuch like Stories, which have no relation at
,, at all with this Fact. Thofe have been cruel
,, to their Enemies who were Foreigners, but
,, without any bafe artifice ; but you have per-
,, petrated a Maffacre upon your moft faithful
,, Subjects, that were unarmed; you have drawn
,, them into your Nets by fo many careffes, tokens
,, of love and friendfhip; you have ftained the
,, honour of Marriage, and trod under your
,, feet

,, feet whatever is moſt ſacred amongſt Men,
,, as well as whatever is moſt reſpected in the
,, King's Majeſty. They add to this, the Con-
,, ſpiration of the Admiral; but to be convin-
,, ced of the injuſtice and falſity of the charge,
,, one needs but to conſider, that he was at-
,, tended only by three hundred Gentlemen,
,, that his two Arms were wounded, one whereof
,, they talk'd of cutting off; that his Bed was al-
,, ways ſurrounded with Phyſicians and Surgeons,
,, who forbad him to think, or to talk of any
,, other affair; and that he was ſurrounded with
,, fifteen hundred Gentlemen, two thouſand Sol-
,, diers of the Guard, and ſixty thouſand Pari-
,, ſians, all armed and full of ſpite and rage againſt
,, the Reformed.

The good Elector, judging by the King's Countenance, that he took theſe Remonſtrances for
threatnings, went on thus: ,, Now Sir, the Ger-
,, man Princes, (thank God) have not as yet
,, ſtained their Hands, nor their Fame with the
,, Blood of thoſe that truſt themſelves to them;
,, and in that, my Religion is of one accord
,, with my Country: I have mentioned theſe
,, things unto you, as a Friend, to deſire you
,, to deteſt for the future bad Counſels, where-
,, by I think you have been moved, rather than
,, by your own nature; deſiring you to ſee what
,, ſervice I can do for you; and I will ſhow you
,, that the Children of God don't bear any ill-
,, will or grudge againſt no body. ,, The King
thanked the Elector, but in a manner which betrayed his ſecret fears. Which was much increaſed in the night; for ſome of the Kitchins in the
Caſtle having taken fire, either accidentally or,
deſignedly, ſuch vaſt crouds of People ran to it;

Vol. III. K k with

with so great a noise, that they thought it was a new Bartholomew's-day (o).

In all other respects the Elector, having unburthened his heart, entertained his royal Guest with great magnificence. The King set out from *Heidelberg* on the 13th of December, and continued his Journey to his Kingdom ; which being so far out of our way, we shall refer our Readers to the Books written upon that Subject.

The Polish Embassadors Request.

But before we leave the Polanders, I must not omit, that amongst other things which the Polish Embassadors, especially the Reformed, insisted upon with King Charles, they required that the Duke of Montpensier's Daughter, retired to the Elector Palatine's Court, should be reconciled to her Father by the King's interposition ; that by the same means, Lady Jaqueline de Monbel D'Entremont, Relict of the late Admiral, who was detained Prisoner at *Turin* by the Duke of *Savoy*, should be set at liberty, and all her Estates restored unto her, and that she might live in perfect Liberty of Conscience in her own House ; and that Charles De Coligny, Son to the Admiral, who was detained Prisoner at *Marseilles*, should be likewise set at liberty : but the King shifted off these demands as he had done most part of the others, which had been tendered by the same in behalf of the French Reformed (p).

The Reformed Petitions.

While the King was at *Villers-Coste-Rets*, he received the Petition of the Reformed Deputies of *Languedoc* and *Guienn*. Tho' the Reformed of these Provinces were included in the Edict published at *Rochelle* after the Siege, nevertheless they had refused to submit themselves to
the

(o) D'Aubigné Tom. 2. liv. 2. ch. 4. (p) Thuan. lib. 57. p. 964.

the terms of it ; and with the King's Licence they held an Affembly at *Nifmes*, and then at *Montauban*, on the 24th of Auguft, (*Bartho-lomew's-Day*) wherein in was unanimoufly a-greed, that there was no provifion made for them in the Edict of *Rochelle*, and that the Articles thereof were captious ; that they were deprived of the moft valuable of their Goods, viz. the free Profeffion of their Religion ; that they were left to the Mercy of their Enemies, and fuch like Grievances too hard for them to bear with. There-fore they agreed to petition the King for re-drefs, and fent their Deputies to Court, viz. Cavagnac, Yollet, and fome others. The fub-ftance of their Petition, was to the following purpofe: That they moft humbly thanked his Majefty for his inclination to Peace, and befought him not to take it amifs, if feeling ftill the dread-ful effects of the *Parifian* Maffacre, they required that a little more regard fhould be had to their own fecurity : That they trufted intirely to the good nature of their Prince, but not to his bad Counfellors, whofe injuftice and great influence were obvious to every one, fince the King ha-ving openly declared by his Letters his utmoft deteftation of the excreable act of Bartholomew's Day, they had obliged him to own it by a pub-lick Edict. Therefore they required, that a ftrong Garrifon of Reformed fhould be maintained at the King's charge in the Cities which they held ; furthermore, that in each Province two more cau-tionary Towns fhould be granted unto them ; again, that the publick Exercife of their Re-ligion fhould be allowed every where all over the Kingdom, without any diftinction of Places ; again, that their Caufes fhould be heard before a Court compofed of Reformed Members ; that their Eftates fhould not be liable to the

Tythes,

Tythes, unleſs for the Maintenance of their Miniſters ; again, that all the Authors, Abettors,
and Executioners of the Maſſacre, ſhould be ri-
gorouſly puniſhed, as Highwaymen, Murderers,
and Diſturbers of the publick Peace ; again, that
all Inſcriptions againſt the Memory of the De-
ceaſed ſhould be eraſed, all Decrees and Sentences
of the Parliament of *Paris* and *Thoulouſe*, given
ſince the Maſſacre, be reverſed ; again, that thoſe
of the Clergy who profeſſed their Religion, and
the Children deſcended from them in lawful
Marriage, ſhould be declared capable of ſuc-
ceeding to any Eſtate, Honours, Dignities, and
Offices, being judged only by Reformed Judges ;
again, that the Tutors and Curators ſhould be
bound to train up their Pupils of the Reformed
Religion, in the ſame ; again, that thoſe of the
Venaiſſine County, and of the Dioceſe of *Avignon*,
ſhould enjoy the ſame Privileges ; again, that
the Ordinances and Statutes of the late Queen of
Navarr, ſhould be inviolably kept in Bearn ; that
all Princes, Magiſtrates and Corporations of the
Kingdom, ſhould be bound by a ſolemn Oath, to
obſerve and keep the Premiſſes (*q*).

That Petition was ſubſcribed by the Viſcounts
Paulin, Gourdon, St. Romain, and ſeveral o-
thers. When it was tendered to the King and
read before him, ſome admired the Petitioners
Boldneſs, others were full of Indignation at it, e-
ſpecially the Queen Mother, who ſaid, *That was
the late Prince of Condé in the Center of the Kingdom, at the head of an Army of twenty thouſand
Horſe and fifty thouſand Foot ſtrong, nay, was he
Maſter of Paris it ſelf, he would not inſiſt on half
of the Articles mentioned in the Petition.*

At

(*q*) Thuan. lib. 57. p. 968. D'Aubigné, tom. 2. liv. 2.
ch. 2.

At the same time the Deputies of *Dauphiné*
and *Provence* tendered their Petition, praying
for a Diminution of Taxes. The King was advised to dissemble at present his Resentment a-
gainst these Petitions and the Petitioners themselves, whereby he thought his Dignity had been
much offended, therefore he eluded their Demands. For he referred those of Languedoc and
Guienn to Damville, who was charged to treat
with them at some convenient Place near *Montauban*, and would answer their Petition conform-
ably to the King's Orders ; and that in the mean
while, he would provide them with impartial
Judges to decide their Causes : and the Duke of
Usez, James of Cruffol, who narrowly escaped from
Bartholomew's Day, by the Duke of Guise's Favour, was ordered to go along with them to *Languedoc*, to the Marshal Duke of Damville.

As to those of *Dauphiné* and *Provence*, the
King excused himself, telling them, that the great
Charges he had been at for the Expences of the
Civil Wars, and the large Dowries and Pensions
he was obliged to pay to the Queen his Mother,
to his Brothers, to the Queen of *Scotland* his
Sifter-in-law, and the Dutchess of Savoy his Aunt,
did not allow him as yet to ease his People from
these heavy Taxes ; but that he would take care
for the future, as soon as Peace should be settled
in the Kingdom, to ease them, and to restore the
Provinces to their ancient Privileges. These two
Answers were delivered to the Deputies of *Guienn*,
Languedoc, *Provence*, and *Dauphiné*, on the 18th
of October.

Those of Languedoc met together at *Millaud*
in *Rouergue*, with Damville's Consent, where
they examined a-new the Matter of their former
Petition ; and far from abating any thing, they
added new Articles to it, by way of Explanation,

and

Charles
IX.
1573.
Pope Gre-
gory XIII

New Regu-
lations of
the Refor-
med in
Languedoc.

and sent them to the Duke of Damville, by the latter end of this Year : and whereas they could not come to any Agreement; they being much exasperated, began to prepare themselves for War (r).

They divided the *Languedoc* High and Low, into two Governments, *Montauban* was the Seat of the first, and *Nimes* of the second; the *Cevennes* and *Vivarets* were put under the Jurisdiction of *Nimes*, and *Quercy* and *Rouergue* under *Montauban*'s. The Viscount of Paulin was declared Governour of *Montauban*, and St. Romain of *Nimes*; they had the general Direction of every thing, but they were accountable to the States of their respective Governments. There were some private Deputies in every Diocese, who met together as often as Affairs required it, and whatever they had decreed was to be brought before the General States to be examined, approved, rejected or altered. These two Governours received Salaries, paid unto them by the General States of their Provinces, and each Government had its own Treasurer. It was agreed, that their Troops should be exactly paid at so much a day, which was for easing the People from Plunder, and that they might enjoy some Quietness amidst these Troubles. For finding out the necessary Supplies, every one was assessed at so much per Head ; besides that, the Catholick Cities, Towns, Boroughs, Villages, Hamlets, were obliged to pay so much into the Treasury, for redeeming themselves, or else they saw themselves exposed to Incursions and Plunders, which they were very glad to avoid ; furthermore, they seized for the same purpose upon the Clergy-Revenues. So in a little time, they had fortified several Places, and provided them with all sorts of

Am-

(r) Thuan. lib. 57. p. 968, 969.

Ammunition, and they had Forces enough of their own to keep them, without calling for any foreign Affiftance, the two Governments being able to maintain twenty thoufand Men. At that Example, many Catholicks grew milder to the Reformed, and defired their Junction for the Reftauration of the State, as we fhall fee hereafter (*s*). I fhall be more particular upon the Civil Government of the Reformed, at the beginning of the next Book.

Several Books, Pamphlets, and Libels were publifhed at that time for and againft the Government, which increafed the Ferment wherein the Kingdom was at that time, to fuch a degree, that at laft having took fire, caufed a general Conflagration all over the Kingdom.

Amongft thefe, was THE WILFUL SLAVERY, written formerly in the Year 1548, by Stephen De La Boëtie (who was then a Youth of about 19 Years old, and was made Counfellor in the Parliament of *Bourdeaux.*) That Book had been written upon the Submiffion of the *Bourdelefians* to the Conftable of Montmorancy, after their Rebellion, mentioned in the 1ft Book of the firft Vol. of this Hiftory. La Boëtie was dead at this time, neverthelefs, his Book was now publifhed to ferve a quite contrary turn, than that meant by the Author himfelf (*t*).

There was likewife another, with the Title of FRANCO-GALLIA, written by Francis Hotoman, a learned Counfellor at Law, wherein he endeavoured to prove, that the Kingdom of France

K k 4 was

(*s*) Dinoth. lib. 5. p. 392. Recueil des Chofes memorables fous Charles IX. p. 487, 488.

(*t*) D'Aubigné hath miftaken grofly when he fpeaks of that Gentleman as living then, and having written out of fpite for an Affront put upon him in the Louvre, that is falfe. See Thuan. lib. V. p. 156-7. Lib. 57. p. 969. Aubigné, tom. 2. liv. 2. ch. 3.

was not hereditary, as private Patrimonies, bu
elective, the General States having Authorit,
and Power of depriving and depofing Kings ; h
evinces this odd Propofition by the Examples o
Philip of Valois, John, Charles V. and VI. and
Lewis XI. And above all, he doth infift upon the
Incapacity of Women for all manner of Adminiftration and Government in the Kingdom.

There was another Book publifhed in Germany
fome years before, during the Siege of *Megae-
bourg*, with this Title, JUNIUS BRUTUS, or Defence againft the Tyrants ; wherein he treats of
Obedience due to the Magiftrate, according to
the Word of God, and demonftrates that our O-
bedience to God muft be infinite, but finite as t
Men ; confequently, that it is lawful for Subjects
to rife in Arms, in their own Defence, againft
Princes and Magiftrates who mifufe their Authority for their Oppreffion. He examines feveral
other Cafes upon that Subject : that Work was
afcribed to Hubert Languet.

The fame Queries were afterwards treated a-
new and confirmed by the Sorbonne, the Congregation of Jefuits, the Affemby of the Clergy, and
the See of Rome, during the League's Wars, to
the great Scandal of every good Chriftian. At
the fame time was publifhed, a Dialogue, under
the Title of THE POLITICIAN, treating of the
Power, Authority and Duties of Princes, and of
the People's Liberty.

The laft whereof I fhall take notice, was that
of one Poncet, known by the Name of Chevalier
of St. Peter, having been knighted by the Pope.
He had been introduced to the King and Queen-
Mother, two Years before, by Chancellor Birague and the Count of Retz ; he had told them,
that having travelled much, he had feen all the
Princes of Chriftendom, and feveral others, but
that

that he had not found one whose Power and Authority was so absolute as the Turk's, and so on. Being asked, how France could be put upon the same foot? he told their Majesties, that the only way was to destroy the Princes, and weaken the Nobility so much, that it should be out of their power to resist, or even gain-say their Sovereign. As to the Princes, says he, which you can't take out of the way, you must keep them the lowest you can, granting no Place, no Dignity, no Favour to any body recommended by them ; and besides that, sowing Division amongst themselves, and such other like base, tyrannical, and devilish Maxims, that really Machiavel was a Saint to Poncet, who was so barefaced and impudent as to publish his Opinions and Counsels. He was answered as he deserved ; but how wicked and detestable soever his Tenets were, they suited so well with Catherine's Temper and Inclination, that she omitted not a Tittle of them, yea she went further still, poisoning those who were suspected by her, increasing the Divisions amongst the Nobility, starving the Natives, and loading the Foreigners, especially Italians, with all the best Preferments of the Kingdom. No wonder, if she was universally hated, and if the Catholicks joined the Reformed, in order to procure a general Reformation in the Political State.

It was likely enough that the King of *Poland's* Absence out of the Kingdom, would contribute to its Tranquillity and Peace, but it happened quite otherwise, thro' the Queen-Mother's Ill-will to the Duke of Alençon her Son, and her Impatience to see him debarred from all his just Pretensions. When she left *Blamont*, being afraid lest Alençon, improving this Opportunity, would ask and obtain the Lieutenancy of the Kingdom, which his Brother had enjoyed, and that by means

means of the King of Navarr, the Prince of Condé, the Montmorancians, and Coffé, he would excite some new Commotions in France, and deprive her of all Adminiftration in the Government, fhe no fooner was arrived from *Blamont*, but fhe whifpered to the King as a matter of Fact, what was only one of her own Sufpicions, to the end that fhe might eftrange the King from his Brother, and that fhe might obtain the Lieutenancy of the Kingdom for the Duke of *Lorrain* her Son-in-law, with whom fhe expected that fhe might do whatever fhe pleafed. As fhe was intent upon that Work, the Duke of Alençon got notice of what fhe was hatching againft his own Intereft, and he refolved to prevent her.

The Duke of Alençon courted by the Fle-mifh.

He had had a fecret Conference at *Blamont* with Lewis of Naffau, and whereas for many good Reafons, becaufe he was a Friend to the late Admiral, and perfecuted at Court upon that account, and becaufe he fhewed himfelf inclined to the Reformed Intereft, the Count took him to be better qualified than his Brother of *Poland*, for a Generaliffimo of the Netherland Forces ; he had treated with him unknown to the Queen, upon that Subject, and had agreed together upon the means of carrying on the War, and the number of Troops neceffary for that purpofe ; all thefe things had been induftriously kept concealed from the Queen. He queftioned not but that the King, who was willing, *(as it was faid abroad)* to refume his Authority, which had been formerly divided between his Mother and Brothers, being now rid of one of them, would be glad to be rid of the other too, who would be employed in a foreign War, whereby he might enjoy Peace at home, and recover by that means, the Authority which he had loft during the Civil Wars.

Now, for the very same Reasons, the Reformed in France had their Eyes fixed upon him, and intreated him, by proper Persons appointed for that purpose, to undertake their Defence, and receive them under his Protection; and to engage him to do it without delay, they produced some Letters, (*intercepted, as they say*) of the Queen-Mother to the King of Spain, and of the King of Spain to her, wherein mention was made of some Device to take him very soon out of the way. To this, the Brothers of the Marshal Duke of Montmorancy, and their Adherents, joined their strong Sollicitations; their Party went by the Name of Politicians and Discontented. They had had an Opportunity of imparting their Thoughts, and discovering themselves one to another during the Siege of *Rochelle*, as above said, and would have run to very great extremes at that time, had it not been for the prudent and wholesome Advices of La Nouë.

What obliged the Reformed at this time to take such a step, (which was always disapproved by the judicious Du Plessis Mornay, who began at this time to appear upon the Stage, and who represented in vain to La Nouë, the dangerous Consequences of such an Union between the Reformed and the Politicians) was the News they received of an Enterprize against *Rochelle*, the Execution of which, the Queen had trusted to Biron, assisted by Puy-gaillard, Landereau, and the Count of Lude.

The Rochellese being acquainted with it by a Deserter just upon the point of Execution, the Mayor sent a Serjeant to summon James Du Lion, the chief of the Traytors, who was at his Country-House; but having refused to follow him, he was killed in his own House, his Papers and Memoirs were seized, whereby the whole Plot and

and the Names of the Complices were known. Several were apprehended and being put to the Torture, they owned the Fact, and were condemned to be broke upon the Wheel, but they recanted at the Place of Execution. Only one Gui le Taillon by name, confessed the Conspiracy, and confirmed whatever had been found written in Du Lion's Memorandum, without any Torture ; and whereas he had been formerly in the Magistracy, he was beheaded. At the same time the Rochellese, with two Ships commanded by Captains Saugeon and Normand, took a Man of War, named the Swallow, which roved on these Coasts, waiting for an Opportunity of doing worse : ten Soldiers of the Crew were hanged, but the Captain, Lichani of *Luca* escaped.

That Enterprize moved the Rochelese to provide for their own Security, and tho' the King approved by his Letters of the Condemnation and Execution of the Traitors, tho' the Queen-Mother, Biron, de Lude, and Puy-gaillard, denied utterly to be any way privy to the Plot, nevertheless they resolved to enter into the general Association of the Reformed Churches, for their common Defence. To which they were strongly exhorted by La Noue, Mirambeau, La Case, and Montguion, who came to Rochelle at that time. It is true, that at first they were something froward, alledging their last Capitulation, their past Miseries, and their present Weakness : But they yielded at last to La Noue's Remonstrances. That Lord having accounted for his past Conduct in the City's Council, to the general Satisfaction of the Publick, made use of such strong Arguments, that he brought them to the desired Point.

Another thing which helped much to that Resolution of theirs, was the News they received of Mont-

Montbrun's wonderful Progress in *Dauphiné*, and *Vivaretz* ; and the taking of the Viscount of Grammont in *Bearn*, which happened as follows.

That Lord had been sent to *Bearn* by the King of Navarr, to restore the Catholick Religion in that Country, as above said ; he was attended with 250 Gentlemen of the Catholick Religion, well armed at his Castle of *Yemau*, ready to execute his Commission by the most violent Methods. The Consternation was general in the City of *Pau*, they celebrated a Fasting-day, and an old Gentleman of above 80 Years, and who had lost his Sight, Baron d'Auros by name, attending the divine Service, was so moved by the Cries of the poor Inhabitants, who expected nothing else but an utter destruction, that he called his Son, and spoke to him to the following purport. *My Son*, says he, *who has given thee Being and Life? It is God, by your means, Sir. Then*, saith the good old Man, *now thy God and thy Father demand again of thee the Life which thou hast received of them. God is able to preserve thee amidst all Dangers, even against all human Appearance: and accepting of the Sacrifice thou shalt make of thy Life for his Service, he will recompence you with another, infinitely better than this. Thy Father here present will follow you very soon, if thou diest, after having published thy Virtue and Obedience, he will bear witness to thee in Heaven, before the Throne of God: Go, do not open your Eyes as yet to see the number of thy Followers, for tho' few, they will be stout and courageous ; don't consider as yet the number of thine Enemies, only to strike them with my Sword, which God will bless in thine hands.* The young Baron received the Sword, the Colling and Kissing of his Father, and went with 38 young Gentlemen to *Yemau*,
and

and without any further Ceremony, he alighted in the Caftle-Yard; and whereas fo many other Gentlemen arrived every minute in order to march the next day to execute the Commiffion, no notice was taken of d'Auras and his Company, being miftaken for fome of the Vifcount's Party. Being entered with others into the Caftle, on a fudden they drew their Swords, killed thofe that made any refiftance, feveral efcaped by jumping out of the Windows, many were made Prifoners, amongft whom was Grammont himfelf; they took fifty or fixty Horfes, and returned with their Prifoners to *Pau*: Grammont was put under Cafe's care, and fo was the *Bearn* preferved at that time. All thefe Advantages got by the Reformed, induced the Rochellefe to liften to whatever La Nouë required of them.

*New Con-
federacy of
the Refor-
med in
Languedoc,
and their
Manifefto.*
By this time the Vifcounts Paulin, Gourdon, Cadenet and Panat, the Barons of Serignac, Forgieres, Bruchieres, and feveral others of the Nobility, held an Affembly at Montauban to refolve upon the Articles of Peace, which they were to petition the King for; but before all, they thought proper to renew a ftrict and perpetual Union amongft themfelves, as well for their civil as for their religious Concerns; to which Confederacy they admitted not only the Natives of the Kingdom, but alfo their Brethren of the Diocefe of *Avignon*, of the Principality of *Orange*, of the Marquifate of *Saluces*, and of the *Meffine* Country, belonging to the Duke of *Lorrain*. They fwore to affift one another for the Maintenance and Defence of the faid Confederacy, and to fpare neither their Goods or Lives for promoting the Kingdom of Chrift, and his Glory, for maintaining the Throne, and reftoring Peace in the Kingdom. And for the better Execution of this their Refolution, they agreed to put Garifons in the

chief Cities of *Languedoc*, and the adjacent untries, for they had notice that the Court intended to raise Forces, not only in the Kingdom, but also in *Germany*, and in the Catholick Cantons of *Switzerland*, to destroy all those that had escaped from the Massacre of Bartholomew's-day, and they thought proper to prevent them.

Another Reason engaged them to take up Arms; for they saw that every thing was promised to them, who trusting in their Arms, repulsed force by force, and that on the contrary, those who submitted themselves patiently, were the most severely treated. Besides that, their Petitions were not tendered to the King, their Enemies not suffering them to have any access to his Majesty. For these Reasons, the Reformed were forced to rise in Arms, having no other means left to divert their utter Destruction.

They published a Manifesto, which they directed to the Nobility, the Governours of the Provinces, and the several Parliaments of the Kingdom. They advised them to consider the Male-Administration of the present Government; that the Princes and great Lords of the Kingdom were not intrusted with the Management, or even with the Cognizance of those Affairs wherein the Publick was so nearly concerned; that the People were loaded with the heaviest Taxes, which however, came not into the King's Exchequer, neither were they laid out for the publick Use; that all Trade was dead, and the Tradesmen reduced to great misery; in a word, that the Natives, of what Rank or Condition soever, were deprived of means of Subsistence, being debarred from all Employments either in State or Church, if they had not Money to bid most for them; that the King's Exchequer was exhausted by extravagant Expences; that the most honourable and

Their Manifesto.

and profitable Offices which ufed formerly to be given only to Princes, were now given to unwor thy Men of the loweft Rank, who fcorned the Nobility, and expofed them to the Dangers and Perils of an unjuft War, kindled to gratify their own Paffions. To cure thefe Evils, there was but one Remedy left, viz. the calling of the States-General, that the King might be acquainted with the Diforders that had fpread themfelves in the Kingdom, either in State or Church *(u)*.

Perplexity of the State-Mi- nifters.

That Manifefto was like a Declaration of War; the Catholick Politicians or Difcontented made no fcruple to join themfelves with the Reformed, already in Arms againft the bad Counfellors and Governours of the Kingdom. Thefe laft having notice of this Confederacy, were in great per plexity, feeing that their Adminiftration was fo generally blamed and cenfured, and that the num ber of the Difcontented increafed every day; but what vexed them the more was, when they heard that the Deputies of the Provinces who had been fummoned to *Compiegne,* having had a free accefs to the King, had reprefented to his Majefty in a very pathetick manner, all the Difeafes of the Kingdom; for they queftioned not but fuch a Boldnefs was infpired into them, by fome of the greateft who countenanced them.

Alençon undertakes the Protec- tion of the Reformed and Poli- ticians.

And indeed the Duke of Alençon, thinking it to be more convenient and agreeable to his own Intereft, had chofen to declare himfelf Protector of the Reformed and Politicians of the Kingdom, having before been refufed the Lieutenancy thereof, by his Mother's Artifices, who deftined that important Dignity for the Duke of Lorrain her Son-in-law.

La Mole, Favourite of Alençon, was the tool made ufe of by Thoré, Meru, Turenne, and
others

(u) Dinoth. lib. 5. p. 396, 397.

others of the same Party, for folliciting his Master, and engaging him to take the steps which they thought convenient. But whereas the Duke of Montmorancy, Brother to the said Thoré, Meru and Damville, and Uncle to Turenne, was a Man of very strict Virtue, of great Prudence, and a true Patriot, an Enemy to all Factions, and seeking only the Peace and Welfare of his Country; La Mole persuaded his Master to consult him, and take his Advice upon dubious Cases, when he himself knew not what course to take; but he was above all very careful not to have him consulted but upon matters that carried with them a shew of Honesty, and that really tended to the publick Good, and no less cautious, that all things of another nature should be kept concealed from him. The next thing which the Duke of Alençon and his Council confidered, was how to begin the Work; and several were of opinion, that he ought to tender only a Petition to the King in the Reformed and the Politician's Name. But having confulted, by La Mole's Advice, with the Duke of Montmorancy upon that Subject, that Lord did not approve at all of that way; for, says he, you will incur unavoidably the King's Displeasure, if following the late Admiral's Example, you do take upon you to petition for the Redrefs of the manifold Grievances and Complaints of his Majesty's Subjects; it would be better, if you do ask the General-Lieutenancy of the Kingdom, and if you desire it so, I will ask it myself for you. By that means, instead of being look'd upon as Chief of any Faction, you will be confider'd as a common Umpire, and one who interposes for the general Pacification of the Kingdom.

*The Duke
of Mont-
morancy
asks the
Lieutenan-
cy for him.*

The Prince relished much that Advice, an
desired no better than to see it executed (*n*
Therefore the Duke went to Court, and pet
tioned the said Lieutenancy for the Duke of A
lençon, shewing forth by many convincing Ar
guments, that the Prince could not be denie
without doing him a great Injury. The Kin
granted the Request, either by force, for avoidin
a greater Mischief, or because he was consciou
that he could not in justice deny it. But at th
same time several things happened, which hin
dered the Effect of that Grant.

What I am going to relate was but a trifle
which nevertheless caused a greater Division be
tween the Montmorancians and the Guisians
One Scævola Ventabran, who had been some tim
in the Duke of Montmorancy's Houshold, ha
ingratiated himself with the Duke of Guise, b
some false Report or other, which had occasion'
Suspicions, Jealousies, and private Grudges be
tween the two Houses; the Duke of Guise hav
ing discovered the Man's ill Temper, had ex
pell'd him, and very often threatned him, that h
would kill him, if he ever met him in his way
Ventabran neglected that Advertisement, and
being at *St. Germain*, he went to meet the Duke
in order to clear himself; the Duke of Guise
being not restrained by the Sacredness of the
Place, drew his Sword and pursued him up the
Stairs of the Castle, and could scarce be hinder'd
by Thoré, whom he met in his way, from running Ventabran through and through.

*The Queen
Mother's
Devices
for pre-
vailing a-
gainst the
said Duke.*

The King incensed at this Audaciousness of
the Duke of Guise, complained of it to the
Queen his Mother; she excused the Fact, and
for appeasing her Son, she caused Ventabran to
be arrested: she went farther, she pretended,
that

(*u*) Thuan. lib. 57. pag. 978, 979.

that the Prisoner had confessed in secret, that he had been suborned by the Duke of Montmorancy for murdering the Duke of Guise, but that afterwards he had recanted; and whereas the Duke of Montmorancy insisted that the Prisoner should be more strictly examined upon that account, the Duke of Guise, who was unwilling to have the Reasons of his secret Hatred against Ventabran known to the Publick, prevailed with the Queen to have him released from his Confinement, upon condition that he should forbear from Court; and the Duke of Montmorancy being affronted at it, retir'd likewise into his own House of *Chantilly*.

But the worst of all this was, that Catharine took from thence a pretence for raising greater Jealousies in the King's mind against his Brother D'Alençon; for she told him, that he could not any longer doubt of his Designs, since Ventabran having attempted to murder the Duke of Guise, the main Support of his Crown, by the Subornation of the Montmorancians, he might depend upon it, that if he did appoint his Brother D'Alençon as his Lieutenant-General in the Kingdom, he would see the Government of it snatch'd out of his own hands. Though the King was moved by these Remonstrances, nevertheless, as he knew that his Mother was entirely devoted to the Faction of the Guises, whom he hated as much as the Montmorancians, and that she spoke not so much out of hatred against these, as out of love for the first, he was still at a stand what to do, whether he should give the Lieutenancy of the Kingdom to D'Alençon, or expose himself to a new Civil War, from which he was much averse.

He was in that anxiety, when the Impatience of Guitry altered entirely his Mind; appearing on

Charles
IX.
1574.
Pope Gre-
goryXIII.

on a fudden, on the 20th of February near St.
Germain, with 200 Horfe, others fay 300, in
order to carry away from Court the Duke of
Alençon, the King of Navarre, and the Prince
of Condé, and to accompany them into fome
place of Security of their own chufing (*x*).

For underftanding this, one muft know, that
by the latter end of the laft Year the Politicians
and the Reformed had agreed together in December laft, that they would rife in arms on a
fudden, in feveral Parts of the Kingdom, and
feize upon as many Places as they could, efpecially that they would procure the Duke of Alençon's Efcape from Court. As to the time appointed, I muft own, that there is a great Am-
biguity in the Relations of Hiftorians, for moft
part agree, that Shrove-Tuefday was appointed
for the Execution of their Scheme, becaufe of
the Diverfions of the day ; but then they add,
that Shrove-Tuefday in that Year fell on the
10th of March, which fpoils all ; for if the 30th
of May, when Charles died, was Whitfunday,
confequently the 20th of February ought to be
Shrove-Tuefday that Year. The Biographer of
Du Pleffis Mornay fpeaks only of the 10th of
March, without mentioning Shrove-Tuefday.
Others fay, that it was fome of the laft Days of
Shrove-Tide, without mentioning the Day of
the Month. So we are left in the dark as to the
precife time appointed ; and all that we can fay
is, that it was not before Shrove-Tuefday, nor
after the tenth of March. However La Noue
was charged with the Affairs of *Poitou, la Rochelle,*
Country of *Aulnix, Xaintonge, Angouleme,* he
went to *Rochelle,* where being arrived by the beginning of January, he prevailed with the Rochelefe to enter into the general Affociation as
above

(*x*) Thuanus ibid. & pag. 980.

above faid, and was acknowledg'd Lieutenant-General of the Provinces above-named, under a Chief, whofe Name was ftill a Secret. Du Pleffis Mornay took upon himfelf the care of procuring the Duke of Alençon's Efcape ; and Colombieres that of caufing an Infurrection in *Normandy*, and fo on.

Now, their Preparations would have been attended with better Succefs, had they not alter'd their time appointed, or had Guitry fubmitted himfelf to that Alteration (*). But for fome private Concerns of his own, (he was told that a Conftable, with his Bailiffs, were coming to arreft him for Debts) he would not tarry any longer, he fent word to La Nouë to rife in arms, becaufe he was going to execute his part. He came indeed, as abovefaid, near St. Germain, and fent Captain Callitrope with a Letter to the Duke of Alençon, acquainting his Highnefs, that he was ready, and exhorting him to improve that opportunity for his Deliverance.

The Duke, with his Council, wondered at this Guitry's Refolution, and refolved at firft to follow his Advice, and to fet out the next Morning with the King of Navarre, &c. on pretence of a Hunting-match, and to go directly to *Mantes*, where De Buhi, Brother to Du Pleffis Mornay, was in garrifon. Accordingly the faid Du Pleffis received Orders of the Duke to be ready early in the Morning to lead them thither.

L l 3

But

(*) This is only a Guefs of mine, that an Alteration had been made in their Scheme as to the time, whereto Guitry refufed to comply, and feems to me the beft way for reconciling the Hiftorians : At firft they appointed Shrove-Tuefday, but for fome reafons, they thought proper to put it off to the 10th of March. Guitry, who knew his own Circumftances, had very likely difpofed of his Affairs in fuch a manner, that he could fet out on Shrove-Tuefday, and no later, and poffibly could not alter his own Scheme.

Charles
IX.
1574.
Pope Gregory XIII.

But a little after the Duke altered his Mind, at La Molle's Persuasion, considering that the number of Guitry's Troops was too great not to be discovered, and too small to protect him against the Pursuits of the Court; and so he resolved to stay, and to wait for a better opportunity.

In the mean while La Molle, who knew very well his Master's Intentions, discovered the Plot to the Queen-Mother, in order to deserve some favour, as he thought, by revealing what could not be kept concealed any longer (y).

Great Confusion of the Court at the Discovery of the Plot.

At this News, the Queen, in order to exasperate the King more and more against his Brother, feigned to be in the greatest fright, and caused all the Apartments of St. Germain's Palace, and all the Corners thereof to be thoroughly searched, even the Duke of Alençon, and the King of Navarre's Beds. She advised the King to depart immediately from so dangerous a place, which was of a very bad Omen, and fatal, as she pretended, grounded upon some Predictions of her Astrologers.

Therefore the Court departed in a great hurry and confusion, the King laid that Night at the Count of Retz in the Suburb of *St. Honoré*, and a few days after he went to the Castle of *Vincennes*, with the Duke of Alençon, and the King of Navarre, who were not as yet under Arrest, but very narrowly watched. Soon after came the News of Insurrections in several Parts of the Kingdom. In *Poitou*, La Noue had surprised *Lusignan* and *Mesle*, by the means of Loche and Baroniere, and *Fontenay*, by the means of St. Stephen and Bessé. He fortified these Places, and put in them a strong Garrison. In *Xaintonge* and

Insurrections in Poitou, &c.

(y) Vie de M. de la Noue, pag. 110, 111, 112, 113. Vie de M. Du Plessis Liv. I. pag. 25, 26, 27. Thuan. Lib. 57. pag. 980, 981.

Angoumois, he furprized likewife *Pons*,
nay-*Charente*, *Roian*, *Talmont*, *St. John de*
ɩgle, *Rochefort* and *Bouteville*, by the means
De Pons de la Caze Lord of Mirambeau,
ɩn de Plaffac, of the illuftrious Houfe of de
ɩs, to whom adjoined themfelves Rochefou-
ɩlt de Monguyon, Uffon, Bertoville, Sau-
ɩ, and another, all Gentlemen of great For-
ɩde and Courage. Thefe Conquefts were
ɩde without any great Refiftance ; and La
ouë being a Man confpicuous for his Mode-
tion, treated the Inhabitants thereof with
eat mildnefs, without impofing upon them any
:w Taxes for the Maintenance of the Garrifons,
hich were paid by other means.

Amidft all thefe Succeffes, happened the Death
f La Caze Lord of Mirambeau, who was killed
ʋith a Mufket-ball before a Caftle, as the Be-
eged asked for a Parley. The great Qualities,
noral and civil, of that Gentleman made him the
nore regretted by all thofe who were acquainted
ʋith him ; but efpecially by La Nouë, who
ɩad a great Value for him, becaufe of a Confor-
nity of Temper and Inclinations, that was between them.

If the Reformed were unfortunate in Velay,
they were recompenfed by their Progrefs in Vivaretz ; the Garrifon of *Villeneuve* having routed
fome of the King's Troops, took *Aubenas*, and
whereas the Garrifon of that Place, was compofed for the moft part of the Murderers of *Lions*,
who had executed the Maffacre upon the Reformed, they were put to the Sword every one ;
they took likewife the Caftle of *St. Pyrauld*,
Audance and *Maleval* in *Forez*, whereby they
furrounded the City of *Lions*, and reduced it to
great ftraits. Therefore Mandelot, Governour
thereof, having affembled fome Forces, went

*In Velay,
Vivaretz,
&c.*

and

Charles
IX.

1574.
Pope Gregory XIII.

Vain Attempt of the Royalists upon Nimes.

Damville's Conduct in Languedoc.

And of Montbrun in Dauphiné.

and besieged the Castle of *St. Pyrauld*, and th
Succours expected from the Lord of St. Roma
coming too late, the Castle was taken by stor
and all its Fortifications were demolished.

St. Jaille attempted upon *Nimes* ; but he w
unsuccessful, and a large Sum of Money, whi
he had paid to Deroni, a Captain of the City, f
admitting him into it, was lost to him, becau
Deroni, who had nothing else in view but
deceive him, acted in concert with St. Roma
whom, from the very first day he had acquaint
with De Jaille's Propositions, and had receiv
of him his Instructions how to behave himse
which he had exactly followed.

Damville Governour of Languedoc, unde
standing what was hatching against him at Cou
and knowing by some intercepted Letters, th
Martinengue, who had been sent to join hi
self with St. Sulpice and Villeroy, had Orders
kill him, if they could not arrest him, he su
prized *Montpelier, Lunel, Beaucaire* and *Pezena*
however, forbearing from any other open A
of Hostility, by which Conduct he lost *Pezena*
which was sold to the Royalists by the Capt
whom he had intrusted with the Guard there
and of a Daughter of his of two Years old ; t
said Captain saying, That he desired to have
Master who stood by one Party, and should n
be wavering and irresolute as Damville was (z).

In *Dauphiné*, the whole Country was in
dread, by the frequent Incursions of Montbru
who made several Conquests, though he misca
ried in his Attempt upon *Montelimar*, whic
cost very dear to the Reformed Inhabitant
thereof. Such was the State of Affairs in th
remotest Provinces.

The

(z) Thuan. lib. 57. pag 981, 982.

They were not in a better Condition in *Normandy*, tho' nearer the Court, where Colombieres, De Guitry, and De Sey, waiting for the Arrival of Montgommery with a Fleet from *Jersey*, surprized in the mean while *St. Lo* and *Domfront.* The Count being landed at *St. Lo*, with De Lorges his Son, and De Refuge Galardon his Son-in-law, marched directly to besiege *Carentan* with what Troops he could assemble, and three days after the Place surrendered it self ; from thence he went to *Valognes*, which surrendered likewise, and by that means he opened a free Passage from one of these Places to another ; he sent Provisions to Carentan, which he intended to fortify (*a*).

Aid of Colombieres, Montgommery, &c. in Normandy.

At this News the King being astonished, set on foot three Armies ; one against Montgommery, under the Command of Matignon Deputy-Governour of *Normandy* ; another against La Nouë, under the Command of the Duke of Montpensier ; and the third to act in the southern Provinces, under the Command of the Prince Dauphin, Son to the Duke of Montpensier ; but before we proceed any farther, we must relate what they were doing at Court.

The fifth Civil War.

The Queen-Mother failed not to publish in the Kingdom and abroad, that a very odious Plot had been discovered against the King's Person and his Government ; that the Plotters intended to murder the King, and to seize upon his Crown. Whereupon the Duke of Alençon and the King of Navarre, in order to clear themselves of such a heinous Imputation, published a Writing on the 24th of March, at the Queen's instance, who thought thereby to put in a dread all those who were any wise concerned in the Association, when they should see themselves disavowed

Alençon and Navarr declare themselves against the Plot.

(*a*) Idem ibidem.

vowed and forsaken, by those whom they thought
would have been their Chiefs. She intended likewise to cast by that means the whole Odium of
the Enterprize upon the Marshal Duke of Montmorancy, and the Marshal of Cossé, whom she
had resolved to arrest Prisoners. So she caused
the Princes her Son and Son-in-law, to declare,
That having understood that they were aspersed
in publick, as if they, forgetting their Dignity
and Duty, had been any wise Accessories to the
Plot of *St. Germain*, they had humbly required
the King's leave for giving account to the Publick of their Will and Intention. Therefore
they desired their Friends to be firmly persuaded,
that it was utterly false that they ever had any
hand at all in the said Plot, nor ever thought of
such a thing, which was very far from their
Mind, being, on the contrary, ready to spend
their Lives, Faculties, and Interest for the King
and Kingdom's Welfare, and to oppose with all
their might, the Efforts of all those that endeavour'd to disturb the Publick's Peace and
Tranquillity, as they were bound by all the Ties
of Nature, and all divine and human Rights.
Which Declaration however was of no effect,
and served only to let the Publick know the
Captivity wherein the Princes were detained.

*The Prince
of Condé's
Escape.*

The Prince of Condé was gone into his Government of *Picardy*, and would have shared the
same fate as the Duke of Alençon, and the King
of Navarr, had he not prevented it by a sea-
sonable Escape ; the Lords of Thoré and Meru,
Brothers to the Duke of Montmorancy, made
likewise their Escape. The Prince of Condé
retired to *Strasbourg*, where he abjured publickly
the Roman Religion, declaring that he had been
forced to embrace it against his own Conscience.

The

The King having had patience till now, flew *Charles* out on a sudden into a violent Passion, and or- *IX.* dered a strict and severe Enquiry to be made into *Pope Gre-* that Conspiracy; for so he called the Duke of A- *gory XIII.* lençon's Correspondence with the Reformed and *Court's* Politicians; and the first President Thuanus, and *Measures* the President Hennequin were deputed for that *for trying* purpose.   Therefore having begun their Pro- *the preten-* ceedings, Brinon, a Man of a good and honour- *ded Con-* rable Family, but much reduced in Paris, and *spirators.* thereby forced to turn an Informer for getting his Bread, caused many to be arrested Prisoners, several of whom were only upon Suspicion.

Joseph de Boniface, Lord of La Molle, the *La Molle,* Duke's Favourite, and Annibal Count of Co- *Coconnas,* connas a Piemontese, Lawrence du Bois Lord *&c. arre-* of St. Martin of the Stones, Peter de Grantrye *ted.* Steward of the King's Houshold, and Counsel- lor of State, Francis de Tourtray, who had been Secretary to Grandchamp, Brother to de Gran- trye, while he was Embassador at Constanti- nople, were arrested.   Thoré, Meru, the Vis- count of Turenne, John Laffin de Beauvais la Nocle, and Grandchamp himself escaped by flight.

On the 11th of April, La Molle and Cocon- *And tried.* nas were interrogated; the first at *Paris* by Thu- anus first President, upon 21 Articles exhibited against him : he denied them all, or said, that he had no Knowledge of these things.   Cocon- nas was brought on the same day to the Castle of *Vincennes,* before the King, and deceived by that difference put between him and La Molle, he flattered himself that he would easily escape, if he complied only with the Queen's Desire, therefore he confessed more than he was asked, and even more than he knew, in order to please their Majesties and to save his Life.

Two

Charles
IX.
1574.
Pope Gre-
goryXIII.

*Alençon
and Na-
varr's dif-
ferent An-
swers.*

Two days after, the Duke of Alençon and the King of Navarr, whom Coconnas had charged, delivered their Declaration in Writing, becauſe their Quality exempted them from following the common courſe in theſe Occaſions; The firſt anſwered like an obedient Son, that makes a general but moſt humble Confeſſion, and was ready to furniſh his Mother with whatever Crimes ſhe could deſire, for compaſſing the Ruin of all his Friends, Clients, and Servants. The other anſwered as a King Captive as to his Perſon, (for he and the Duke had Guards ſet upon them) but always free as to his Dignity; he bitterly inveighed againſt the Queen in her own Preſence, and before the Chancellor and other Commiſſaries, complaining of the many Plots laid againſt his Life, even from his Cradle, of the many Wrongs and Injuſtices, of the many Affronts put upon him ſince his coming to Court, whereby his Patience had been quite worn out, therefore he had reſolved to fly from a Place wherein he could not live any longer with honour; and indeed, ſays he, what Security could I expect in a Place, where the capital Enemies of my Houſe bore the ſway? where the Lorrainers are raiſed to the higheſt pitch of Favour; where the Duke of Guiſe, at the Recommendation of the King of *Poland*, is to enjoy the Dignity of Conſtable; where Innocence can find no Security or Protection againſt the Frauds, Calumnies, Ambuſhes, &c. of the Wicked; where, in a word, I do receive every day friendly Advices to provide for myſelf, becauſe the Duke of Alençon, and the Prince of Condé and I are deſtined to a certain Death? He added ſeveral other Truths, which put the Queen out of countenance; and he reiterated the ſame things five days after at a ſecond Interrogation
before

before her Majesty, the Cardinal of Bourbon, the Chancellor, and the Commissaries (*b*).

Though that Prince spoke with so great assurance, nevertheless he was almost persuaded that he was undone, and that this was only a Device for hastening his Ruin ; and I do find in Agricola (*Le Laboureur*) that the said Prince, in order to avert the threatning Danger, if possible, had advised the Duke of Alençon to feign to be sick, and to send for his Mother, and then, under pretence that they both had some Secret to tell her, they would desire her Majesty to send her Attendants out of the Room, and then they would strangle her. That his Reasons were that of their own Preservation ; the King's Death which was not far off ; the great Interest which their Friends would get thereby ; and that the political Views which engaged her to renounce the Laws of Nature and of Blood, for procuring the Destruction of her own Son and her Son-in-law, dispensed them by a much greater Consideration than that of Ambition to govern, from feeling any Horror for an Action, whereby two Princes, necessary to the State, were saved by the Death of her who disturbed the Peace thereof, and hasten'd its Ruin. The Duke (*continues my Author*) wanted Courage for the Execution, as well as Discretion to conceal that Advice from his Mother ; for some time after he told her of it, and it is the true Cause of the insuperable Hatred which that Princess conceived against the King of Navarr ; to gratify which, she made no scruple afterwards to conspire with the Guises against her own darling Henry III. when she saw that he had no Issue ; and that, for hindering Henry IV. from succeeding

(*b*) Thuan. lib. 57. 983, 4, 5. Agricola Additions aux Mem. de Casteln. Tom. II. liv. 6. ch. 2. pag. 354—581.

ceeding to the Crown, and for placing upon the Throne Henry Duke of Lorrain, her Grandson, by her Daughter the Duchess of Lorrain (*c*).

But, let it be said with all the Reverence due to the Memory of the judicious Author, such a Plot is of too black a Dye, and too base and odious in itself, to have ever entered into so noble and generous a Soul as that of the King of Navarr. Had King Charles himself called his Mother to give account of her Administration; had he delivered her to the Power of the Law to try her, and do with her as the Law directed; had he delivered her to suffer the Punishment, which her manifold and most heinous Crimes deserved, he had a Right to do it, as supreme Magistrate, obliged in that Character to do Justice without any Partiality; nevertheless his Behaviour, in that respect, would have been justly censured, and in his own Time, and throughout all the Ages to come; nay, that would have compleated his wicked Character, as Agrippina's Murder compleated Nero's. How much more so, had the Duke of Alençon and the King of Navarr, who were but Subjects, attempted such a thing? Therefore I may wish, that Agricola had named his Authorities for what he says; he speaks of certain Memoirs, but he don't name the Authors, or from what hand he had them, he had left us in the dark not able to judge of their Authenticity, but inclined to question the Veracity, not of Agricola, but of his Memoirs. A Charge so grave as this must be grounded upon the best Foundation, especially when the whole Character of a Prince contradicts it. This is nothing but what, in justice, I owe to Henry IVth's Memory.

To

(*c*) This last Tom. II. liv. 2. ch. 2. pag. 352.

Charles
IX.
1574.
Pope Gregory XIII.

*La Molle,
Coconnas,
Tourtray
condemned,*

To make an end of La Molle, Coconnas, and others Trials, it is to be obſerved, that, though whatever could be inferred from the ſeveral Depoſitions of the Witneſſes, amounted to no more than a Deſign of helping the Duke of Alençon to eſcape from Court, and of obſtructing the King of Poland's Return into the Kingdom, for placing the ſaid Duke upon the Throne after King Charles's Death, neverthelefs they were condemned as guilty of High Treaſon. La Molle was charged with having compaſſed the King's Death by Magick Arts, becauſe of a Wax-Image, which, as they pretended at Court, had been done for King Charles, and was pierced through the Heart with a Needle; but La Molle ſays to the laſt, that it had been done for a young Lady in *Provence,* which he loved deſperately, in order to engage her to return love for love; and that Coſmo Rugieri, a famous Aſtrologer of that time, had been the Artificer thereof.   However De la Molle and Coconnas were condemned to be beheaded, after having been put to an extraordinary Torture; for the Queen neglected nothing to force them to confeſs that they had conſpired againſt the King's Life. Tourtray was condemned to be hanged, (Thuanus, and thoſe who have copied after him, ſay, to be broke upon the Wheel.)   The Sentence was executed with all the Rigour of the Law on the 30th of April.   Coſmo, by the Queen's favour, who was paſſionately fond of ſuch ſort of Men, was condemned to the Galleys, but lived at *Marſeilles* with as much Freedom and Eaſe, as he could have done at *Paris;* Grantrye was ſpared by the favour of the Biſhop of Limoges, Brother to his Mother.

What is very obſervable in the Depoſitions of theſe pretended Criminals, was, that moſt of them

them agreed in this point, that the King had received a Packet from *Spain*, and another from *Rome*; by the first, Philip II. advised him to put to death the Duke of Alençon and the King of Navarr; by the second, the Pope sent a Dispensation and Absolution for that Fratricide.

The Marshals of Montmorancy and Cossé arrested.

Tho' there was no proof against the Duke of Montmorancy and the Marshal of Cossé, nevertheless the Queen seeing the King grow worse and worse every day, and being certain, that his Death was very near, being afraid, left these Lords should obstruct the King of Poland's Return, raised Suspicions and Jealousies in the King's Mind, who, in the condition he was in, was more apt than ever to receive those Impressions of Distrust and Fear, which his Mother was willing to make upon him, and extorted from him an Order for them to repair to Court, which was sent to the Duke of Montmorancy at *Chantilly*, by Torcy; they obey'd at the first Summons, notwithstanding their Ladies and Friends Intreaties. Being arrived at *Vincennes*, they were lodged in the Castle, in full liberty; and tho' they received Warnings of their Friends to make speedily their Escape, if they had a mind to avoid the Danger, yet trusting to their Innocence, they neglected these wholesome Advices, and three days after their Arrival they were arrested Prisoners by the Viscount D'Auchy, who brought them to the Bastile at *Paris*, to the great Joy of the Parisians, who offered and furnished eight hundred Men for the Prisoners Guard.

Operations of the three Armies.

While the Court was tossed by these Commotions, the three Armies under the Command of their respective Generals were in action in the several Provinces wherein they had been sent, with various Success. The Duke of Montpensier's Army

Army made at first very small progress in *Poitou*. Biron was in *Xaintonge* at *St. John d'Angely*, spying the first opportunity to do service to the King, or rather to the Queen, and not being able to do better, he made an attempt upon *Tonnay-Charente*; he was in hopes of taking it by the Intelligence he had with a Publick-Notary of the Place, but the Traitor having been discovered, was seized and punished according to his deserts, and his Accomplices fled away, whereby Biron was disappointed, and obliged to retreat. The Duke of Montpensier having sojourned a few days at *Parthenai* and *Coulonges*, was come to *St. Hermine*, to draw La Nouë, if he could, to an Engagement, which La Nouë declining, he sent part of his Army under the Command of Puygaillard, to besiege *Talmont*; and he himself went to besiege *Fontenay*, whereof St. Stephen was Commander, from whom he had received of late, a great Affront. *Talmont* having capitulated, Puigalliard led his Troops to Montpensier's Army, before *Fontenay*, but for all that, after two general Assaults, wherein he lost many of his best Troops, he was forced to raise the Siege.

Before this, the Court not forgetting its old Artifices, had hired two Assassines, MAUREVEL, and one St. MARTIN, to murder La Nouë; but tho' they came with that design to *Poitou*, nevertheless they could not execute it (d).

In *Languedoc*, the War was more fierce than any where else, the Reformed being Masters of several of the best Places, and being confirmed by the hopes which the Prince of Condé gave them of speedy Succours from the Protestant Princes of Germany, they rejected, as dangerous, all Propositions of Peace made by the Court.

The

(d) Thuan. lib. 57. p. 986.

M m

The Prince being arrived at *Strasbourg*, as a-
boveſaid, reſolved to follow the ſteps of his Father, and meeting in that City a Deputy of the
Reformed in *Languedoc*, who was treating for a
certain number of Reïſters, he ſent Gaſques to
France, with Letters of the 4th of May, directed
to the Reformed of Languedoc, and to the Lord
of St. Romain, one of their Governours; whereby he gave them notice of his and Thoré's ſafe
Arrival in *Germany*, and promiſing to undertake
their Defence, as his Father had done, and to
ſend them the Auxiliaries as ſoon as they had
remitted the neceſſary Sums for that purpoſe.
Thoré wrote by the ſame Meſſenger to his Brother Damville, and uſed his beſt Endeavours to
perſuade him to declare himſelf openly now, and
to avert the threatning Danger he was in, to be
ſerved in the ſame manner as their Brother of
Montmorency was, and may be, to fare worſe.
But Damville, tho' moved by theſe Exhortations,
was afraid leſt the Marſhal Duke his Brother
ſhould be made anſwerable for all the ſteps he
might take, therefore he was in a great perplexity,
and wavered between two Parties: he wrote to
the King, and made great Proteſtations of Fidelity and Obedience, declaring that the Duke his
Brother would certainly make his Innocence appear in a little time; but whatever ſhould be his
Caſe and his Fate, he was in hopes that he would
not be involved under the ſame Condemnation,
that he was ready to clear himſelf before any impartial Judges, and to reſign his Government and
Marſhal's Staff into the King's hands, to diſpoſe
of them as his Majeſty pleaſed, after he had ſuf-
ficiently evinced his Innocence. But his Deputy
arriving at Court when the King drew near to
his end, that Affair was ſuperſeded till after his
Death. As to the Army under the Command
of

of the Prince Dauphin, Son to the Duke of Mont-pensier, it made very little progress either in *Languedoc* or *Dauphiné*, till after the King's Death, and therefore I refer the Relation of them to the next Volume.

But in *Normandy*, Matignon and Fervaques having joined their Forces together, came to *St. Lo*, from whence they came to *Damfront*, where they had understood that Montgommery was, and besieged it. At first, the Besieged made a brave resistance, but seeing that the Place was not tenable, some of them being disheartened, forsook the Count, and surrendered themselves to the Royal Army. The Queen-Mother having notice that the said Count was in the Nets, sent more Troops to reinforce Matignon, and sent likewise Orders to those that besieged St. Lo, to march directly to Damfront, the Castle whereof was battered with six Cannons, for five hours together, on the 23d of May, and made a Breach of 45 Paces; then the Count saw himself deserted by most part of his Men, nevertheless he withstood a furious Assault for five hours together, wherein the Royalists were worsted; but at last, seeing that he was almost alone in the Place, with some wounded, and that there was no Ammunition or Provisions in it, he yielded to the strong Sollicitations of Vassey, one of his near Relations, who served in the Royal Army, and surrendered upon Capitulation, that their Lives should be safe, and that they should march out with their Clothes, their Swords and Daggers. But as for himself, he should remain for some time in the hands of Matignon and Vassey, and that he should be treated honourably, and his Life safe.

On the 26th of May, Matignon and Vassey went to fetch the Count out of the Castle, and

Charles
IX.
1574.
Pope Gregory XIII.

the reft marched out on the fame day. None of the Capitulation-Articles were obferved, for feveral were killed, fome hanged, and the reft, three or four excepted, were ftript. The Count himfelf, a few days after, was fent to Paris by the Queen's Orders, and there tried, condemned, and executed; but this happened at the beginning of the next Reign.

The King drawing near his end, declares his Mother Regent.

Now the King was a dying, and on the 29th of May, the Queen-Mother, in order to fettle her Authority, caufed Letters to be fent in the King's Name, to the Governours of Provinces, notifying unto them, that during his Sicknefs, being not able to take care of the Government, he intrufted his Mother with it, and commanded them to obey her in every thing as himfelf, and in cafe he fhould die, to pay a ftrict Obedience to her Commands, till his Brother the King of *Poland* fhould arrive in *France*. The next day, 30th of May, which was Whit-Sunday, the Queen not thinking thefe Letters of the 29th fufficient to declare her Regent of the Kingdom, during the King of *Poland*'s abfence, ordered Chancellor Birague to fpeak to the King about it (e). The King, who was in his Agony, fent for the Secretaries of his Commands, and the Captains of his Guards, and bid them to do whatever the Queen his Mother fhould command them, and to obey her Orders as his own; then the

(e) Papyrius Maffo and Brantome, who had tranfcribed him, and fome others, fay that he did this of his own accord, and had fent for Birague, &c. Thuanus fays only, that the Letters-Patent conftituting the Queen-Mother Regent, were drawn on Whit-Sunday, without fpecifying whether he did it by his own accord, or by the Impulfion of others; I have followed thofe who fay that he did it by Birague's Impulfion, becaufe, methinks it is not likely that being in fuch Agonies, as it is faid he was in, he could think of any fuch things.

Charles IX. 1574. Pope Gregory XIII.

he Duke of Alençon and the King of Navarr
were fent for, to let them know that the Queen-
Mother was intrufted with the Regency of the
Kingdom during the King's Sicknefs, and if he
died, during his Succeffor's abfence. Letters-
Patent of it were drawn out of hand, which
however, could not be regiftered in Parliament
till the 3d of June, becaufe of the Holidays ; and
for gratifying the Queen's Ambition, it was in-
ferted in the Acts, that the reading, publifhing,
and regiftering of the faid Letters had been done
at the King's Attorney-General's Inftance ; then
the Queen took upon her the Title of Regent,
and the fupreme Adminiftration of the Kingdom,
being required fo to do, by the Duke of Alençon
and the King of Navarr, who were forced to
it, as well as by the Cardinal of Bourbon, the
Prefidents and Counfellors of the Parliament,
which that Court had deputed for that purpofe.

Mean while, the King after having fuffered the *King Charles's Death.*
bittereft Pains, and the fevereft Agonies, died at
three in the Afternoon, on the very fame day
that the Letters-Patent had been drawn, having
lived 23 Years, eleven Months, and three Days,
being born on the 27th of June, 1550 (*f*). He
came to the Crown on the 5th of December,
1560.

That Prince was born with all thofe Qualifica- *His Character.*
tions requifite to make a Hero, when they are
curioufly cultivated and carefully improved to
their true and right ufe ; but his Mother's immoderate and criminal Ambition incited her to
neglect his Education, and to truft him into the
hands of Perfons of bad Principles and bad Morals ;

M m 3

(*f*) Thuanus his Copift, d'Aubigné, and fome others,
fay that he was in the 25th Year of his age, and neverthelefs
they all agree that he was born on the 27th of June, 1550.

rals, and to entertain him in all manner of Diſſoluteneſs.

He was born at the Caſtle of St. Germain en
Laye, on the 27th of June 1550, at half an hour
after Five ; it is ſaid that Michel de *Salon*, ſur-
named NOSTRADAMUS, having caſt his Nativity,
foretold that his Reign would be bloody and unfortunate, which was verified by the event.
Maximilian, then Arch-Duke of Auſtria, was
his Godfather, and he was chriſtened by the
Name of Maximilian, which was afterwards
changed into that of Charles.

He was tall, but a little crooked, and carried
his Head awry, his Looks were ſharp, his Noſe
hawked, his Complexion was pale and leaded,
his Hair black, his Neck ſomething long, he
was full cheſted, all his Body well proportioned,
his Legs excepted, which ſome ſay, were too big,
and was born with a ſtrong Conſtitution, which
he ſpoiled intirely by his too frequent and too violent Exerciſes, as we ſhall ſay.

He was naturally of a great Spirit, of a quick
and piercing Wit, of a ſharp Judgment, of a
ready Memory, of an incredible Activity, and
had a fine, noble, and rich way of expreſſing himſelf.

His Writing-Maſter was one Peter Hammon,
of *Blois*, who was afterwards hanged at *Paris*
for his Religion, during the Civil Wars. Amiot
Abbot of *Belloſane*, and then Biſhop of Auxerre,
well known by his Verſion of Plutarch's Lives,
was his Tutor, he loved him intirely, and ſhewed
always great regard for him, tho' he jeered him
ſometimes upon his Avarice, and great Penu-
riouſneſs, living moſtly upon Neat's Tongues.
He learned the Grammar under him, and liked
Learning well enough in his Childhood, but as
ſoon as he aſcended the Throne, he neglected
his

his Studies, neverthelefs he had always a great regard for the Learned. Amongft the Sciences, he was particularly a great Admirer of Mufick and Poetry; befides the ordinary Salary which his Band of Muficians received, he rewarded them with very rich Livings, efpecially one LE ROY an Eunuch, who excelled in his Art. Amongft the Poets, he had a great value for DAURAT, who wrote in Latin, and for RONSARD, the moft celebrated amongft the French Poetsof his Age, and JOHN ANTHONY BAIF, Son of Lazarus; his Gifts to them were but fmall, but frequent, and his reafon for it was, to keep them always in play, and oblige them to work conftantly, for he compared Poets to fine Horfes, which muft be fed but not fattened: he himfelf made Verfes tolerably good. As to his moral Qualities, he was liberal, magnificent, very fober, he eat but very little, and abftained from Wine fince he had been once put out of order with it, he drank commonly but Water or Hipocras. He flept but very little, and very often he was up before Midnight. Tho' his Court was the Receptacle of all the Filthinefs in the World, I don't find that he had been much inclined to Lewdnefs; he had but one Miftrefs, which he conftantly loved, MARY TOUCHET was her Name, Daughter (not of an Apothecary of *Orleans*, as almoft all the Hiftorians have faid) but of John Touchet Sieur de Beauvais and du Quillart, one of the King's Council, and private Lieutenant of the Bailiwick and Prefidialfhip of *Orleans (g)*, fhe was a perfect Beauty; the King had a Son by her named Charles of Valois, Count of *Auvergne* and *Ponthieu*, Duke of *Angouleme*. It is true that before his Marriage, he ufed very often to enter

M m 4 into

(g) Agricola addit. aux Mem. de Caftelnau, Tom. II. Liv. vii. p. 605.

into the Apartments of the Maids of Honour, and other Ladies of the Court, in the Morning, and to whip them in their Beds, but this was a Frolick of his. He was constant enough in his Friendship, whereof he gave a great Instance in behalf of Ambrosius Paré his first Surgeon, and of his own Nurse; tho' they both professed the Reformed Religion, nevertheless he had always for them the same regard, the same Affection, and took them under his Protection at the time of the Massacre, for he sent for the first, on the first Night, and bad him to stay in his Wardrobe, saying, that it was not reasonable that a Man who could be useful to a little World, should be massacred, he never required of him to change his Religion. As to his Nurse, he was always so kind to her that he never refused her any thing which she could ask, either for herself or for her Relations and Friends; he left her always at full liberty as to her Religion, only he desired that she would acknowledge her Errors for the good of her own Soul: Papyrius Masso says, that she renounced her Religion at Bartholomew's-time, being frightened by the Massacres; but Brantome, and after him Agricola, say, that she was not in earnest, and did it only out of Complaisance to the King: I am surprized that her Name hath not been recorded by any of the Historians that I have seen, either Roman Catholicks or Reformed; I find only that she was a Country-Woman, very subtle and cunning, but likewise very civil and affable, and that she acquired so much Wit and Sagacity at Court, that she became able to judge of every thing. I have made mention of her in the second Volume, when I spoke of the Battel of Dreux.

Till now we have seen nothing in King Charles, but what is either commendable, or indifferent in
itself,

itfelf, or at leaft tolerable in a Prince. But his Vices muft not be concealed, tho' moft part of them had been contracted either by Education and bad Examples, or by his way of living, and violent Exercifes. He was naturally paffionate and cholerick, but that Difpofition was not only fomented in him, but alfo increafed to an exceffive degree by his Exercifes, efpecially Hunting, Forging and Hammering. He had fo ftrong a Paffion for the firft, that he forgot eating, drinking, fleeping, for it, and was Days and Nights rambling in the Woods, and founding the Horn himfelf, he was very fkilful in catching of the wild Beafts, and compofed a Book about the Train and Equipage belonging to Venery, and about the means of catching the wild Beafts, and hunting them out of their Holds ; the Book was tranflated into Latin by his Orders, but I don't know whether it had ever been publifhed. When he returned from hunting, he went to his Forge, and there he worked as hard as any Blackfmith's Journeyman could do, and put himfelf all in a fweat, to make fometimes a Horfe-Shoe, fometimes a Gun, at other times other things, according to his fancy ; thefe Exercifes ftirred up his Paffion to fuch a degree, that he was furious and mad in his Anger : and his being almoft continually bent againft the Beafts, which he was ufed to draw, and dip his Arms into their Blood, made him cruel, bloody, and blood-thirfty, not only againft the Beafts, but even againft Men, (notwithftanding what Papyrius Maffo fays to the contraty) for tho' it don't appear that he had ever killed any Man with his own Hands, how many Executioners had he not in his pay ? And what fhows that Eagernefs, was his going to look upon the Admiral hanging at *Montfaucon*, to look upon Briquemaut and Cavagnes when they

were

were executed, and causing Candles to be put all
over the Gibbet, that he might see what Mouths
and Faces they made in dying, for firing over the
River *Seine* upon his poor Subjects that endeavoured to escape from the Massacre, either by
swimming or otherwise: Indeed if these are not
some of the greatest Instances of Cruelty in a
Prince, I don't know what is. He was used to
kill Hogs, to draw them, and to dress them himself, as well as any Butcher could have done ; all
these things heated his natural Dispositions, and
prompted him to the most violent Acts. He
was one of the most heinous Swearers and Blas-
phemers, this he had learnt of his Governors
Cipierre, and the Count of Retz, especially the
last, but had so far improved that base and wicked
Habit, that he never spoke two Words, but one
was a Curse or an Oath, and he took that for an
Ornament of Speech, rather than for a Vice ;
from whence it came to pass that he made no
scruple of forswearing himself frequently, and that
he had no great regard for his most sacred Promises and Engagements: he was in that respect
a plague to his Kingdom, for the Courtiers following his Example, the City conformed itself
to the Court, and the Provinces to the chief City
of the Kingdom. He was thoroughly Master
in the Art of dissembling, so well he had improved in his Mother's School! Nay, he carried
it so far, that according to Thuanus himself, who,
speaking of the Massacre, pretends that Charles
was naturally so cholerick and passionate, that it
was impossible for him to dissemble so long, and
yet he says, when he relates his last Farewell to
his Mother, IN EO ETIAM DISSIMULATIONE U-
SUS; QUIPPE CUM CONSTARET, EUM SI DIU-
TIUS VIXISSET, &c. that is, wherein he dissembled likewise, seeing that it is certain, that had he
lived

lived any longer, he was refolved to make ufe of
his own Judgment and to govern himfelf, and
to remove his Mother from all manner of Adminiftration in his Kingdom. He tells us, fome
lines before, that he had refolved to fend his
Mother away for a time, on the fpecious pretence
of paying a Vifit to her beloved Son the King of
Poland. We need not obferve, that his Reign
was one of the moft unhappy and miferable that
had ever been feen in France; but to do him
juftice, we muft own, that it was rather the Fault
of others than his own; he was fenfible, but too
late, of the bad Adminiftration of his Mother; he
fadly felt the pernicious Effects of the bloody
Counfels of his bad Counfellors, and was fully
refolved, as he faid, to remove them out of
Council. He knew at laft, that the Civil Wars
which had raged in his Kingdom during his Reign,
had been kindled by a Spirit of Faction, rather
than of Religion, and was refolved to deftroy the
Houfe of Guife and Montmorancy, for he hated
them both equally, without any regard to the Juftice of the Pretenfions of the laft, who certainly deferved better of the Crown than the firft. But
his Death put a ftop to all his Defigns. He was
faying two or three days before, that he was very
glad to die without any male Iffue, becaufe he
knew by his own Experience, how miferable is
the Condition of a King minor, and how lamentable would be the Fate of the Kingdom, under
the Government of a Regent, or other Adminif-
trators, that the State of the Kingdom was fuch,
that it required a Man and not a Child to govern
it. Neverthelefs, he had no great Opinion of
his Brother the King of Poland, for he faid, that
the great hopes conceived of him not only by the
French but alfo by foreign Princes, would be certainly fruftrated, and that he would be known,
fuch

such as he was, as soon as he should ascend the Throne. Tho' it was thought that he spoke those Words out of Jealousy against his Brother, nevertheless they were verified by the Event. He was taken ill of a Fever in October, 1573, just when his Brother set out for Poland, and not two days after he had been in so violent a Passion against his Mother and Brother, which occasioned the Report of his having been poisoned. AGRICOLA, having related what Anguishes the Queen-Mother was in at the parting of her beloved Son, the great Apprehensions she had of losing her Credit and Authority, leaves his Reader at full Liberty to think whatever he pleases concerning King Charles's Death. However, he suffered the most exquisite Pains, and was seen almost swimming in his own Blood, which came out of his Body through all the usual Passages, and thro' the Pores; but who could express the Remories and Tortures of his poor Soul? *Ah! Nurse, my dear*, says he, the day before his Death, *Ah! Nurse, how much Blood, how many Murders, ah! that I have followed a bad Counsel, O my God, do forgive me, and vouchsafe to be merciful unto me; I don't know where I am, so great is my Perplexity and Trouble, what will become of all this? What shall I do? I am undone, I know that very well.* His Nurse endeavoured to comfort him; at last he died, having recommended the Queen his Consort, and the Princess his Daughter, to his Mother. His Corpse was opened the next Day, before the Magistrates, no Contusion nor Spot was found in it, and Brantome says, that he and Strozzi asked PARÉ what he thought of the King's Death, what had occasioned it? who answered, that the too frequent sounding of the Horn had been the occasion of it. And it appears, by a Letter of the Queen-Mother to the

French

French Ambaſſador in England, that his Lungs were much offended, but that all other parts of his Body were very intire and wholeſome. Neverthelefs, the Publick perfiſted in the belief of his having been poiſoned either by his Mother, or Brother of *Poland*, or by the mutual Conſent of both. And the ſtrong Suſpicion againſt the Queen-Mother occaſioned the following Lines ;

De quadam Maga.

Eſſe quid hoc dicam : quondam MEDICÆA
   Virago
  Uſa fuit medicis, ut bene fœta foret.
Sicque virum medicè, numeroſâ prole beavit,
  Sicque fuit Natis illa beata novem.
Hanc tamen effœtam, medicè quos edidit ante,
  E medio medicè tollere fama refert.
Sic fœcunda parens uſa eſt medicamine THUSCO
  Ut MEDÆA foret, quæ MEDICÆA fuit.

The ſame Vices of Lewdneſs, Luxury, Irreligion, Impiety, and magick Abominations which had reigned under Henry II. triumphed under Charles IX. with an unbridled Licence : and beſides theſe Diſorders, Treaſon, Poiſoning, Aſſaſſinations became ſo rife and common, that it was but a Joke to deſtroy by theſe means, thoſe whoſe Death could be any ways ſerviceable. In his Reign was ſeen what never before was ſeen, Women provoking Men ! and that openly, and without the leaſt Decency, not only the common ſort of People, but the greateſt Ladies of the Court, as the Queen of Navarr complain'd of it to her Son Henry. No wonder, if ſo many heinous Vices complicated one with another, drew upon the Kingdom the heavieſt Judgments of God, what we have ſeen is but a beginning of Pain ; I refer my Reader to the next Book.

N. B.

N. B. Whatever I have said about King C
Character, is extracted out of Thuanus, I
pag. 989, 990. Agricola's Addit. to the Me
of Castelnau, Vol. III. Disc. de la Vie de
Henry III. pag. 32, 33.　Brantome Ed
Charles IX. Papyrius Masso **Hist.** Vitæ
Valesii Gall. Reg. ejus Nominis *noni conc*
1575. Agricola Nouvelles Addit. aux Me
de Castelnau, Tom. III. pag. 406. *Men*
pour servir a l'Hist. de France, Tom. I. pag
Recueil des Choses memorables sous Henry I
Henry IV. pag. 502—507. Mezeray 3 Pr
Tom. V. pag. 182—185.

F I N I S.

ERRATA.

Page 80, the laſt Line in the Note, for *Loula*, read *Loyola*.
82. l. 1. *the World*, r. *the whole World.* P. 97. l. 21. *Re-action*, r. *Retractation.* P. 99. l. 27. *firſt*, r. *fifth.* P. 105.
19. *Kultembourg*, r. *Kullembourg.* P. 126. l. 28. *ſaid*, r.
d. P. 132. l. 18. *them*, r. *themſelves.* P. 134. l. 17. *to
> it*, r. *to do.* P. 166. l. 27. *Poſſeſſion*, r. *Profeſſion.* P. 194.
36. *reſolve*, r. *reſolved.* P. 202. the laſt line, *Thorn*, r. *of
be Thorn.* P. 222. l 5. *Seſſion*, r. *Juſſion.* P. 234. l. 22.
is own Life, r. *with his own Life.* P. 240. l. 14. *Cipierre*,
Sipierre. P. 281. l. 11. *with Prince*, r. *with that of Prince.*
?. 308. l. 25. *Orez*, r. *Ortez.* P. 314. l. 2. *in the Aſſiſtance*,
their Aſſiſtance. P. 318. l. 8. *to obey*, r. *as to obey.* P 321.
l. 5. *riſe*, r. *riſes.* l. 24. *but*, r. *for.* P. 331. l. 13. *Father
and Son*, that muſt be underſtood of *Lewis* Prince of *Condé*,
murdered at the Battel of *Baſſac*, during this War, and of
Henry his Son. P. 350. l. 19. *Queen Navarr*, r. *Queen of
Navarr.* P. 357. l. 1. *at Bearn*, r. *in Bearn.* P. 364. l. 28.
carrying on of the War, r. *carrying the War.*

CPSIA information can be obtained
at www.ICGtesting.com
Printed in the USA
BVHW080219190819
556172BV00015B/1737/P

9 781406 971880